Paragraphs
and the Short Theme

P. Joseph Canavan
Mount San Antonio College

D. C. HEATH AND COMPANY
A Division of Raytheon Education Company
Lexington, Massachusetts

Cover design by Studio 4, Inc.

Acknowledgments are to be found following each chapter.

Library of Congress Number 69–20460

Contents

Contents

Prefatory note

This book provides the student in a writing class with knowledge of the principles, techniques, and practices necessary to write effective expository paragraphs and short themes — types of writing required in most beginning writing courses. The organizational pattern of the book reveals its purpose; it begins with an overall view of the short theme, stressing the function and organization of the separate parts and their relationship to the whole. It moves next to a detailed treatment of the different kinds of paragraphs, and then to methods of writing the short theme. The text and exercises focus on organization and effective presentation of a student's ideas into meaningful paragraph units and then into unified wholes, often by step-by-step explanations which the inexperienced writer can follow. Special emphasis is given prewriting or planning as an essential part of written communication.

Throughout the book are numerous professional and student models of paragraphs and short themes. These selections offer the student an opportunity for classroom analysis and discussion, illustrate the basic rhetorical concerns, and serve as sources for his own written assignments. Exercises are included in the book to help the student recognize principles and practices that he can employ in his own writing. In addition, many written assignments afford him a chance to practice what he has been studying.

P. J.C.

Viewing the whole

Writing is commonly divided into four principal classes: *exposition, description, narration,* and *argumentation.* In most writing, however, the different forms shade so smoothly one into another that the reader is seldom aware which form dominates. A writer's purpose is the main determiner of the forms he uses.

A writer of exposition, for example, usually gives information or explains his subject. In order to help with understanding, he addresses himself to the reader's intellect with logical explanations and valid support. He may be giving facts and specifics to explain an event like the invasion of France, the roles which society forces one to play, or the dangers of a certain action. He may be informing in order to explain how an event happened, such as a revolution or an earthquake. He may be instructing his reader on how to do something or how something is done — a process, for instance, like making steel.

In description, a writer appeals to a reader's imagination and perceptive senses. He wishes his reader to see, hear, taste, smell, and feel as he presents a vivid word picture of the subject. He may be describing a sunset, a sinking ship, an individual, or a dying elephant. Whatever the subject, a writer's purpose in description is the same: to appeal to the imagination, the emotions, and the senses.

The writer of narration tells a story; he writes about an incident or a series of incidents in which action dominates. In argumentation, a writer attempts to persuade his reader to accept his opinions or his view concerning some controversial subject.

The whole theme

Perhaps you have already discovered that in college most of your writing will be expository. You have probably written one or more essay examinations, term reports, themes, "compositions" for English writing classes, and numerous out-of-class papers in many of your courses. Papers like these are usually limited to the treatment of one point of view or purpose. They usually try to develop one central idea in a few well-aimed and well-constructed paragraphs. Notice in the following section how the writer expresses his thesis (the central idea) in the first paragraph, the "introduction." The thesis is: integration offers opportunities and benefits for both the Negro and white citizens.

INTEGRATION: OPPORTUNITY AND OBLIGATION
by Whitney M. Young, Jr.

[1] One of the obstacles to progress in the civil rights movement is a tendency to view change primarily in terms of problems rather than opportunities and advantages. Of course integration poses problems; but also it offers great opportunities. We will start making true progress when we begin to see it this way. Obviously, it offers Negro citizens the chance they want — and are entitled to — for better homes, better jobs, better education. But many people fail to understand that integration offers benefits for white citizens, as well.

[2] For one thing, integration brings them the chance to rid themselves of the fears and hatreds which segregation has bred between the races. Segregation is artificial, imposed upon the natural instincts of men to congregate and know each other. In this country, special interest groups relied on the powerful motives of greed and bigotry to bring about segregation as we know it — in our neighborhoods, schools, labor unions, offices. But in addition to moral objections to segregation, it is well to remember that it doesn't even make economic sense.

[3] Integration can double our rate of national economic growth, adding vastly to the prosperity of all Americans. At the present time, Negroes earn only about half of what white Americans earn each year. By improving their skills, education, and employment opportunities, their increased purchasing power would add at least $20 billion a year to our economy.

[4] Integration in housing is also an opportunity to rid our cities of the costly and ugly slums which are corroding metropolitan areas and making them less habitable for all people.

[5] The ghetto conditions in which Negroes have had to live have often led to the breakup or demoralization of their families,

to high rates of crime and delinquency, and, as the slums spread, to the flight of an increasing number of white citizens to the suburbs, thus undermining the tax base of central urban areas and their ability to support themselves.

⁶Negroes, who did succeed in educating themselves and in finding adequate jobs, often had no decent housing to move to, ~~anyway~~. Thus their interest in work was undermined. By offering better housing opportunities to Negro families, the disastrous price we pay for city slums could be ended, and more communities could improve their home values.

⁷For Negro children integration brings the chance for self-fulfillment — the chance to go as far in education and work as each person's capabilities permit. For white children, integration means learning to live in the natural, diversified setting which will prepare them for the multi-racial world they will have to get along in. A white youngster who grows up with a notion of superiority attributed to race, or even with an uncomfortable feeling among people who are different, is under a severe handicap in a world where seventy-five per cent of the population is non-white.

⁸Segregation doesn't shut some people out, it fences in the people who believe in it. Integration tears down fences. In making normal those contacts which yesterday were fearful, and today are still painful to some, integration leads to a better, more profitable, and pleasant tomorrow.

⁹Congress has made integration possible; it is up to each community to make it work. We must make integration a matter-of-fact part of our lives, because, as John F. Kennedy once said, "It is right." Our religious beliefs, our political principles, our national and international well-being require it.

¹⁰I believe that as Americans we have a particular obligation today to the Negro citizen. In the longer view, our responsibility is to all our citizens. Avoiding integration avoids meeting our immediate and our long-term responsibilities. Promoting integration adds to the legitimate pride we can take in our nation — for its strength, unity, and justice. [1]

DISCUSSION

This selection, which runs a little over 500 words, illustrates how effective is a well organized and skillfully structured short piece of writing. The writer begins with an introductory paragraph in which he points out that "one of the obstacles to the civil rights movement is a tendency to view change primarily in terms of problems rather than opportunities and advantages." Such a beginning, differing from traditional views of civil rights situations, should gain reader interest. In addition, the writer states clearly his point of view in the early sentences by announcing the thesis: integration offers great opportunities for both Negro and white citizens.

The middle or body of the paper consists of eight well-structured paragraphs which develop and support the central idea of opportunities and advantages for both Negro and white citizens. Many of the paragraphs are simply organized around beginning topic sentences that express a main idea, such as "For one thing, integration brings them the chance to rid themselves of the fears and hatreds which segregation has bred between the races" (paragraph 2); "Integration can double our rate of national growth, adding vastly to the prosperity of all Americans" (paragraph 3); "... it is up to each community to make it [integration] work" (paragraph 9). Each of these paragraphs relates to and develops the thesis of opportunities and advantages.

In the concluding paragraph, Mr. Young repeats the thesis idea: "I believe that as Americans we have a particular obligation today to the Negro citizens. In the longer view, our responsibility is to all our citizens." In the last lines, he writes of the benefits which will result if Americans accept his views.

In diagram form, the structural pattern of "Integration: Opportunity and Obligation" looks something like the following:

Integration: Opportunity and Obligation

I.   Introduction
        Thesis: Integration offers great opportunities for both
        Negro and white citizens.
II.   " ... Integration brings them [white citizens] the chance to
        rid themselves of the fears and hatreds which segregation
        has bred between the races.
III. ⎤
IV. ⎥
V. ⎬   Main idea suggested: Economic Benefits
VI. ⎦
VII. ⎤
VIII. ⎦   Main idea suggested: Individual Benefits
IX.   Part of Conclusion
X.   Concluding Paragraph

R∈M∈MB∈R

The organizational and structural pattern of this short selection illustrates an effective plan for structuring your own short themes. It suggests a plan that beginning writers would probably be wise to follow. However, it only suggests. If your subject requires modification of this plan and you feel capable of changing it, do so. Add or delete a paragraph. Omit the introduction or expand the simple one-thesis sentence introduction to a paragraph with other material. Omit a conclusion or make your final remarks part of the last supporting paragraph. As you become more experienced in writing, you will undoubtedly wish to make other modifications. Once you have learned the various methods of organizing and developing thought, you will discover that the materials of the theme, not the writer, determine the best kind of organizational structure.

Study the following unified division of a larger piece of writing. Afterwards, answer the questions concerning its structural organization.

WHAT SLANG IS?
by Paul Roberts

[1] Slang is one of those things that everybody can recognize and nobody can define. Not only is it hard to wrap slang in a definition; it is also hard to distinguish it from such similar things as colloquialisms, provincialisms, jargon, trade talk. As we shall see, these areas blend into one another, and it is often a waste of time to look for the boundary.

[2] One characteristic of a slang term is that it exists side by side with another, more general term for the same thing. Take for example the word *chick*, which has been used by some speakers in the meaning *girl* or *young woman*. The difference between *chick* and *girl* can be stated only in reference to the people who use the words: some say, "This chick is my sister"; others "This girl is my sister." *Chick* is slang and *girl* is not, because *chick* is used by a limited part of the population, mostly young people, whereas *girl* is used by everybody, including those who use *chick*.

[3] It is often said that a slang term ceases to be slang when it is "accepted by the dictionary." This is not really the test. You will find many slang terms duly registered in dictionaries and still slang terms. The term ceases to be slang when it drives out of use its respectable synonym, or when it acquires a meaning that cannot be expressed otherwise. If, for instance, people ceased to use the word *girl* and used *chick* instead, then *chick* could no longer be called a slang term.

⁴Such things have happened. The term *hot dog* was once a slang term, but it couldn't be considered so now. No one in America would go up to a counter and order a "sausage sandwich." Similarly *varsity*, originally a slang contraction of *university*, has acquired special meaning which only it expresses and is no longer slang. Jazz, when it means a particular kind of music, is scarcely a slang term, since there is no more respectable word meaning that kind of music.

⁵Certainly respectability must enter into any discussion of slang. Slang is essentially not respectable. There is always a more elegant way of saying the thing but one chooses the slang term for reasons. The reason may be a desire to be thought witty or clever or up-to-date. More often it is a desire to show, by a particular use of language, that one is a member in good standing of a particular group of people. [2]

QUESTIONS AND DISCUSSION

1. What does the title indicate about the writing?
2. What is the function of the first paragraph?
3. Does the writer make clear his purpose in a concisely stated thesis sentence?
4. Does the writer fulfill his purpose? By what means?
5. Does he have a conclusion? Is one necessary?

The title indicates that the writer will define slang. Roberts' first paragraph serves to introduce the subject by pointing out that slang is a difficult word to define. He does not have a definite thesis sentence; however, he makes clear the purpose of the writing by the introductory paragraph. The writer's purpose is to define slang; he does this by mentioning characteristics. His second paragraph discusses the fact that slang exists side by side with another, more general term for the same thing. He supports this generalization with examples. His next paragraph of development considers the question of when slang ceases to be slang. The third paragraph moves onward with additional examples of when slang ceases to be slang. The final paragraph — still a paragraph of development — discusses the respectability of slang. A conclusion for this kind of treatment is unnecessary. In planning and organizing your own expository themes, follow these suggestions:

1. Find a suitable subject.
2. Limit the subject.
3. Express your point of view or purpose in a thesis statement.

4. Introduce the topic in the first paragraph. Phrase your purpose in the form of a thesis sentence placed at the beginning or end of paragraph 1.
5. Write a short series of well-developed paragraphs — the middle or body of the theme — that relate to and support the thesis.
6. Bring the theme to an effective conclusion.

Selecting a subject

What shall I write about? Most beginning writers are constantly asking this question. Most experienced writers, you will find, begin with an interest in and knowledge of some subject and a desire to share a particular point of view about that subject with their readers. Beginning writers, however, find it difficult to get started because they feel that they have nothing important to write about. More often than not, the true problem is that the beginning writer has not used his imagination in selecting an appropriate subject for an audience that should be interested in what he has to say.

In selecting a subject, draw first from your own experiences. Many things that you have done, seen, heard, felt in your lifetime must have left an impression on you. From these experiences, select one that interests you, that is still vivid, or that you have a knowledge of, and that you believe will interest your readers. It might be surfing. It might be fashions or clothes. It might be cheating in classes, student government, a current event, a happening on campus or at home, a personal discovery about yourself, a friend, your parents, or life in general. With some thought, you will find a number of suitable subjects for the short theme. Listed below are some broad general subjects which, *when limited*, become suitable subjects for student themes.

Accidents	Brotherhood	Comics
Actors	Camping	Countries
Animals	Cars	Courage
Architecture	Censorship	Crime
Art	Cities	Customs
Athletics	Clothes	Dance
Beauty	College	Dating
Birth	Comedians	Death

Drama	Hobbies	Radio
Drugs	Inventions	Religion
Education	Jobs	Schools
Entertainment	Language	Sex
Ethics	Literature	Social Problems
Faith	Love	Space
Family	Movies	Sports
Freedom	Music	Television
Friends	Nature	Theater
Games	People	Travel
Groups	Philosophy	War
History	Prejudices	

Read this list again. Add any subjects that you have found interesting and that you consider suitable for theme topics.

Remember, this kind of listing is simply a means of getting you started. Such subjects are, for the most part, too broad and general to be adequately treated in the short theme. In addition you would probably find that you do not possess enough knowledge to develop fully most of them and that the task of researching them would be too time-consuming. Suppose, for example, you are interested in a subject like "Rome," and you decide to write on "The Story of Rome." Read the selection which follows. As you read the selection, keep these comments about it in mind. This excerpt was actually a "Summary" at the end of a chapter of thirty-one pages titled "The Ascendancy of Rome." It illustrates the impossibility of treating broad subjects adequately in a short theme. Even in the space available for this summary, the writers were able to present, for the most part, a series of generalizations covering a number of topics, any one of which would require a thousand or more words for complete treatment. To illustrate the problem of the broad subject, let us consider the writers' statement which reads: "the tradition of a representative democracy is seen in the development of the Roman law and political theory" (Paragraph 3). Separate aspects of this thought are many, such as "The Extension and Reform Under the Antonines," "Justinian Law," "The Applications of Roman Law," "The Influence of Roman Law," "The Supremacy of Roman Law," and "The Concept of Social Contract." Any one of these topics would require treatment beyond the limits of the short theme.

THE STORY OF ROME
by T. Walter Wallbank and Alastair M. Taylor

[1] The story of how Rome rose from the insignificant status of a muddy village along the banks of the river Tiber to the mighty position of master of the Mediterranean world will always remain one of the most fascinating epics in world history. Emerging from obscurity about the middle of the eighth century before Christ, the Latin people, clustered about Rome and its seven hills, succeeded in 509 B.C. in ousting their Etruscan overlords from power and establishing a republic. The next four hundred years of Roman history concerned two dominant themes: the democratization of the government and the conquest of the Mediterranean.

[2] Following the expulsion of the Etruscan kings, the aristocratic Senate took charge of the state. Only the nobles exercised political rights, and the people — the plebeians — had no voice in the affairs of government. During the next two centuries, however, the plebeians succeeded in breaking down the privileged position of the patricians by obtaining recognition of their fundamental rights as citizens and by acquiring a progressively more important share of political power. Yet these gains, significant as they were, proved largely illusory, for the rank and file of citizens never gained actual control of the government of the republic — and the latter eventually was transformed into a principate and then a monarchy.

[3] However, the tradition of a representative democracy is seen in the development of Roman law and political theory. Under the Antonines, the extension and reform of the legal system made the most progress, and under Justinian the law was codified to become an influence upon all subsequent legal thought. The Romans gave us the concepts of the supremacy of the law, of social contract, the sovereignty of the people, and the separation of governmental powers.

[4] The other theme in the early history of Rome was the conquest of the Mediterranean. Between the years 509 and 270 B.C. the Romans managed to crush all resistance in Italy. They then turned their attention to Carthage, Rome's only remaining rival in the western Mediterranean, and after a herculean struggle marked by the brilliant tactics but final defeat of Hannibal, Carthage was completely destroyed in 146 B.C. Having conquered the west, the Romans now became involved in disputes in the east, and in short order the petty and inefficient successors of Alexander the Great were defeated, and their territory came under the rule of the Roman republic. But when the western world was conquered, it soon became evident that Rome herself faced civil war and degeneration. The wars of conquest had resulted in the disappearance of the sturdy Roman far-

mers, the cities were filled with parasites and loungers who demanded free bread, and the government was corrupt.

[5] Several patriotic reformers, such as the Gracchi brothers, tried to get the Senate to enact necessary reforms, but to no avail. After the Gracchi a series of military heroes came to the fore in Roman history. Marius, Sulla, Pompey, and Julius Caesar mark the appearance of one man rule and the end of the republic. Augustus, the heir of Caesar, ruled Rome wisely and well. On the surface the old republican characteristics of government, such as the Senate, were preserved, but Augustus wielded the real power in the new government, which was thenceforth called the principate. For two hundred years, during the *Pax Romana,* the people of Italy and the many other millions of subjects in the empire's provinces enjoyed peace and prosperity.

[6] Through the Roman achievement of a single empire and a cosmopolitan culture, the Greek legacy was preserved, synthesized, and disseminated — and the Romans were able in their own right to make important contributions. For the first time in the western world, secular architecture on a monumental scale evolved with the erection throughout the empire of baths, government buildings, stadia, and triumphal arches. In other arts, the Romans contributed realistic portrait sculpture, historical reliefs, stone and stucco decoration, and realistic painting.

[7] The Romans accomplished little in abstract thought and pure science, because they had slight interest in scientific speculation or experimentation. Borrowing Hellenistic science wholesale, they applied it to meet their practical needs. They were the first to have hospitals, public medical service, efficient sewage systems, and a workable calendar. In philosophy the Romans got their thought ready-made from Greece. Epicureanism and Stoicism appealed most to the Romans; in their hands the latter was given new force and dignity. In literature the Romans evolved few new forms except the satire, but their sonorous prose set a standard for later centuries. The Latin language, throughout the Middle Ages the vehicle of literature, law, and the Church, is the foundation of the modern languages spoken by more than 200,000,000 people. [3]

Limiting a subject

If you are to write an effective short theme, you must learn to limit a subject or select a subject that is already limited for treatment in approximately 500 words. If you select broad subjects like religion, sports, fashions, or crime, you will undoubtedly end up with a disorganized series of generalizations with no specific point of view. Instead of selecting "Religion," treat one part of it and write about a religious experience of your own, such as "What Prayer Has Meant to Me" or "I Was a Child of a Missionary in Africa." Instead of writing about an ambitious subject like "Sports," select a topic, such as "Sports Are Overemphasized at Hewton Elementary School" or "Little League Baseball Is Really for Adults." If you stick to one idea, you can develop it fully in a short theme. If you limit your subject successfully, you will find that you can build a unified whole with a few well-structured paragraphs.

To help you limit a subject, here are some suggestions:

1. A subject can be limited by concentrating on one particular angle of interest. Thus, a broad subject like "Religion" was effectively de-limited when the writer decided to present a child's view of religion as the son of a missionary in Africa.

2. A subject can be limited by time. An over-ambitious subject such as "Crime" becomes a feasible topic for a short theme if limited to "Crime in the 1960's" or "Chicago During the Days of Prohibition."

3. A subject can be limited by process. Instead of wandering aimlessly in the vast regions of "Space" or the "Oceans," concentrate on less expansive subjects as "How A Space Ship Re-enters Our Atmosphere," or "How To Dock a Cabin Cruiser in High Seas."

4. A subject like "Dancing" can be treated effectively in a short theme if you limit to one aspect or part; for example, "Folk Dancing is Fun," "I Learned to Appreciate Ballet," or "Choreography is an Art."

5. Subjects can be limited by space. Thus, "Racial Tensions in America" could be limited to "Racial Tensions in My Home Town," "Racial Tensions on My Campus," or "There Are No Racial Tensions in My Neighborhood."

6. Subjects can be limited by causes and effects. "Depressions" or "Crime" or "Divorce" are broad subjects that become interesting cause and effect relationship themes, such as "The Causes of the Great Depression," "The Effects of The Crash in 1929," "The Causes of Divorce," "The Causes of Juvenile Crime Today."

7. Many general subjects may be limited by comparisons and contrasts, such as "British Education and American Education," "Hitler and Mussolini," "The Economic Resources of the North and South in 1860."

8. Other subjects can be limited by definition. "What Is Poetry?" "The Meaning of the Term *Nihilism.*" "What is an 'Ivory Tower'?"

9. Subjects may be limited by breaking them down into kinds or types, such as "Kinds of Clouds," "Types of Poetry," "Kinds of Apples," "Types of Volcanoes," "Classes of People."

10. Subjects may be limited by any combination of these methods. "Racial Tensions in Chicago Last Summer," for example, is a subject, "Racism" limited by time, place, and by partition (one part or aspect).

Limiting a subject with a step-by-step process can be a valuable method of finding a topic that you can handle in approximately 500 words. The process is simple. Begin with a broad subject and continue to limit the scope at each step until you have a topic which you consider appropriate for development in a short theme. The plan diagrammed below may be helpful:

Subject:	Rome
Step One:	Roman Law
Step Two:	The Justinian Code
Possible Topics:	(1) The Nature of the Justinian Code
	(2) Some Contributions to Civilization of the Justinian Code
	(3) The History of the Justinian Code

Subject:	Government
Step One:	Government in Germany
Step Two:	Dictatorship
Step Three:	Hitler
Possible Topics:	(1) Hitler's Greatest Moment
	(2) Hitler and Mussolini
	(3) Was Hitler Mad?
	(4) The Death of Adolph Hitler
	(5) Does Hitler still live?
	(6) The Mistakes of Adolph Hitler

In selecting and limiting a subject, ask yourself the following questions:

1. Do I know enough about the subject to develop it fully? If not, can I research it for additional information?
2. Can the subject be treated adequately in the space available? Most college assignments involve writing single paragraphs of approximately 100 words or short papers of approximately 500 words.
3. Is the subject interesting to me?
4. Will the subject be interesting for the reader?

EXERCISES

1. Limiting a subject

Which of the following subjects is suited for both the writer and his reader? Place a "S" in front of the sentence number if you consider the subject suitable.

1. A college student writes about fraternities for a group of his high school friends.
2. A female college student writes about politics for the local Shakespeare Club.
3. A physician writes about drugs for a college publication.
4. A parent writes about children's behavior for the P.T.A.
5. A major in drama writes about commercialism in athletics for a group of coaches.
6. A novelist discusses medicine with a group of scientists.
7. A politician defines the term, "conservative," for the Young Democrats.
8. An FBI agent writes about the proposed gun laws for a hunting club.
9. A female college student writes about cooking for hotel chefs.
10. A college student writes about his "Freshman Days" for a newspaper in his home town.

2. Limiting a subject

Using the step by step method, limit the following subjects:

1. Habits   2. Cars   3. Wealth   4. Kindness
5. Love

3. Limiting a subject
    Under the following broad, general subjects, list at least four limited topics. Study the following example:

> *Athletics or Sports*
>   1. In Defense of the Fullback
>   2. College Athletics: Education or Show Business?
>   3. The Decline of Sport
>   4. The Scramble for College Athletes

1. Family 2. Hobbies 3. Accidents 4. Recreation 5. Friends

4. Limiting a subject (titles)
    Under the general subject heading, place the appropriate title.

>   1. Rebellion
>   2. Crime
>   3. Drugs
>   4. Poverty
>   5. Education
>   6. Censorship
>   7. Theater
>   8. Religion
>   9. Travel
>   10. Recreation

1. New York City in the Summer
2. Camping in Louisiana
3. Censorship and Obscenity: What's Happened to Taste?
4. Should God Die?
5. 1 in 7: Drugs on Campus
6. You Force Kids to Rebel
7. Verdict Guilty—Now What?
8. Where the Real Poverty Is: Plight of the American Indian
9. What's the Use of Educating Women?
10. The Theater of Edward Albee

5. Limiting a subject
    Under each title, indicate the kinds of limitations.
Example: Racial Tensions in Chicago Last Summer
Answer: by parts (partition), by place, by time

1. Folk Music in the Ozarks Today
2. How to Build a Patio
3. Lee and Grant: A Study in Contrasts
4. Reasons for Napoleon's Defeat at Waterloo
5. What Religion Meant to the Ancient Greeks
6. Social Classes in Suburbia in the 1960's
7. I Rode on a Torpedo
8. The Assassination of a President
9. Capone's Gangster Empire
10. Education in a Danish Gymnasium (high school)

Thesis statement

Interest in and knowledge of a subject are not enough for a good beginning. And limiting a subject is not the entire story. In your planning, including the limiting of the subject, you should have developed a point of view or purpose for writing. Perhaps you will be motivated sufficiently about something to have a purpose that will be the reason for writing, rather than deciding on a purpose to fulfill a writing assignment. With a definite purpose in mind, you will find that limiting the subject and structuring the paper are easier to do. Your purpose, whether explicitly stated in a thesis sentence or *not* spelled out in the paper, must be phrased before you begin to organize and develop the topic, for the thesis is a concise statement of the central theme or underlying thought of the whole theme.

Read the following thesis statements:

1. Computer registration destroys student choice.
2. School spirit is present on our campus only during football season.
3. Reading is a complex process of many skills.
4. Radio is still an important news medium.
5. Television can be educational.

A good thesis is clear, specific, and limiting. It should express clearly the writer's purpose or point of view, limit or narrow the subject, and express the central thought (the underlying point) of the paper. An effective thesis sentence should be concise and complete, a declaration, not a question. It should have a strong subject and a predicate that expresses an attitude or point of view. The thesis sentence may appear anywhere in the paper or it may not be expressed. It appears frequently as the first or last sentence of the introductory paragraph. In a theme where the movement of the writer's thought is from the specifics to a final conclusion, the thesis comes in the final paragraph.

EXERCISES

6. Thesis sentence
What is wrong with each of the thesis sentences below in light of what you have learned? Write a good thesis sentence on the same subject as each sentence.
1. Is smoking harmful?
2. Crime is costing the American citizens millions of dollars each year.
3. Literature is a very old art.
4. Most television commercials are too long and unimaginative.
5. Sports are good builders of character.
6. Tennis is a great pastime.
7. My paper is about drama.
8. Socialism is an interesting economic ideology.
9. Our trip to Yellowstone (or some other place).
10. College coaching is hard work.

7. Thesis
Write a thesis sentence for each of the following subjects.
1. Compact Cars
2. Teen-age Marriages
3. Alcoholism
4. Politics
5. Football (or any other sport)
6. Clothes or Fashions
7. Customs or Manners
8. School Spirit
9. Campus Clubs
10. A Social Problem

Outlining

Outlining can be a valuable aid in planning and organizing your paper. To organize with an outline, you must first think about your subject, gather material by researching the subject in your library when you cannot draw from your own experiences, and define clearly your point of view or purpose. Too many beginning writers begin writing before limiting the subject, phrasing the thesis, or considering some effective methods of organizing and developing the material. The most common kinds of outlines are the *topic* and *sentence* outlines. Each of these types is structured in the same way. Each major heading is numbered with Roman numerals: I, II, III and so forth. The subheads use capital letters: A, B, C .... Additional subdividing requires small letters: a, b, c .... If further subdividing is necessary, follow with Arabic numerals in parentheses (1), (2), (3) and small letters in parentheses: (a), (b), (c). Periods are used after the figures and letters except for those in parentheses. The headings in any one group are equally important. In longer papers, one might include an *introduction* and a *conclusion*. No single heading should stand alone; that is, a major heading "I" requires a major heading "II" and a minor heading "A" requires a minor heading "B" and so forth.

A topic outline indicates topics simply with a word or a group of words. The form is as follows:

Title: Crime and slang
(space)

Thesis Statement: Criminals are prolific producers of slang.

I. Reasons for use of slang
    A. Multiplying language differences
    B. Differences for practical purposes
    C. Criminal groups in other centuries
II. Criminal slang today
    A. Relating to money
        1. Money in general
        2. Different denominations
    B. All familiar to many people
    C. More common in criminal districts
III. Slang in games
    A. Most common in disreputable games
        1. Poker
            a. General names for cards
            b. Another set, such as *bull* or *bullet*
        2. Dice

IV. Dope racket
   A. Dope
   B. Within the racket
     1. Marihuana and heroin
     2. H or big H
     3. A fix
     4. Mainline
     5. Pusher
     6. Junkie
     7. To kick the habit

       The sentence outline indicates each heading and sub-heading with a complete sentence. It is better for beginning writers because it demands more pre-organization.

Title: Crime and slang

Thesis Statement: Criminals are prolific producers of slang.

I. There are reasons why criminals use slang.
   A. They deliberately widen the gulf by multiplying language differences.
   B. They often use the differences for practical purposes.
   C. Criminal groups of seventeenth- and eighteenth-century England developed large vocabularies of slang which rendered their talk almost meaningless to an outsider.
II. Much of the slang in common use today comes ultimately from characters on the other side of the law.
   A. This will be recognizable in words relating to American money.
     1. For "money" in general, we have such terms as *dough, lettuce,* the *green* or the *big green, folding stuff,* and various others.
     2. The different denominations all have their slang terms: *singles* or *fish* for one dollar bills; *fin* for a five; *sawbuck* for a ten and *double sawbuck* for a twenty and so forth.
   B. All of these are old, well-weathered terms and are familiar to many people.
   C. It is clear that they have their highest frequency in those districts where policemen would prefer to go in pairs.
III. In games slang is common everywhere.
   A. Slang is most common in disreputable games.
     1. Poker has a wide variety of slang terms.

      a. Many slang terms for general names for the cards, such as *ace, deuce, king.*

      b. Another set of slang terms are the following: *bull* or *bullet* for "ace," *cowboy* for "king," *a pair of ducks* for "a pair of deuces."

    2. Dice has a higher incidence of slang terms.

IV. The connection between slang and the criminal elements is seen again in the dope racket.

  A. The word *dope* itself is originally slang, but it is now in more general use than *narcotics.*

  B. Within the racket terms abound.

    1. The words *marihuana* and *heroin* seem scarcely to occur among users or peddlers of drugs.

      a. They say *H* or *big H* or *horse* or *caballito* (a Spanish word meaning "little horse" or "horsey.")

      b. *Marihuana* is referred to by several slang terms, of which *hay* seems to be the most enduring.

    2. An injection is a *fix.*

    3. To inject it in the vein is *mainline.*

    4. A salesman or peddler is a *pusher.*

    5. An addict is a *junkie.*

    6. To rid oneself of an addiction is *to kick the habit.*

  C. It will be seen that a narcotic addict can discuss his troubles at some length without being understood by anyone outside the circle.

    The article on which this outline was based appears in Chapter 8, *Crime and Slang* by Paul Roberts.

ASSIGNMENTS

1. Outlining
    Make a sentence outline for the article "A Vote for Student Protest," in Chapter 2.

2. Outlining
    Make a topic outline for a short article that you can find in a contemporary magazine.

The title

    Although the title may not be written until the paper is nearly completed, it is wise to begin with a tentative title since it helps in limiting the subject. A good title should be brief, fresh, informative, cogent, and interesting. A good title, therefore, must gain the reader's attention, reveal something about the theme, and grasp the reader's interest.

Underline the titles below which you consider effective.

1. Stranger in the Valley
2. Grading
3. The Unbanning of the Books
4. What's Happening to America?
5. The West
6. Tragedy and the Common Man
7. Schoolboy Racketeers
8. Student Government
9. Oil in the Wastelands
10. How to Face a Bad Grade

In your writing of a title, then, avoid vague, indefinite, and long titles. Do not enclose a title in quotation marks unless the title is itself a quotation. Do not end a title with a period. Do not indirectly refer to the title in the first sentence with such words as *this, that, such.*

Introductions

A good introductory paragraph should indicate the thesis, gain the reader's interest, and get the theme moving. Introductions may be as varied and effective as the ingenuity and competence of the writer. Some writers begin with a direct statement of the thesis, some with a question; others with a contrast emphasizing the thesis or background material and then the thesis. Still others begin with an exciting incident, a startling statement, or a happening to capture the reader's attention and interest. Study the model introductions which follow.

Model 1 — A STARTLING INCIDENT

It is a melancholy object to those who walk through this great town or travel in the country, when they see the streets, the roads, and cabin-doors crowded with beggars of the female sex, followed by three, four, or six children, all in rags, and importuning every passenger for an alms. These mothers, instead of being able to work for their honest livelihood, are forced to employ all their time in strolling to beg sustenance for their helpless infants, who, as they grow up, either turn thieves for want of work, or leave their dear native country, to fight for the Pretender in Spain, or sell themselves to the Barbadoes. [4]

Model 2 — AN EVENT *AWKWARD* *SENT.*

The earthquake shook down in San Francisco hundreds of thousands of dollars' worth of walls and chimneys. But the conflagration that followed burned up hundreds of millions of dollars' worth of property. There is no estimating within hundreds of millions the actual damage wrought. Not in history has a modern imperial city been so completely destroyed. San Francisco is gone. Nothing remains of it but memories and a fringe of dwelling-houses on its outskirts. Its industrial section is wiped out. Its business section is wiped out. The factories and warehouses, the great stores and newspaper buildings, the hotels and the palaces of the nabobs, are all gone. Remains only the fringe of dwelling-houses on the outskirts of what was once San Francisco.

Within an hour after the earthquake shock the smoke of San Francisco's burning was a lurid tower visible a hundred miles away. And for three days and nights this lurid tower swayed in the sky, reddening the sun, darkening the day, and filling the land with smoke. [5]

Model 3 — SERIES OF QUESTIONS

Are you a reader? Then how do you evaluate writers and the material they publish? If you are a concerned citizen, what do you make of today's authors? What will be their effect on our nation and society? It is a controversial and confusing subject because readers may also be writers, and you can be sure that all writers are readers. [6]

Model 4 — DIRECT STATEMENT OF THE THESIS

Most of the important discoveries which bring about revolutionary advances in science are made by men under 35. Young men are the ones who have taken giant strides on which human advancement is made. [7]

Model 5 — ANALOGY AND PLAN OF DEVELOPMENT

College and University Presidents, faculty representatives, athletic directors, coaches — all those who have anything whatsoever to do with intercollegiate athletics — are keenly aware of the fact that they have a tiger by the tail. They are afraid to hold on to it, and they are afraid to let it go. My own judgment is that we should hold on to the tail but get more control of the whole tiger.

With this positive affirmation about intercollegiate athletics, I have probably lost approximately one-third of my readers. I base this estimate upon my own experience of faculties. Roughly one-third of any faculty has either a congenital or an experiential aversion to intercollegiate athletics, and tends to view the whole subject with alarm. For the remaining two-thirds, the plan of this article is to discuss briefly (1) values in intercollegiate athletics, (2) present abuses, (3) corrective measures in the recent past, (4) present trends, and (5) steps which need to be taken in the future. [8]

Model 6 — BACKGROUND MATERIAL

I was interested in the letter of Five Bewildered Freshmen, and in the discussion it gave rise to. The freshmen say they have been engaged in the intellectual life for more than two months and don't know what it's all about. This is bad, but who is to blame? Some say the students are to blame, and some say the professors. What is to be done about it? You suggest a foundation or an orientation course such as is given in other universities. [9]

Model 7 — BACKGROUND AND THESIS

Twenty years ago the United States joined in founding the United Nations in order "to reaffirm faith in fundamental human rights . . . to promote social progress . . . to unite our strength to maintain international peace and security." The U.N. has indeed done many of these things — repelling aggression in Korea, cushioning the breakup of colonial empires, fighting diseases as malaria and yaws. Today an overwhelming majority of Americans — almost 80 percent according to a Gallup poll — favor U.S. support of the U.N. as a major force for world peace.

In such a soothing atmosphere of benevolence, it is easy to be lulled into the pleasant assumption that the U.N. will somehow take care of things. In actual fact, the first part of the U.N.'s latest session provided little but bickering. In the debate on the Congo, both white and black delegates accused each other of racism. In a debate on Malaysia, Indonesia angrily announced it was quitting the U.N. outright. Every regional quarrel was rehashed — but nobody could vote on anything. Because of the dispute over whether Russia lost its voting rights by its refusal to pay assessments, the delegates decided on the bizarre "solution" of not holding any votes at all until some compromise could be reached. One irate delegate summed up the situation neatly: "A farce." [10]

The middle

If you have done this much planning before writing, a basic organizational plan or plans of developing your material should have taken place, providing that you are familiar with the variety of methods and combination of methods of structuring writing. This section of the theme — the middle or body — is very important. If the whole is to be successful, you must support and develop the central thought with well-structured paragraphs that relate to and make meaningful the thesis. In this chapter, the middle part of the paper will be considered only briefly; the remainder of the book will treat the middle in great detail. As you study the model short piece of writing which follows, observe the function of the middle: those paragraphs which support and develop the thesis.

BASKETBALL BRIBES AND SPORTS DE-EMPHASIS
by Dwight Keith

[1] The recent basketball bribe scandals have brought shocking disappointment to coaches, educators and all true sportsmen. It is too bad that a few gamblers plus a small minority of the players can cast such a dark shadow over the great game of basketball, the game which had its origin in the United States and has done so much for the American youth. It is a game which reaches all the way from the big coliseums to the country hamlets where the game is played on an outdoor court.

[2] This column realizes that it is a problem to be faced but we were disappointed to hear proposals that the game be curtailed or even eliminated if necessary. These proposals come from people who seize a situation like this to attack sports or else lack the imagination needed to solve the problem.

[3] Certainly the administrators feel the responsibility to meet the problem squarely and, in their urgency to do so, they propose de-emphasis. Surely you can burn down the barn to rid it of mice, but then you have no barn and the mice move elsewhere. You will not improve a boy's character by locking the gym door. This is a battle that must be fought in the boy's heart and mind. His chances of growing morally stronger are enhanced when he comes under the influence of a good coach.

[4] In the recent price fixing cases brought against big business, no one proposed that we discontinue manufacturing the products of the companies involved. You even sometimes find immorality in the church, but no one recommends de-emphasis of religion.

Sometimes you find cribbing in the classroom, but no one suggests that we de-emphasize education or close the school.

[5]With a few remote exceptions, the athletic coaches of America are men of high character who are dedicated to their profession and to the moral and physical welfare of the players in their charge. The overwhelming majority of players are high type youngsters who could never be tempted by a bribe. It is grossly unfair to deprive them of the recognized benefits of sports because of the weakness of a few players.

[6]A better solution would be to place *greater emphasis* on sports, along with more attention being given to recruiting methods. We have always felt that, as a matter of policy, schools should recruit only in their own geographical areas. However, it would not be fair to impose a ban on students coming from other areas as that sometimes involves sons of the alumni of the institution and other worthy applicants who are seeking the course best suited to their needs. Most important of all, let's not make the mistake of de-emphasizing things that have proven benefits and should receive *greater emphasis!* [11]

QUESTIONS

1. What is the thesis of this selection?
2. What is the function of the first paragraph?
3. What is the main point of the second paragraph? What relationship to the whole does this point have?
4. How many supporting paragraphs are there? Write the main idea of each of the supporting paragraphs.
5. What is the function of the last paragraph?

Conclusions

Conclusions like introductions vary with the ability of writers. A common means of concluding a piece of writing is with a statement or restatement of the thesis idea. Some writer will close with a summary of the main points of the discussion; others will indicate future action that the point of view demands. Still others will omit a formal conclusion, preferring to mention the thesis in the last supporting paragraph or to end the paper with a meaningful quotation.

Read the model conclusions which follow.

Model 1 — FROM "...HOLD THAT TIGER!"

A further positive program needs to be inaugurated by means of which the values in intercollegiate athletic participation may be made available to greater numbers of young men and women. The number of persons acquiring these values now is far too costly, but it would be worth the price. The tiger is valuable — if we get positive and effective control of it and lead it in the right direction. [12]

In concluding his discussion of intercollegiate athletics, Frank N. Gardner offers positive programs to control it. He makes use again of his opening analogy of the tiger.

Model 2 — FROM "WHERE ARE WE?"
This effort to find out what it's all about is, in our time, more difficult than ever before. The reason is that the old foundations of assured faith and familiar custom are crumbling under our feet. For four hundred years the world of education and knowledge rested securely on two fundamentals which were rarely questioned. These were *Christian philosophy* and *Classical learning*. For the better part of a century Christian faith has been going by the board, and Classical learning into discard. To replace these we have as yet no foundations, no certainties. We live in a world dominated by machines, a world of incredibly rapid change, a world of naturalistic science and of physico-chemico-libido psychology. There are no longer any certainties either in life or in thought. Everywhere confusion. Everywhere questions. Where are we? [13]

Model 3 — FROM "WHAT'S WRONG WITH THE U.N."
A presidential study group would naturally consider and evaluate many such suggestions, but reform of the U.N. cannot long be delayed. If we simply go on "supporting" the U.N. without enabling it to function realistically, it will die as surely as the League of Nations died — because it will become irrelevant to the problems we face. [14]

Model 4 — FROM "BEETLES, BATS, AND BALLISTIC BEASTS"
I plead for patience with the Air Force biologist when he uses strange specimens of animal life. [15]

Model 5 — FROM "THE MORAL SENSE OF THE SCIENTISTS"
And Lynn T. White, Jr., another historian, argued that "both our present science and our present technology are so tinctured with Christian arrogance toward nature" — the attitude that it exists for the service of man — that "the remedy must also be essentially religious." Science and technology, he said, cannot answer all the questions they raise." [16]

Model 6 — FROM "THE COMPUTER AND THE POET"
The poet reminds men of their uniqueness. It is not necessary to possess the ultimate definition of this uniqueness. Even to speculate on it is a gain. [17]

Norman Cousins closes his discussion of the computer and the poet with a statement of his thesis.

ASSIGNMENTS

3. Overall view

Select any one of the following topics and write the following: (1) a thesis sentence, (2) an introductory paragraph, (3) a concluding paragraph.
1. Law Enforcement
2. The Right to Vote
3. Crime Prevention
4. Automobile Accidents
5. Deadly Insecticides
6. Modern Fashions
7. Drug Addiction
8. My Campus
9. Entertainment
10. Movies or Television

4. Overall view

Read the two short student themes below, both entitled "Why I Came to College." Write a paragraph criticizing each. Give reasons in your criticism why you think the theme is good or bad.

My primary reasons for coming to college was to try to get into a position where I would have enough education to find a good job. A good job that would support my family and I confortaly for the rest of are lives.
I want to be an engineer is another reason I came. Because engineering offers good money and security in the years ahead and it will give me the things I want.
While in college I have followed along the way I wanted to but I have not done as well as I would like to in all classes I have been takeing.

A college education can mean many things to different people. My purpose in coming to college was to acquire an education.

I want to be able to associate with educated people and carry on an intelligent discussion without difficulty.

Finding a husband is another point to consider. A girl has more of a chance to meet someone on her own level if she increases her knowledge. She will also share interests that will be common to both.

A broader education means choosing a career that is interesting and rewarding. It is important to enjoy your work because you can't be happy doing something you don't like.

College is necessary in planning a future. At this time in your life you have to make adult decisions and stick to them.

5. Overall view

Write a theme of approximately 500 words on the subject "Why I Came to College."

CHAPTER ONE   *References*

1. "Integration: Opportunity and Obligation" by Whitney M. Young, Jr. Copyright 1966 by *Parents' Magazine*. Reprinted by permission.

2. From *Understanding English* by Paul Roberts. Copyright © 1958 by Paul Roberts. Reprinted by permission of Harper & Row, Publishers.

3. From *Civilization: Past and Present,* Volume I, by T. Walter Wallbank and Alastair M. Taylor. Copyright 1954 by Scott, Foresman and Company.

4. From "A Modest Proposal" by Jonathan Swift.

5. From "The San Francisco Earthquake" by Jack London.

6. From "Second Thoughts About Readers," by Alma Boice Holland in *The Writer's Digest* (July, 1967). Reprinted by permission of the author.

7. From "Young Men Lead in Science Discovery" in *Science Digest* (January, 1961). Reprinted with permission from *Science Digest*. © The Hearst Corporation.

8. From "The Place of Intercollegiate Athletics in Higher Education: Hold That Tiger!" by Frank N. Gardner. Copyright © 1960 by The Ohio State University Press and reprinted with its permission.

9. From "Where Are We?" by Carl Becker in *The Cornell Daily Sun*. Reprinted by permission of *The Cornell Daily Sun*.

10. From "What's Wrong With the U.N.?" Editorial in *The Saturday Evening Post* (February, 1965). Reprinted with the permission of *The Saturday Evening Post*. © 1965 The Curtis Publishing Company.
11. "Basketball Bribes and Sports De-Emphasis," by Dwight Keith, in *Coach & Athlete* (June, 1961). Reprinted by permission of *Coach & Athlete*.
12. From "The Place of Intercollegiate Athletics in Higher Education: Hold That Tiger!" by Frank N. Gardner. Cf. 8.
13. From "Where Are We?" by Carl Becker. Cf. 9.
14. From "What's Wrong With the U.N.?" Cf. 10.
15. From "Beetles, Bats, and Ballistic Beasts," by B. G. Holzman in *Science Digest* (February, 1961). Reprinted with permission from *Science Digest*. © The Hearst Corporation.
16. From "The Moral Sense of the Scientists," by J. V. Reistrup, *Science,* Volume 155 (January 20, 1967). Copyright 1967 by The American Association for the Advancement of Science, and reprinted with their permission and *The Washington Post*.
17. From "The Computer and the Poet," by Norman Cousins. Copyright 1966 Saturday Review, Inc. By permission.

TWO

Writing the paragraph

In the last chapter, the importance of well-structured paragraphs to effective writing was mentioned many times. What is a paragraph? What are its functions? How does one structure effective paragraphs? These are some of the questions that will be answered in this chapter and in Chapter 4.

Characteristics of a paragraph

A paragraph consists of sentences (usually more than one), each with its own structural pattern, in a series that develops one single idea. Generally, a paragraph consists of a main idea in the form of a generalization with supporting material that enables the reader to accept the generalization. The model paragraph that follows, excerpted from a letter written to a college newspaper by a college professor, illustrates this kind of organization and development.

This effort to find out what it's all about is, in our time, more difficult than ever before. The reason is that the old foundations of assured faith and familiar custom are crumbling under our feet. For four hundred years the world of education and knowledge rested securely on two fundamentals which were rarely questioned. These were *Christian philosophy* and *Classical learning*. For the better part of a century Christian faith has been going by the board, and Classical learning into the discard. To replace these we have as yet no foundations, no certainties. We live in a world dominated by machines, a world of incredibly rapid change, a world of naturalistic science and of physico-chemico-libido psychology. There are no longer any certainties either in life or in thought. Everywhere confusion. Everywhere questions. Where are we? [1]

DISCUSSION

The writer Carl Becker begins with stating his main idea in the form of a generalization: *This effort to find out what it's all about is, in our time, more difficult than ever before.* He then cites reasons — a series of factual statements — why his belief is true. He closes this final paragraph with a restatement of the thesis of the whole piece of writing: "Everywhere confusion. Everywhere questions. Where are we?"

As you read the model paragraph which follows, taken from an editorial in "The Sporting News," look for the main idea and observe the kinds of supporting material, particularly the example.

It's unfortunate that the sports fraternity lacks imagination as well as frankness in announcing appointments to positions of eminence. How regrettable it was, for example, that the promotion of Phil Bengtson into the shoes of the incomparable Vince Lombardi at Green Bay failed to inspire Bengtson beyond the usual: "It's a great challenge." [2]

Read the following paragraph, excerpted from an article in *The Atlantic Monthly* but written by a student.

The human fact is that a student of any age cannot read analytically the works of Locke, Jefferson, Ortega, Shaw (much less Sartre, Osborne, or Baldwin) without recognizing much that is stupid and evil in our society. In the way of people who are young, free, and relatively innocent of the adult world's experience, he believes that there's no point arguing because no one listens to him anyway, so he makes his anger known in other ways. His righteous wrath and insistence that society take steps to improve itself immediately are not the products of inflammatory texts or teachers; they are the inevitable concomitants of the intelligent student's attempt to relate what he hears in class to himself and his world. [3]

DISCUSSION

This paragraph illustrates a main idea that must be inferred by the reader. The inference is not difficult to make when one knows that this paragraph is part of a short piece of writing

titled "A Vote For Student Protest." (See page 32.) The writer
cites reasons why students have a right to protest.

_____

Here is a longer and more fully developed paragraph,
excerpted from a textbook in history.

Their [the men who overthrew James II] course was
dangerous. They agreed on the fundamentals of what had to be done,
but on very little else. For a decade they had been divided into two
embattled parties, Whigs and Tories; only a great crisis could have
brought the two together, and even in the crisis they threatened to
turn on each other again. Many issues separated them. The Tories
were traditionally the champions of the crown and of the Church of
England, the Whigs the champions of parliament and the dissenters,
or Protestants outside the Anglican Church. Although both Tories
and Whigs disliked Roman Catholics, until the Revolution the Tories,
professing blind obedience to the Catholic James, muted their hostility to Rome in order to remain obedient. On foreign policy the two
parties were as far apart as on domestic. The Whigs, partly because of
their ties with domestic interests and partly because of their stalwart
Protestantism, were belligerent toward France, which was becoming
Britain's chief commercial rival and was the major Catholic power of
the Continent; the Tories, who drew strong support from the rural
gentry, had no desire to be drawn into a French war, from which the
merchants would profit and for which the gentry would be taxed.
These were the major issues, and so divisive that nothing short of a
political miracle could have induced the two parties to collaborate. [4]

DISCUSSION

This model paragraph begins with a statement of the
main idea in the form of an opening generalization: *Their course
was dangerous.* The writer next recounts some of the history of
that time, stressing the differences between the two parties. With
the statement "Many issues separated them," he begins to offer
support. He organizes and develops the support by citing disputes
over domestic and foreign policy. He concludes with a transitional sentence that leads the reader onward to the thought of the
following paragraph.

Functions of paragraphing

Besides presenting distinctive styles of organization
and development of thought, the model paragraphs just preceding

have illustrated two important functions of paragraphing. First, paragraphing enables a writer to organize and develop effectively a single important idea. Frequently, a writer will express this main idea in the form of a generalization known as a *topic sentence* or *statement sentence*. Occasionally, he lets the reader infer the main idea from the contents of the paragraph. He develops his main idea by a number of sentences known as *support*.

Second, paragraphing enables a writer to effectively develop the thesis of a longer piece of writing. Just as a group of sentences relate to one another and to a main idea, so a group of paragraphs relate to one another and to the thesis of a theme or an even longer piece of writing. Just as sentences develop the main idea of a paragraph, so paragraphs develop the thesis around which they are organized. A paragraph or a group of paragraphs can serve as one link in a chain of thought. Each paragraph must contribute something directly to the thesis; otherwise it is a digression and should be eliminated.

Let us see the role a paragraph plays in writing by placing a model paragraph back into the longer piece of writing from which it was excerpted for the purposes of illustration.

A VOTE FOR STUDENT PROTEST
by Mary N. Gonzales
¹In the present era university students and their professors, who are, it must be immediately established, only older students paying their debt to scholarship by inducting a new generation, have been passionately involved in debating and protesting the political and social events of their time.

²The students who demonstrated on campuses across the country last year against the U.S. position in Vietnam were acting within their rights as citizens. Where they infringed the constitutional rights of others — by breaking up assemblies of fellow students or inhibiting the free speech of others — they deserved to be, and were, punished. But the fact that some of the students who demonstrated were rowdy (or dirty or bearded or *wrong*) is no more logical as an argument against demonstrations than the fact that Americans have often elected incompetent men to office can be considered a reason for abandoning democratic elections.

³The human fact is that a student of any age cannot read analytically the works of Locke, Jefferson, Ortega, Shaw, Ibsen (much less Sartre, Osborne, or Baldwin) without recognizing much that is stupid and evil in our society. In the way of people who are

young, free, and relatively innocent of the adult world's experience, he believes that there's no point arguing because no one listens to him anyway, so he makes his anger known in other ways. His righteous wrath and insistence that society take steps to improve itself immediately are not the products of inflammatory texts or teachers; they are the inevitable concomitants of the intelligent student's attempt to relate what he hears in class to himself and his world.
    [4]No pat on the head for youthful idealism is intended here. Youthful idealism is widely known to curdle into middle-aged cynicism, and both are diffuse, unproductive ways of meeting social problems. The past year's crop of demonstrators made it clear that they were not claiming to have answers to problems that have required years of persistent effort and will require many more to produce results. They wanted to express their attitude on issues of the greatest importance — war and peace, and foreign intervention, the rights of small nations and defenseless citizens — and to communicate these attitudes as widely as possible.
    [5]Any student who can sit through four years of college without once getting excited enough about the war in Vietnam or Communism in Cuba, voting discrimination in the South or the plight of the Jews in Russia to investigate the problem (study) and find others who agree with him and make some public protest — any student so dense or just plain selfish that he has not perceived the relation between his university education and the pressing questions of his society has undoubtedly been wasting his time. [5]

DISCUSSION

    Mrs. Gonzales' short piece of writing shows clearly the functions of paragraphing. She organizes and develops her supporting material — the middle of the paper — around a thesis stated clearly and cogently in the final paragraph.
    She begins her discussion with a short introductory paragraph pointing out that professors and students "have been passionately involved in debating and protesting the political and social events of their time."
    She supports and develops the thesis — students' right to protest — by three well-structured paragraphs, consisting essentially of examples and statements defending their rights to protest. The first supporting paragraph mentions their rights to protest as citizens. The second paragraph of support stresses strongly that protests "are the inevitable concomitants of the

intelligent student's attempt to relate what he hears in class to himself and his world." The third paragraph of support points out that students do not think that they have the answers to the problems; she adds, however, that they want to express their "attitudes on issues of the greatest importance . . . ."

She uses the final paragraph to state the thesis: *students have the right to protest.* She moves her developing thought onward through details and specifics to a conclusion — a method of developing thought known as *induction.*

The structural organization of "A Vote For Student Protest" shows how effective and important good paragraphing is to the total process of written communication. Each paragraph or paragraph unit plays a special role in the organization and development of the whole. It may introduce the subject or bring the subject to a conclusion. It may function simply as a transitional device to carry the reader logically and smoothly from one phase of the writer's developing thought to another. Finally, a paragraph or paragraph unit may play the very important role of supporting the thesis in order that the reader will accept the writer's point of view concerning the subject.

With these facts in mind about paragraphing, read now the next short selection from which the second model paragraph in this chapter was taken.

LET'S HAVE THAT AGAIN . . . SLOWLY
The Sporting News

[1] Of all the bromides which our paragons of the sports world have worn to a frazzle, the stalest is the refrain of the newly-hired coach, manager or executive. The traded player also is an enthusiastic member of this society. Invariably, upon discussing his most recent connection, the ball of fire proclaims: "I regard it as a challenge." Chances are he also considers it an opportunity to keep on eating, but such an admission would be shockingly candid in this era of credibility gaps.

[2] It's unfortunate that the sports fraternity lacks imagination as well as frankness in announcing appointments to positions of eminence. How regrettable it was, for example, that the promotion of Phil Bengtson into the shoes of the incomparable Vince Lombardi at Green Bay failed to inspire Bengtson beyond the usual: "It's a great challenge."

³The future, however, is not completely desolate. Potential job hunters might take a cue from Alex Hannum, who now directs the Philadelphia 76ers, but apparently is casting about for a new command. Hannum displayed a talent for obscuring the obvious with his remark that "I am interested in an opportunity for more total involvement." Are we to assume that Alex' involvement now is total, but that he would like it to be "more total"?

⁴At least, Hannum avoided the trite, but he is not yet in the big leagues of obfuscation. For the ultimate in bewildering word structure, we must go to Wall Street and the builders of the conglomerates, those stock-market darlings which only recently began to look more like fallen angels. In that league, the wheeler-dealers speak of "the synergy of the free-form company and its interface with change and technology." Think that over, Alex, baby.

⁵The I-like-a-challenge school and the more-total-involvement theme differ only in technique. The result is similar: A bland statement or a maze of word mixology nobody is likely to contest or criticize. The real sports rarity is the guy who says what he means and means what he says. In this category, Clete Boyer stands virtually alone, the master of the blunt message. In some amazingly succinct quotes on Page 28 of this issue, Clete dispatches Rico Carty as a loafer, Billy Hitchcock as an incompetent manager and the Braves as a hopeless case in the pennant race unless some players change their attitudes.

⁶Clete won't win any popularity contests with those remarks, but when he speaks, nobody has to ask: "What did he say?" [6]

QUESTIONS

1. What is the thesis?
2. Is the thesis expressed in a clearly written thesis sentence?
3. What is the main idea in each of the supporting paragraphs?
    (2)
    (3)
    (4)
    (5) The real sports rarity is the guy who says what he
        means and means what he says.
4. What relationships does the last sentence — a one-sentence conclusion — have to the thesis?

Finally, observe how the model paragraph excerpted from the history text fits into the structural organization of that particular division of Chapter 1.

THE GLORIOUS REVOLUTION
by William B. Willcox

[1] Between November, 1688 and March, 1689, England went through the rare experience of a revolution that was initiated and controlled by conservatives. The only man in the kingdom in 1688 who was a true revolutionary, in the sense of desiring fundamental change, was the King himself, and the change that James II desired was reactionary. He wanted to reestablish a form of government and a church that the British political world had long since rejected. His dream of making the royal prerogative superior to parliament had died on the scaffold with his father, Charles I; his dream of returning Britain to Roman Catholicism had died with his great-grandmother, Mary, Queen of Scots, and its ghost had been laid at the time of the Popish Plot, which at the end of the 1670's had almost upset his brother's throne. James, from the moment of his accession in 1685, worked stalwartly and stupidly to realize his dreams; and by the close of 1688 he was an exile in France. His departure set great changes in motion, but the men who overthrew him were no lovers of change. They acted in order to conserve what they had gained since the restoration of the monarchy in 1660. James threatened their gains and consequently, in their eyes, threatened to subvert the established constitution. To defend it they turned against him, and used revolutionary means to *prevent* revolutionary change.

[2] Their course was dangerous. They were agreed on the fundamentals of what had to be done, but on little else. For a decade they had been divided into two embattled parties, Whigs and Tories; only a great crisis could have brought the two together, and even in the crisis they threatened to turn on each other again. Many issues separated them. The Tories were traditionally the champions of the crown and of the Church of England, the Whigs the champions of parliament and the dissenters, or Protestants outside the established Anglican Church. Although both Tories and Whigs disliked Roman Catholics, until the Revolution the Tories, professing blind obedience to the Catholic James, muted their hostility to Rome in order to remain obedient. On foreign policy the two parties were as far apart as on domestic. The Whigs, partly because of their ties with the mercantile interests and partly because of their stalwart Protestantism, were belligerent toward France, which was becoming Britain's chief commercial rival and was the major Catholic power of the Continent; the Tories, who drew strong support from the rural gentry, had no desire to be drawn into a French war, from which the merchants would profit and for which the gentry would be taxed. These were major issues, and so divisive that nothing short of a political miracle could have induced the two parties to collaborate.

[3] James worked the miracle. When he tried to use his prerogative not only to establish despotism but to return the church to Rome, he forced the Tories to choose between the two basic articles of their creed: loyalty to the crown and to Anglicanism — for the two were now in conflict. Most Tories responded, however reluctantly, by discarding their theory that the king could do no wrong and by allying with the Whigs to safeguard the familiar institutions of the country. The alliance was precarious, for within it all the old stresses were still at work; but the cost of letting them come to the surface was clear — to put the nation, in all likelihood, on the road it had followed in 1642, through civil war to the destruction of the whole known order. The men of 1688, with the lesson of the Cavaliers and Roundheads fresh in memory, were so determined to keep their own revolution from getting out of hand that they were willing to forget past quarrels and temporarily compromise their differences.

[4] They had their awkward moments. In the autumn of 1688 they faced a real threat of civil war, but James saved them by fleeing the kingdom. Then came the problem of who should succeed him. The Convention Parliament, summoned to determine the question, argued long and bitterly before it agreed to settle the crown on James's elder daughter, Mary, and her husband and first cousin, William, Stadtholder of the Netherlands and grandson, through his mother, of Charles I. Once William III and Mary II were proclaimed as joint sovereigns, the revolution in England was virtually complete. It still had a stormy course to run in Scotland and an even stormier one in Ireland, as will soon be seen, but by the spring of 1689 the danger was over that the attack on James would, like the attack on his father, Charles I, unloose the flood of radicalism.

[5] The Revolution was adroitly managed, but this was not the principal reason why it was orderly. It also commanded a large degree of consensus among the oligarchs, the small group of Whigs and Tories who were the political world of the day. Violently as these men disagreed on specific issues, they agreed on the fundamental point that their own position must be secured against royal encroachment. A few Tories, for whom their old principles were more important than their position as oligarchs, remained loyal to their exiled King; for them, as for Shakespeare,

> The breath of worldly men cannot depose
> The deputy elected by the Lord.

These nostalgic royalists were known as Jacobites, from the Latin form of James, and they and their descendants continued to make intermittent trouble for more than half a century. But they found little support among their fellow oligarchs, whose power the Revolution confirmed and who therefore found it profoundly satisfying. [7]

DISCUSSION

This selection is a division of chapter 1 of a book *The Age of Aristocracy 1688 to 1830* by William B. Willcox. It consists of five well-organized and fully developed paragraphs — paragraph 2 is the model paragraph. The author states his thesis in the first sentence of paragraph 1: "Between November, 1688 and March, 1689, England went through the rare experience of a revolution that was initiated and controlled by conservatives." Paragraph 2 develops one aspect of that thesis: "Their course was dangerous." The relatedness of the paragraphs in the selection may be studied further by means of a paragraph outline — a simple listing of the main idea of each paragraph.

The glorious revolution

Thesis: Between November, 1688 and March, 1689, England went through the rare experience of a revolution that was initiated and controlled by conservatives.

1. An introductory paragraph including a statement of the thesis.
2. Their course was dangerous.
3. James worked miracles.
4. They had their awkward moments.
5. It was an orderly revolution.

A paragraph, then, has two important functions in a theme: (1) to give order and completeness to the thought developing its own main idea, and (2) to relate to and develop the thesis of the longer piece of writing of which it is a part.

Most modern writers divide any sizable piece of writing into paragraphs. They use paragraphing because it is an effective means of presenting their ideas clearly, giving order to their flowing thoughts, emphasizing important points, and indicating beginnings and endings of each related part of a whole piece of writing. Modern writers use paragraphing also because they know it will help their readers. They realize that page after page of unbroken thought can be dull and tiresome reading. They indent separate phrases of their thought so that the reader will be able to see more clearly each link in that chain of thinking. They know that their readers will grasp meaning more easily and rapidly, maintain interest in the writing, and sense relationships among the separate parts and between each part and the whole if their writing consists of skillfully organized and fully developed paragraphs.

Paragraph unity: The topic sentence

How do you structure the kinds of paragraphs that we have been discussing? First, you must learn to phrase a good topic sentence. A topic sentence will help give a paragraph unity. You would not have too much difficulty in determining the subject matter of paragraphs beginning with the following topic sentences:

The authority of parents has weakened.

Surfing is a dangerous sport.

Animals use color chiefly for protection.

Water conservation should be the concern of all people.

Cape Cod is unique.

College athletics is public entertainment.

Most meteorites are of two kinds.

Basic to all Greek achievement was freedom.

You should be realizing by now that a good topic sentence is essential to effective paragraphing. It unifies a number of sentences into a cohesive unit, as the thesis unifies a number of paragraphs into a whole theme. In addition, the topic sentence may serve as a sort of introduction to what follows since it may indicate what the paragraph is about and reveal something of the subject matter. This kind of planned sentence also limits the scope of the paragraph for both writer and reader. You will be better able to achieve unity by developing a single idea. A good topic sentence, then, is the statement which unifies a number of sentences. It provides the focal point around which you can develop your central thought.

Notice the loss of unity and conciseness when these same topic sentences are poorly phrased.

The authority of parents has become a problem.

Surfing is a fascinating sport.

Animals make good use of color.

Water conservation is a concern.

Cape Cod is in Massachusetts.

College athletics is a controversial issue.

Meteorites are "happy travellers" in space.

The Greek experiment was an important one.

How does a writer structure a good topic sentence? He must first have a definite purpose or point of view. He must have a strong reason for stressing a particular aspect of his thought about a subject. In thinking about his visit to Saigon, a writer recalls many details. One condition, however, left a deep impression on him — the corruption. He wishes his readers to know about such corruption. He phrases a topic sentence stressing this idea: "Saigon today is a corrupt city." It is the idea of *corrupt,* not the rest of the sentence, that he will develop fully. He could have expressed a number of other dominant impressions about Saigon in much the same way, such as "Saigon is a city of intrigue," "Saigon is an immoral city," "Saigon is a beautiful city," "Saigon is a city in transition." Any one of these statements would make a good topic sentence because it is limited and expresses an attitude or point of view.

Statements like the following, on the other hand, would probably be weak topic sentences because they are simply statements of fact.

Shakespeare is an Elizabethan writer.

Boston is the capital of Massachusetts.

Saigon is a city in Southeast Asia.

Each of these statements is merely factual; it would be very difficult, therefore, to develop them as topics for a paragraph. The statements which follow would probably make poor topic sentences because they are too broad for adequate development in paragraph length.

Literature presents a mirror of life.

The dictionary has an interesting history.

Rome has a glorious and tragic story.

The difference between a poor topic sentence and a good one is that the poor topic sentence does not have a clearly stated main idea which shows the writer's purpose or point of view. A poor topic sentence, as we have already seen, is too limited or too broad and general to be developed into an effective paragraph. A sentence, for example, like "Saigon is a city in Southeast Asia" is sufficient in itself. A writer would find it difficult to say anything else. And a statement like "Every individual in the U.S. is entitled to free public education," on the other hand, is too broad to treat adequately in a short theme.

In phrasing a topic sentence, a writer must make his main idea unmistakably clear. Many writers, therefore, phrase the main idea in a word, phrase, or clause that dominates the topic sentence.

Saigon is a *dangerous* city *at night*.

Integration will *benefit* the *white* citizen.

A college student has the *right* to *protest*.

Saigon is a *beautiful* city *at dawn*.

Animals use colors chiefly *for protection*.

In my early school years, teachers *frightened* me.

But above all, the Continental Congress adopted two measures *which pointed straight toward a breach with the British ministry*.

It was toward the very end of the period of apparent placidity *that Walter Bagehot provided his classic account of the English constitution*.

Between November, 1688 and March, 1689, England went through the rare experience of a revolution *that was initiated and controlled by conservatives.*

Writers also phrase their main idea in a question sentence.

Why are writers active enemies of sociology, economics, and other social sciences?

How was the literature of eighteenth-century England related to the political and social conditions of that time?

What was the meaning of Democracy in the Age of Pericles?

Read the model paragraph which follows, written by a student. Is the main idea unmistakably clear?

Very shortly police officers are going to be forced to ask permission of the person they wish to arrest before the arrest can be made legally. Laws are being passed to protect the guilty and not to protect the innocent. No wonder the crime rate in the nation has risen so high; the criminals know they have a very good chance of not being convicted of their crime. Today, it is extremely difficult to convict a person of a crime because somewhere between their arrest and conviction, a police officer will make a human error allowing the arrested person to go free from punishment for the crime he has committed against society.

DISCUSSION

The paragraph is confusing because the main idea is not clearly thought out. As a result the paragraph consists of four somewhat unrelated sentences, each expressing a different idea. If the writer had stated a main idea, such as "Many of our present laws protect the criminal," he would still have to limit the subject to the one particular law concerning procedures when a police officer makes an arrest. This is the main idea that he is apparently trying to develop.

Read the next student paragraph.

The right to vote can be given only to those people who can understand what it means to vote. Therefore, there must be an age limit. In California, one must be at least 21 years of age to vote in state or national elections. Although there are some people who are trying to bring this age down to 18 years of age.

DISCUSSION

The main idea in this paragraph — "the right to vote can be given only to those people who can understand what it means to vote" — is a poor topic sentence because it is too involved and does not state clearly a main idea. The writer probably meant "An individual must be twenty-one to vote in state and national elections." Such a statement would also be a poor topic sentence since it is essentially a factual statement. A writer with this kind of main idea has nothing else to say. As a result he is very likely to digress into a discussion of points irrelevant to the main idea as does the writer of the model paragraph in his discussion of the lowering of the voting age.

EXERCISES

1. Topic sentence

Read the model student paragraph below. Answer the subsequent questions.

Funerals in the United States are big business. From the moment the mortician is selected, a subtle but forceful pressure begins to separate the bereaved family from as much money as possible. The best casket, the finest "view" plot in the cemetery and the longest, newest Cadillacs for the procession are some of the expensive items that are objects of a "hard sell" campaign directed at persons who are at an emotional nadir. Included in the service — if it is a reasonably expensive one — is a half-hour eulogy said by one who probably did not know the deceased at all and heard by either those who don't know whether it is true or not or who are too busy observing the trappings to hear the words.

1. What is the topic sentence?
2. What point of view does the main idea establish?
3. Do you feel that the writer makes clear his main idea?
4. Are you willing to accept his point of view on the basis of the evidence he presents?

2. *Topic sentence*

Read the following statements. If you believe that the statement would make a good topic sentence, place (A) in front of the sentence number. Underline the word or words that reveal the writer's attitude or point of view.

1. A teacher like a salesman must learn the art of selling.
2. The old wharf is an exciting place to be when the fishing fleet returns home.
3. Ice fishing is a cold job.
4. Roman emperors were very cruel.
5. The Painted Desert is especially beautiful when the sun sets.
6. Lincoln was assassinated while he was watching a play.
7. Mt. Vesuvius is still an active volcano.
8. Surfing can be dangerous.
9. The changes in dress during the last decade of this century were many and extreme.
10. Bismarck was a famous German military leader.

3. *Topic sentence*

Read the following statements. If you believe that the statement would make a good topic sentence, place (A) in front of the sentence number. Underline the word or words that reveal the writer's attitude or point of view.

1. Our current ethic is a curious mixture of superstition and rationalism.
2. Barry Goldwater is a conservative in his political thinking.
3. President John F. Kennedy was assassinated in Dallas, Texas.
4. Their route to the Northwest was hazardous.
5. High school is an exciting four years.
6. My first high school dance was a frightening experience.
7. Comics are badly written.
8. Exemption from the draft for brains is discriminatory.
9. Capital punishment is wrong.
10. Capital punishment is not a deterrent to murder.

4. Topic sentence

Write a main idea under fifteen of the following topics.

1. college football	11. friends
2. comics	12. parents
3. art	13. civil rights
4. clothes	14. minority groups
5. sewing	15. space
6. occupations	16. weather
7. school politics	17. gardening
8. dates	18. cooking
9. music	19. religion
10. games	20. social groups

Where is the most effective position in a paragraph for the topic sentence? The main idea is commonly expressed in the first sentence of a paragraph. It is emphatic in that position and it can function also as a kind of introduction. However, a series of paragraphs, all beginning with topic sentences, can produce a stultifying mechanical effect. A writer, therefore, obtains variety and emphasis by placing his topic sentence in other positions. In developing a paragraph inductively, a writer ends his discussion with a statement of the main idea so that he can emphasize or summarize the preceding thought. Sometimes a writer will place his topic sentence in the middle of the paragraph so that he can reverse the direction of the developing thought. Occasionally, a writer will place his topic sentence in other positions than the beginning, middle, or end. At times a writer will begin with a statement of the main idea and restate it in slightly different words in the final sentence in order to emphasize the central thought.

Read the model paragraphs and observe the kind of topic sentence and its position. Ask yourself: Is the topic sentence too limited? Is the topic sentence too broad? Does the topic sentence indicate the writer's purpose or point of view? Does the topic sentence reveal something of the contents of the paragraph? Does the position give the main idea emphasis?

Model 1

The invasion never came. Hitler repeatedly postponed the date for a number of reasons, the most important of which may well have been the heroic resistance of the British air fighter command.

Outnumbered four to one, the intrepid Hurricane and Spitfire pilots destroyed two German planes for every one of their own. "Never in the field of human conflict," declared Churchill, "was so much owed by so many to so few." German air superiority over the Channel was not achieved, and an increasing number of German invasion transports and barges were sunk in port. Neither industrial production nor civilian morale had been damaged by air raids to the degree that German planners had anticipated. Londoners digging in the rubble after a severe air raid often found King George VI at hand to commiserate or else a defiant Churchill puffing a cigar, his fingers formed in a "V for Victory" sign. [8]

DISCUSSION

The writer begins with a brief, emphatic statement of his main idea: "The invasion never came." His purpose is informative: to explain why the invasion did not take place. He gives the following reasons as supporting material: (1) the heroic resistance of the British fighter command; (2) German superiority over the Channel was not achieved; (3) industrial production and civilian morale was not affected by the air raids to the extent that the Germans had planned; (4) the courage of the British symbolized by the figure of the undaunted Churchill.

This model paragraph is well written. It is unified, organized effectively, and complete. Yet the plan of organization and development is simple — a topic sentence stating a result followed by a number of reasons explaining that occurrence.

Model 2

Parents may not realize how much they contribute to their youngsters' dishonest behavior. For one thing, more and more parents virtually do their children's homework for them, without stopping to consider if such help really helps the student. Some parents are scrupulously honest themselves, and refrain from actually doing their children's work for them, but they may place the youngsters under such heavy pressure to excel in school that they turn to cheating in order to get the grades they couldn't otherwise make. [9]

QUESTIONS

1. What is the topic sentence?
2. Does the topic sentence reveal something of the contents of the paragraph?

3. Write a title for a theme in which this paragraph would fit.

Model 3

This luxuriant blooming of the Army bureaucracy has been a much-noted feature of the American effort in Vietnam. The junior officers with the Vietnamese combat units have done valiant work, but they are a small minority. There are a round dozen American generals in Vietnam, each with his subordinate colonels, majors, and so on down. Correspondents on the spot have reported that at least half the 22,000 uniformed Americans in Vietnam are in Saigon, doing staff and housekeeping chores. One result is that, as reporter Joseph Kraft noted after a visit to Vietnam, the American Army there is like "an elephant (trying) to act like a mouse." Another result is that the "American presence" in Saigon is all too visible, lending color to Communist propaganda about American "neocolonialism."

The same elephantine staff system prevails in Europe. Colonel Crosby writes: "The commander of a combat division in Europe has no less than five staffs breathing down his neck — a corps headquarters, 7th U.S. Army, U.S. Army Europe, European Command, and hovering in the background, SHAPE. Never have so few been commanded by so many." [10]

QUESTIONS

1. What is the main idea? Is it expressed?
2. What is the main idea of the second paragraph?

Model 4

Millions of years ago, a volcano built a mountain on the floor of the Atlantic. In eruption after eruption, it gushed up a great pile of volcanic rock, until it had accumulated a mass a hundred miles across at its base, reaching upward toward the surface of the sea. Finally its cone emerged as an island with an area of about 200 square miles. Thousands of years passed, and thousands of thousands. Eventually the waves of the Atlantic cut down the cone and reduced it to a shoal — all of it, that is, but a small fragment which remained above water. This fragment we know as Bermuda.[11]

QUESTIONS

1. Where in the paragraph is the topic sentence?
2. What process is the writer describing?

Model 5

A good deal of cheating, therefore — but not all — is done to get good grades. There are also the "anything for kicks" youngsters who cheat for somewhat the same reasons that they drag race cars, shoplift, or wreck property — because they have nothing more constructive they want to do or can do, and because such flouting of rules is considered smart by their friends. Generally, those who consider it smart to cheat will voice as a defense, "Everybody does it, why shouldn't I?"[12]

QUESTIONS

1. Is the topic sentence concisely expressed?
2. What is the main idea being developed?

Model 6

(Is it possible, one may ask, to guess at the identity of the first great pioneer and radical who came to dry land? . . .)

Well, if the paleontologists are right — and their evidence seems pretty good — we can answer this question. As a matter of fact, I met only the day before yesterday one of the almost unchanged relatives of the first air-breathing creatures, and he did not seem especially proud. He crawled on eight legs out from under a board in my storeroom and I confess that, though I do not do such things lightly, I put my foot upon him. Before he was crushed into nothing he was about two inches long and pale straw in color. He carried two pincers before him and over his back he carried a long tail with a sting at its end. He was, in short, one of the least popular of desert dwellers — a scorpion.[13]

DISCUSSION

The writer of this selection begins with a question — a one sentence paragraph — which introduces the subject. He develops this subject by relating an incident concerning a relative of the first desert inhabitants and by presenting a detailed description of the creature. He concludes the unit with his main idea — the answer to the question — a scorpion.

The main idea is not always stated as briefly and concisely as in some of the model paragraphs which you have just read. Sometimes a writer may not wish to limit himself to just one main idea; his topic sentence may be phrased to include two or more main ideas. A writer, for example, might wish to develop the point of view that Karl Marx was a social scientist and a reformer; therefore, he phrases the following topic sentence: "Karl Marx was a social scientist and a reformer." In developing topic sentences with more than one main idea, writers develop one idea in the first half of the paragraph and follow with the development of the second main idea in the second half.

Read the next model paragraph.

Model 7

A plant or animal that one finds at any location either evolved there or was introduced by some means or another. The Monterey Cypress is found naturally on the coast of Monterey Bay, California, and nowhere else in the world. Presumably it evolved there. On the other hand, the English sparrow was brought to the United States only about one hundred years ago (1850), and it can now be found in almost every part of the country. Many of our cultivated plants and all of our domestic farm animals except the turkey were brought from Europe or Asia. Most of these can survive only under the care of humans. But many of man's introductions, the English sparrow, for example, are well enough adapted to the climate and conditions of the location to which they have been transported to get along on their own.[14]

DISCUSSION

The writer makes his topic sentence emphasize two main ideas: "A plant or animal that one finds at any location either (1) evolved there or (2) was introduced by some means or another." He then develops his first main idea by using the example of the Monterey Cypress which is found nowhere else in the world except on the coast of Monterey Bay, California. Next, he develops his second main idea by citing an example of the English Sparrow that was brought to the United States only about 100 years ago (1850).

In addition to achieving unity, you must also organize your flowing thought logically by giving order to your writing. You must adequately develop your main ideas with explanations and various kinds of support, such as details, examples, illustrations, facts, statistics, anecdotes, testimony. These supports make the central thought clear and acceptable, so that each paragraph or paragraph unit makes meaningful the thesis of the whole piece of writing (completeness). You must learn skills which will enable you to show relationships and tie ideas together so that you can move your reader smoothly through your developing thought (coherence). In addition, you must show the relative importance of your various ideas by stressing important thought and subordinating the less important ideas (emphasis). In short, effective writing means that you must learn the skills and techniques by which you can gain unity, completeness, order, coherence, and emphasis — the five characteristics of effective writing.

Although each of these skills is treated separately in this book for your convenience in learning them, they overlap in the actual process of writing. Unity, the concern of the previous discussion, for example, is very necessary for completeness, our next concern, and for order, the discussion of which follows in the next few chapters. Without an orderly and logical progression of thought, there can be no true unity. At the same time unless main ideas and theses are unmistakably clear, any kind of progression would be difficult. Completeness means full development of the thesis and the main idea. It would be meaningless unless it consists of an orderly and fully-developed series of sentences in separate paragraphs or paragraph groups which in turn relate to and develop the thesis. And parallel structure, repetition of key words and expressions, along with other devices for gaining emphasis, will at the same time add considerably to coherence.

Completeness

How long should a piece of writing be? This question troubles many beginning writers. Sadly enough, there is no satisfactory answer. Most teachers of writing feel that a theme of approximately 500 words is a good length for beginning writers. Most modern paragraphs are from seventy-five to 300 words long (six to twenty-five sentences). Many contemporary paragraphs, especially those in newspapers and magazines (such as *Time*), may be only one or two sentences in length; other paragraphs in textbooks, learned journals, and magazines such as "Harper's" and "The Atlantic" may be a page or more. Word or sentence count, therefore, may serve only as a guide for the length of your average paragraph.

Theme or paragraph completeness is a much better way of viewing length. How complete should a piece of writing be? This question can be answered. A good paragraph fulfills its function of developing fully the main idea: A short theme or any piece of writing longer than a paragraph is complete when it fulfills its function of developing a thesis fully. You must, therefore, develop the central thought until you feel that it is sufficiently clear and acceptable, whether it requires a sentence, a paragraph, or four or five pages. With some subjects you will be able to accomplish your purpose with little supporting and explanatory material. With most subjects, you will need much more complete development. Incompleteness, not over-development, is common with beginning writers. The short theme — a piece of writing that develops a single central thought — can usually be developed effectively in about 500 words.

Let us first discuss paragraph completeness, since the whole depends on the separate parts. In your opinion is the following paragraph complete? Does the writer make clear and support the main idea?

These opportunities to fight satisfied the essentially bellicose side of his [Michelangelo] character. He loved Julius II because, during those years, the tempestuous Pope had given him many such chances. [15]

DISCUSSION

This paragraph begins with a clear statement of the main idea: these opportunities to fight satisfied the warlike nature of Michelangelo. It reveals the writer's purpose, which is to show the bellicose side of Michelangelo's character. However, the main idea lacks sufficient support to make the generalization acceptable. Thus, it remains simply an opinion. This kind of subject would require many more supporting sentences for completeness.

The original paragraph is a well-organized and fully developed piece of writing consisting of major and minor supporting statements of the central thought.

These opportunities to fight satisfied the essentially bellicose side of his character. He had loved Julius II because, during those years, the tempestuous Pope had given him many such chances. He would have despised a patron who had let him follow his own caprices; that would have sent him back to his pessimism. Giving what a participant in war was required to give nourished his vigor and his vitality. His was a quarrelsome nature and this made him unpleasant to other artists, whose gifts he failed to recognize with that curious blindness common to men of genius — a somehow natural and perhaps even necessary state, preventing great artists from appreciating what is not of their own creation, or at least out of their line. He had nothing but contempt for Leonardo, and he was completely unjust to Titian whom he did not understand. He said that Raphael had learned all he knew from him, regarded Perugino as of no account whatever, and once, having encountered one of Francesco Francia's handsome sons in the street, he complimented him and bade him tell his father that he was more successful with children than with pictures. [16]

In the model paragraph which follows, the writer opens with his topic sentence, and follows with two sentences of support.

It is ironic that the thin upper crust of cultivated Orientals is already getting a global education still unavailable to most Americans. The educated Syrian reads his Koran and Voltaire; the Chinese knows Mencius, Dewey, and Bertrand Russell; the Hindu is familiar with the Bhagavad-Gita and Dickens. At times this produces a mere glib cosmopolitanism, but those of us who are fortunate enough to meet a good many educated Asiatics often have an uncomfortable sense of being intellectually outclassed: they have encompassed more of human experience than we. [17]

The model paragraph above is only three sentences in length. Is it complete? In other words, does the writer fulfill his purpose of showing that "the thin upper crust of cultivated Orientals is already getting a global education still unavailable to most Americans"?

Who determines whether a paragraph is complete or not? The answer to this question is probably obvious to you by now — both the writer and the reader. As a writer, if you believe that you have developed the main idea so that it is clear and acceptable, you will consider the paragraph complete. But you cannot be sure. A better test, therefore, is to place yourself in the position of the reader. If the reader feels that a writer has supported adequately the main thought, he will consider the paragraph complete. If the reader feels that the main idea lacks sufficient explanation and support, he will consider the paragraph incomplete.

Read the following paragraph. It consists of a simple opening statement of the main idea. Next comes the support. In your opinion, is the paragraph complete?

Then came the fateful day predicted by Michelangelo. The *condottiere* [leader of the mercenary soldiers] went over to the enemy and the gates of Florence were opened wide to receive the Medicis, now the conquerors of the city from which an angry populace had driven them. [18]

A reader would probably consider this paragraph complete since the writer fulfills his purpose. He wishes to explain that the "fateful day" predicted by Michelangelo arrived. Since the subject does not require extensive support, he offers two facts "the *condottiere* went over to the enemy" and "the gates of Florence were opened wide to receive the Medicis . . . ."

A writer, then, gains completeness by fully explaining and supporting his main idea. He structures his paragraph so that his explanations and support revolve around and develop a main idea. Some of the sentences in a paragraph explain, clarify, or elaborate on the main idea. Other sentences function as *major support* of the central thought. At times, a writer also will phrase his statements of major support in the form of a generalization. In such cases, he will offer specifics to convince his reader that the generalization is valid. Such sentences are called *minor support*. Still other sentences explain or clarify major and minor supporting statements. A paragraph, then, consists of a topic sentence, statements of major and minor support, sentences explaining, clarifying or elaborating on the main idea or major and minor supporting statements. Some paragraphs end with a restatement of the main idea in slightly different words.

A structural view of this very common type of organizational pattern might look something like the following partial outline form.

I. statement of the main idea
    (two sentences of explanation, clarification or elaboration)
    A. first major supporting statement
       (one sentence for clarification)

B. second major supporting statement
  1. first minor supporting statement
      (two sentences of clarification or explanation)
  2. minor support
C. major support
D. major support
      (restatement of the opening generalization)

The organizational pattern of the following paragraph illustrates effective use of major support. It consists of a topic sentence with three supporting statements concerning religion, morality, and studies. Each of these statements of major support develops the main idea: "At seventeen we were disillusioned and weary." The last of these major supporting statements, the writer explains further by mentioning authors, especially Shakespeare, who "were unpleasant to our palates."

At seventeen we were disillusioned and weary. In the midst of basketball, puppy love and discussions of life — washed down with chocolate sodas on warm afternoons — we had come to question almost everything we were taught at home and in school. Religion — we argued about it so much, Catholics against agnostics against Lutherans against Christian Scientists, that we were all converted to indifferentism. Morality, which we identified with chasteness, was a lie told to our bodies. Our studies were useless or misdirected, especially our studies in English Literature: the authors we were forced to read, and Shakespeare most of all, were unpleasant to our palates; they had the taste of chlorinated water. [19]

An outline view of this paragraph reveals a simple but effective pattern of development:

I.   At seventeen we were disillusioned   ____ main idea
     and weary.
   A. In religion we were all converted to   ____ major support
      indifferentism.
   B. Morality was a lie to our bodies.   ____ major support
   C. Our studies, especially English   ____ major support
      Literature, useless and misdirected.
   (Next follows, sentences elaborating on the statement)

In reading the following model, look for major and minor support.

The connection between slang and the criminal element is seen again in the dope racket, the terms of which have been made more or less generally familiar by the movies and television. The word *dope* itself is originally slang, but it is now in more general use than *narcotics*. Within the racket, terms abound. The words *marihuana* and *heroin* seem scarcely to occur among users or peddlers of the drugs, as is suggested by the fact that addicts speaking of heroin on a television program pronounced it to rhyme with *groin*. Usually, apparently, they say H or big H or *horse* or *caballito* (a Spanish word meaning "little horse" or "horsey.") Marihuana is referred to by several slang terms, of which *hay* seems to be the most enduring. An injection of a narcotic is a *fix*. To inject it in the vein is *mainline*. A salesman or peddler is a *pusher*. An addict is a *junkie*. To rid oneself of an addiction is *to kick the habit*. It will be seen that a narcotics addict can discuss his troubles at some length without being understood by anyone outside the circle. [20]

Read now an outline form for this paragraph.

I. The connection between slang and the criminal element is seen again in the dope racket . . . .
  A. The word *dope* itself is originally slang, but it is now in more general use than *narcotics*.
  B. Within the racket, terms abound.
    1. The words *marihuana* and *heroin* seem scarcely to occur among users or peddlers of drugs . . .
    2. They say H or big H or *horse* or *caballito* (a Spanish word meaning "little horse" or "horsey.") *Marihuana* is referred to by several slang terms, of which *hay* seems to be the most enduring.
    3. An injection of a narcotic is a *fix*.
    4. To inject it in the vein is *mainline*.
    5. A salesman or peddler is a *pusher*.
    6. An addict is a *junkie*.
    7. To rid oneself of an addiction is *to kick the habit*.
  C. It will be seen that a narcotics addict can discuss his troubles at some length without being understood by anyone outside the circle. (Repetition of the main idea)

Read now these two paragraphs by students. Is the first paragraph complete enough? What is wrong with the structural organization of the second paragraph?

Model 1

What amazes me the most is the differences of opinions these boys have on the draft. For instance, some are very much against it because of the policy of the U.S. involvement in Vietnam. On the other hand, some feel the draft is the only way that the U.S. can fill the ranks in the armed forces.

Model 2

One of the biggest obstacles in recruiting personnel for the police department in large populated cities is that those who qualify are also qualified for many other jobs in the federal government. The city which offers the best example of this is the District of Columbia. If you are a man that has to choose between two jobs, only one having weekends off, you are going to take the weekend job. Unfortunately the police department does not offer this type of benefit.

Read now this next paragraph by a student. Is it a better written paragraph than the first two? If you think so, give the reasons for your judgment.

Model 3

Wearing a white shirt and tie is one of the oldest traditions of this country. Some people say that tie is for hiding the buttons on the shirt, but others say that it brings out a clean cut appearance. Wearing a tie is a tradition inherited from England; today it is customary to wear a white shirt and tie in most business areas. Different countries have other traditions as to what should be the formal dress. American society expects people to dress semiformally in business and social life. My personal opinion is that a white shirt and tie is a must to get along in today's business world. White shirts and ties are becoming more acceptable in most sections. There are public and private areas where one is not permitted after certain hours without a tie. The Play Boy Club is one private spot where one cannot enter without a tie. Disneyland is one public ground where one has to wear a tie after dark. On the other hand, some organizations will not accept a tie and will take drastic measures to eliminate them. Some restaurants will not accept ties; their workers will ring a loud bell and cut off a persons tie. Teachers are expected to wear a white shirt and tie and they accept this. Should a teacher violate this rule he would be looking for employment elsewhere. In centuries to come, this old tradition might be forgotten but I feel this to be unlikely. The tie will be a hard custom to forget, unless the style changes completely in the next era.

ASSIGNMENT

1. Paragraph unity
With a red pencil or pen with red ink, make corrections in the model paragraph 3.

Read the following student model paragraph. Answer the ensuing questions.

Tipping is an overworked custom in the United States. Almost everybody in a service type occupation expects a tip. A waitress will expect a ten percent tip or better, and she will claim she has been "stiffed" if she doesn't get more than a dollar tip on a ten dollar ticket. A customer is expected to leave a tip even if he thinks the service or food is bad. Bellboys will stand and wait for a tip, and if one only has large bills they will go and get change. Barbers are also beginning to expect a quarter tip for a two dollar trim and shave. Most people in a service occupation don't regard the tip as a gift but as a must. If people would be more discriminating about the way they tip a tip would be more meaningful.

QUESTIONS

1. What is the topic sentence?
2. Does the student repeat the main idea?
3. Do you consider the paragraph complete?
4. What would be a good title for a theme in which this paragraph plays a role in supporting a thesis?
5. How many major supporting statements are there?
6. What sentences would you classify as explanations or clarification?

Completeness in the longer piece of writing

Though much will be said about completeness in the longer piece of writing later in the book, it will be helpful now if you relate what you have learned about paragraph completeness to theme completeness. One may ask the same question: Who determines whether a longer piece of writing is complete or not? The answer is the same as for paragraph completeness. Both the writer and the reader. As a writer, if you believe that you have

developed the thesis so that your point of view is clear and acceptable, you will consider the development complete. But again,
you cannot be sure. You must, therefore, place yourself in the
position of a reader. Ask yourself: (1) Have I developed the central
thought adequately enough? (2) Is each paragraph complete
enough and does it contribute something to the whole? Are there
any digressions? Read the model short student theme which
follows. Is it a good theme? Is the thesis idea unmistakably
clear? Is the thesis idea developed completely enough? Can you
recognize main ideas? Are the main ideas related to the thesis?
Is the paragraph development complete? Does the writer digress
from his thesis?

ARE SOME CUSTOMS NECESSARY?
a student theme

[1] One of the customs which has been handed down from
father to son is the concept of courtship. Why is it that a young man
is expected to open doors for his date, push in her chair when she
sits at the table, and provide for her transportation? Certainly it is
tradition or a custom. But is it necessary?

[2] At one time I dated a young woman who was only one-
half inch shorter than I am and was probably as strong. Feeling very
foolish, I was still expected to help her with her coat and to open the
doors for her. She was every bit as capable of opening the door as I
was, but custom demanded that I open it.

[3] Whenever we went out, we always took her car because
I didn't have one, and she provided the money because I never had
any. This system was very satisfactory to us, but I took a large amount
of kidding from my friends because this arrangement was contrary
to custom.

[4] Boys and girls should be able to work out the arrangement which works best for them, regardless of custom. If the girl
has the car and the money, why should a stigma be attached to them
because they make the best of the situation? It is foolish for the
couple to forego the pleasure they derive from a date while they wait
for the boy to secure the necessary money and transportation. If
the boy and girl enjoy their relationship together, is it so terrible
because the girl has to open doors, put on her own coat and order
her own dinner? No! In most cases she does not always have a young
man around to do these things for her, and she is perfectly capable
of doing them for herself. But the moment a young man comes in
contact with her, she becomes instantly helpless.

[5] Are some customs really necessary?

Read the longer piece of writing that follows. Observe that the completeness of each paragraph contributes to the development of the central thought of the whole.

WORDS THAT LAUGH AND CRY
by Charles A. Dana

[1] Did it ever strike you that there was anything queer about the capacity of written words to absorb and convey feelings? Taken separately they are mere symbols with no more feeling to them than so many bricks, but string them along in a row under certain mysterious conditions and you find yourself laughing or crying as your eye runs over them. That words should convey mere ideas is not so remarkable. "The boy is fat," "the cat has nine tails," are statements that seem obviously enough within the power of written language. But it is different with feelings. They are no more visible in the symbols that hold them than electricity is visible on the wire; and yet there they are, always ready to respond when the right test is applied by the right person. That spoken words, charged with human tones and lighted by human eyes, should carry feelings, is not so astonishing. The magnetic sympathy of the orator one understands; he might affect his audience, possibly, in a language they did not know. But written words: How can they do it!

[2] Suppose, for example, that you possess remarkable facility in grouping language, and that you have strong feelings upon some subject, which finally you determine to commit to paper. Your pen runs along, the words present themselves, or are dragged out, and fall into their places. You are a good deal moved; here you chuckle to yourself, and half a dozen lines further down a lump comes into your throat, and perhaps you have to wipe your eyes. You finish, and the copy goes to the printer. When it gets into print a reader sees it. His eye runs along the lines and down the page until it comes to the place where you chuckled as you wrote; then he smiles, and six lines below he has to swallow several times and snuffle and wink to restrain an exhibition of weakness. And then some one else comes along who is not so good a word juggler as you are, or who has no feelings, and swaps the words about a little, and twists the sentences; and behold the spell is gone, and you have left a parcel of written language duly charged with facts, but without a single feeling.

[3] No one can juggle with words with any degree of success without getting a vast respect for their independent ability. They will catch the best idea a man ever had as it flashes through his brain, and hold on to it, to surprise him with it long after, and make him wonder that he was ever man enough to have had such an idea. And often they will catch an idea on its way from the brain to the pen

point, turn, twist, and improve on it as the eye winks, and in an instant there they are, strung hand in hand across the page and grinning back at the writer: "This is our idea, old man; not yours!"

[4] As for poetry, every word that expects to earn its salt in poetry should have a head and a pair of legs of its own to go and find its place, carry another word, if necessary, on its back. The most that should be expected of any competent poet in regular practice is to serve a general summons and notice of action on the language. If the words won't do the rest for him, it indicates that he is out of sympathy with his tools.

[5] But you don't find feelings in written words unless there were feelings in the man who used them. With all their apparent independence they seem to be little vessels that hold in some puzzling fashion exactly what is put into them. You can put tears into them, as though they were so many little buckets; and you can hang smiles along them, like Monday's clothes on the line, or you can starch them with facts and stand them up like a picket fence; but you won't get the tears out unless you first put them in. Art won't put them there. It is like the faculty of getting the quality of interest into pictures. If the quality exists in the artist's mind he is likely to find means to get it into his pictures, but if it isn't in the man no technical skill will supply it. So, if the feelings are in the writer and he knows his business, they will get into the words; but they must be in him first. It isn't the way words are strung together that makes Lincoln's Gettysburg speech immortal, but the feelings that were in the man. But how do such little, plain words manage to keep their grip on such feelings? That is the miracle. [21]

EXERCISES

5. *Completeness*

Read the model paragraph below. With complete sentences, complete the outline form below it.

The railroad moguls, moreover, were adept in protecting their privileged position. They would issue free passes to journalists, legislators, and other public men. They would bribe judges and legislatures, maintain powerful lobbies, and elect their own "creatures" to high office. They would also contribute freely to the campaign funds of "friendly" politicians, who in turn would support the "railroad rascals." [22]

I.

    A.

    B.

    C.

6. Completeness

Read the model paragraph below. Answer the questions that follow it. Make a structural outline of its organizational pattern if you think it will help you.

The danger in those studies where the main emphasis is upon acquisition of skill is just the reverse. The tendency is to take the shortest cuts possible to gain the required end. This makes the subjects *mechanical*, and thus restrictive of intellectual power. In the mastery of reading, writing, drawing, laboratory technique, etc., the need for economy of time and material, of neatness and accuracy, for promptness and uniformity, is so great that these things tend to become ends in themselves, irrespective of their influence upon general mental attitude. Sheer imitation, dictation of steps to be taken, mechanical drill, may give results most quickly and yet strengthen traits likely to be fatal to reflective power. The pupil is enjoined to do this and that specific thing, with no knowledge of any reason except that by so doing he gets his result most speedily; his mistakes are pointed out and corrected for him; he is kept at pure repetition of certain acts till they become automatic. Later, teachers wonder why the pupil reads with so little expression, and figures with so little intelligent consideration of the terms of his problem. In some educational dogmas and practices, the very idea of training the mind seems to be hopelessly confused with that of a drill which hardly touches *mind* at all — or touches it for the worse — since it is wholly taken up with training skill in external execution. This method reduces the 'training' of human beings to the level of animal training. Practical skill, modes of effective technique, can be intelligently, non-mechanically *used* only when intelligence has played a part in their *acquisition.* [23]

1. What is the topic sentence?
2. How many major supporting statements are there?
3. What sentences serve the purposes of explanation and clarification?
4. Does the writer use minor support? Where?
5. Is the main idea repeated for emphasis? Where?
6. Do you consider the paragraph complete? Why?

7. Completeness

Make a structural outline of the paragraph below.

The straight arrows in the class of 1972 will be balanced by plenty of students with something else [that is, something besides classroom performance] to offer. The University of Pennsylvania found one in a senior at Massachusetts' Phillips Academy with a generally undistinguished academic record. He impressed Penn officials by mentioning in his application his deep love of sailing, which, he rhaposodized, occupies his attention "from the first wakening sail in early April to the last frostbite stint in late October." Columbia passed over applicants with stronger academic credentials to accept a practicing Buddhist from upstate New York, a New Jersey student who arranged music for an off-Broadway show and a Long Island youth who accompanied his application with photographs of his sculpture. It also agreed to accept Vladimir Gulevich, 20, of Paterson, N.J., who graduated from his local high school two years ago with below-average grades, went on to a Manhattan business school. Gulevich caught the notice of admission officials by writing the required essay about himself in the form of an extended poem, then by showing interviewers a sheaf of first-rate translations of Russian verse. [24]

Study the outline form which follows:

I.   The straight arrows in the class of 1972 will be balanced by plenty of students with something else to offer.
     A. The University of Pennsylvania found one in a senior at Massachusetts' Phillips Academy with a generally undistinguished academic record.
        1. He impressed Penn officials by mentioning in his application his deep love of sailing . . . .
     B. Columbia passed over applicants with stronger academic credentials to accept . . . .
        1. A practicing Buddhist from upstate New York
        2. A New Jersey student who arranges music for an off-Broadway show
        3. A Long Island sculptor
        4. Vladmir Gulevich who translates Russian poems

8. *Organization*
     Fill in the missing support with complete sentences of your own structuring. If necessary, research the subject.

I.   Concord, Massachusetts, is an historic town.
     A. It was one of the earliest settled regions.
        1.

2.
B. Concord can claim many famous poets and writers as its own.
   1.
   2.
   3.
   4.
C. At Concord, the shot was fired "heard round the world."

9. *Organization*
Fill in the missing support with complete sentences of your own structuring. If necessary, research the subject.

I. Citizens in a democracy must be willing to pay a price for freedom.
   A. They must accept the economic burdens of democracy.
      1.
      2.
   B. They must accept the political responsibilities that go with representative government.
      1.
      2.
   C. They must accept the disadvantages as well as the advantages of democracy.
      1.
      2.
   D. They must be willing to defend their way of life when it is threatened by forces within or from outside the country.
      1.
      2.
      3.

10. *Organization*
Fill in the missing support with complete sentences of your own structuring. If necessary, research the subject.

I. Michelangelo was a truly amazing man.
   A. He was an inventor.
      1.
      2.
      3.
      4.

B. Michelangelo is one of the world's greatest painters.
   1.
   2.
   3.
   4.
C. He was also an outstanding military strategist.
   1.
   2.
D. He was a highly controversial figure in his day.
   1.
   2.
   3.

11. Organization

Fill in the missing support with complete sentences of your own structuring. If necessary, research the subject.

I. New York is a fascinating city.
   A. It is a city of towering buildings.
      1.
      2.
      3.
   B. New York is a city of contrasts.
      1.
      2.
      3.
      4.
   C. New York is a great commercial giant.
      1.
      2.
      3.
   D. New York is a city of broken dreams.
      1.
      2.
      3.
      4.
   E. New York represents America at its best and worst.
      1.
      2.
      3.
      4.

ASSIGNMENT

2. *Organizing for completeness*
Write a paragraph from 100 to 150 words using the outline that you constructed for one of the previous exercises as a guide to the structural pattern.

CHAPTER TWO *References*

1. From "Where Are We?" by Carl Becker in *The Cornell Daily Sun*. Reprinted by permission of *The Cornell Daily Sun*.
2. From "Let's Have That Again . . . Slowly," Editorial in *The Sporting News* (February 24, 1968). By permission.
3. From "A Vote for Student Protest," by Mary N. Gonzales in *The Atlantic Monthly* (November, 1965). Reprinted by permission of the author.
4. From *The Age of Aristocracy: 1688 to 1830* by William Willcox. Copyright © 1966 by D. C. Heath and Company.
5. "A Vote for Student Protest," by Mary N. Gonzales. Cf. 3.
6. "Let's Have That Again . . . Slowly," Cf. 2.
7. From *The Age of Aristocracy: 1688 to 1830* by William Willcox. Cf. 4.
8. From *Britain Yesterday* by Walter L. Arnstein. Copyright © 1966 by D. C. Heath and Company.
9. From "What To Do When Children Cheat," by Orville Palmer, *Parents' Magazine* (January, 1966). Reprinted by permission of Parents' Magazine Enterprises, Inc.
10. From "What's Wrong With Our Army?" by Stewart Alsop, in *The Saturday Evening Post* (February, 1965). Reprinted by permission of the author.
11. From *The Sea Around Us* by Rachel L. Carson. Copyright © 1950, 1951 by Rachel L. Carson. Reprinted by permission of Oxford University Press, Inc.
12. From "What To Do When Children Cheat," by Orville Palmer. Cf. 9.
13. From *The Voice of the Desert* by Joseph Wood Krutch. Reprinted by permission of William Morrow and Company, Inc. Copyright © 1954, 1955 by Joseph Wood Krutch.
14. From *Biology*, Second Edition, by Relis B. Brown. Copyright © 1961 by D. C. Heath and Company.

15. From *Michelangelo* by Marcel Brion, translated by James Whital. Copyright 1940. Reprinted by permission of the author.
16. From *Michelangelo* by Marcel Brion. Cf. 15.
17. From "Educating Women in a Man's World," by Lynn White, Jr., in *The Atlantic Monthly.* Reprinted by permission of the Atlantic Monthly Company and the author.
18. From *Michelangelo* by Marcel Brion. Cf. 15.
19. From *Exile's Return* by Malcolm Cowley. Copyright 1934, 1935, 1941, 1951, copyright © renewed 1962, 1963 by Malcolm Cowley. Reprinted by permission of The Viking Press, Inc.
20. From *Understanding English* by Paul Roberts. Copyright © 1958 by Paul Roberts. Reprinted by permission of Harper & Row, Publishers.
21. "Words That Laugh and Cry," by Charles A. Dana.
22. From *The American Pageant,* Third Edition, by Thomas A. Bailey. Copyright © 1966 by D. C. Heath and Company.
23. From *How We Think* by John Dewey. Copyright © 1933 by John Dewey, published by D. C. Heath and Company.
24. From "Universities: The Search for Something Else," in *Time* (April, 1968). Copyright © 1968 by Time, Inc., and reprinted with their permission.

THREE

Gaining additional rhetorical effectiveness

Even though writing may possess unity, completeness, and order, it may not necessarily be effective. Writing needs also *variety* to keep the reader from tiring easily from the same monotonous word choice and sentence constructions, *emphasis* to enable the reader to readily discern what is important, what is less important, and what is simply transitional, and *coherence* to move him smoothly and logically along with the flowing thought. The examples which follow are grammatically correct, yet they lack effectiveness.

I was a white man with a gun. I was standing in front of a crowd of unarmed natives. I was the leader. Yet I was really their prisoner.

A foolish optimist denies the present crisis.

Recall some event that has left a powerful impression on you, such as two people talking.

We set our sail. The rising wind drove us along. We could hardly move the lee oars fast enough to keep them from being torn from the rowlocks.

In world affairs I would be a good neighbor.

The true complexity of reading is revealed by comparison.

Compare the example sentences that you have just read with the original models. Observe how variety, emphasis, and coherence give the writing additional meaning and richness.

Here was I, the white man with his gun, standing in front of the unarmed native crowd — seemingly the leading acto of the piece — but in reality I was only an absurd puppet pushed to and for by the will of those yellow faces behind. [1]

Only a foolish optimist can deny the dark realities of the moment. [2]

Recall, then, some event that has left a distinct impression on you — how at the corner of the street, perhaps you passed two people talking. A tree shook; an electric light danced; the tone of the talk was comic, but also tragic; a whole vision, an entire conception, seemed contained in that moment. [3]

Our sail was now set, and with the still rising wind, we rushed along; the boat going with such madness through the water, that the lee oars could scarcely be worked rapidly enough to escape being torn from the row-locks. [4]

In the field of world policy, I would dedicate this Nation to the policy of the good neighbor — the neighbor who resolutely respects himself and because he does so, respects the rights of others — the neighbor who respects his obligations and respects the sanctity of his agreements in and with a world of neighbors. [5]

"We have only to compare" — with these words the cat is out of the bag, and the true complexity of reading is admitted. [6]

Variety

1. By introductory phrases and clauses
2. By varying the internal structure of the sentence
3. By varying the beginning of a sentence
4. By varying kinds of sentences
5. By varying their length

Variety in the length and structure of sentences contributes considerably to effective writing. Too many sentences beginning with the same word, phrase, or clause and too many sentences of one kind will soon tire the reader, just as much as he would tire from sameness in anything else. To hold the reader's interest, the experienced writer varies sentence length, sentence beginnings, and sentence constructions. He avoids short, choppy sentences by carefully subordinating less important ideas and coordinating the truly important ideas. He varies beginnings by using introductory words, phrases, and clauses; thus he avoids such common, overworked beginnings as *there is, there are, it is, this, that, the, he, she, we,* or some noun. He mixes up the different kinds of sentences because his thought is complex enough for such varied patterns. He uses interrogative, exclamatory, imperative, periodic sentences as well as the common declarative and loose sentence constructions. In addition, he uses the middle part of his sentences for modifying words, phrases, clauses, and sentence interrupters, such as *however, therefore, moreover, nevertheless, I believe, I am sure, on the other hand,* and so forth.

Use the following models in learning to gain variety in your own writing.

Introductory phrases and clauses

As for my own feelings in the matter, it's not that I fear buck fever, it's more that I can't seem to work up a decent feeling of enmity toward a deer. [7]

However complex, shifting and ambivalent these definitions of youth, they have in common a fundamental indifference to politics. [8]

If you could write lucidly, simply, euphoniously and yet with liveliness you would write perfectly: you would write like Voltaire. [9]

As the custodians of the history of our times, we can do no less. [10]

Read these same models again; notice this time the variety of sentence constructions.

Varying the internal structure of the sentence

The most common sentence pattern in English is the subject — transitive verb–object pattern. Experienced writers gain variety and emphasis by varying the internal structure of their sentences.

> The bloodiest portion — make no mistake about it — of this war for Great Britain and the United States lies ahead of us. [11]

> Their [Scott and Zelda Fitzgerald] generation had been defeated by life — so it seemed at the time — and yet in their own defeat they were still its representative figures. [12]

> The path to peace lies through thickets of conflict and the biggest obstacle in the path, the most overwhelming danger of all, is the onrushing arms race. [13]

> Thus, this dangerous episode, which, although on a small scale compared with the vast movement of the war, might have been the cause of endless discussion detrimental to our affairs, came to a satisfactory conclusion. [14]

Varying the beginning of a sentence

> Theoretically — and secretly, of course — I was all for the Burmese and all against their oppressors, the British. [15]

> Only a foolish optimist can deny the dark realities of the moment. [16]

> But we tire of rubbish-reading in the long run. [17]

> And his [Toscanini] rage is quite terrifying. It seems like a combination of indignation, contempt, and heartbreak. [18]

> Now the Hill [the Hill on which Parliament stood in Ottawa, Canada] was melting in the spring. [19]

> Serene, suave, handsomely venerable in his sixty-ninth year, a prominent specimen of Northern upper-class distinction, Everett was a natural choice of the Pennsylvania commissioners, who sought an orator for a solemn national occasion. [20]

Varying the kinds of sentences

According to the kind of thought they express, sentences may be classified as declarative, interrogative, exclamatory, and imperative. According to clauses, sentences may be classified as simple, compound, complex, and complex-compound. Sentences are also classified as loose and periodic. An experienced writer gains variety and emphasis by using different kinds of sentences. In addition *by varying their length,* he avoids short, choppy sentences that indicate by their numbers immature thinking and that soon tire the reader. Study the following models.

The dictum that style is the man is well known. It is one of those aphorisms that say too much to mean a great deal. Where is the man in Goethe, in his bird-like lyrics or in his clumsy prose? And Hazlitt? [21]

To the backward and forward pendulum swing of a tall old clock in a quiet corner they might read those cadenced words [Lincoln's words at Gettysburg] while outside the windows the first flurry of snow blew across the orchard and down over the meadow, the beginnings of winter in a gun-metal gloaming to be later arched with a star-flung sky. [22]

What profound depths we visit then — how sudden and complete is our immersion! [23]

Once upon a time, long long ago, I learned how to reduce a fraction to its lowest terms. Whether I could still perform that operation is uncertain; but the discipline involved in early training has its uses, since it taught me that in order to understand the essential nature of anything it is well to strip it of all superficial and irrelevant accretions — in short, to reduce it to its lowest terms. [24]

When they went ashore the animals that took up a land life carried with them a part of the sea in their bodies, a heritage which they passed on to their children and which even today links each land animal with its origin in the ancient sea. [25]

Periodic sentences begin with less important details and end with a climactic statement of the central thought; the *loose* sentence begins with the central thought and ends with the less important details.

Those who roused the people to resistance, who directed their measures through a long series of eventful years, who formed, out of the most unpromising materials, the finest army that Europe had ever seen, who trampled down King, Church, and Aristocracy, who, in short intervals of domestic sedition and rebellion, made the name of England terrible to every nation on the face of the earth, were no vulgar fanatics. [26]

Observe the variety in the memorable last paragraph excerpted from Churchill's address to the House of Commons on the evacuation of 335,000 men from the beaches of Dunkirk, June 4, 1940.

I have, myself, full confidence that if all do their duty, if nothing is neglected, and if the best arrangements are made, as they are being made, we shall prove ourselves once again able to defend our Island home, to ride out the storm of war, and to outlive the menace of tyranny, if necessary for years, if necessary alone. At any rate, that is what we are going to try to do. That is the resolve of His Majesty's Government — every man of them. That is the will of Parliament and the nation. The Brisith Empire and the French Republic, linked together in their cause and in their need, will defend to the death their native soil, aiding each other like good comrades to the utmost of their strength. Even though large tracts of Europe and many old and famous States have fallen or may fall into the grip of the Gestapo and all the odious apparatus of Nazi rule, we shall not flag or fail. We shall go on to the end, we shall fight in France, we shall fight on the seas and oceans, we shall fight with growing confidence and growing strength in the air, we shall defend our Island, whatever the cost may be, we shall fight on the beaches, we shall fight on the landing grounds, we shall fight in the fields and in the streets, we shall fight in the hills; we shall never surrender, and even if, which I do not for a moment believe, this Island or a large part of it were subjugated and starving, then our Empire beyond the seas, armed and guarded by the British Fleet, would carry on the struggle, until, in God's good time, the New World, with all its power and might, steps forth to the rescue and the liberation of the old. [27]

EXERCISES

1. Variety

Read the first two paragraphs of the selection, by Whitney M. Young, in Chapter 1, seeking examples of variety. Classify the example material under the following headings. It is not necessary to write an entire sentence; write only a sufficient number of words to make it identifiable.

1. Introductory phrases and
   clauses
2. Varying the internal
   structure
3. Varying beginnings
4. Varying sentence length

5. Varying kinds of sentences
   a. simple
   b. compound
   c. complex
   d. complex-compound

2. *Variety*

Read the paragraph used as model 2 on page 25, Chapter 1. Under the headings below, write one example, or wherever possible two examples, of the devices used for variety.

1. Short sentences
2. An interrogative sentence
3. Beginning phrases

4. Effective fragments
5. Complex sentences
6. Simple sentences

Emphasis

1. By position
2. By varying the order of words in a sentence
3. By using figures of speech
4. By occasional short sentences
5. By arranging items in a series in order of climax
6. By using words in special ways
7. By using the periodic sentence
8. By repeating key words and phrases
9. By using parallel structure

Emphasis means stressing important words and ideas and subordinating less important material. Experienced writers, therefore, place important words, expressions, and ideas in certain positions in sentences and paragraphs, not only to gain variety but also to show their degrees of importance. Thus, in the models that follow, many of the devices suggested for achieving sentence and paragraph emphasis will also enable a writer to gain variety.

By *placing words and phrases in the end position and the beginning position in a sentence,* a writer gains emphasis.

This tiny occurrence demonstrates an important fact concerning the air ocean — one that is only now becoming the practical knowledge of practical airfaring men: there are winds which blow neither east nor west, neither north nor south, but in the third dimension: straight up. [28]

Beginnings are apt to be shadowy, and so it is with the beginnings of that great mother of life, the sea. [29]

All human activity is prompted by desire or impulse. [30]

The other terror that scares us from self-trust is our consistency. [31]

What is serious about excitement is that so many of its forms are destructive. [32]

Read the first model again; note this time the role punctuation plays in emphasis. In the models that follow be alert to the function of punctuation in aiding emphasis.

By *varying the order of words in a sentence,* a writer gains emphasis. Frequently, experienced writers will place adverbial modifiers in the beginning position, saving the end position for the truly important material.

On the beach itself, high and dry, were all kinds of wrecked vehicles. [33]

At the end of this terrific room, across an enormous space of carpet, sat "the governor." [34]

In movement, he was rather graceless. [35]

With consistency, a great soul has simply nothing to do. [36]

For nonconformity, the world whips you with its displeasure. [37]

For the past 500 million years, however, the rocks have preserved the fossil record. [38]

By *using figures of speech,* a writer can gain emphasis as well as enrichment for his writing.

The fierce old hen sat still, brooding over the English nation, whose pullulating energies were coming swiftly to ripeness under her wings. She sat still; but every feather bristled; she was tremendously alive. [39]

By *occasional short sentences,* a writer achieves emphasis.

She (Queen Elizabeth) swore; she spat; she struck with her fist when she was angry; she roared with laughter when she was amused. And she was often amused. [40]

He talked his prose, Agee prose. [41]

Night was his time. [42]

And suddenly pure space looms into view. [43]

By *arranging items in a series in order of climax,* a writer can gain emphasis.

These members (who do not conform) are those who have fallen below, or risen above, the ordinary herd. They are: idiots, criminals, prophets, and discoverers. [44]

I didn't know that, for a new arrived European, there was a "New York sickness," like sea-sickness, air sickness, and mountain sickness. [45]

By *using words in special ways,* a writer can gain emphasis.

Celine has remarked of New York that "it is a vertical city." [46]

This is true, but it seemed to me, at first, like a lengthwise city." [47]

I have never heard of a war that proceeded from dance halls. [48]

Writers gain emphasis by *using the periodic sentence.* A periodic sentence is constructed so that its true meaning is not revealed until the end. The important parts, therefore, such as subject, main verb, and objects, are placed at the end or very near the end in such a sentence construction.

When I think of old people I remember, people whose first memories were rich with stories of how Nelson stood and how Nelson fell; who saw the prentices marching with marrow-bones and cleavers through the streets of the City in 1821,[1] and heard the great bell of St. Paul's tolling in 1901; of the next generation, whose span covered the last stagecoach and the first airplane, who had sat waiting for news from Lucknow and Sebastopol, and lived to listen for the guns defending London; when I consider their assured morality, their confident acceptance of the social order, their ready undertaking of its obligations; I have a sense of solidity, tenacity, and uniformity, which all the time I know to be in large part an illusion of distance, and I shall have failed of my purpose if I have not made it clear that the very word "Victorian" may be used to mask a fallacy and a misconception. [49]

Writers gain emphasis also by *repeating key words and phrases*. Study the models which follow. Underline the words or phrases that are repeated.

Defense can not be static. Defense must grow and change from day to day. Defense must be dynamic and flexible, an expression of the vital forces of the nation and of its resolute will to meet whatever challenge the future may hold. For these reasons, I need hardly assure you that after the adjournment of this session of Congress, I will not hesitate to call the Congress into special session if at any time the situation of the national defense requires it. . . . [50]

You ask, what is our policy? I say it is to wage war by land, sea and air. War with all our might and with all the strength God has given us, and to wage war against a monstrous tyranny never surpassed in the dark and lamentable catalogue of human crime. That is our policy.
You ask, what is our aim? I can answer in one word. It is victory. Victory at all costs — victory in spite of all terrors — victory, however long and hard the road may be, for without victory there is no survival. [51]

Writers gain emphasis by *using parallel structure*. Parallelism is a technique of writing by which a noun is paralleled with a noun, an adjective with an adjective, an adverb with an adverb, a phrase with a phrase, a main clause with a main clause, a subordinate clause with a subordinate clause, a sentence with a sentence. In the model which follows, observe the emphatic power of the continued parallelism.

[1] This much we pledge — and more.

[2] To those old allies whose culture and spiritual origins we share, we pledge loyalty of faithful friends. United, there is little we cannot do in a host of new cooperative ventures. Divided, there is little we can do — for we dare not meet a powerful challenge at odds and split asunder.

[3] To those new states whom we welcome to the ranks of the free, we pledge our word that one form of colonial control shall not have passed away merely to be replaced by a far more iron tyranny. We shall not always expect to find them supporting our view. But we shall always hope to find them strongly supporting their own freedom — and to remember that, in the past, those who foolishly sought power by riding the back of the tiger ended up inside.

[4] To those peoples in the huts and villages of half the globe struggling to break the bonds of mass misery, we pledge our best efforts to help them help themselves, for whatever period is required — not because the Communists may be doing it, not because we seek their votes, but because it is right. If a society cannot help the many who are poor, it cannot save the few who are rich.

[5] To our sister republics south of our border, we offer a special pledge — to convert our good words into good deeds — in a new alliance for progress — to assist free men and free governments in casting off the chains of poverty. But the peaceful revolution of hope cannot become the prey of hostile powers. Let all our neighbors know that we shall join with them to oppose aggression or subversion anywhere in the Americas. And let every other power know that this hemisphere intends to remain the master of its own house.

[6] To that world assembly of sovereign states, the United Nations, our last best hope in an age where the instruments of war have far outpaced the instruments of peace, we renew our pledge of support — to prevent it from becoming merely a forum for invective — to strengthen its shield of the new and the weak — and to enlarge the area in which its writ may run.

[7] Finally, to those nations who would make themselves our adversary, we offer not a pledge but a request: that both sides begin anew the quest for peace, before the dark powers of destruction unleashed by science engulf all humanity in planned or accidental self-destruction.

[8] We dare not tempt them with weakness. For only when our arms are sufficient beyond doubt can we be certain beyond doubt that they will never be employed.

[9] But neither can two great and powerful groups of nations take comfort from our present course — both sides overburdened by the cost of modern weapons, both rightly alarmed by the steady spread of the deadly atom, yet both racing to alter that un-

certain balance of terror that stays the hand of mankind's final war.
[10] So let us begin anew — remembering on both sides that
civility is not a sign of weakness, and sincerity is always subject to
proof. Let us never negotiate out of fear. But let us never fear to
negotiate. [52]

EXERCISES

3. *Emphasis*

Write what you consider to be the kind or kinds of
emphasis the writer uses in the models below.

Her response to every stimulus was immediate and rich:
to the folly of the moment, to the clash and horror of great events,
her soul leapt out with a vivacity, an abandonment, a complete awareness of the situation, which made her, which makes her still, a fascinating spectacle. [53]

Interwoven with many other political motives are two
closely related passions to which human beings are regrettably
prone: I mean fear and hate. [54]

4. *Emphasis*

What seem to be the kind or kinds of emphasis the
writers use in these models?

How often the taxi-drivers, willing to take passengers
from north to south, flatly refuse to take any for the east and west! [55]

What's gone wrong in our own nation that so many of
our women should doubt, resent, or repudiate their womanhood? [56]

On the Cape, too, he could be elementally refreshed. [57]

5. *Emphasis*

What do you consider to be the kind or kinds of emphasis the writer uses in each of these models?

If I had, at that time, ventured to offer a remedy for all
these ills, every one of them, by advising the afflicted nation to take
active part in the greatest and bloodiest human war ever conceived —
a war that destroys more property and brutally butchers more innocent people than the worst human butchers have ever enjoyed in
their most gorgeous dreams; if I had recommended that mad procedure, guaranteeing the almost complete cure of all such ills within

ten years, and the practical attainment of all the high goals I have implied, it is quite likely that both my advice and I should have been (to understate it) deplored. [58]

And what does one do to make a success?
Well, the answer is very simple: one learns how, or one consults an expert. [59]

When a vivid man does a sufficient number of things that are unfailingly characteristic, legend begins to attach itself to his name. [60]

Many of the methods of paragraph organization and development, which you learned about in the previous chapter, contribute also to emphasis.

1. By movement from general to particular
2. By movement in climactic order
3. By stating the topic sentence
4. By repeating the topic sentence at the end
5. By giving more space to important ideas
6. By proper coordinating and subordinating of the thought

Study the following selection. Observe the variety and emphasis the writer gains by organization and by definite rhetorical techniques.

[1]Though I have often seen, as well as heard, Toscanini conduct, I never cease to be fascinated and excited to trembling by what is, I think, the greatest artistic performance that one can see and hear anywhere in the world today.
[2]Artistic perfection is something so rare, and so strange, that one is tongue-tied before it. One must feel it, and I am afraid that as I attempt to describe it, it will evaporate.
[3]But there is, of course, an explanation of why Toscanini gets out of a group of ninety-two men, first-rate musicians, gathered together, as they are, from a dozen orchestras, something that no other conductor on earth can evoke. The explanation lies in the person of Toscanini himself. He is the perfect, the complete, artist of music, and in him is combined complete passion, complete self-offering, with complete control. Everything functions at its highest potency — feeling, the feeling for music, something which comes out of one's insides, out of one's emotions and sensibilities, and isn't

written in the score — but that feeling is always disciplined and re-strained by the most complete consciousness, the highest technique, and by consummate musical knowledge.

[4]Now, you see that as you watch this slim, small black figure hold ninety-two men in a kind of magical unity.

[5]The sword-like slash, the impassioned swing of that baton seems to pull the orchestra out of itself, and in the great sym-phonic passages to evoke out of it, and out of the audience, and out of the very air, ecstasy and rapture.

[6]But watch the left hand. It is one of the most beautiful and eloquent hands in the world. A large hand, with a square palm, long square fingers, and a wide-springing thumb.

[7]Watch that hand. For while the swinging right arm pulls out the uttermost in every player, that left hand is held aloft in a ges-ture restraining, governing, controlling. It seems to say: I want all that is in you, and all that is in this music. I want the fullest expression of it that can be brought forth. But not too much. Not more than is there. Everything given . . . and everything under control. The right arm stimulates. The left hand restrains.

[8]And the result is the incomparable experience that you listen to on Saturday evenings. [61]

Coherence

1. By overall planning
2. By paragraph unity and order
3. By transitional words and expressions
4. By pronoun reference
5. By repetition of key words and ideas
6. By parallel structure
7. By maintaining a consistent point of view

Coherence is essentially a technique of connecting ideas smoothly and logically in written communication. In a co-herent piece of writing, the writer leads his reader clearly and logically from one idea to another in his developing thought. He weaves his ideas so skillfully together that the reader can see quickly the relationship of one idea to another and to the central thought of the whole.

By *overall planning, a writer gains coherence.* Intro-ductions, occasional summaries that mark the end of one particular train of thought, transitional sentences and paragraphs that lead the reader smoothly onward to another link in the developing chain of thought, and conclusions — all play significant roles in coherence.

But *paragraph unity and order* are most important for coherence. By arranging sentences in a clear, logical order, whether it be by time, space, climax, question to answer, or any other arrangement of ideas, a writer gives his thought the continuity necessary to carry his reader easily from sentence to sentence and paragraph to paragraph. Clarifying his main ideas by placing them in brief, emphatic topic sentences, a writer can also skillfully guide his reader, for the topic sentence highlights the main idea of its own paragraph and serves as a link to the thought of the preceding and subsequent paragraphs and to the central idea of the whole piece of writing.

But other gaps in thought must also be bridged; therefore, experienced writers rely on transitional words and expressions, pronoun reference, repetition of key words and ideas, parallel structure, and consistent viewpoint to gain this kind of paragraph and sentence coherence.

Consider this selection:

What is masculinity? One dictionary defines it as: manly, virile, robust. Masculinity as a composite of these terms would be: resolute, dignified, honorable, sexually potent, sturdy, healthy, lusty, and most important, male. All these qualities are not visible to the naked eye. Social mores play an important part in interpretation. Ancient Grecian society accepted homosexuality as perfectly natural. Our society regards it as illegal and an unhealthy approach to life. Tchambuli tribesmen of New Guinea, reformed headhunters, are artists. They enjoy painting, music, drama. They spend much time ornamenting themselves, conducting neighborhood plays, and gossiping. We do not consider such conduct masculine. In the early days, the Eastern man wore a powdered wig, ruffled shirt, ornamented breeches, and the Eastern man carried a jeweled snuff-box. This man regarded the frontiersman as not far above an animal. The frontiersman looked upon the Eastern man as a soft, unreliable Fop. This country could not have endured without both. Today it is becoming increasingly more difficult to tell which is the male and which is the female. The older generation has firm convictions as to what constitutes masculinity. Shoulder–length hair, ring be-decked fingers, necklaces, and dirty unshod feet do not meet established specifications. The Nehru jacket and the necklace are fast becoming masculine attire.

Role playing is necessary to any society. Man's role
should remain one of authority. The role does not possess a fixed
image. The role has, is, and will be modified by society. Masculinity
is nothing more than a reflection of authority.

This writing has unity, order, and completeness. In
addition, it concerns a contemporary topic of some significance.
Yet it is not effective because it lacks coherence. The writer does
not carry his reader smoothly from one idea to another or relate
each separate idea to others and to the central thought of the
whole. Instead, he thinks in separate sentences, adding new ideas
as he moves onward without bridging gaps in thought or showing
logical and necessary relationships. As a result, the reader cannot
grasp meaning easily and soon tires from the monotonous search
for understanding.

Read now the student's model as it was originally
written. Observe the smoothness in the flow of thought that the
writer gains with obvious attempts at coherence, such as transitional words like *therefore, for example, nevertheless,* pronoun
reference, repetition of the key word *masculinity* and its synonyms, and an attempt at parallel structure concerning the Eastern
man and the frontiersman. Perhaps the writing lacks consistency
in point of view, but it does indicate a definite improvement over
the original model through use of transitional and linking devices.

WHAT IS MASCULINITY?
a student theme

What is masculinity? One dictionary defines it as: Manly;
virile; robust; therefore, a composite of these definitive terms would
be: One who is resolute, dignified, honorable, sexually potent, sturdy,
healthy, lusty, and most important, male. It is immediately obvious
that all of these qualities are not visible to the naked eye; moreover,
social mores would play an important part in interpretation. For example, ancient Grecian society accepted homosexuality as perfectly
natural, but our society regards it as illegal and certainly an unhealthy
approach to life. Tchambuli tribesmen of New Guinea, reformed headhunters, are artists who enjoy painting, music, and drama. They spend
much of their time ornamenting themselves, conducting neighborhood plays, and gossiping. Certainly not the type of conduct we consider masculine. During the early expansion of this country, the
Eastern man, with his powdered wig, ruffled shirt, ornamented
breeches, and jeweled snuff-box regarded the frontiersman as not
far above an animal; for his part, the frontiersman looked upon his

Eastern counterpart as a soft, unreliable Fop; nevertheless, this country could not have endured without both. Currently, it is becoming increasingly more difficult to tell which is the male and which is the female among our younger generation. Previously conditioned by two wars, the older generation has firm convictions as to what constitutes masculinity. Shoulder–length hair, ring be-decked fingers, necklaces, and dirty unshod feet do not meet established specifications. However, the Nehru jacket, named for a man who appeared neither sexually potent, sturdy, healthy, or lusty, and the necklace are fast becoming masculine attire.

By *using transitional words and expressions and pronoun reference,* a writer gains coherence. In the model paragraph that follows, observe the way the writer gives his flowing thought direction by transitional words and expressions, such as *two, one, both, or, in any case, finally, still others* and pronouns, such as *he, his, they, this,* and *that.*

To the vexing question of how one can know precisely what the words really mean, two contrasting answers are frequently given. One is that only the author knows; the other, that each reader must decide on the meaning for himself. Plausible as these sound in theory, both answers actually leave us helpless. For the author — Chaucer, Spenser, or Shakespeare — may no longer be available for comment. Or, when he has left explanatory statements, as Milton has in his prefaces to *Paradise Lost* and *Samson Agonistes,* or Keats in his various letters, these may help to explain only certain limited aspects of the work. In any case, they show what the writer thought he was doing or intended to do rather than what he has actually achieved. Finally, if the author is our contemporary and can be asked about his work, he may be reluctant to comment, or he may even take a certain diabolic pleasure in making confusing and contradictory statements. As for leaving the decision to each individual reader, this answer presents the problem that innumerable different readings may result, some perhaps very full, perceptive, and knowledgeable, others rather more private and associative, and still others actual misinterpretations. How, then, is one to distinguish the partial or erroneous from the valid readings?
Under the circumstances, it seems best to discard both these theoretical answers and to take a frankly pragmatic position. We can recognize the difficulty of determining the precise meaning of the words, but we can nonetheless aim at more than a private or haphazard reading . . . . [62]

DISCUSSION

The paragraph is simply and effectively organized and developed. The writers present "the vexing question of how one can know precisely what words mean." Then they present the answers. They follow with the topic sentence: "Plausible as these sound in theory, both answers actually leave us helpless." They support with examples and explanations. They close the paragraph with a transitional sentence that leads the reader onward to the thought of the next paragraph.

To help the reader bridge the gaps in thought, the writers use effectively certain transitional words, such as *one, the other, both, or, as Milton has, in any case, rather than, finally, as for leaving, still others,* and *then.* The writers also use pronoun reference as a means of maintaining coherence. In three places the pronoun *he* takes the reader back to the word *author;* in another sentence *he* refers to the word *writer.* The pronoun *they* along with the forms *us, his, himself, our* and *one* are also used effectively for coherence. Although the writers have used many transitional devices for gaining coherence, they have used them so skillfully that the reader is scarcely aware of their influence on the flow of thought.

Study the following list of transitional words and phrases; use them in filling in the gaps in your own thought.

TO INDICATE ADDITION: again, also, and, and then, besides, equally important, finally, first, further, furthermore, in addition, indeed, in fact, in the second place, likewise, moreover, next, too, secondly

TO INDICATE COMPARISON (LIKENESSES): at the same time, in the same way, in like manner, likewise, similarly

TO INDICATE CONCESSION: although this may be true, at the same time, after all, certainly, doubtless, granted that, I admit, I concede, naturally, no doubt, surely

TO INDICATE CONSEQUENCES OR RESULT: all in all, accordingly, after all, and so, as a consequence, as a result, at last, consequently, finally, hence, in conclusion, so, therefore, then, thus

TO INDICATE CONDITION: as if, if, as though, even if

TO INDICATE CONTRAST: and yet, although true, at the same time, but, conversely, for all that, however, in contrast, nevertheless, notwithstanding, on the one hand, on the other hand, rather, still, whereas, yet

TO INDICATE EXAMPLES: especially, for example, for instance, for one thing, frequently, in general, in particular, in this way, namely, occasionally, specifically, that is, to illustrate, thus, usually

TO INDICATE REASON: because, since, for

TO INDICATE REPETITION: and so again, as has been said, in fact, indeed, in other words, to recapitulate, to repeat, I repeat

TO INDICATE SUMMARY: in brief, in short, to sum up, to summarize, in conclusion, to conclude

RELATIVE PRONOUNS, DEMONSTRATIVE ADJECTIVES, AND OTHER PRONOUNS: this, that, these, those, who, whom, whose, which, what, that, it, they, them, few, many, most, several, he, she, and so forth.

In the paragraphs which follow, observe *the repetition of the main idea* "Bowl games." Notice also the use of pronoun reference to carry the reader back to the dominant noun *Bowl games*.

Consider the Bowl games. They are important influences on athletic policies and at the same time irrefutable evidence that athletics, so far as the Bowls are concerned, have no educational significance whatsoever. So far as I know, no one seriously claims that they do.

All of the Bowls for obvious reasons are located in the South or in winter vacation areas. They are immensely successful business promotions; there is nothing about them remotely related to education. As one man put it: "Rose Bowl, Sugar Bowl, Orange Bowl — all are gravy bowls!" A half-million people saw the games in the eight major bowls last January 1, and it is estimated 70 million more heard them on radio or saw them on television. Receipts were almost $2.5 million. The distribution of the money follows a kind of formula in each conference — a large percentage to each school participating in the Bowl, a smaller percentage to each school in the conference and to the conference treasury itself. A more subtle formula to ensure support for Bowl games could hardly be devised. Participation in one of the Big Four Bowls — Rose, Sugar, Cotton, and Orange — may bring each participating school as much as $125,000. Everyone profits — except the players, whose amateur status has thus far confined them to such grubby rewards as gifts of gold watches, blankets, free tickets which can be scalped, sometimes a little cash — the last usually secretly. Under pressure from the players and perhaps from a sense of institutional guilt at the indefensible exploitation, the rewards to players are improving, but they still are far below the A.S.C.A.P. and Equity pay scales for big-time entertainers. [63]

In the paragraph which follows, the writer places his main idea in the first sentence, and he develops this main idea with supporting material in the form of contrasts between man's existence and a woman's life. He uses simple, short sentences with effective parallel structure. He keeps the dominant nouns *man* and *woman* in the reader's mind by repetition of the words and pronoun substitutes. In addition he uses such transitional words as *after, first,* and *yet.* He leads the reader onward to the thought of the following paragraph by a final transitional sentence. Then, he opens the second paragraph with a transitional word *moreover* to indicate to the reader that he will offer additional supporting evidence for his viewpoint.

A woman must be educated to handle options more fundamental than any which ever confront a man. The pattern of a man's existence is fairly simple. He is born; he is educated partly to be a person and partly to earn a living; he earns a living, gets a wife, begets children, and works until he dies. The pattern of a woman's life today is essentially different. After she graduates from college she is faced with her first major choice: family or career (although "career" is a glamour word for the kind of jobs most women can get!). If a man marries he must work harder than ever at his career; there is no conflict. Yet, despite all the brave phrases which are currently fashionable, a married woman who tries to combine the two usually has either a token career or a token family, at least so long as her children are young.

Moreover, the woman who marries and takes her family seriously must be prepared to face a second distinctively feminine option. Twenty or twenty-five years after marriage, when normally she is in her forties, she may still have a husband about the house who needs some care and affection, but the children, who have taken the bulk of her time since she left college, have grown up and established their own homes. What is she to do with her released energies and intelligence during the next three decades? For the second time in her life she must choose as a man never chooses; for even to do nothing is to choose. [64]

In the model paragraph which follows, observe the effective use of *parallel structure*.

We cannot go back, we cannot go back to the old prisons, the old systems of mere punishment under which when a man came out of prison he was not fitted to live in our community alongside of us. We cannot go back to the old systems of asylums. We cannot go back to the old lack of hospitals, the lack of public health. We cannot go back to the sweatshops of America. We cannot go back to children working in factories. Those days are gone. [65]

A writer gains coherence *by maintaining a consistent point of view*. Unnecessary, sudden, and illogical shifts in point of view; that is, in subject, person, number, tense, voice, and mood, affect sentence and paragraph relationships; thus obscuring meaning. Avoid shifts in the following:

1. Shifts in subject or voice

SHIFT: The store was robbed by the two wanted criminals as we enter it.
[*A shift in subjects from* store *to* we; *a shift in voice from passive to active*]

IMPROVED: We saw the two wanted criminals robbing the store as we entered it.
[*Both verbs in active voice*]

SHIFT: John ran to his right, and the ball nestled in his glove.
[*Shift in subject from* John *to* ball]

IMPROVED: John ran to his right, and he caught the ball in his glove.
[*pronoun substitute*] [*same subject*]

IMPROVED: John ran to the right and caught the ball in his glove.
[*One subject only*]

SHIFT: Jane disliked Paris, but London was enjoyed by her.
[*Shift in subject and voice*]

IMPROVED: Jane disliked Paris, but she enjoyed London.
[*One subject only; both verbs in active voice*]

2. Shifts in tense

SHIFT: Helen opened the door and rushes into the yard after William.
[*A shift from past tense to present tense*]
IMPROVED: Helen opens the door and rushes into the yard after William.
[*Both present tenses*]

SHIFT: The curtain opens and the play began.
[*Shift from present tense to past tense*]
IMPROVED: The curtain opened and the play began.
[*Both verbs in the past tense*]

3. Shifts in mood

SHIFT: Raise the ball onto your fingertips, and then you should lay it gently against the backboard.
[*Shift from the imperative to the indicative mood*]
IMPROVED: Raise the ball onto your fingertips and then lay it gently against the backboard.
[*Both verbs in the imperative mood*]

4. Shifts in person

SHIFT: When *you* pass his examination, *one* should feel a little proud.
[*A shift from second person to third person*]
IMPROVED: When *you* pass his examination, *you* should feel a little proud.
[*Both in the second person*]
IMPROVED: When *one* passes his examination, *he* (or *one*) should feel a little proud.
[*Both in the third person*]

SHIFT: A *student* needs to study long hours for Professor White's class. *You* will find the lectures filled with facts and the examinations difficult.
[*A shift from third person to second*]
IMPROVED: A *student* needs to study long hours for Professor White's class. *He* will find the lectures filled with facts and the examinations difficult.
[*Both in the third person*]

5. Shifts in number

SHIFT: If a *person* follows those suggestions, *they* will get into difficulty.

[*A shift from singular to plural number*]

IMPROVED: If a *person* follows those suggestions, *he* will get into difficulty.

[*Both third person singular*]

In the student model which follows, notice that frequent shifts in subject and person cause confusion. Observe also the shifts in tense and voice.

Good study habits are necessary for success in college. The art of studying must be learned in order to excel in anything. Two hours for each hour of class time is required but is not enough if you are careless and haphazard in your study habits. He is just putting in time that is of little or no use. A student must have much self-discipline and motivation to learn to the best of their ability.

This paragraph is very badly written. Why? Answer the following questions; they will help you identify the mistakes.

1. What is the main idea?
2. Is the main idea developed?
3. How many different subjects are there?
4. What is the voice of the verbs in sentences 2 and 3?

Study the model paragraphs which follow. Observe the various uses of transitional devices. Notice especially the manner in which Huxley relates the thought of one paragraph to another by transitional sentences as the first sentence of some paragraphs.

¹ So much, then, by way of proof that the method of establishing laws in science is exactly the same as that pursued in common life. Let us now turn to another matter (though really it is but another phase of the same question), and that is, the method by which, from the relatiohs of certain phenomena, we prove that some stand in the position of causes towards the others.

² I want to put the case clearly before you, and I will therefore show you what I mean by another familiar example. I will suppose that one of you, on coming down in the morning to the parlour of your house, finds that a teapot and some spoons which had been

left in the room on the previous evening are gone — the window is open, and you observe the mark of a dirty hand on the window frame, and perhaps, in addition to that, you notice the impress of a hobnailed shoe on the gravel outside. All these phenomena have struck your attention instantly, and before two seconds have passed you say, "Oh, somebody has broken open the window, entered the room, and run off with the spoons and the teapot!" That speech is out of your mouth in a moment. And you will probably add, "I know he has; I am quite sure of it!" You mean to say exactly what you know; but in reality you are giving expression to what is, in all essential particulars, an hypothesis. You do not *know* it at all; it is nothing but an hypothesis rapidly framed in your own mind. And it is an hypothesis founded on a long train of inductions and deductions.

[3]What are those inductions and deductions, and how have you got at this hypothesis? You have observed, in the first place, that the window is open; but by a train of reasoning involving many inductions and deductions, you have probably arrived long before at the general law — and a very good one it is — that windows do not open of themselves; and you therefore conclude that something has opened the window. A second general law that you have arrived at in the same way is, that teapots and spoons do not go out of a window spontaneously, and you are satisfied that, as they are not now where you left them, they have been removed. In the third place, you look at the marks on the window sill, and the shoemarks outside, and you say that in all previous experience the former kind of mark has never been produced by anything else but the hand of a human being; and the same experience shows that no other animal but man at present wears shoes with hobnails in them such as would produce the marks in the gravel. I do not know, even if we could discover any of those "missing links" that are talked about, that they would help us to any other conclusion! At any rate the law which states our present experience is strong enough for my present purpose. You next reach the conclusion that, as these kinds of marks have not been left by any other animal than man, nor are liable to be formed in any other way than by a man's hand and shoe, the marks in question have been formed by a man in that way. You have, further, a general law, founded on observation and experience, and that, too, is, I am sorry to say, a very universal and unimpeachable one — that some men are thieves; and you assume at once from all these premises — and that is what constitutes your hypothesis — that the man who made the marks outside and on the window sill, opened the window, got into the room, and stole your teapot and spoons. You have now arrived at a *vera causa* [real cause]; you have assumed a cause which, it is plain, is competent to produce all the phenomena you have observed. You can explain all these phenomena only by the hypothesis of a thief.

But that is a hypothetical conclusion, of the justice of which you have no absolute proof at all; it is only rendered highly probable by a series of inductive and deductive reasonings. [66]

EXERCISES

6. *Coherence*
Study the paragraphs below. Underline any transitional words or phrases and encircle any repetitions of key words or phrases.

[1]Intelligence tests seek to avert bias, first by avoiding, so far as possible, test items which favor one group as against another, and secondly by taking care that subjects used in the standardization of these tests shall be representative of the populations to whom the tests will be subsequently administered.

[2]Thus, in getting up a vocabulary list, one would avoid words with which individuals of a higher status group would be more familiar than would a lower status group — "peignoir," "chutney" and "litigation," for example. Again, in testing a person for ability to detect missing parts, one would use a picture of a horse rather than a yak, a drum rather than a base viol. Similarly in planning questions of general comprehension one must take into consideration the customs and attitudes of different places. Thus the questions "Why are shoes made of leather?" and "Why does the state require people to get a marriage license?" would be suitable for Europeans and Americans but might be quite incomprehensible to persons living where shoes are not worn and where the state is not so particular.

[3]However, there is considerable evidence to show that so-called "race" differences have been greatly overestimated. General intelligence seems to be a very general commodity. It is not so much the significance of the differences in ability found between groups as the exploitation of these differences which have sometimes given intelligence tests a bad reputation. [67]

7. *Coherence*
Read the paragraph below. Encircle any repetitions and underline transitional words or phrases.

What is it that we mean by *literature*? Popularly, and amongst the thoughtless, it is held to include everything that is printed in a book. Little logic is required to disturb *that* definition; the most thoughtless person is easily made aware that in the idea of *literature* one essential element is — some relation to a general and common interest of man, so that what applies only to a local — or professional — or merely personal interest, even though presenting itself in the shape of a book, will not belong to literature. So far the definition is easily narrowed; and it is as easily expanded. For not only is much that takes a station in books not literature; but inversely, much that really *is* literature never reaches a station in books. The weekly sermons of Christendom, that vast pulpit literature which acts so extensively upon the popular mind — to warn, to uphold, to renew, to comfort, to alarm, does not attain the sanctuary of libraries in the ten thousandth part of its extent. The drama again, as, for instance, the finest of Shakspere's plays in England, and all leading Athenian plays in the noontide of the Attic stage, operated as a literature on the public mind, and were (according to the strictest letter of that term) *published* through the audiences that witnessed their representation some time before they were published as things to be read; and they were published in this scenical mode of publication with much more effect than they could have had as books, during ages of costly copying or of costly printing. [68]

8. Coherence

Revise the following sentences by eliminating shifts in subject, voice, person, number, mood, and tense.

1. Airplanes could be heard as we approached the field.
2. After you finish the inventory, one reports to the manager.
3. The waves were very strong, and the boat was damaged by it.
4. He sat down in front of the painting and begins to copy it.
5. When one receives praise from him, you should feel fortunate.
6. Take the book back to the library and then you should pay the fine.
7. When I asked Jim for the answers, he does not hear me.
8. If a student develops good study habits, they will have a better chance of success in college.
9. You should follow his suggestion, and much time will be saved.
10. When a person reaches the edge of the canyon, a deep river can be seen about a mile below.
11. Fill out the application and then you should hand it to his secretary.

12. James enjoyed sailing, but swimming was also enjoyed by him.
13. We have arrived at a decision, and the money was returned.
14. The student will find the cafeteria a great convenience. You need not leave the campus for meals or evening snacks.
15. The teacher scolded Walter and walks hurriedly away.
16. First return the materials and then you should buy new ones.
17. A person should never let their friends suffer.
18. Smith liked athletics, but studying was disliked by him.
19. She inquires about William and received a vague answer.
20. A man must accept responsibilities if you are going to win their respect.

9. Coherence

Read the paragraphs below. Underline once any transitional sentences. Encircle any transitional words or expressions. Draw a rectangle about any repetitions.

[1] But precisely how and why this matching of student to college takes place remains unclear. Certainly the "image" of a college has a great deal to do with the selective application of the "right" type of student. But in no college is the match between student needs and capacities and the institution's provisions and demands perfect.

[2] Nor should a perfect match be viewed as the ideal. Education, after all, aims at inducing change in students; and some disparity between what the entering freshman is and what the college thinks he should become by graduation is necessary if college is to be more than stagnation or play. But no one really knows how to define the optimal disparity. If the gap between what the student wants and expects and what the college provides and asks is too great, then frustration, a sense of failure, or discontent is likely to result. But if what the student brings with him to college and what the college expects from him are too perfectly matched, the result is likely to be that stagnation which some observers think characteristic of student development at many major American colleges.

[3] Furthermore, an ideal match for men students may not be at all ideal for women; yet little is known about the educational differences between the sexes. Most studies concentrate on one or the other sex, yet generalize to both. But anyone who has taught both sexes can personally document the enormous difference between their educational outlooks, concerns, and motivations. It is not yet clear, for example, to what extent student development as described in two classic studies of Bennington and Vassar should be generalized to most students, most liberal-arts students, most female students, or most female liberal-arts students. Other accounts of contemporary students seem relevant primarily to men; thus, for example, very few of the "activists" in the present generation are drawn from among co-eds. Whether we consider it a result of anatomy or social conditioning, women view their educations and their lives very differently than do men. [69]

ASSIGNMENTS

1. Coherence

Rewrite the following student paragraph to improve the coherence, especially the shifts in subject and voice.

Color creates or is associated with moods or feelings Blue is usually associated with sadness or loneliness. And red and yellow are usually associated with violence or cause you to feel violently toward the object that these colors are on. We also associate such colors as blue, green, and purple with ice or snow as being cool colors. In the same way, they associate yellow, red, and orange with warm colors.

2. Coherence

Write a brief paragraph explaining why you believe that parallel structure is effective in the following selection.

[1] But neither can two great and powerful groups of nations take comfort from our present course — both sides overburdened by the cost of modern weapons, both rightly alarmed by the steady spread of the deadly atom, yet both racing to alter that uncertain balance of terror that stays the hand of mankind's final war.

[2] So let us begin anew — remembering on both sides that civility is not a sign of weakness, and sincerity is always subject to proof. Let us never negotiate out of fear. But let us never fear to negotiate.

[3] Let both sides explore what problems unite us instead of belaboring those problems which divide us.

⁴Let both sides, for the first time, formulate serious and precise proposals for the inspection and control of arms — and bring the absolute power to destroy other nations under the absolute control of all nations.

⁵Let both sides join to invoke the wonders of science instead of its terrors. Together let us explore the stars, conquer the deserts, eradicate disease, tap the ocean depths, and encourage the arts and commerce.

⁶Let both sides unite to heed in all corners of the earth the command of Isaiah — to "undo the heavy burdens . . . [and] let the oppressed go free."

⁷And if a beach-head of cooperation may push back the jungles of suspicion, let both sides join in creating a new endeavor, not a new balance of power, but a new world of law, where the strong are just and the weak secure and the peace preserved.

⁸All this will not be finished in the first one hundred days. Nor will it be finished in the first one thousand days, nor in the life of this Administration, nor even perhaps in our lifetime on this planet. But let us begin.

⁹In your hands, my fellow citizens, more than mine, will rest the final success or failure of our course. Since this country was founded, each generation of Americans has been summoned to give testimony to its national loyalty. The graves of young Americans who answered the call to service surround the globe. [70]

3. *Variety, emphasis, coherence*

After reading the following selection, be prepared to discuss and analyze techniques of variety in sentence structure and methods of achieving emphasis and smooth transitions.

QUEEN ELIZABETH

by Lytton Strachey

¹Certainly no more *baroque* figure ever trod this earth than the supreme phenomenon of Elizabethanism — Elizabeth herself. From her visible aspect to the profundities of her being, every part of her was permeated by the bewildering discordances of the real and the apparent. Under the serried complexities of her raiment — the huge hoop, the stiff ruff, the swollen sleeves, the powdered pearls, the spreading, gilded gauzes — the form of the woman vanished, and men saw instead an image — magnificent, portentous, self-created — an image of regality, which yet, by a miracle, was actually alive. Posterity has suffered by a similar deceit of vision. The great Queen of its imagination, the lion-hearted heroine, who flung back the insolence of Spain and crushed the tyranny

of Rome with splendid unhesitating gestures, no more resembles the Queen of fact than the clothed Elizabeth the naked one. But, after all, posterity is privileged. Let us draw nearer; we shall do no wrong now to that Majesty, if we look below the robes.

[2]The lion heart, the splendid gestures — such heroic things were there, no doubt — visible to everybody; but their true significance in the general scheme of her character was remote and complicated. The sharp and hostile eyes of the Spanish ambassadors saw something different; in their opinion, the outstanding characteristic of Elizabeth was pusillanimity. They were wrong; but they perceived more of the truth than the idle onlooker. They had come into contact with those forces in the Queen's mind which proved, incidentally, fatal to themselves, and brought her, in the end, her enormous triumph. That triumph was not the result of heroism. The very contrary was the case: the grand policy which dominated Elizabeth's life was the most unheroic conceivable; and her true history remains a standing lesson for melodramatists in statecraft. In reality, she succeeded by virtue of all the qualities which every hero should be without — dissimulation, pliability, indecision, procrastination, parsimony. It might almost be said that the heroic element chiefly appeared in the unparalleled lengths to which she allowed those qualities to carry her. It needed a lion heart indeed to spend twelve years in convincing the world that she was in love with the Duke of Anjou and to stint the victuals of the men who defeated the Armada; but in such directions she was in very truth capable of everything. She found herself a sane woman in a universe of violent maniacs, between contending forces of terrific intensity — the rival nationalisms of France and Spain, the rival religions of Rome and Calvin; for years it had seemed inevitable that she should be crushed by one or other of them, and she had survived because she had been able to meet the extremes around her with her own extremes of cunning and prevarication. It so happened that the subtlety of her intellect was exactly adapted to the complexities of her environment. The balance of power between France and Spain, the balance of factions in France and Scotland, the swaying fortunes of the Netherlands, gave scope for a tortuosity of diplomacy which has never been completely unravelled to this day. Burghley was her chosen helper, a careful steward after her own heart; and more than once Burghley gave up the puzzle of his mistress's proceedings in despair. Nor was it only her intellect that served her; it was her temperament as well. That too — in its mixture of the masculine and the feminine, of vigour and sinuosity, of pertinacity and vacillation — was precisely what her case required. A deep instinct made it almost impossible for her to come to a fixed determination upon any subject whatever. Or, if she did, she immediately proceeded to contradict her resolu-

tion with the utmost violence, and, after that, to contradict her contradiction more violently still. Such was her nature — to float, when it was calm, in a sea of indecisions, and, when the wind rose, to tack hectically from side to side. Had it been otherwise — had she possessed, according to the approved pattern of the strong man of action, the capacity for taking a line and sticking to it — she would have been lost. She would have become inextricably entangled in the forces that surrounded her, and, almost inevitably, swiftly destroyed. Her femininity saved her. Only a woman could have shuffled so shamelessly, only a woman could have abandoned with such unscrupulous completeness the last shreds not only of consistency, but of dignity, honour, and common decency, in order to escape the appalling necessity of having, really and truly, to make up her mind. Yet it is true that a woman's evasiveness was not enough; male courage, male energy were needed, if she were to escape the pressure that came upon her from every side. Those qualities she also possessed; but their value to her — it was the final paradox of her career — was merely that they made her strong enough to turn her back, with an indomitable persistence, upon the ways of strength.

[3] Religious persons at the time were distressed by her conduct, and imperialist historians have wrung their hands over her since. Why could she not suppress her hesitations and chicaneries and take a noble risk? Why did she not step forth, boldly and frankly, as the leader of Protestant Europe, accept the sovereignty of Holland, and fight the good fight to destroy Catholicism and transfer the Spanish Empire to the rule of England? The answer is that she cared for none of those things. She understood her true nature and her true mission better than her critics. It was only by an accident of birth that she was a Protestant leader; at heart she was profoundly secular; and it was her destiny to be the champion, not of the Reformation, but of something greater — the Renaissance. When she had finished her strange doings, there was civilisation in England. The secret of her conduct was, after all, a simple one: she had been gaining time. And time, for her purposes, was everything. A decision meant war — war, which was the very antithesis of all she had at heart. Like no other great statesman in history, she was, not only by disposition, but in practice, pacific. It was not that she was much disturbed by the cruelty of war — she was far from sentimental; she hated it for the best of all reasons — its wastefulness. Her thrift was spiritual as well as material, and the harvest that she gathered in was the great Age, to which, though its supreme glories were achieved under her successor, her name has been rightly given. For without her those particular fields could never have come to ripeness; they would have been trodden down by struggling hordes of nationalists and theologians. She kept the peace for thirty years

— by dint, it is true, of one long succession of disgraceful collapses and unheard-of equivocations; but she kept it, and that was enough for Elizabeth.

[4]To put the day of decision off — and off — and off — it seemed her only object, and her life passed in a passion of postponement. But here, too, appearances were deceitful, as her adversaries found to their cost. In the end, when the pendulum had swung to and fro for ages, and delay had grown grey, and expectation sunk down in its socket . . . something terrible happened. The crafty Maitland of Lethington, in whose eyes the God of his fathers was "ane bogle of the nursery," declared with scorn that the Queen of England was inconstant, irresolute, timorous, and that before the game was played out he would "make her sit upon her tail and whine, like ane whippet hound." Long years passed, and then suddenly the rocks of Edinburgh Castle ran down like sand at Elizabeth's bidding, and Maitland took refuge from the impossible ruin in a Roman's death. Mary Stuart despised her rival with a virulent French scorn; and, after eighteen years, at Fotheringay, she found she was mistaken. King Philip took thirty years to learn the same lesson. For so long had he spared his sister-in-law; but now he pronounced her doom; and he smiled to watch the misguided woman still negotiating for a universal peace, as his Armada sailed into the Channel.

[5]Undoubtedly there was a touch of the sinister about her. One saw it in the movements of her extraordinarily long hands. But it was a touch and no more — just enough to remind one that there was Italian blood in her veins — the blood of the subtle and cruel Visconti. On the whole, she was English. On the whole, though she was infinitely subtle, she was not cruel; she was almost humane for her times; and her occasional bursts of savagery were the results of fear or temper. In spite of superficial resemblances, she was the very opposite of her most dangerous enemy — the weaving spider of the Escurial. Both were masters of dissimulation and lovers of delay; but the leaden foot of Philip was the symptom of a dying organism, while Elizabeth temporised for the contrary reason — because vitality can afford to wait. The fierce old hen sat still, brooding over the English nation, whose pullulating energies were coming swiftly to ripeness and unity under her wings. She sat still; but every feather bristled; she was tremendously alive. Her super-abundant vigour was at once alarming and delightful. While the Spanish ambassador declared that ten thousand devils possessed her, the ordinary Englishman saw in King Hal's full-blooded daughter a Queen after his own heart. She swore; she spat; she struck with her fist when she was angry; she roared with laughter when she was amused. And she was often amused. A radiant atmosphere of humour coloured and softened the harsh lines of her destiny, and buoyed her up along the

zigzags of her dreadful path. Her response to every stimulus was immediate and rich: to the folly of the moment, to the clash and horror of great events, her soul leapt out with a vivacity, an abandonment, a complete awareness of the situation, which made her, which makes her still, a fascinating spectacle. She could play with life as with an equal, wrestling with it, making fun of it, admiring it, watching its drama, intimately relishing the strangeness of circumstance, the sudden freaks of fortune, the perpetual unexpectedness of things. "Per molto variare la natura è bella" was one of her favourite aphorisms.

[6]The variations in her own behaviour were hardly less frequent than nature's. The rough hectoring dame with her practical jokes, her out-of-doors manners, her passion for hunting, would suddenly become a stern-faced woman of business, closeted for long hours with secretaries, reading and dictating despatches, and examining with sharp exactitude the minutiae of accounts. Then, as suddenly, the cultivated lady of the Renaissance would shine forth. For Elizabeth's accomplishments were many and dazzling. She was mistress of six languages besides her own, a student of Greek, a superb calligraphist, an excellent musician. She was a connoisseur of painting and poetry. She danced, after the Florentine style, with a high magnificence that astonished beholders. Her conversation, full, not only of humour, but of elegance and wit, revealed an unerring social sense, a charming delicacy of personal perception. It was this spiritual versatility which made her one of the supreme diplomatists of history. Her protean mind, projecting itself with extreme rapidity into every sinuous shape conceivable, perplexed the most clear-sighted of her antagonists and deluded the most wary. But her crowning virtuosity was her command over the resources of words. When she wished, she could drive in her meaning up to the hilt with hammer blows of speech, and no one ever surpassed her in the elaborate confection of studied ambiguities. Her letters she composed in a regal mode of her own, full of apophthegm and insinuation. In private talk she could win a heart by some quick felicitous *brusquerie;* but her greatest moments came when, in public audience, she made known her wishes, her opinions, and her meditations to the world. Then the splendid sentences, following one another in a steady volubility, proclaimed the curious workings of her intellect with enthralling force; while the woman's inward passion vibrated magically through the loud high uncompromising utterance and the perfect rhythms of her speech. [71]

CHAPTER THREE   *References*

1. From "Shooting an Elephant" by George Orwell.
2. From "First Inaugural Address" by Franklin Delano Roosevelt.
3. From *The Second Common Reader* by Virginia Woolf. Reprinted by permission of the publisher, Harcourt, Brace & World, Inc.
4. From *Moby Dick* by Herman Melville.
5. From "First Inaugural Address" by Franklin Delano Roosevelt.
6. From *The Second Common Reader* by Virginia Woolf. Cf. 3.
7. From *One Man's Meat* by E. B. White.
8. From *The Autobiography of Lincoln Steffens* by Lincoln Steffens.
9. From *The Summing Up* by W. Somerset Maugham.
10. From "Custodians of History" by Adlai E. Stevenson.
11. From *Closing the Ring* by Winston Churchill.
12. From "Introduction" to *The Stories of F. Scott Fitzgerald* by Malcolm Cowley.
13. From "Custodians of History" by Adlai E. Stevenson.
14. From *Closing the Ring* by Winston Churchill.
15. From "Shooting an Elephant" by George Orwell.
16. From "First Inaugural Address" by Franklin Delano Roosevelt.
17. From *The Second Common Reader* by Virginia Woolf. Cf. 3.
18. From "On the Record" by Dorothy Thompson.
19. From *Canada, Tomorrow's Giant* by Bruce Hutchinson.
20. From *Abraham Lincoln: The War Years* by Carl Sandburg. Reprinted by permission of the publisher, Harcourt, Brace & World, Inc.
21. From *The Summing Up* by W. Somerset Maugham.
22. From *Abraham Lincoln: The War Years* by Carl Sandburg. Cf. 20.
23. From *The Second Common Reader* by Virginia Woolf. Cf. 3.
24. From "Everyman His Own Historian," by Carl Becker, in *The American Historical Review*. Reprinted by permission of The American Historical Association.
25. From *The Sea Around Us* by Rachel L. Carson. Published by The Oxford University Press, Inc.
26. From "Essay on Milton" by Thomas Babington Macaulay.
27. From "Address to the House of Commons," by Winston Churchill.
28. From "Winds That Blow Straight Up" by Wolfgang Langewiesche.
29. From *The Sea Around Us* by Rachel L. Carson. Cf. 25.
30. From "Human Society in Ethics and Politics" by Bertrand Russell.
31. From "Conformity and Noncomformity" by Ralph Waldo Emerson.
32. From "Human Society in Ethics and Politics" by Bertrand Russell.
33. From *Brave Men* by Ernie Pyle.
34. From *Of Time and the River* by Thomas Wolfe.
35. From *Let Us Now Praise Famous Men* by James Agee and Walker Evans.
36. From "Conformity and Nonconformity" by Ralph Waldo Emerson.
37. Cf. 36.
38. From *The Sea Around Us* by Rachel L. Carson. Cf. 25.
39. From *Elizabeth and Essex, A Tragic History* by Lytton Strachey. Copyright 1928 by Lytton Strachey, copyright 1956 by James Strachey. Reprinted by permission of Harcourt, Brace & World, Inc.
40. From *Elizabeth and Essex, A Tragic History* by Lytton Strachey. Cf. 39.

41. From *Let Us Now Praise Famous Men* by James Agee and Walker Evans.
42. Cf. 41.
43. From *Literary and Philosophical Essays* by Jean-Paul Sartre.
44. From "Human Society in Ethics and Politics" by Bertrand Russell.
45. From *Literary and Philosophical Essays* by Jean-Paul Sartre.
46. Cf. 45.
47. Cf. 45.
48. From "Human Society in Ethics and Politics" by Bertrand Russell.
49. From *Victorian England: Portrait of an Age* by G. M. Young. By permission of Oxford University Press, London.
50. From "Speech to Congress, May 16, 1940" by Franklin Delano Roosevelt.
51. From "Speech to House of Commons, May 13, 1940" by Winston Churchill.
52. From "Inaugural Address, January 20, 1961" by John F. Kennedy.
53. From *Elizabeth and Essex, A Tragic History* by Lytton Strachey. Cf. 39.
54. From "Human Society in Ethics and Politics" by Bertrand Russell.
55. From *Literary and Philosophical Essays* by Jean-Paul Sartre.
56. From "Educating Women in a Man's World" by Lynn White, Jr., in *The Atlantic Monthly*. By permission.
57. From "'Kitty' of Harvard" by Rollo Walter Brown.
58. From "A Design for Fighting" by Harlow Shapley. Based on a Phi Beta Kappa address, the essay appears in *The View from a Distant Star*, 1963, Basic Books.
59. From "Love in America" by Raoul De Roussy De Sales.
60. From "'Kitty' of Harvard" by Rollo Walter Brown.
61. From "On the Record" by Dorothy Thompson.
62. From *An Introduction to Literary Criticism* by Marlies K. Danziger and W. Stacy Johnson. Copyright © 1961 by D. C. Heath and Company.
63. From "College Athletics: Education or Show Business" by Harold W. Stoke, in *The Atlantic Monthly* (March, 1954). Copyright © The Atlantic Monthly Company, Boston, Mass. By permission of the author.
64. From "Educating Women in a Man's World" by Lynn White, Jr., in *The Atlantic Monthly*. Cf. 56.
65. From "The Philosophy of Social Justice Through Social Action" by Franklin Delano Roosevelt.
66. From "The Method of Scientific Investigation" by Thomas Henry Huxley.
67. From "Measuring the I.Q. Test" by David Wechsler. Copyright © 1957 by The New York Times Company. Reprinted by permission of The New York Times Company and the author.
68. From "Literature of Knowledge and Literature of Power" by Thomas De Quincy.
69. From "The Faces in the Lecture Room" by Robert S. Morison, in *Daedalus*, 1966. Reprinted by permission of *Daedalus*.
70. From "Inaugural Address, January 20, 1961" by John F. Kennedy.
71. "Queen Elizabeth," from *Elizabeth and Essex, A Tragic History* by Lytton Strachey. Cf. 39.

FOUR

Giving order to your flowing thought

Mastering the skills of writing concise and cogent topic sentences will help you achieve paragraph unity, and structuring valid and sufficient major and minor support will give your paragraphs completeness. But you will need also some kind of consistent and logical order or arrangement of your ideas to give your flowing thought coherence and direction. The brief paragraph which follows, for example, begins with a succinctly stated main idea which is supported adequately; nevertheless, the thought is confused.

Cape Cod is unique. It was then molded for more than 100 centuries by winds, waves, tides and currents. You can even pick up pebbles brought by glaciers from the Laurentian Mountains in Canada. A peninsula which stands farther out to sea than any other portion of our Atlantic coast, it was created, geologists say, by mile-high glaciers which dropped deposits here in the last Ice Age — about 11,000 years ago. You can see mile after mile of original glacial deposits sliced by the elements into clean-sloping cliffs. Layers, some as distinct as in a cake, show the advances and retreats of the ice.

Something is wrong. The writer expresses several ideas which are in themselves interesting and important. Yet, the relationship of one idea to another and to the central thought of the entire passage is confusing. The paragraph lacks a smooth and logical development; it has no consistent order or pattern of development.

In contrast, the original paragraph illustrates a smooth flow of thought from the opening topic sentence through the support. The writer plans a concise topic sentence and develops the main idea with two orders or patterns which rise naturally from the supporting material and his purpose.

Cape Cod is unique. A peninsula which stands farther out to sea than any other portion of our Atlantic coast, it was created, geologists say, by mile-high glaciers which dropped deposits here in the last Ice Age — about 11,000 years ago. It was then molded for more than 100 centuries by winds, waves, tides and currents. You can see mile after mile of original glacial deposits sliced by the elements into clean-sloping cliffs. Layers, some as distinct as in a cake, show the advances and retreats of the ice. You can even pick up pebbles brought by glaciers from the Laurentian Mountains in Canada. [1]

DISCUSSION

The writer makes clear his purpose with the topic sentence "Cape Cod is unique." A glance at his supporting material indicates the two kinds of development that are logical: by time and by cause and effect. He begins, therefore, about 11,000 years ago with discussing the mile-high glaciers (a cause) which formed the Cape (an effect or result). He moves onward through time for more than 100 centuries citing additional causes — the winds, waves, tides, and currents — which have molded the Cape. Finally, he describes the Cape as it looks today — the result of those causes.

Read the following student paragraph. As you read, try to determine the topic sentence and the method of development.

The twentieth century is the age of progress. Without a college education we would be unable to cope with the changing times. It would be impossible to develop skills essential to satisfy the daily needs of the public. How would a doctor perform an operation without a college education? Or a teacher teach his class without being better educated than his students,

DISCUSSION

Although the first sentence appears at first glance to be the topic sentence, the second sentence states the main idea: a college education enables one to cope with the changing times. It is a poor topic sentence because it is too general. With revision this main idea could be the thesis of a longer piece of writing. In addition, the writer does not support the generalization with material that makes it acceptable. His support consists first of a somewhat confusing generalization about skills essential to satisfy the daily needs of the public; however, he does not mention specific skills or any definite needs. He concludes his paragraph with two questions which he does not answer; the reader, therefore, is again lost as to what he means. The writer, on the other hand, has attempted to write a general to a particular paragraph; the structural pattern is obvious.

Effective development of a main idea, then, is the result of skillfully organizing various methods of structuring thought into some kind of a consistent pattern or patterns. In this chapter, some simple methods involving essentially an arrangement of sentences into logical and emphatic orders of development will be discussed. In the remainder of the book, some more complex orders of development will be considered.

Because the emphasis on developing fully a main idea is on methods of structuring thought, you may forget that your material and your purpose actually determine the kind of development. In writing a paragraph or even a longer piece of writing, you do not arbitrarily impose on the material a certain kind or kinds of orders. You do not, for example, decide that you will develop a particular main idea by comparison, another by time order, still another by deduction with examples and statistics as supporting material. Instead, you will find that after you have defined clearly in your own mind the purpose and have phrased the topic sentence, the material as support will actually dictate the kind of development.

The topic sentence

Study the following topic sentence. In your opinion what kind of development would be the most natural?

Most of these meteorites are of two kinds.

The arrangement of ideas into a paragraph with this kind of main idea and purpose would be obviously into a discussion of the two kinds of meteorites. The writer can break his subject meteorites down into two component parts for the purpose of analysis (See analysis by partition in Chapter 7.) The paragraph from which this topic sentence was excerpted follows.

Most of these meteorites are of two kinds. One is stony in nature, like a piece of rock from the sky. The largest of these that we have yet found is at Norton, Kansas, and it is estimated to weigh 1 ton. The other kind is composed of an alloy of nickel and iron, similar to what is believed to make up the interior of the Earth. The largest known nickel-iron meteorite is in Grootfontein, in Africa. Its weight is probably more than 60 tons. [2]

When a writer has written his topic sentence and studied his supporting material, he does not need to ask "Shall I develop this main idea by time? or by comparison? or by definition? or by climax? He finds that the order or orders of development come naturally from the material itself and his purpose, providing that he has defined clearly that purpose and can recognize and develop various orders.

In the model paragraph which follows, observe that the material dictates a description of the "sight full of quick wonder and awe!"

It was a sight full of quick wonder and awe! The vast swells of the omnipotent sea; the surging, hollow roar they made, as they rolled along the eight gunwales, like gigantic bowls in a boundless bowling-green; the brief suspended agony of the boat, as it would tip for an instant on the knifelike edge of the sharper waves, that almost seemed threatening to cut it in two; the sudden profound dip into the watery glens and hollows; the keen spurrings and goadings to gain the top of the opposite hill; the headlong, sledlike slide down its other side — all these, with the cries of the headsmen and harpooneers, and the shuddering gasps of the oarsmen, with the wondrous sight of the ivory *Pequod* bearing down upon her boats with outstretched sails, like a wild hen after her screaming brood — all this was thrilling. Not the raw recruit, marching from the bosom of his wife into the fever heat of his first battle; not the dead man's ghost encountering the first unknown phantom in the other world; — neither of these can feel stranger and stronger emotions than that man does, who for the first time finds himself pulling into the charmed, churned circle of the hunted sperm whale. [3]

The topic sentences which follow suggest the kind of development which might follow them.

Not all robins receive a lethal dose, but another consequence may lead to the extinction of their kind as surely as fatal poisoning.

This kind of topic sentence indicates movement from cause to a rather complete discussion of the consequences (effects).

Babylonian astrology became a second celestial religion, but it was quite unlike the first, that of ancient China.

Obviously, the material for this topic sentence will be organized by points of contrast between Babylonian religion and Chinese religion.

That faith overwhelmed the Greeks at the time their own cultural forces were running dry.

The movement here will be from the generalization (the topic sentence) through particulars as support. Examples and illustrative details will probably make up most of the support.

Certain happenings in the nineteenth century and early twentieth century have contributed heavily to the dominant tone of naturalism in much of contemporary literature.

This paragraph will probably be organized by time order; the writer will begin undoubtedly with early events and move forward in time to the more recent events showing the way each happening contributed to the dominant tone of naturalism in contemporary literature.

Among the most common kinds of simple orders of paragraph development are the following: general to particular, particular to general, and question to answer.

General to particular (deduction)

General to particular is the most common of all orders. It gives a structural order to deductive thinking. A writer begins with a generalization, then moves through the support. In the model paragraph which follows, the writer begins with the generalization: "I hate women because they almost never get anything exactly right." He then supports this generalization with a number of humorous examples.

I (to quit hiding behind the generalization of "the male") hate women because they almost never get anything exactly right. They say, "I have been faithful to thee, Cynara, after my fashion" instead of "in my fashion." They will bet you Alfred Smith's middle name is Aloysius, instead of Emanuel. They will tell you to take the 2:57 train, on a day that the 2:57 does not run, or, if it does run, does not stop at the station where you are supposed to get off. Many men, separated from a woman by this particular form of imprecision, have never showed up in her life again. Nothing so embitters a man as to end up in Bridgeport when he was supposed to get off at Westport. [4]

Study the following model paragraph. The movement is from the generalization "Man is just now beginning to plumb the ocean's depths" through a number of statements supporting that generalization.

Man is just now beginning to plumb the ocean's depths. Through most of his history he has been preoccupied only with its surface, as a source of food and as an avenue for travel. For much of recorded history he thought it was much smaller than it is. He did not, in fact, begin to apprehend its enormous size until the 14th and 15th Centuries. Ancient theories that the earth was a sphere were again coming to the fore, leading Columbus' discovery of the Western Hemisphere in 1492, and culminating in Magellan's epochal feat of sailing around the world in 1519–1522. Even so, Mercator, the great map maker, believed as recently as 375 years ago that the earth was about equally divided between land and water, and that there was an immense land mass in the Southern Hemisphere to balance the masses of Europe, Asia and North America that lie in the Northern Hemisphere. Awareness of how watery the world really is came only with the voyages of the Dutch navigator Abel Tasman (for whom Tasmania is named) and England's illustrious explorer of the Pacific, Captain James Cook. Tasman and Cook proved that the southern seas were so huge and so empty that a luckless ship could conceivably sail around and around the world forever in southern latitudes without sighting land. [5]

EXERCISE

1. General to particular order
        Read the model paragraph below. Answer the questions that follow it.

> College athletics *is* public entertainment. Last year football audiences numbered 40 million, and now basketball is outstripping football in attendance. It is estimated that the public pays $100 million a year to the colleges for admission tickets, and television has added enormously to the number of spectators and to the revenue. Public interest as measured in publicity, newspaper coverage, and attention is far beyond that given to any educational activity. In no major school does the attention given to the appointment of a president compare with that given to the appointment of a coach, and the general public can name many more coaches than presidents. [6]

        1. What is the topic sentence?
        2. How many major statements are in support of the generalization?
        3. In your opinion is the paragraph complete?

Repeat of the topic sentence
        Writers will frequently vary this basic pattern by beginning with a generalization, presenting adequate support, and finally repeating the main idea in slightly different words in the last sentence. The model which follows illustrates this variation of the general to particular pattern. The writer begins with the generalization "The Jews did not need astronomers." He follows this apparent topic sentence with an explanatory statement. He then moves onward to the support which consists of one factual statement about the nature of the God of Israel, a "jealous God who would permit no other God before him and who forbade them to make graven images." He concludes with an emphatic restatement of the main idea of the topic sentence: "If they were obedient to their Law, the Jews had to renounce astrology, and hence astronomy." This slight variation of the general to particular is effective when a writer wishes to emphasize again the main idea. In addition, restatement of the main idea in the final sentence serves as a climatic conclusion to the developing thought.

> The Jews did not need astronomers. This may seem sur-

prising, since their culture derived from Babylon, including their story of the Creation, their Paradise and Deluge. But they had the God of Israel, the jealous God who would permit no other gods before him and who forbade them to make graven images. Signs of the zodiac and likenesses of the deified planets surely came under this prohibition. If they were to be obedient to their Law, the Jews had to renounce astrology, and hence astronomy. [7]

Study the following model which illustrates the same kind of variation: the repetition of the main idea in slightly different words as a conclusion. Observe how the repetition drives home the extreme individualism of "Dada."

Dada, in art and life, was the extreme of individualism. It denied that there was any psychic basis common to all humanity. There was no emotion shared by all men, no law to which all were subject; there was not even a sure means of communication between one man and another. Morality was a snare, "a plague produced by the intelligence." — "Thought is a fine thing for philosophy, but it is relative. There is no final Truth." — "Logic is a complication. Logic is always false." — "Everything one looks at is false." In a word, nothing is real or true except the individual pursuing his individual whims, the artist riding his hobbyhorse, his *dada*. [8]

The model paragraph which follows also illustrates the effectiveness of repeating a generalized statement in more specific terms.

Soon after the spraying had ended there were unmistakable signs that all was not well. Within two days dead and dying fish, including many young salmon, were found along the banks of the stream. Brook trout also appeared among the dead fish, and along the roads and in the woods birds were dying. All the life of the stream was stilled. Before the spraying there had been a rich assortment of the water life that forms the food of salmon and trout — caddis fly larvae, living in loosely fitting protective cases of leaves, stems or gravel cemented together with saliva, stonefly nymphs clinging to rocks in the swirling currents, and the wormlike larvae of blackflies edging the stones under riffles or where the stream spills over steeply slanting rocks. But now the stream insects were dead, killed by the DDT, and there was nothing for a young salmon to eat. [9]

The reversal type of development
Another variation of the general to particular pattern

is the reversal paragraph. With this method of development, a
writer begins with a statement that is apparently the topic sentence which he develops in the first part of the paragraph. Then,
toward the middle of the paragraph, he writes the true topic sentence which qualifies or contrasts sharply with his opening
sentence. He continues onward developing this main idea in the
remainder of the paragraph. In the following model, the writer
begins with what appears to be his main idea, " . . . women were
frail, foolish, and inferior." He then continues onward elaborating
on this thought. However, with the sentence "During the years
1558–1560 this happy and dulce order of things was sadly upset
by a plethora of ladies who failed to fit the normal female pattern," he reverses the thought. He develops the main idea with
many supporting statements.

>   The role of womankind was perfectly clear: in sermon,
> book, and Bible it was stated that women were frail, foolish, and
> inferior. Their ordained function was to bear children "till they die
> of it; that is what they are for." Without doubt God had created man
> to rule, and it was a wife's duty "if she saw her husband merry, then
> she was merry; if he were sad, she was sad." During the years 1558–
> 1560 this happy and dulce order of things was sadly upset by a pleth-
> ora of ladies who failed to fit the normal female pattern. In France,
> England, and Scotland the realms were afflicted with what John
> Knox called that enormity of nature — "The monstrous regiment of
> women." It was against all human and divine law that "a woman
> should reign and have empire above men." Yet Mary of Guise was
> regent of Scotland, Catherine de Medici was regent and queen
> mother of France, Mary Stuart was queen of Scotland, and Elizabeth
> Tudor succeeded her sister on the throne of England. No one ques-
> tioned that the consequences of such an unnatural and undesirable
> situation would be discord, inconstancy, and civil strife. The regent
> of Scotland died in the midst of civil war; Catherine de Medici be-
> queathed to her heirs a kingdom convulsed by religious conflict and
> human atrocities; and Mary Stuart perished on the execution block.
> Only Elizabeth was an exception to the rule, and Englishmen were
> quite certain that the cause lay with the special interference of God
> and the divine genius of their sovereign lady. [10]

In the next model paragraph, the writer begins with
the question: "Why, one may ask, has Islamic civilization in
modern times failed to retain its cultural supremacy?" He follows
with reasons for the failure. Then with the sentence "But a new

day is at hand for Modern Islam," he reverses the thought, discussing the dynamic awakening taking place in the Moslem world.

Why, one may ask, has Islamic civilization in modern times failed to retain its cultural supremacy? One reason was the influx of semibarbarous peoples into Islamic lands during the Middle Ages. Another was the stagnation that accrued from a too rigid interpretation of the Koran, so that a ban was placed on material change and progress. Still another reason was the corrupt and despotic rule of such Moslem dynasties as the Ottomans in Turkey, who destroyed all progressive political and economic movements. But a new day is at hand for Modern Islam. The Moslems have amply proved that they have the intellectual and administrative gifts to make themselves a great people, and the rejuvenation of Turkey after the First World War under the able guidance of the late Mustapha Kemal Ataturk has indicated a possible road for the modern descendants of Mohammed the Prophet. In addition to the Turks, other Moslem people have been on the march in recent times. The Arab peoples of the Middle East and north Africa — Tunisians, Moroccans, Egyptians, Iraqis, and Syrians — not to mention other Moslem peoples such as Iranians, Pakistanis, and Indonesians have experienced a remarkable and dynamic awakening. These people have resurrected the memories of their glorious past; they are determined to enjoy complete political independence and to see to it that the Moslem world will play an important part in international affairs. This Moslem revival will constitute one of the major themes dealt with in our narrative of the twentieth-century world. [11]

Study the model paragraph which follows. What sentence reverses the thought?

The potato was, moreover, the most universally useful of foods. Pigs, cattle, and fowl could be raised on it, using the tubers which were too small for family use; it was simple to cook; it produced fine children; as a diet, it did not pall. Yet it was the most dangerous of crops. It did not keep, nor could it be stored from one season to another. Thus, every year the nearly two and a half million laborers who had no regular employment more or less starved in the summer, when the old potatoes were finished and the new had not come in. It was for this reason that June, July, and August were called "meal months"; there was always the danger that the potatoes would run out and meal would have to be eaten instead. The laborers would then have to buy it on credit, at exorbitant prices, from the petty dealer and usurer who was the scourge of the Irish village — the dreaded "gombeen-man." [12]

EXERCISES

2. General to particular order

Read the paragraphs below. Answer the questions that follow them.

Probably few of the freshmen who try out for the team realize how much of their time will eventually be exacted by football. I remember discovering with dismay, as a freshman, that if I were to keep up with the rest of the men who were competing for positions on the varsity I would have to report for spring practice. Practicing football for six weeks during the warm and budding spring did not strike me as being either a glorious or a worth-while occupation, but I needed to do it during both my freshman and sophomore years if I was to get in the line-up. I was engaged in actual practice on the field for about twenty hours a week during the spring semester, and during the fall my working week was boosted to about twenty-eight hours. Of course this includes only the time actually spent on the field, and does not include such things as evening movies of the next week's opponent, study time wasted because of fatigue, extra time demanded by game trips to other schools, and time spent in whirlpools and under heat lamps in the training room.

The four-year total actually spent on the field, counting three extra weeks of Rose Bowl practice, comes to about 1350 hours. Although it was hard for me to realize it at the sophomoric height of my athletic zeal, my reason now tells me that football is only a single, minor, and unacademic part of a college education, and that it should not be more important than other single parts of college — such as, for example, the study of history. At Michigan I took six courses in history, each of them meeting three times a week for fifteen weeks, and each requiring an average of two hours of study for each hour in class. The total number of hours here is 810, about half of the time that I spent on the gridiron. [13]

1. What would be a good title for this selection?
2. What is the function of the second sentence in paragraph 1?
3. Does the second paragraph have a new topic sentence or does it develop further the main idea in paragraph 1?
4. What supporting point receives most space in paragraph 1?
5. Do you think the comparison in paragraph 2 helps the writer's point of view?

3. General to particular order

Read the model paragraph below. Make a topic outline of its structural organization. Then explain why you think it is a well organized paragraph or a poorly organized paragraph.

The antelope, too, have adjusted their lives to the sage. They are primarily animals of the plains, and in winter when the first snows come those that have summered in the mountain move down to lower elevations. There the sage provided the food that tides them over the winter. Where all other plants have shed their leaves, the sage remains evergreen, the gray-green leaves — bitter, aromatic, rich in proteins, fats, and needed minerals — clinging to the stems of the dense and shrubby plants. Though the snows pile up, the tops of the sage remain exposed, or can be reached by the sharp, pawing hoofs of the antelope. Then grouse feed on them too, finding them on bare and wind-swept ledges or following antelope to feed where they have scratched away the snow. [14]

4. General to particular order

Read the paragraph below. Complete the structural outline that follows it.

Father Wilhelm Kleinsorge, of the Society of Jesus, was, on the morning of the explosion [the atomic bomb], in rather frail condition. The Japanese wartime diet had not sustained him, and he felt the strain of being a foreigner in an increasingly xenophobic Japan; even a German, since the defeat of the Fatherland, was unpopular. Father Kleinsorge had, at thirty-eight, the look of a boy growing too fast — thin in the face, with a prominent Adam's apple, a hollow chest, dangling hands, big feet. He walked clumsily, leaning forward a little. He was tired all the time. To make matters worse, he had suffered for two days with Father Cieslik, a fellow-priest, from a rather painful diarrhea, which they blamed on the beans and black ration bread they were obliged to eat. Two other priests then living in the mission compound, which was in the Nobori-cho section — Father Superior LaSalle and Father Schiffer — had happily escaped this affliction. [15]

Title

Writer's purpose: _____

I.   Main idea
     A.
     B.
     C.

    D.

    E.

    F.

5. *Planning the paragraph*

Listed below are some of the thoughts a writer might jot down in preparing to write a paper on the subject of reading. From this list, select those from which you could write a paragraph of 100 to 150 words moving from the general to particular. You may add additional points if you wish.

1. What will be the future of reading?
2. These are audio-visual days in education.
3. One college president predicted that in fifty years "only five per cent of the people will be reading."
4. Reading is a very complex process.
5. Many individuals will not need to read since television supplies what newspapers once did.
6. Future inventions will do the reading.
7. Is reading really necessary?
8. Reading stimulates thinking.
9. Reading is pleasurable.
10. Audio-visual devices require "no discipline of the mind."
11. There are too many persons in our society who cannot read efficiently.
12. "Programed learning" is too impersonal.

ASSIGNMENTS

1. *General to particular order*

Listed below are ten possible topic sentences. From this list select one and write a paragraph of approximately 125 words moving from the general to the particular. Consult reference sources for background material if you find it necessary.

1. Fascism has played a significant role in the history of the past fifty years.
2. The increase in accidents on the U.S. highways is alarming.
3. In the U.S. crime by individuals under twenty-one years of age has become a major problem.
4. Forest fires are unbelievably destructive.
5. Commercialism has hurt competitive athletics in our colleges and universities.

6. Motion pictures are better (worse) than ever.
7. The U.N. has been (has not been) a successful peace-keeping body.
8. Mountain-climbing (skin-diving, water-skiing, etc.) is a dangerous sport.
9. Television can be educational.
10. This country needs more vocational schools.

2. Deduction

Study again the essays in the first half of this chapter that were developed by deduction — movement from the statement of the thesis in the opening paragraph through paragraphs of support. Write a theme of approximately 500 words beginning with a statement of the thesis in the first paragraph followed by supporting paragraphs.

WHICH

by James Thurber

[1]The relative pronoun "which" can cause more trouble than any other word, if recklessly used. Foolhardy persons sometimes get lost in which-clauses and are never heard of again. My distinguished contemporary, Fowler, cites several tragic cases, of which the following is one: "It was rumoured that Beaconsfield intended opening the Conference with a speech in French, his pronunciation of which language leaving everything to be desired . . ." That's as much as Mr. Fowler quotes because, at his age, he was afraid to go any farther. The young man who originally got into that sentence was never found. His fate, however, was not as terrible as that of another adventurer who became involved in a remarkable which-mire. Fowler has followed his devious course as far as he safely could on foot: "Surely what applies to games should also apply to racing, the leaders of which being the very people from whom an example might well be looked for . . ." Not even Henry James could have successfully emerged from a sentence with "which," "whom," and "being" in it. The safest way to avoid such things is to follow in the path of the American author, Ernest Hemingway. In his youth he was trapped in a which-clause one time and barely escaped with his mind. He was going along on solid ground until he got into this: "It was the one thing of which, being very much afraid — for whom has not been warned to fear such things — he . . ." Being a young and powerfully built man, Hemingway was able to fight his way back to where he had started, and begin again. This time he skirted the treacherous morass in this way: "He was afraid of one thing. This was

the one thing. He had been warned to fear such things. Everybody has been warned to fear such things." Today Hemingway is alive and well, and many happy writers are following along the trail he blazed.

[2]What most people don't realize is that one "which" leads to another. Trying to cross a paragraph by leaping from "which" to "which" is like Eliza crossing the ice. The danger is in missing a "which" and falling in. A case in point is this: "He went up to a pew which was in the gallery, which brought him under a colored window which he loved and always quieted his spirit." The writer, worn out, missed the last "which" — the one that should come just before "always" in that sentence. But supposing he had got it in! We would have: "He went up to a pew which was in the gallery, which brought him under a colored window which he loved and which always quieted his spirit." Your inveterate whicher in this way gives the effect of tweeting like a bird or walking with a crutch, and is not welcome in the best company.

[3]It is well to remember that one "which" leads to two and that two "whiches" multiply like rabbits. You should never start out with the idea that you can get by with one "which." Suddenly they are all around you. Take a sentence like this: "It imposes a problem which we either solve, or perish." On a hot night, or after a hard day's work, a man often lets himself get by with a monstrosity like that, but suppose he dictates that sentence bright and early in the morning. It comes to him typed out by his stenographer and he instantly senses that something is the matter with it. He tries to reconstruct the sentence, still clinging to the "which," and gets something like this: "It imposes a problem which we either solve, or which, failing to solve, we must perish on account of." He goes to the water cooler, gets a drink, sharpens his pencil, and grimly tries again. "It imposes a problem which we either solve or which we don't solve and . . ." He begins once more: "It imposes a problem which we either solve, or which we do not solve, and from which . . ." The more times he does it the more "whiches" he gets. The way out is simple: "We must either solve this problem, or perish." Never monkey with "which." Nothing except getting tangled up in a typewriter ribbon is worse. [16]

WHEN MONEY WAS IN FLOWER
by Charles W. Morton
[1]Anything written about the effect of money on life in the United States ought to be in the past tense. There was a time, that is, when money really meant something. A dollar was not an infinitesimal sum; neither was a nickel. One recalls a reverse-English witticism, "It's only money," which was mentioned when a price seemed

exorbitant, and which might even get a laugh from those who hadn't heard it before. But nowadays, the same line would be played straight, and all within hearing would amiably concur: it's only money, and what it will buy is very little indeed.

²To begin thinking about prices as, for example, they stood at the beginning of World War I is to be overwhelmed by reminders of what a dollar used to do for its owner. Many daily papers cost a cent, and a nickel on Sunday, and home delivery to the subscriber was a matter of about $5.00 a year for what costs today just nine times as much. As a schoolboy I used to lodge at the McAlpin when I was hard up, in a comfortable room, well kept, for $2.00 a day, and when in funds, at the Waldorf, a block away, for $3.50. The Ritz-Carlton was a little too steep for me at $4.00 to $5.00, and I still regard the Thirty-fourth Street Waldorf as the most glamorous and exciting hotel in my experience.

³The treat for a schoolboy at the Waldorf was a pot of chocolate in the Men's Café; the portion consisted, simply, of a large silver pot of rich bittersweet chocolate, a large silver pot of scalded milk, and a long silver dish piled with heavy whipped cream — all grouped on a silver tray at a tariff of thirty-five cents. As a generous tipper, appreciative of good service, one gave a waiter or bellboy a quarter. There were no hotel maids; at any rate, they worked when no one was around and without demanding cash in advance for straightening up a room.

⁴To return briefly to the nickel: it would buy, in packages of ten, Hassan or Mecca cigarettes, with a colored photograph thrown in of a celebrated ballplayer or prizefighter of the time; a variety of domestic cigars (when Havana cigars were about three for a half-dollar); a ride in the subway; and much of the contents of what was, in all truth, the five-and-ten-cent store. The hottest competition at this price was among the saloons, most of which boasted of putting out the biggest five-cent schooner of beer in town.

⁵The real competition by saloons lay in the nickel beer and equally in the quality and variety of the free lunch offered with it. A certain amount of etiquette, no doubt, governed how heartily one might feed on the basis of a single schooner without a lift of the bartender's eyebrow, yet the free lunch in a first-class saloon was a vast assortment of cold dishes, possibly a hot delicacy or two like melted cheese on toast, but often flanked by a standing roast of beef and a ham, both of towering dimensions.

⁶In a Chicago bar called Righeimer's, the free lunch was a ham or roast beef sandwich of extraordinary quality, prepared by an elderly Negro who used a slicing knife in each hand and turned out elegantly thin sandwiches without handling them, offering them to

the customer on the extended blade of a knife; the style and dexterity in this operation were as attractive as the sandwich itself.

[7] Theater tickets, for the thirty or forty attractions available of a winter evening in New York, were somewhere around $2.00 to $2.50 for the best seats and considerably less in the balconies. After the theater one went not to a nightclub but to a cabaret such as Shanley's, Churchill's, or perhaps — a few years later — the Midnight Frolic on the New Amsterdam roof. For two or three dollars a head, one found not only first-rate entertainment in these places but also notably good food and drink; the competition among their kitchens was just as serious as that among the good restaurants. One other quip of that period points up what a dollar would do: the man who was complaining to the waiter about being charged a dollar for an order of corned beef and cabbage and who said, "You couldn't *lift* a dollar's worth of corned beef and cabbage." [17]

Particular to general (induction)

Another common order in organizing and developing the expository paragraph is particular to general. Sometimes this pattern is called *inductive order* since the writer leads his reader through various kinds of support to a concluding statement. By presenting the support first, a writer can gain a reader's interest, lead the reader to accept the final conclusion on the strength of the evidence, or emphasize the point he is making by a cogent climactic statement. In the model paragraph which follows, the writer Bruce Catton leads his reader through a series of events which occurred from April 5 to April 7 — the closing days of the Battle of Shiloh. Each specific leads the reader to accept the emphatic conclusion: "To all intents and purposes, the Confederacy had lost the middle Mississippi."

Nothing remained now but to pick up the pieces. On the morning of April 5 — the beautiful spring day when the soldiers around Shiloh were firing their guns to see how rain had affected loaded muskets — Pope had transports and one gunboat on the river below New Madrid and he could get on with the job, which he promptly did. Troops went aboard the stern-wheelers that had come down through the cutoff, Walke discarded his hay barge and his hot-water hoses, and the Federals went down to cross the river. *Carondelet's* guns knocked the Confederate river batteries to bits, and before long John Pope had soldiers over on the Tennessee shore around Tiptonville and Island Number Ten had been cut off. The Confederates along the river took to the brush to escape capture, Foote sent U.S.S.

Pittsburgh down to join *Carondelet* — once Walke had done it, everybody could see how simple it was — and late on the evening of April 7 Island Number Ten surrendered and the victory that had just been won at Shiloh was made complete. To all intents and purposes, the Confederacy had lost the middle Mississippi. [18]

Study the following passage by Malcolm Cowley who describes his meeting with James Joyce.

Having been granted an interview, I went to his hotel. He was waiting for me in a room that looked sour and moldy, as if the red-plush furniture had fermented in the twilight behind closed shutters. I saw a tall, emaciated man with a very white forehead and smoked glasses; on his thin mouth and at the puckered corners of his eyes was a look of suffering so plainly marked that I forgot the questions with which I had come prepared. I was simply a younger person meeting an older person who needed help. [19]

DISCUSSION

First, Malcolm Cowley gains his reader's interest by describing vividly the "sour and moldy room" and the "tall, emaciated man" whose thin mouth and "the puckered corners of his eyes" showed his suffering. Cowley next explains why he forgot to ask Joyce questions. He then follows with a mildly surprising conclusion. The final sentence is not exactly what the readers would expect; yet it is a magnificent statement of an experience true to life. Cowley was no longer the young man seeking an interview with the famous James Joyce, a legend among figures. He was simply "a younger person meeting an older person who needed help."

Study the model paragraph which follows. Observe the brief but very effective conclusion.

He (Michelangelo) rushed into revolution and war with his customary violence; his soul was weary, but he welcomed any form of action. It was an effective antidote, a timely escape from the stupefying melancholy of the tombs. The dramatic uproar of battle afforded his heart and mind, and his body too, the excitement they needed. Had he been left to himself, the pessimism fundamental to his nature would have wrecked him. Events and the will of others now obliged him to undergo danger, and he entered the combat wholeheartedly, with the unreasoning violence of the man of action who cares nothing for the objections of the thinker, the mutterings of the sceptic, or the reasonings of the philosopher on the quality, use, and valor of action. He acted. [20]

Study this model passage:

What makes the revolt of modern youth serious is that it bears little resemblance to what was once viewed as juvenile delinquency. There was a time when the difference between a bad boy and a playful boy was merely one of degree. Today the crimes of violence in which the young indulge can never be mistaken for boyish pranks. The many cases of malicious destruction of property that have entailed great loss to the public are not the cumulative consequence of youthful exuberance but the product of calculated and planned mischief. The many assaults with dangerous weapons, some of which have had fatal consequence, are the acts of irresponsible desperadoes which differ little from the planned attacks on society by adult outlaws.

More alarming are the thefts and holdups. The petty pilferings that once represented a boy's transgressions were largely restricted to doormats, ash barrels, and milk bottles. But in the past few years I have had an eighteen-year-old boy in my court who, while employed by a wholesale electric supply house, loaded $10,000 worth of electric equipment on a freight elevator, lowered the elevator to the ground floor, and then secured a truckman to cart away the loot. Three boys, all seventeen years of age, were before me charged with breaking and entering and larceny. After getting an automobile, these boys broke into a Surplus War Goods Store and carted away $3500 worth of merchandise. Two others in the same age group looted the warehouse of a jewelry novelty wholesaler and carried away $6000 worth of merchandise. After making their getaway they stored the loot in a safe place and canvassed the community until they found an operator of a jewelry store who would buy the goods from them. There is nothing "juvenile" about this kind of delinquency. [21]

DISCUSSION

Sometimes more than one paragraph is needed to develop fully the main idea. In the paragraph above, the writer Judge Adlow considers one aspect of his subject, juvenile delinquency. He finds it necessary to devote two complete paragraphs to making clear his main idea. He moves through a number of telling particulars to his final statement: "There is nothing 'juvenile' about this kind of delinquency."

Read the model paragraph which follows. You will find the real meaning of the paragraph in the last line.

"Why, sir," the student asks, "does Achilles drag the body of Hector around the walls of Troy?" "That sounds like a stimulating question. Most interesting. I'll bite," says the professor. "Well, you see, sir, the *Iliad* is full of circles — shields, chariot wheels and other round figures. And you know what Plato said about circles. The Greeks were all mad for geometry." "Bless your crew-cut head," says the professor, "for such a beautiful thought. You have exquisite sensibility. Your approach is both deep and serious. Still I always believed that Achilles did it because he *was* angry." [22]

Ideas in order of increasing importance

A writer can achieve a very effective modification of the particular to general pattern by simply arranging his ideas in the paragraph in order of increasing importance. In the following paragraph, Rachel Carson's intent was to establish the fact that man is indifferent to the preservation of his natural resources — especially water. She leads gradually to her most important point: "water along with other resources has become the victim of his indifference."

Of all our natural resources water has become the most precious. By far the greater part of the earth's surface is covered by its enveloping seas, yet in the midst of this plenty we are in want. By a strange paradox, most of the earth's abundant water is not usable for agriculture, industry, or human consumption because of its heavy load of sea salts, and so most of the world's population is either experiencing or is threatened with critical shortages. In an age when man has forgotten his origins and is blind even to his most essential needs for survival, water along with other resources has become the victim of his indifference. [23]

Study the paragraph which follows. Observe the way in which Edith Hamilton leads the reader to the final climactic statement "That was not the Greek way" by placing her more important ideas toward the end of the paragraph.

That kind of education is not geared to mass production. It does not produce people who instinctively go the same way. That is how Athenian children lived and learned, while our millions learn the same lessons and spend hours before television sets looking at exactly the same thing at exactly the same time. For one reason and another we are more and more ignoring differences, if not trying to obliterate them. We seem headed toward a standardization of the mind, what Goethe called "the deadly commonplace that fetters us all." That was not the Greek way. [24]

EXERCISES

6. *Particular to general*

Read the model paragraph below. Make a topic outline of its structural organization.

But with the "improvement" instituted by the Forest Service, the willows went the way of the sagebrush, killed by the same impartial spray. When Justice Douglas visited the area in 1959, the year of the spraying, he was shocked to see the shriveled and dying willows — the "vast, incredible damage." What would become of the moose? Of the beavers and the little world they had constructed? A year later he returned to read the answers in the devastated landscape. The moose were gone and so were the beaver. Their principal dam had gone out for want of attention by its skilled architects, and the lake had drained away. None of the large trout were left. None could live in the tiny creek that remained, threading its way through a bare, hot land where no shade remained. The living world was shattered. [25]

7. *Particular to general*

Read the model paragraph below. Answer the questions that follow it.

So Michelangelo reappeared in the streets of Florence. He had never left the city. With the help of the parish-priest he had concealed himself in the bell-tower of the church of San Niccolo oltr' Arno during the reprisals. No one thought of looking for him there, and the good priest had done the best to feed him and care for his comfort. Now that there was no further danger he left his tower and went back to his studio. The time for heroism had passed. [26]

1. What would be a good title for this paragraph?
2. Where is the topic sentence?

8. Organization

Arrange the sentences below into the most effective particular to general pattern of development.

1. The history of the recent centuries has its black passages — the slaughter of the buffalo on the western plains, the massacre of the shorebirds by the market gunners, the near-extermination of the egrets for their plumage.
2. Now, to these and others like them, we are adding a chapter and a new kind of havoc — the direct killing of birds, mammals, fishes, and indeed practically every form of wildlife by chemical insecticides indiscriminately sprayed on the land.
3. As man proceeds toward his announced goal of the conquest of nature, he has written a depressing record of destruction, directed not only against the earth he inhabits but against the life that shares it with him.

9. Organization

Read the model paragraph below. Compare its structural organization with the one you completed for exercise 8. Answer the ensuing questions.

As man proceeds toward his announced goal of the conquest of nature, he has written a depressing record of destruction, directed not only against the earth he inhabits but against the life that shares it with him. The history of the recent centuries has its black passages — the slaughter of the buffalo on the western plains, the massacre of the shorebirds by the market gunners, the near-extermination of the egrets for their plumage. Now, to these and others like them, we are adding a chapter and a new kind of havoc — the direct killing of birds, mammals, fishes, and indeed practically every form of wildlife by chemical insecticides indiscriminately sprayed on the land. [27]

1. Write a good title for this passage.
2. List the sentences in order of their importance.
3. What particular guide word helped you in putting the sentences in the proper order?
4. Would you accept the point of view of the writer on the basis of the evidence she presents?

10. Planning

From the statements below, eliminate irrelevant thoughts, add additional sentences of support, clarification, or elaboration, and organize the material into an outline for a particular to general paragraph or paragraphs.

1. Many comic books glorify the wrong kinds of people.
2. T.V. has more violence than comic books.
3. Comic books are full of violence.
4. Many comic books are too expensive for young people.
5. Comic books are written for the most part in sub-standard English.
6. Comics keep children away from T.V.
7. Adults also find comic books interesting.
8. Comics are a deterrent, not an incentive to good reading.
9. Comics hurt a child's eyes.
10. Comics keep children from more valuable recreational pursuits.

11. Planning

Write a particular to general paragraph or paragraphs on the belief that capital punishment is wrong. From the list of ideas below, eliminate those that are irrelevant and add any additional supporting sentences or sentences for clarification, elaboration, and explanation as you develop the main idea.

1. Many murderers have become valuable members of the prison society.
2. Many murderers on parole have become valuable members of society.
3. The death penalty is inhuman.
4. The death penalty takes the life of persons who are really sick.
5. The death penalty is not a deterrent to crimes of violence.
6. There are not enough understanding prison wardens.
7. Prisons are too overcrowded.
8. The taking of a person's life is degrading to all concerned, especially to society as a whole.

9. Few women murderers have received the death penalty.
10. The death penalty is simply a form of revenge.

12. *Organization*

Arrange the sentences in the list below in a logical order moving from the particular to general.

1. Consequently, we reason that our athletic problems would be solved if institutions elsewhere followed our pattern.
2. Procedures which may fit the needs and circumstances of an Ivy League school may not meet those of a school in Texas or Oregon.
3. Most of us tend to view the present situation in athletics from the perspectives of our own collegiate situation, our region or tradition, or our own procedures and practices.
4. But the United States is a complex society, and its universities and colleges display amazing diversity, not only in their regional environment, but in their academic and athletic programs.

Read now the paragraph as it was originally written.

Most of us tend to view the present situation in athletics from the perspectives of our own collegiate situation, our region or tradition, or our own procedures and practices. Consequently, we reason that our athletic problems would be solved if institutions elsewhere followed our pattern. But the United States is a complex society, and its universities and colleges display amazing diversity, not only in their academic and athletic programs. Procedures which may fit the needs and circumstances of an Ivy League school may not meet those of a school in Texas or Oregon. [28]

ASSIGNMENTS

3. *Particular to general*

Write a particular to general paragraph with one of the following thoughts as an effective concluding sentence.

1. personality of a city
2. a fascinating study, subject, situation, etc.
3. "the ocean is a capricious lady"
4. importance of education today
5. college — a playground for teenagers

6. college — not a playground for teenagers
7. "career women"
8. crime in the streets
9. violence in our age
10. learning through doing

4. Induction

Study the model induction essays on pages 118–122. Write a theme of approximately 500 words with movement from the support to the statement of the thesis (induction).

5. Induction

Read again "A Vote for Student Protest" in Chapter 2, on page 32. Write a paragraph of 100 to 150 words in which you agree or disagree with her viewpoint.

ENOUGH IS A WARM TOO MUCH
by William K. Zinsser

[1] Not long ago I went into a bookstore and saw, side by side on one table, 18 different books by Charles Schulz, creator of *Peanuts*. Some were small paperbound reprints of the *Peanuts* comic strips that had originally run in newspapers. One, an item called *Snoopy and the Red Baron*, was described as Schulz's "first full-length novel," the full length being 58 pages. Next to it, in still another format, was *A Charlie Brown Christmas*, which briefly recounted Charlie Brown's search for "the true meaning of Christmas." Finally there were the little square manuals of instant philosophy — *Happiness Is a Warm Puppy*, *Security Is a Thumb and a Blanket*, etc. — in which the *Peanuts* characters dispense tiny aphorisms to help the rest of us tilt with emotional problems that have vexed mankind since Job.

[2] A few days later I revisited the bookstore and the Wizard of Is had struck again. *Love Is Walking Hand in Hand* had joined the crowd, and so had *Home Is on Top of a Dog House*, which offered a dog's-eye view of the human plight, or the dog plight, or whatever plight it is that Snoopy has staked out as his psychological domain. Looming over them both was a giant *Peanuts* calendar-and-appointment book for 1967.

[3] Not long afterward I went back and, sure enough, like crabgrass, new patches of Schulz were creeping along the table. A set of four diminutive books had sprouted overnight — *The Wisdom of Charlie Brown*, *Linus on Life*, *The World According to Lucy* and *Snoopy's Philosophy* — and two other newcomers were nearby. *I Need All the Friends I Can Get*, despite its title, turned out

to be an "Is" book ("A friend is someone who likes you even when the other guys are around"), and beside it in a larger format was *Charlie Brown's All-Stars,* wherein Charlie Brown's baseball experiences were woven into a semblance of narrative running 44 pages and costing $2.50.

[4]This put the number of available *Peanuts* books near 30 — not counting the *Peanuts* dolls that were propped around the various volumes, or the record album called *You're a Good Man, Charlie Brown* — and gave Schulz a comfortable edge over his nearest rival in the "Is" derby, Joan Walsh Anglund, author and illustrator of *A Friend Is Someone Who Likes You, Love Is a Special Way of Feeling, Spring Is a New Beginning* and a mere 13 other tiny books, including *A Joan Walsh Anglund Sampler* and *A Pocketful of Proverbs.* Mrs. Anglund, however, was well ahead in sugar content. At any rate, I felt that the time has come for Schulz to take his merchandise out of the bookstores and open a separate outlet for them — like Sears, Roebuck — in every major town, perhaps renting a corner in each one to Mrs. Anglund. (Love is a shop with a heart.)

[5]Now from all of this you might well assume that I am against love and that I hate *Peanuts.* On the contrary, I am for love, and *Peanuts* has been my favorite comic strip since it began. The recesses of my desk still yield yellow *Peanuts* strips from the early 1950's, clipped out of a newspaper because at some moment they coddled the Charlie Brown in me. To this day, in fact, I share so many of Charlie Brown's bright hopes that I often slip into the illusion that he exists. Last summer, trying to organize Sunday baseball in a small community, I invariably arrived ahead of time and stood on the pitcher's box (a wooden board), peering across the fields to see if anybody else, by any possible chance, might turn up. In this vigil I took comfort in the thought that somewhere Charlie Brown was doing the same.

[6]But my affection no longer runs as deep, and it is not because Charlie Brown is any less my alter ego or the truths in *Peanuts* are any less true. It is because the sub-product is smothering my love of the product. I love comic strips as an art form, and I love books, and I love bookstores, and in cases like this I feel that something is going out of all three — and therefore out of our lives.

[7]Schulz first took a part of Charlie Brown away from me when he used his *Peanuts* characters in a series of ads for Falcon cars. I was hurt and puzzled to open a grown-up magazine and see my small friend touting a grown-up automobile. And why wouldn't I be? If there is one quality about Charlie Brown that particularly binds him to us as a character, it is his own hurt and puzzlement when innocence is betrayed. Few figures in fiction are so pure in heart. He will never stop believing Lucy when she promises not to

snatch away the football that he is about to kick. And Lucy will never stop snatching it away.

[8] We know this about them as surely as we know how our own children will act. This is the special genius of a good comic strip: It is a daily play that involves us in the lives of another set of people. Chic Young's *Blondie*, for instance, has almost become our second family. We have spent so many years watching Blondie and Dagwood react to each other and to their children, to Mr. Dithers and Herb Woodley and salesmen at the door, that we identify with them in all the ordinary situations that we ourselves face. They tell us more about human nature than most novels or dramas.

[9] Blondie and Dagwood, of course, have also strayed beyond their comic strip into richer pastures. This is, after all, the age of the "tie-in," and rare is the manufacturer of a pop hero — whether human (Mary Poppins), superhuman (James Bond) or subhuman (Mickey Mouse) — who has not inundated us with related toys, dolls and sweatshirts. Still, when Blondie and Dagwood venture out into a movie or a comic book, they at least remain within a story line, true to their origins. I don't recall Dagwood's native wit ever being codified and sold as a separate piece of goods. He doesn't keep turning up in little books to tell us that happiness is a six-decker sandwich at midnight, or that love is saying you like your wife's outlandish new hat.

[10] But the real danger with these little books of pop uplift — and with all the other little books of instant wisdom that have begun to flood America — is that they are too easy. I don't only mean that they are too easy for the Schulzes and the Anglunds and their publishers to crank out and for the booksellers to sell. They are also too easy for us to swallow. No truth worth knowing will surrender without a tussle, and the whole point of art is that an artist has worked long and hard to catch his private vision and we must share the journey. If we love a Bach fugue, say, or a Picasso painting or a Nabokov novel, it is because we have teased its meaning out — slowly and with a certain reverence. To have great poets there must be great audiences, Walt Whitman said, perhaps because he had so few. Or, as Thoreau wrote, "It takes two to speak the truth — one to speak, and another to hear."

[11] Plenty of poets in our midst are trying to speak the truth today, or at least to grope for it. Edward Albee comes to mind because his latest play, *A Delicate Balance,* is a painful search into the very themes that are so dear to Schulzville. In the play, a family whose HAPPINESS has eroded finds its capacity for LOVE challenged when two FRIENDS unexpectedly move in because they "got frightened" — i.e., lost their SECURITY. (They don't have a DOG.)

[12]The play is imperfect and often cloudy, but I enjoyed it. Albee is our best current playwright, a serious artist with a saving vein of humor, and I like to watch him tackling the big subjects, rebounding from old failures and risking new ones, trying to grow. He doesn't pamper himself or his audience, and I expect him to speak many truths in the years ahead that we will hear and value. Meanwhile I'm grateful to him in *A Delicate Balance* for confirming one belief that I was already fairly sure of: Happiness is not a warm puppy. [29]

Question to answer

In the question to answer order of development, a writer begins with a question and answers it with sufficient facts and other material until he feels that the answer is acceptable to the reader. This kind of paragraph has no stated topic sentence; however, the question itself reveals the writer's purpose. Study the model paragraphs which follow.

Model 1

Why does the spider mite appear to thrive on insecticides? Besides the obvious fact that it is relatively insensitive to them, there seem to be two other reasons. In nature it is kept in check by various predators such as ladybugs, a gall midge, predaceous mites and several pirate bugs, all of them extremely sensitive to insecticides. The third reason has to do with population pressure within the spider mite colonies. An undisturbed colony of mites is a densely settled community, huddled under a protective webbing for concealment from its enemies. When sprayed, the colonies disperse as the mites, irritated though not killed by the chemicals, scatter out in search of places where they will not be disturbed. In so doing they find a far greater abundance of space and food than was available in the former colonies. Their enemies are now dead so there is no need for the mites to spend their energy in secreting protective webbing. Instead, they pour all their energies into producing more mites. It is not uncommon for their egg production to be increased threefold — all through the beneficent effect of insecticides. [30]

DISCUSSION

The structure of this paragraph is relatively simple. The writer begins with a question. She answers the question by giving three reasons.

Model 2

A bright-eyed woman, whose sparkle was rather more of eagerness than of intelligence, approached me at a party one afternoon and said; "Why do you hate women, Mr. Thurberg?" I quickly adjusted my fixed grin and denied that I hated women; I said I did not hate women at all. But the question remained with me, and I discovered when I went to bed that night that I had been subconsciously listing a number of reasons I do hate women. It might be interesting — at least it will help pass time — to set down these reasons, just as they came up out of my subsconscious. [31]

Model 3

Did it ever strike you that there was anything queer about the capacity of written words to absorb and convey feelings? Taken separately they are mere symbols with no more feeling to them than so many bricks, but string them along in a row under certain mysterious conditions and you find yourself laughing or crying as your eyes run over them. That words should convey mere ideas is not so remarkable. "The boy is fat," "The cat has nine tails," are statements that seem obviously enough within the power of written language. But it is different with feelings. They are no more visible in the symbols that hold them than electricity is visible on the wire; and yet there they are, always ready to respond when the right test is applied by the right person. That spoken words, charged with human tones and lighted by human eyes, should carry feelings, is not so astonishing. The magnetic sympathy of the orator one understands; he might affect his audience, possibly, in a language they did not know. But written words: How can they do it! [32]

EXERCISE

13. Question to answer
Read the model paragraph below. Answer the questions that follow it.

What is it (the protests on the campus) all about? One thing is fairly clear: the teach-ins, the sit-ins, the lay-downs, the mass picketing, and all the rest are not *merely* about Vietnam, or civil rights, or the size of classes at Berkeley, or the recognition of Red China. They are about these issues surely, and most sincerely. But there is, transparently, a passion behind the protests that refuses to be satisfied by the various topics which incite it. This passion reaches far beyond politics, as we ordinarily understand that term. Anyone who believes the turbulence will subside once we reach a settlement in Vietnam is in for a rude surprise. Similarly, anyone who thinks of present-day campus radicalism as a kind of over-zealous political liberalism, whose extremism derives from nothing more than youthful high spirits, is deceiving himself. What we are witnessing is an event in American politics, but not *of* it. [33]

1. Does the writer answer the question directly?
2. What would be the meaning of the paragraph if we omitted the last sentence?
3. What may we expect the writer to discuss in the next few paragraphs?

ASSIGNMENT

6. *Question to answer*

Write a question to answer paragraph or paragraphs on any one of the following subjects.

1. smog
2. traffic accidents
3. famous persons
4. great moments in sports, theater, concert hall, etc.
5. dreams
6. cigarettes
7. emotions
8. dating
9. clubs
10. family

CHAPTER FOUR *References*

1. From "They're Saving America's Priceless Seashore," by Don Wharton. Reprinted from The August 1966 *Reader's Digest*. Copyright 1966 by The Reader's Digest Association, Inc.
2. From *The Mysterious Sky* by Lester del Rey, copyright © 1964 by Lester del Rey. Reprinted by permission of Chilton Books.
3. From *Moby Dick* by Herman Melville.
4. From "The Case Against Women" by James Thurber. Copyright © 1937 James Thurber. Copyright © 1964 Helen W. Thurber and Rosemary Thurber Sauers. From *Let Your*

Mind Alone, published by Harper and Row, New York. Originally printed in *The New Yorker.*

5. From "The Sea" in *Life Nature Library* by Leonard Engel and the Editors of *Life.* Copyright © 1961 by Time, Inc. Reprinted by permission of Time-Life, Inc.

6. From "College Athletics: Education or Show Business," by Harold W. Stoke, *The Atlantic Monthly* (March, 1954). Copyright © The Atlantic Monthly Company, Boston, Mass. By permission of the author.

7. From *And There Was Light* by Rudolf Thiel, translated by Richard and Clara Winston. Copyright © 1957 by Alfred A. Knopf, Inc. By permission.

8. From *Exile's Return* by Malcolm Cowley. Copyright 1934, 1935, 1941, 1951, copyright © renewed 1962, 1963 by Malcolm Cowley. Reprinted by permission of The Viking Press, Inc.

9. From *Silent Spring,* by Rachel L. Carson. Copyright 1962. By permission of the publisher, The Houghton Mifflin Company.

10. From *This Realm of England* by Lacey Baldwin Smith. Copyright © 1966 by D. C. Heath and Company.

11. From *Civilization: Past and Present,* Volume I by T. Walter Wallbank and Alastair M. Taylor. Copyright 1954 by Scott, Foresman and Company.

12. From *The Great Hunger* by Cecil Woodham-Smith (Harper & Row, 1962). Reprinted by permission of Harper & Row, Publishers.

13. From "Too Much Football," by Allen Jackson, in *The Atlantic Monthly* (October, 1951). Copyright © 1952 by The Atlantic Monthly Company, Boston, Mass. Reprinted by permission of the author.

14. From *Silent Spring,* by Rachel L. Carson. Cf. 9.

15. From *Hiroshima* by John Hersey. Copyright © 1946 by John Hersey. Reprinted by permission of Alfred A. Knopf, Inc.

16. "Which" by James Thurber. Copyright © 1931, 1959 James Thurber. From *Ladies' and Gentlemen's Guide to Modern English Usage,* in *The Owl in The Attic,* published by Harper & Row, New York. Originally printed in *The New Yorker.*

17. "When Money Was in Flower" by Charles W. Morton, in *The Atlantic Monthly* (April, 1962). Copyright © 1962, by The Atlantic Monthly Company, Boston, Mass. and reprinted with their permission.
18. From *Terrible Swift Sword,* by Bruce Catton. Reprinted by permission of Doubleday and Company, Inc.
19. From *Exile's Return* by Malcolm Cowley. Cf. 8.
20. From *Michelangelo* by Marcel Brion, translated by James Whital. Copyright 1940. Reprinted by permission of the author.
21. From "Teen-Age Criminals" by Judge Elijah Adlow, in *The Atlantic Monthly* (July, 1955). By permission of the Atlantic Monthly Company and the author.
22. From "Plain Style" by Saul Bellow, from *Deep Readers of the World, Beware,* originally published in *The New York Times Magazine.* Copyright © The New York Times Company, 1959.
23. From *Silent Spring* by Rachel L. Carson. Cf. 9.
24. From "Lessons of the Past" by Edith Hamilton, in *The Saturday Evening Post* (September 27, 1958). Reprinted by permission of Doris Fielding Reid.
25. From *Silent Spring* by Rachel L. Carson. Cf. 9.
26. From *Michelangelo* by Marcel Brion. Cf. 20.
27. From *Silent Spring* by Rachel L. Carson. Cf. 9.
28. From "The Place of Intercollegiate Athletics in Higher Education: Hold That Tiger!" by Frank N. Gardner. Copyright © 1960 by The Ohio State University Press and reprinted with its permission.
29. "Enough Is a Warm Too Much" by William K. Zinsser in *Look* (February 21, 1967). Copyright © 1967 by William K. Zinsser. Reprinted by permission of The Sterling Lord Agency.
30. From *Silent Spring* by Rachel L. Carson. Cf. 9.
31. From "The Case Against Women" by James Thurber. Cf. 4.
32. From "Words That Laugh and Cry" by Charles A. Dana.
33. From "What's Bugging the Students" by Irving Kristol in *The Atlantic Monthly* (November, 1965). Reprinted by permission of The Atlantic Monthly Company, Boston, Mass., and the author.

FIVE

Moving through time and space

Time order (narration)

Perhaps the simplest order of paragraph or theme organization and development is by a time sequence of the events or happenings. It is a natural order for telling a story (narration) and explaining how to do something (process). In addition, time or chronological order (as it is frequently called) is a logical and effective method of organizing the supporting material in expository paragraphs.

Expository paragraphs

In the model that follows, the writer moves his reader by time sequence to the final sentence — the statement of the main idea: "Their generation had been defeated by life — so it seemed at the time — and yet in their own defeat they were still its representative figures." Notice the guide words and phrases that indicate time divisions — *in the afternoon, dinner, after dinner, afterward.*

That was in the spring of 1933, a few weeks after the banks had closed all over the country. The Fitzgeralds were living at La Paix, a brown wooden late-Victorian lodge on a thirty-acre estate near Baltimore — "La Paix (my God!)" Scott wrote at the head of a letter. In the afternoon the house had been filled with little sounds of life — the colored cook and her relatives arguing in the kitchen, Zelda talking to her nurse or rustling about her studio as she painted furiously. Scott somewhere in a back room dictating to his secretary, then their daughter coming home from school and playing under the big oak trees on the lawn. Zelda wasn't well enough to come down to dinner, but the visitor was taken to see her afterward; her face was emaciated and twitched as she talked and her mouth twisted into unhappy shapes. After dinner the sounds of life died away from the house. Little Scottie was put to bed, the cook and her friends went home. Zelda had to rest and Big Scott wandered from room to room with a glass in his hand, explaining that it was water; then, as he started another trip to refill the glass in the kitchen, he confessed that it was gin. There was not enough furniture, there were no carpets to absorb the inhuman noises of the night. Everything creaked and echoed. The visitor sat alone in the one big chair in the almost empty living room and thought the house was the perfect setting for a ghost story, with Scott and Zelda as ghosts, the golden boy of 1920 and the belle of two states. Their generation had been defeated by life — so it seemed at the time — and yet in their own defeat they were still its representative figures. [1]

In the model paragraph which follows, the writer supports her topic sentence by examples and repetitions in a time pattern of development.

Basic to all the Greek achievement was freedom. The Athenians were the only free people in the world. In the great empires of antiquity — Egypt, Babylon, Assyria, Persia — splendid though they were, with riches beyond reckoning and immense power, freedom was unknown. The idea of it never dawned in any of them. It was born in Greece, a poor little country, but with it able to remain unconquered no matter what manpower and what wealth were arrayed against her. At Marathon and at Salamis overwhelming numbers of Persians had been defeated by small Greek forces. It had been proved that one free man was superior to many submissively obedient subjects of a tyrant. Athens was the leader in that amazing victory, and to the Athenians freedom was their dearest possession. Demosthenes said that they would not think it worth their while to live if they could not do so as free men, and years later a great teacher said, "Athenians, if you deprive them of their liberty, will die." [2]

DISCUSSION

The writer Edith Hamilton begins this paragraph with a generalization "Basic to all the Greek achievement was freedom." She follows her statement of the main idea with a repetition of that thought in the second sentence. Then she offers her first major supporting statement by citing examples of ancient

empires without freedom — Egypt, Babylon, Assyria, and Persia.
Her next sentence, clarifying the previous one, carries the reader
onward to another sequence in time — the birth of freedom in
Greece. She moves up in time quickly to the battles of Marathon
and Salamis where the superiority of men who believed in freedom was proved. Then she closes with the words of Demosthenes
and the words of a great teacher, a few years later, who said:
"Athenians, if you deprive them of their liberty, will die."

Sometimes the time order may be used simply to develop the support of a writer's generalization that is not necessarily a topic sentence. In the model which follows, the writer
discusses the free elective system that allowed the student wide
ranges of choice in a college program of studies. In speaking of the
products of such a system, he states that they "came into social
or economic or cultural or political power in this republic some
ten or twenty years after being graduated." To support this
statement, he discusses pertinent events in chronological order.

Products of the free elective system, graduating any year
between 1895 and 1915 (my dates are approximate, or, as the New
Critics would say, symbolical only), came into social or economic
or cultural or political power in this republic some ten or twenty years
after being graduated. They fought World War I. They carried forward
the technological revolution that accompanied or followed that
catastrophe. They were in the saddle during the administrations
of Wilson, Harding, and Coolidge, and you can, if you like, say they
are responsible for the twenties, for the stock-market crash of 1929,
and for a variety of other sins. Perhaps I have no defense. All I can
murmur is that American literature, American art, American music,
American science, and American technology came of age during this
quarter-century; and though I am as ready as the next historian to
admit that 1929 was a catastrophic year, I am not persuaded that the
world-wide depression setting in at the end of the twenties was the
direct result of the old, free elective system. [3]

EXERCISES

1. Time order
Arrange the sentences below into a paragraph that
moves onward by time order.

1. They were in much the same position that Masséna had been in before Lisbon: the enemy hung on their flanks, their lines of communication were stretched to the limit, and they faced starvation.
2. Half a million had disappeared, and with them had gone the foundation of the Napoleonic Empire.
3. In June 1812 Napoleon's vast horde crossed the Russian frontier and rolled eastward.
4. Out of the host that had entered Russia some 20,000 men returned, and they were more dead than alive.
5. It failed by a narrow margin to encircle the defending army, which fell back before it and like the Portuguese, laid waste the countryside.
6. As soon as he did so his whole supply system disintegrated, and his nightmare began.
7. Napoleon's overtures for peace were met by silence.
8. In mid-September the French entered Moscow, and there they stayed for a month.
9. He had to retreat.
10. In December he reappeared in the west, and only then did Europe learn what was behind the rumors that had been circulating for weeks.

2. Time order

Make a sentence outline of the model paragraph below. Check its organizational structure with your written version of the paragraph in exercise 1. In the paragraph below, underline the words and phrases that indicate time sequences.

In June 1812 Napoleon's vast horde crossed the Russian frontier and rolled eastward. It failed by a narrow margin to encircle the defending army, which fell back before it and, like the Portuguese, laid waste the countryside. In mid-September the French entered Moscow, and there they stayed for a month. They were in much the same position that Masséna had been in before Lisbon: the enemy hung on their flanks, their lines of communication were stretched to the limit, and they faced starvation. Napoleon's overtures for peace were met by silence. He had to retreat. As soon as he did so his whole supply system disintegrated, and his nightmare began. In December he reappeared in the west, and only then did Europe learn what was behind the rumors that had been circulating for weeks. Out of the host that had entered Russia some 20,000 men returned, and they were more dead than alive. Half a million had disappeared, and with them had gone the foundation of the Napoleonic Empire. [4]

3. Time order

Read the model paragraph below. Answer the questions that follow it.

The moment the pressure of the Civil War ended in 1646, the radicals, who had taken over the control of the army, had to face the consequences of victory; they were in danger of having won themselves out of a job. In 1647 the conservatives struck at the wartime political leadership of such radicals as Sir Henry Vane and Oliver St. John, and tried to dissolve the New Model Army. In retaliation the military occupied London, and in August the House of Commons was purged at bayonet point of eleven of its most conservative Presbyterian members. Government by coup d'etat had commenced, but the final defeat of the conservatives was delayed until the summer of 1648. In the face of mounting radical pressure from the army and the extremists in parliament, the conservative Presbyterian members made their last bid to stem the tide of revolution and to turn the clock back to the days of 1641. They made common cause with Charles, who promised to reform the Church of England along Presbyterian lines, and they found the military means to defy the New Model Army by alliance with the Scots, who suddenly remembered that after all Charles was a Stuart and a Scotsman. The unholy league of conservative parliamentarians, Scottish Presbyterians, and Anglican Charles Stuart was no match for the soldiers of righteousness, and the Scottish forces were badly defeated in August of 1648 at the battle of Preston Pans. In December Cromwell and his victorious army returned to London, surrounded the ancient palace of Westminster, and purified parliament of the fearful of heart, the sinful of soul, and the uncertain of politics. Colonel Pride excluded 143 members from Commons, and the Long Parliament of 1641 became very short of members, only 78 remaining of whom 20 refused to take their seats. [5]

1. What is the main idea of this paragraph?
2. Mention some phrases that indicate time sequence of events.

Expository narration

Narration tells a story. Whether the purpose is to inform or entertain or both, narration emphasizes action — what is happening. In its most highly developed forms, the novel, and the short story, narration stresses refinements, such as conflict, characterization, setting, suspense, and climax. *Expository narration*, the concern of this book, however, is not so complex.

In writing expository narration, a writer's development depends upon his purpose and the space available. Therefore, his problem is essentially one of selectivity. He must focus on an incident or a series of happenings related to his reason for telling the story; he must choose specifics relevant to his purpose, emphasize important details, subordinate less important particulars, and eliminate the irrelevant specifics. He tells his story in time (chronological) order.

This fact is worth stressing. Narration, whether it be a complete story or an individual paragraph, is organized chronologically. The model which follows is about the arrival of a steamboat from *Life on the Mississippi* by Mark Twain. His purpose is to make the reader understand the feelings of a small town boy about steamboats. With vivid descriptive details and skillful organization of events in order of their happening, Mark Twain captures the glorious expectancy with the steamboat's arrival, the exciting climax as it docks and takes on passengers and supplies, and the emptiness in the boy and the entire town after its departure.

Once a day a cheap, gaudy packet arrived upward from St. Louis, and another downward from Keokuk. Before these events, the day was glorious with expectancy; after them, the day was a dead and empty thing. Not only the boys, but the whole village, felt this. After all these years I can picture that old time to myself now, just as it was then: the white town drowsing in the sunshine of a summer's morning; the streets empty, or pretty nearly so; one or two clerks sitting in front of the Water Street stores, with their splint-bottomed chairs tilted back against the walls, chins on breasts, hats slouched over their faces, asleep — with shingle-shavings enough around to show what broke them down; a sow and a litter of pigs loafing along the sidewalk, doing a good business in watermelon rinds and seeds; two or three lonely little freight piles scattered about the "levee"; a pile of "skids" on the slope of the stone-paved wharf, and the fragrant town drunkard asleep in the shadow of them;

two or three wood flats at the head of the wharf, but nobody to listen
to the peaceful lapping of the wavelets against them; the great
Mississippi, the majestic, the magnificent Mississippi, rolling its
milewide tide along, shining in the sun; the dense forest away on the
other side; the "point" above the town, and the "point" below,
bounding the river-glimpse and turning it into a sort of sea, and withal
a very still and brilliant and lonely one. Presently a film of dark smoke
appears above one of those remote "points"; instantly a negro dray-
man, famous for his quick eye and prodigious voice, lifts up the cry,
"S-t-e-a-m-boat a-comin'!" and the scene changes! The town
drunkard stirs, the clerks wake up, a furious clatter of drays follows, every house and store pours out a human contribution, and
all in a twinkling the dead town is alive and moving. Drays, carts,
men, boys, all go hurrying from many quarters to a common center,
the wharf. Assembled there, the people fasten their eyes upon the
coming boat as upon a wonder they are seeing for the first time. And
the boat *is* rather a handsome sight, too. She is long and sharp
and trim and pretty; she has two tall, fancy-topped chimneys, with
a gilded device of some kind swung between them; a fanciful pilot-
house, all glass and "gingerbread," perched on top of the "texas"
deck behind them; the paddle-boxes are gorgeous with a picture
or with gilded rays above the boat's name; the boiler-deck, the
hurricane-deck, and the texas deck are fenced and ornamented with
clean white railings; there is a flag gallantly flying from the jack-
staff; the furnace doors are open and the fires glaring bravely; the
upper decks are black with passengers; the captain stands by the big
bell, calm, imposing, the envy of all; great volumes of the blackest
smoke are rolling and tumbling out of the chimneys — a husbanded
grandeur created with a bit of pitch pine just before arriving at a
town; the crew are grouped on the forecastle; the broad stage is run
far out over the port bow, and an envied deck-hand stands pictur-
esquely on the end of it with a coil of rope in his hand; the pent
steam is screaming through the gauge-cocks; the captain lifts his
hand, a bell rings, the wheels stop; then they turn back, churning
the water to foam, and the steamer is at rest. Then such a scramble
as there is to get aboard, and to get ashore, and to take in freight and
to discharge freight, all at one and the same time; and such a yelling
and cursing as the mates facilitate it all with! Ten minutes later the
steamer is under way again, with no flag on the jack-staff and no black
smoke issuing from the chimneys. After ten more minutes the town
is dead again, and the town drunkard asleep by the skids once
more. [6]

Read the narration again, observing Mark Twain's selection and
organization of details and events to make vivid and meaningful

the purpose: the importance of the arrival of a steamboat for a small town boy.

Point of view

Point of view in narration is important. Point of view in narration means through whose eyes and mind the reader gets the story. Is the story by the major character? a minor character? Or the author himself with an all-knowing (omniscient) view of the happenings? Point of view, therefore, involves person and number. In the example that follows, Washington Irving tells the story of "Rip Van Winkle" in the third person.

As he was about to descend, he heard a voice from a distance, hallooing, "Rip Van Winkle! Rip Van Winkle!" He looked round, but could see nothing but a crow winging its solitary flight across the mountain. He thought his fancy must have deceived him, and turned again to descend, when he heard the same cry ring through the still evening air: "Rip Van Winkle! Rip Van Winkle!" — at the same time Wolf bristled up his back, and, giving a loud growl, skulked to his master's side, looking fearfully down into the glen. Rip now felt a vague apprehension stealing over him; he looked anxiously in the same direction, and perceived a strange figure slowly toiling up the rocks, and bending under the weight of something he carried on his back. He was surprised to see any human being in this lonely and unfrequented place; but supposing it to be some one of the neighborhood in need of his assistance, he hastened down to yield it.

On nearer approach he was still more surprised at the singularity of the stranger's appearance. He was a short, square-built old fellow, with thick bushy hair and a grizzled beard. His dress was of the antique Dutch fashion — a cloth jerkin, strapped round the waist — several pair of breeches, the outer one of ample volume, decorated with rows of buttons down the sides, and bunches at the knees. He bore on his shoulder a stout keg, . . . [7]

In the next model, Henry David Thoreau tells the story of the ant war in the first person.

One day when I went out to my woodpile, or rather my pile of stumps, I observed two large ants, the one red, the other much larger, nearly half an inch long, and black, fiercely contending with one another. Having once got hold they never let go, but struggled and wrestled and rolled on the chips incessantly. Looking farther, I was surprised to find that the chips were covered with such combatants, that it was not a *duellum,* but a *bellum,* a war between two races of ants, the red always pitted against the black, and frequently two red ones to one black. The legions of these Myrmidons covered all the hills and vales in my woodyard, and the ground was already strewn with the dead and dying, both red and black. It was the only battle which I have ever witnessed, the only battlefield I ever trod while the battle was raging; internecine war; the red republicans on the one hand, and the black imperialists on the other. On every side they were engaged in deadly combat, yet without any noise that I could hear, and human soldiers never fought so resolutely. I watched a couple that were fast locked in each other's embraces, in a little sunny valley amid the chips, now at noonday prepared to fight till the sun went down, or life went out. The smaller red champion had fastened himself like a vice to his adversary's front, and through all the tumblings on that field never for an instant ceased to gnaw at one of his feelers near the root, having already caused the other to go by the board; while the stronger black one dashed him from side to side, and, as I saw on looking nearer, had already divested him of several of his members. They fought with more pertinacity than bulldogs. Neither manifested the least disposition to retreat. It was evident that their battle cry was "Conquer or die." In the meanwhile there came along a single red ant on the hillside of this valley, evidently full of excitement, who either had dispatched his foe, or had not yet taken part in the battle; probably the latter, for he had lost none of his limbs; whose mother had charged him to return with his shield or upon it. Or perchance he was some Achilles, who had nourished his wrath apart, and had now come to avenge or rescue his Patroclus. He saw this unequal combat from afar — for the blacks were nearly twice the size of the red — he drew near with rapid pace till he stood on his guard within half an inch of the combatants; then, watching his opportunity, he sprang upon the black warrior, and commenced his operations near the root of his right foreleg, leaving the foe to select among his own members; and so there were three united for life, as if a new kind of attraction had been invented which put all other locks and cements to shame. I should not have wondered by this time to find that they had their respective musical bands stationed on some eminent chip, and playing their national airs the while, to excite the slow and cheer the dying combatants. I was myself excited somewhat even as if they had been men. The more you think of it, the less the difference. And certainly there is not the fight recorded in Concord history, at least, if in the history of America, that will bear a moment's comparison with this, whether for the numbers engaged in it, or for the patriotism and heroism displayed. For numbers and for carnage it was an Austerlitz or

Dresden. Concord Fight! Two killed on the patriots' side, and Luther Blanchard wounded! Why here every ant was a Buttrick — "Fire! for God's sake fire!" — and thousands shared the fate of Davis and Hosmer. There was not one hireling there. I have no doubt that it was a principle they fought for, as much as our ancestors, and not to avoid a three-penny tax on their tea; and the results of this battle will be as important and memorable to those whom it concerns as those of the battle of Bunker Hill, at least. [8]

The first person plural "we" and the third person plural "they" are occasionally used. (See the selection on page 210.) The second person "you" is rarely used except in process. (p. 153)

As you read the model narrations which follow, keep in mind the following points of information:

1. The writer's purpose
2. The selectivity of happenings to fulfill his purpose
3. The role of time order in coherence
4. The point of view or points of view
5. The emphasis on important details and the sub-ordination of the less important specifics
6. The emphasis on action

NIGHT WATCH
by Roy Popkin

[1] The story began on a downtown Brooklyn street corner. An elderly man had collapsed while crossing the street, and an ambulance rushed him to Kings County Hospital. There, during his few returns to consciousness, the man repeatedly called for his son.

[2] From a smudged, oft-read letter, an emergency-room nurse learned that the son was a Marine stationed in North Carolina. Apparently, there were no other relatives.

[3] Someone at the hospital called the Red Cross office in Brooklyn, and a request for the boy to rush to Brooklyn was re-layed to the Red Cross director of the North Carolina Marine Corps camp. Because time was short — the patient was dying — the Red Cross man and an officer set out in a jeep. They located the sought-after young man wading through marshy boondocks on maneuvers. He was rushed to the airport in time to catch the one plane that might enable him to reach his dying father.

[4] It was mid-evening when the young Marine walked into the entrance lobby of Kings County Hospital. A nurse took the tired, anxious serviceman to the bedside.

[5] "Your son is here," she said to the old man. She had to repeat the words several times before the patient's eyes opened.

Heavily sedated because of the pain of his heart attack, he dimly saw the young man in the Marine Corps uniform standing outside the oxygen tent. He reached out his hand. The Marine wrapped his toughened fingers around the old man's limp ones, squeezing a message of love and encouragement. The nurse brought a chair, so the Marine could sit alongside the bed.

[6]Nights are long in hospitals, but all through the night the young Marine sat there in the poorly lighted ward, holding the old man's hand and offering words of hope and strength. Occasionally, the nurse suggested that the Marine move away and rest a while. He refused.

[7]Whenever the nurse came into the ward, the Marine was there, oblivious of her and the night noises of the hospital — the clanking of an oxygen tank, the laughter of night-staff members exchanging greetings, the cries and moans and snores of other patients. Now and then she heard him say a few gentle words. The dying man said nothing, only held tightly to his son through most of the night.

[8]Along toward dawn, the patient died. The Marine placed on the bed the lifeless hand he had been holding, and went to tell the nurse. While she did what she had to do, he smoked a cigarette — his first since he got to the hospital.

[9]Finally, she returned to the nurse's station, where he was waiting. She started to offer words of sympathy, but the Marine interrupted her. "Who was that man?" he asked.

[10]"He was your father," she answered, startled.

[11]"No, he wasn't," the Marine replied. "I never saw him before in my life."

[12]"Why didn't you say something when I took you to him?" the nurse asked.

[13]"I knew right off there'd been a mistake, but I also knew he needed his son, and his son just wasn't here. When I realized he was too sick to tell whether or not I was his son, I figured he really needed *me*. So I stayed."

[14]With that, the Marine turned and left the hospital. Two days later, a routine message came in from the North Carolina Marine Corps base informing the Brooklyn Red Cross that the real son was on his way to Brooklyn for his father's funeral. It turned out there had been two Marines with the same name and similar serial numbers in the camp. Someone in the personnel office had pulled out the wrong record.

[15]But the wrong Marine had become the right son at the right time. And he proved, in a uniquely human way, that there *are* people who care what happens to their fellow man. [9]

FIVE MISSED CHANCES AT PEARL HARBOR
by Walter Lord

[1] Ever since December 7, 1941, we've been arguing about who was to blame for Pearl Harbor — and with reason. For the surprise attack by some 353 Japanese planes was surely one of the cheapest military victories in history. By the time it was over, a matter of two hours, all eight of our battleships in the harbor were sunk or damaged. Many of our cruisers and destroyers were hit. All six of our major air bases on Oahu were wrecked. Nearly all of our planes were gone. More than 2400 American lives were lost. As the Japanese planes winged back to their carriers they could count a loss of only 29 planes and 55 men.

[2] Many learned men have spent a great deal of time on the military aspect of the subject. But far more fascinating to the layman is the role played by human nature in our failure to avoid calamity on December 7. For entirely apart from the question of whether Washington sent enough information, or whether the Hawaiian command made adequate use of the information and equipment it did have, there were five golden opportunities in the last few hours to avoid disaster. But because human beings are only human beings, all five opportunities were lost.

[3] The first came at 6:30 the evening before the blow fell, with the Japanese fleet still 500 miles away. As Honolulu basked in its last peacetime sunset, Lt. Col. George Bicknell, Intelligence Officer, hustled up to Lt. Gen. Walter Short, the Commanding General, with a most interesting message. A telephone conversation had been monitored by the FBI — a call from Tokyo to a Japanese in Honolulu. Tokyo asked about planes, searchlights, ships, the weather ... and flowers. "Presently," the Japanese in Honolulu offered, "the flowers in bloom are fewest out of the whole year; however the hibiscus and poinsettia are in bloom now."

[4] The two officers thought about it. Why on earth would anyone spend the money for a transpacific phone call to talk about flowers? Yet if this were espionage, why would anybody use anything as easily monitored as a telephone?

[5] Even today we're not sure of the significance of that Tokyo phone call, although with the advantage of hindsight it looks most suspicious. But at the time General Short, after debating with his staff about an hour, reached a very human conclusion: he decided to sleep on it and take it up again the following day. And so the evening wore on. A quiet evening, not a night of revelry and debauchery as has often been thought.

[6] At 3:42 the next morning, with the Japanese fleet now only 275 miles away, the small mine sweeper *Condor* sighted a

periscope outside the mouth of Pearl Harbor. She flashed a warning
to the destroyer *Ward* on patrol. The *Ward* dashed over and searched
for an hour but could find nothing.

[7] The *Condor* never reported this sighting to headquarters
because the skipper, humanly enough, thought he must be mistaken
if they couldn't find anything in an hour. The *Ward* never reported it
because the *Condor* didn't, and after all she was the ship that said
she saw something. The naval radio station, which was listening in
all the time, never reported it because the *Ward* and the *Condor*
didn't, and after all it was *their* business. So well-meaning, decent
men who later proved themselves brave, resourceful and intelligent,
let another opportunity slip by, for the periscope was indeed Japanese. It was one of the midget subs that were to coöperate with the
air attack. And as the last message flashed back and forth between
the *Condor* and the *Ward,* the first Japanese planes were already
taking off from their carriers 230 miles away.

[8] Now it was 6:45 in the morning, with the Japanese
air armada only 180 miles off. Just outside Pearl Harbor the *Ward*
— still on patrol — saw the conning tower of a strange submarine.
She raced over, fired at it, dropped depth bombs on it, sank it. A
Navy patrol plane joined in the fight, dropped some bombs of its own.
Both the *Ward* and the plane radioed the shore that a submarine
had been sunk in forbidden waters. The shore reacted in a very human
way: telephone calls back and forth between high officers. What did
this mean? Was it true? Was it not? They decided that perhaps it was
a spar or a buoy the *Ward* had seen. They decided that, Heaven
forbid, it might be an American submarine that had been sunk
by mistake. They ordered the ready-duty destroyer to the *Ward's*
assistance, and decided — so humanly — to await further developments.

[9] At seven o'clock the Japanese planes were only 137
miles away and a couple of Army privates at the Opana radar station
picked up more blips than they had ever seen before — so many they
thought the machine was broken. But they quickly found this wasn't
the case — it was an enormous fleet of planes sweeping down on
the islands. They telephoned the information center. There, a young
lieutenant was on duty. He had handled this assignment only once
before in his life and he knew nothing of radar. The officers who were
normally above him didn't have duty this day. The men who were below him had all gone to breakfast.

[10] So everything hung on a young officer who was about
as helpless as a soldier could be — no one above him, no one below
him, no knowledge of the problem. But he did remember that coming
to work for the 4 to 8 a.m. shift he had heard, on his car radio, station
KGMB playing Hawaiian records, and he also remembered that when

planes were coming in from California the station played all night to beam them in. So he decided that these were American planes. A very human decision, and he gave a very human answer to the men at the radar station: don't worry about it. The two privates continued watching the planes come in: 7:15, 92 miles away; 7:25, 62 miles away. Finally at 7:39 they lost contact on the radarscope because the planes were too close to be picked up any more.

[11] Just about that time a young messenger boy, Tadao Fuchikami, was walking out of the RCA cable office in Honolulu with a message addressed to the Commanding General. It had been drafted an hour and a half before by Gen. George Marshall in Washington. He had just learned that the Japanese were finally breaking off all diplomatic negotiations with the United States and that one o'clock was the time their emissaries were ordered to advise Secretary of State Cordell Hull in Washington. Obviously something was going to happen somewhere at one o'clock Washington time, and it very quickly was apparent that this was 7:30 in the morning at Pearl Harbor — the ideal time for a surprise air attack.

[12] The General had one thought in mind: send out a warning. He wrote a message at once, but he didn't pick up a telephone that was right beside him. The phone had a direct scramble line to Honolulu. It was a human decision that he didn't, because he was afraid he would endanger the security of his communication system. And so the message was to be sent by radio, which was — well — almost as fast. But this morning there was a lot of atmospheric disturbance. This might ruin reception, and the message was much too important to risk that. So some well-meaning communications officer decided to send it by commercial cable instead.

[13] The cable got to Honolulu an hour and a half after General Marshall drafted it, and it was now 7:33. Even then the envelope had nothing that indicated urgency, and when Tadao Fuchikami came out with it in his hand, he whiled away a few minutes with the boys in the parking lot across the street. Then he got on his two-cylinder Indian motorcycle and started off. But as he did, he saw angry clouds of black smoke boil up over Pearl Harbor, and antiaircraft fire pock the morning sky. So it was too late; the attack was on.

[14] And today the arguments still ramble on. But in the midst of the name-calling let's not forget that whatever the high command in both Washington and Pearl Harbor did or did not do, there were these chances to avoid disaster. Chances missed, not because of wickedness or incompetence, but because human beings are, after all, human beings.

[15] And so it has always been. At the Sepoy Mutiny against the British in India, blazing arrows seared the night sky in warning

before disaster broke. At Johnstown, wise men foretold that the dam would collapse. On the Titanic, six wireless messages were received warning of icebergs ahead.

[16]The student of human nature, after studying the strange ways that people behave, comes away thinking not of policy and strategy but that man's best chance to avoid disaster is very simple indeed: we have only to learn to recognize danger signals when we see them. [10]

ASSIGNMENTS

1. *Point of view*

Rewrite the following incident as if you were the leading character.

[1]On waking, he found himself on the green knoll whence he had first seen the old man of the glen. He rubbed his eyes — it was a bright sunny morning. The birds were hopping and twittering among the bushes, and the eagle was wheeling aloft, and breasting the pure mountain breeze. "Surely," thought Rip, "I have not slept here all night." He recalled the occurrences before he fell asleep. The strange man with a keg of liquor — the mountain ravine — the wild retreat among the rocks — the woebegone party at nine-pins — the flagon — "Oh! that flagon! that wicked flagon!" thought Rip; "what excuse shall I make to Dame Van Winkle?"

[2]He looked round for his gun, but in place of the clean well-oiled fowling-piece, he found an old firelock lying by him, the barrel incrusted with rust, the lock falling off, and the stock worm-eaten. He now suspected that the grave roysters of the mountain had put a trick upon him, and, having dosed him with liquor, had robbed him of his gun. Wolf, too, had disappeared, but he might have strayed away after a squirrel or partridge. He whistled after him, and shouted his name, but all in vain; the echoes repeated his whistle and shout, but no dog was to be seen.

[3]He determined to revisit the scene of the last evening's gambol, and, if he met with any of the party, to demand his dog and gun. As he rose to walk he found himself stiff in the joints, and wanting in his usual activity. "These mountain beds do not agree with me," thought Rip; "and if this frolic should lay me up with a fit of the rheumatism, I shall have a blessed time with Dame Van Winkle." With some difficulty he got down into the glen: he found the gully up which he and his companion had ascended the preceding evening; but, to his astonishment, a mountain stream was now foaming down it — leaping from rock to rock, and filling the glen with babbling murmurs. He, however, made shift to scramble up its sides, working

his toilsome way through thickets of birch, sassafras, and witch-
hazel, and sometimes tripped up or entangled by the wild grape-
vines that twisted their coils or tendrils from tree to tree, and spread
a kind of network in his path. [11]

2. Time order
Write a general to particular paragraph of approximately 150 words. Organize the supporting material chronologically.

3. Narration
Write a narration of approximately 500 words on one
of the following topics.

1. An accident	5. A humorous happening
2. Capturing a criminal	6. A personal experience
3. A day at the fair	7. An adventure
4. A date	8. An exciting moment

4. Expository narration
Write an expository narration of approximately 500
words on some subject which you feel needs discussing.

Process
Process is a method of organizing and developing
thought by breaking down a subject, step by step, to show how to
do something or how something is done. The making of steel is
one process; the steps in giving a speech is another; the procedure
for impeaching a President is still another, and the method of scientific investigation is also a process. A process can be as simple
as giving directions for assembling a child's bicycle or submitting
a paper to an instructor and as complex as explaining how life
began, building a space ship, or the Battle of Waterloo.

Instructional process
Process is commonly divided into two kinds: the *instructional process* (How To Do It) and the *informational process*
(How Something Is Done). The writer's purpose will determine
his choice. If you wish to explain how to build a dog house, assemble a swing set, repair a television, change a tire, prepare metal for
painting, you write an instructional process.

In writing effective processes, you break the operation into a series of orderly and logical steps and present each step or stage — a series of related steps — usually in time order. You explain each step in enough detail so that the reader can understand your directions, defining terms and expanding explanations and instructions whenever necessary for clarity. You will be more effective if you tell the reader why certain procedures are necessary and emphasize negative orders — things not to do. Keep the language simple and repeat key directions.

Study now the instructional process which follows:

Assuming that you have the proper outfit, you now are ready to learn walking or sliding on level ground. Here we go! Lunge forward on one foot, keeping the weight well on the front ski. Before the skis stop, lunge forward again and slide on the other ski, transferring your weight. The chief points to remember are: Never lift the skis from the ground, and *keep sliding.*

Propel your skis with easy, dipping motions of the legs and manage your weight with corresponding balancing motions of the arms. The action somewhat resembles skating, except that the feet are not turned sideways to make a forward push, but are kept in a straight line. [12]

DISCUSSION

The writer Strand Mikkelsen explains how to walk on skis with a series of simple, orderly, and effective steps. He groups steps into two separate stages: getting started and moving on the skis. He emphasizes negative directions in the admonition: "Never lift the skis from the ground, and keep sliding."

In writing process analysis, clarity is most important. If you fail to make clear the directions at any given step, the reader will become confused, and the whole process will be a failure. Select a subject, therefore, with which you are very familiar — preferably one that you have done yourself many times. Keep the steps in exact order; group related steps into meaningful stages or divisions wherever possible and use illustrations to establish clearness with complicated operations. If certain materials are needed before beginning the operation, specify them. Make sure that the reader is familiar with new terms and techniques as you proceed with your explanations. Always keep in mind that you are the expert and that you are writing for someone who does not know how to do what you have done many times.

Study the following model process. It was excerpted from *Make the Team in Basketball* (p. 19), written for boys by Clair Bee. Coach Bee gives instructions as he introduces a series of picture drills and learning aids which make up the contents of Chapter 3 of his book.

[1] The practice and learning aids presented in this chapter are but a few of the stunts and drills you may use alone or with the aid of one or two friends in getting ready to make the team. Naturally, when you become a member of a team, the coach will prescribe the drills necessary to develop your basketball skills. However, few of these exercises and drills will conflict with those of the coach, and their use in your free time may shorten your learning spell.

[2] You must keep in mind that the best way to learn any game is to *play it*. And it is wise to remember that the right start is necessary, because it is disastrous to practice a skill incorrectly until it becomes a habit. Habits are hard to break! So, when you practice, be sure you are practicing the correct way. Once you develop the habit of executing a skill the right way, you can concentrate on speed, timing, and greater accuracy.

[3] To make sure you are starting right, first ask your coach what techniques he prefers you to use in executing a skill. Second, watch a great player *play* basketball and try to take away with you a mental picture of his execution of the skills. Third, try always to play with and against players who are better players than yourself. You will learn little from playing with or against fellows who are inferior to yourself. In fact, playing with or against such competition may be harmful because the skills that work with or against inferior competition may not work with or against skillful players.

[4] Now take a look at the practice and learning aids, choose those you think will be of help to you — and get busy! The only fellow worse than the quitter is the one who won't start! [13]

EXERCISES

4. Time order
Read the model paragraph below. Answer the questions that follow it.

Many students encounter difficulty in getting started. Unfortunately, your listeners form impressions of you during the first few minutes more than they do later in the speech. Getting off to a good start also affects your poise and self-confidence. If you feel an audience respond early in your speech, you tend to lose your feelings of apprehensions as you gain interest in your subject. Consider the following suggestions:

Use deliberation in beginning. Upon being introduced, raise slowly and walk to the speaker's stand with a firm step, an erect body, a pleasant expression, and a direct and assuring look at your audience. If you slouch up to the speaker's stand, you may give the impression that your speech will be as listless as your walk. If you look away from your audience, you announce that you are sure of neither yourself, your material, nor your desire at the moment. Conversely, do not leap from your chair and charge to the stand like a warrior to battle. Your audience will be likely to conclude that you are apprehensive. Either extreme in approaching the speaker's stand calls attention to itself and causes unfavorable impressions.

Upon taking your position at the speaker's stand, pause momentarily before beginning your speech. Arrange your notes on the lectern, adjust the microphone, or put your watch on the table. A brief pause causes your audience to turn their attention from their thoughts of the moment and to polarize their attention on you. Sometimes speakers start talking before an audience is ready to listen. This condition is likely to happen if you start speaking as you walk to the speaker's stand. Show deliberation in beginning your speech. [14]

1. What would be a good title for these two paragraphs?
2. Into what two divisions does the writer divide the discussion?
3. Frequently in writing process, a writer will give negative directions — things not to do. What are some of the admonitions in this process?

5. Time order

Read the model paragraph below. Answer the questions that follow it.

Start the book at a time when you will be able to lose yourself in it daily for a period of about two weeks. First read the front pages — the dedication, the table of contents, the list of illustrations, the foreword, and the prologue — in order to get into the mood, to get a motivating taste of the flavor of the book. Then turn to the end pages and read the suggestions under the caption "On How to Use This Book." Next, riffle through the pages and examine the multitude of delightful black-and-white and water-color drawings and read the scintillating captions under each. These mood-inducing activities — which, incidentally, should be your habitual way of preparing to read any books as long, as deep, and as inclusive as this one — will prepare you for the actual reading of the text.

Now divide the book into as many approximately equal parts as the number of days you expect to devote to it. To get the most enjoyment and value out of a book of this nature, plan on ten to twenty consecutive days' reading. Develop the discipline of returning religiously to the book every day, or nearly every day, until you have finished it. After the first few days, this will not be a hard discipline to enforce. [15]

1. Write a good title for this paragraph.
2. What guide words help the reader understand the separate steps?
3. How many parts make up the front pages?

FLOWER ARRANGING
by Adrienne Green

[1]When gathering flowers from the garden, it is a good idea to cut them when the sun is not at its warmest — late in the afternoon or early in the morning. As you know, cut flowers need water to stay fresh, so take a pailful along, and as soon as you cut a stem, pop it into water. As you cut, select flowers in different stages of development; this variety will add interest to your arrangements. When you come into the house, sort your kinds and colors and put them into separate containers of deep water. (Large juice cans are good for this purpose.) Having the kinds sorted will make arranging easier later on. Leave the materials in a cool place free of drafts for a couple of hours or overnight.

[2]While the flowers are conditioning, assemble your mechanical aids: Containers, shears, needle-point holders, floral clay, and Oasis.

[3]To help you decide which containers to use, you might try holding your containers in turn near your cut flowers. This is how we discovered that containers we had around the house, not originally intended for flowers, could be used. For possible containers, look over your silver and pewter as well as your casseroles, baskets, and cooking utensils. A plain container that does not offer too much competition with the flowers is usually easier to use than a highly decorated one. Neutral containers such as gray, black, and soft green ones are suitable for any color flower.

⁴Now you are ready to begin your arrangements. Place a piece of paper, a sheet of plastic, or an old cloth on the table to help in tidying up later. Plan to sit down to arrange. This is a creative hobby, and you should relax and enjoy your time with the flowers.

⁵Like other forms of artistic expression, flower arranging is guided by the elements and principles of good design. In brief outline we will review these and relate them to flower arranging. The design elements that we think about are space, line, form, pattern, texture, and color. *Space* refers to the area your arrangement is going to fill. An arrangement is like a piece of sculpture. If you are doing a tall arrangement, it will look best in a vertical space. On the other hand, a low arrangement would be better suited to a horizontal space, such as a coffee table. Take the container and a couple of branches or flowers to the space you are planning to fill, and do just a rough sketch by putting the tallest placement you expect to use in the container and standing back to evaluate the relationship. [16]

Steps in the instructional process
1. Select a subject with which you are familiar.
2. Specify the materials that are necessary for the operation.
3. Define terms or technical words.
4. Decide on a pattern of development — time order is very common.
5. Use illustrations to aid your explanations of complicated directions.
6. Group steps into meaningful stages whenever possible.
7. Keep the language simple and explanations as brief as possible.
8. Explain reasons for the procedures whenever you believe such explanations will help.
9. Stress things the reader should not do.

Informational process
      If you wish to tell your reader how something happened or how something is done, you write an *informational process.* You might, for example, wish to explain how Wellington won the Battle of Waterloo, how the ocean got its water, how Hilary scaled Mount Everest, or to describe the excitement and wonder of the making of steel. Informational process is narration to a large extent, but it is narration with a different intent. The writer is not telling a story simply to narrate; he uses narrative to

show how something happened or how something is done. Study the model which follows:

> The birth of a volcanic island is an event marked by pro-
> longed and violent travail: the forces of the earth striving to create,
> and all the forces of the sea opposing. The sea floor, where an island
> begins, is probably nowhere more than about fifty miles thick — a
> thin covering over the vast bulk of the earth. In it are deep cracks
> and fissures, the results of unequal cooling and shrinkage in past
> ages. Along such lines of weakness the molten lava from the earth's
> interior presses up and finally bursts forth into the sea. But a sub-
> marine volcano is different from a terrestrial eruption, where lava,
> molten rocks, gases, and other ejecta are hurled into the air through
> an open crater. Here on the bottom of the ocean the volcano has
> resisting it all the weight of the ocean water above it. Despite the
> immense pressure of, it may be, two or three miles of sea water, the
> new volcanic cone builds upward toward the surface, in flow after
> flow of lava. Once within reach of the waves, its soft ash and tuff are
> violently attacked, and for a long period the potential island may
> remain a shoal, unable to emerge. But, eventually, in new eruptions,
> the cone is pushed up into the air and a rampart against the attacks
> of the waves is built of hardened lava. [17]

DISCUSSION

Rachel Carson, the writer, announces her informa-
tional process in the first sentence: the birth of a volcanic island.
By relying heavily on descriptive details she tells the story of the
birth of a volcanic island. The intent of Rachel Carson, however,
is the distinguishing feature that enables us to determine the kind
of development. Her purpose is to inform, to show how a volcanic
island pushes up into the air from the ocean depths.

EXERCISES

6. Process

Read the sentences below and arrange them into a
coherent informational process.

1. Thousands of years passed, and thousands of
   thousands.
2. Million of years ago, a volcano built a mountain
   on the floor of the Atlantic.
3. This fragment we know as Bermuda.
4. Finally its cone emerged as an island with an area
   of about 200 square miles.

5. Eventually the waves of the Atlantic cut down the cone and reduced it to a shoal — all of it, that is, but a small fragment which remained above water.
6. In eruption after eruption, it gushed up a great pile of rock, until it had accumulated a mass a hundred miles across at its base, reaching upward toward the surface of the sea.

7. Process

    Make an outline of the structural organization of the paragraph below that was used also in Exercise 6. Answer the questions that follow it.

    Millions of years ago, a volcano built a mountain on the floor of the Atlantic. In eruption after eruption, it gushed up a great pile of volcanic rock, until it had accumulated a mass a hundred miles across at its base, reaching upward toward the surface of the sea. Finally its cone emerged as an island with an area of about 200 square miles. Thousands of years passed, and thousands of thousands. Eventually the waves of the Atlantic cut down the cone and reduced it to a shoal — all of it, that is, but a small fragment which remained above water. This fragment we know as Bermuda. [18]

1. What would be a good title for this paragraph?
2. In what position is the topic sentence?
3. What process is the writer describing?

8. Process

    Read the paragraph below. Answer the questions that follow it.

    There was yet no sea. The primeval ocean was created when the temperature of the earth's surface fell below the boiling point of water. Water was present on earth from the beginning, but pent-up in the interior rock, and was released by processes occurring in the infant earth. Water vapor rose in great cloud masses that enveloped and darkened the earth. For a time the new planet's surface may have been so hot that no moisture could fall without immediately being converted to steam. Yet even this "rain" helped carry away heat from the hot rocks, and sped the cooling of the planet by transferring heat from the earth to the upper layers of the atmosphere, where it could be dissipated into space.

    For perhaps thousands of years the great overhanging cloud masses prevented the sun's rays from reaching the face of the earth. It took that long for the crust to cool from the freezing point of rocks (1,000 to 2,000 degrees Fahrenheit) to the boiling point of water (212 degrees Fahrenheit). Finally the day came when the falling raindrops did not hiss away in steam, but stayed to start filling the crevices and corners of the naked planet. Then it rained, and the accumulation of the seas began. The accumulation did not take place (in the opinion of modern geologists) through "the greatest deluge of all time" that has so often been described. So far as anyone can tell, it may merely have rained as it rains today. Nature has plenty of time. It probably took a billion years to fill the oceans. William Rubey, of the United States Geological Survey, thinks that the low valleys and shallow depressions that formed the early seas contained only 5 to 10 per cent of the volume of water in the sea today. But as the eons have passed, water vapor has kept coming up through volcanoes and fumaroles, adding to the moisture of the atmosphere and thus to the bulk of the seas.

All this may help explain how the ocean got its water. [19]

1. In what sentence would you find a good title for the selection?
2. List the time divisions that make the writing coherent.

ASSIGNMENTS

5. *Process*

Put yourself in the position of a teacher of writing and correct the following student theme. Then, write a theme of your own on the same subject and develop by process.

HOW TO STUDY

a student theme

[1] Good study habits are necessary for success in college. Studying is an art that must be learned in order to excell in anything. It is not enough for a student to study two hours for each hour of class you have careless or haphazard study habits. He is just putting in time that is of little or no use. A student must have self-discipline and motivation to learn to the best of their ability.

[2] The first step to good study habits is finding the time to study. By making a schedule of your free time, you can see how long you have to study. After that, divide that time into subject areas. Be flexible in your budgetting of time in case that you have extra long reading assignments in some subjects, but do not neglect the other subjects. Do not be afraid to revise your completed schedule later in

the semester if you feel you need to work harder in certain places.

[3]Next, you choose a place to study. The best place is in a well lighted room where you are free from distractions. Absolute quiet is not necessary if you concentrate on your work. Try to study in the same place all the time; new distractions are caused by new surroundings. Also study in a chair or in an upright position; studying in bed almost always turns out to be a failure.

[4]The most important aspect of studying is a good method. If a good method of studying is not worked out, the previous suggestions are of little importance. To start quickly look over your material to be covered. Pay careful attention to underlining, pictures, and headings. After you first survey, cover the material again more slowly. This time, read the parts you have questions about. Studying your notes along with the text is suggested during this step; it may clarify your material or make note translation easier. Another idea to keep in mind is to read summaries and outlines carefully; it is very good as review, if you know the material.

[5]There are many other habits that make studying more efficient and easier. One tip is to take breaks; if you get tired and let your mind wander, your studying is not doing you any good. Another tip is to date your class notes and study the material that was covered in class, as soon as possible after class. Also it is very good to review the previous class notes. Also neatness helps very much. Clear, precise notes kept in an organized fashion will make studying easier.

[6]Once this system is mastered and becomes more or less a habit with the student, good grades are almost certain to result.

6. Process

Write an instructional process of approximately 500 words on one of the following topics.

1. How to build something like a bird house
2. How to do something like throwing a curve ball or doing a dance
3. How to interview a person
4. How to use your library efficiently
5. How to study
6. How to play something well like tennis or some phase of it

7. Process

Write an informational process of approximately 500 words on one of the following subjects. If you find it necessary, go to your library and research the topic.

1. How Nazism rose
2. How a certain teacher teaches
3. How a student leader gets votes
4. How an athlete wins games or wins a special event
5. How some custom started
6. How to improve prisons
7. How a jury is selected
8. How some natural phenomenon occurred
9. How some economic ideology began
10. How some famous person accomplished a great deed

Space order (description)

Space or spatial pattern of development is movement by some kind of natural and logical order through space. It is most common in *description*. A writer, for example, wishes to describe what he sees: a person, place, or thing. He begins at some point in space and moves about as his eyes move from one aspect of the whole to another. To avoid confusing his reader, a writer must give this movement some kind of logical and natural order which the reader can recognize and follow easily. Study the model paragraph which follows. Mark Twain describes a Missouri farm from memory. How does he give order to the picture he creates? Can you easily follow the movement as he takes you around the farm? Does he make the scene vivid and real?

The farmhouse stood in the middle of a very large yard, and the yard was fenced on three sides with rails and on the rear side with high palings; against these stood the smoke-house; beyond the palings was the orchard; beyond the orchard were the negro quarters and the tobacco fields. The front yard was entered over a stile made of sawed-off logs of graduated heights; I do not remember any gate. In a corner of the front yard were a dozen lofty hickory trees and a dozen black walnuts, and in the nutting season riches were to be gathered there. [20]

DISCUSSION

Mark Twain takes his reader first to the dominant feature — the farmhouse in the middle of a very large yard. Then he moves to the fence with rails which encloses three sides of that yard. Next, to the rear fence with high palings and the smoke-house standing against it. From that place he moves beyond to the orchard and still farther beyond that position in space to the negro quarters and the distant tobacco fields. Having taken the reader as far in that direction as necessary, Mark Twain moves to the front yard and the entrance over "a stile made of sawed-off logs of graduated heights." Finally, he describes a corner of the front yard where stand a "dozen lofty hickory trees and a dozen black walnuts."

Word choice

        To write good descriptions, you must be able to use words discriminatingly. You will need to be objective if you are to present for your reader a reasonably true picture of what you see. Therefore, you must select words that are precise and factual. On the other hand, some descriptions demand evocative words to capture impressionistic feelings about a person or thing. Thus, you will need to use words that will create for the reader an emotional feeling about the subject. To create pictures with words, you must first know something about the power of words. Words in the English language may be classified into words with denotative meanings and connotative meanings. The denotative meaning of a word is its dictionary meaning. A "house," for example, is defined as "a building intended as a dwelling for human beings." The denotation of a word, then, means what the word stands for. It is the precise, literal, factual meaning. A "cat," defined literally, is, according to *Webster's New World Dictionary,* "a small, lithe, soft-furred animal, domesticated since ancient times and often kept as a pet or for killing mice." "To hiss" in its literal sense means "to make a sound like that of a prolonged *s,* as of a goose, or snake, or of escaping steam, air, etc. If a writer's purpose is to present exact information, he will use words with denotative meanings.

> Those houses were built in the early '50's.
> That cat was nearly hit by an automobile yesterday.

        The connotative meaning of a word, on the other hand, is what the word suggests. The word "home," for example, though it means the same as "house," suggests something more than "a building intended as a dwelling." It means in its connotative sense "a place where an individual's affections are centered." "Cat" has also the connotative meaning of "a spiteful woman."

Two words, therefore, may share the same denotative meaning, but they may have connotative meanings quite different. Consider the words in the list which follows. Observe the shades of meaning around the denotative meaning.

imitate, copy, forge, mirror, counterfeit, reproduce
small, little, stunted, puny, dwarfish, tiny
stout, corpulent, fat, obese, plumb, chubby, fleshy
thin, slender, slim, lean, lank, gaunt, emaciated
dog, mongrel, pup, puppy, mutt, canine, whelp
old, ancient, stale, obsolete, antique, elderly, senile
late, tardy, slow, dilatory, belated, overdue

What do the following words or phrases connote to you personally?

church	oily	mother	honesty
rose	ocean	love	examination
snow	eternal	test	youth

| censorship | suppression of news | free press |
| citizen | politician | statesman |

| Zest | Mr. Clean | Tide |
| Filter Tip | Easy Off | Mountain Grown |

Words may be classified also as *abstract* (general) or concrete (specific). An abstract or general word names a group or a class. A concrete word names a particular object, quality, event — a member of a class or group. The word *emotion*, for example, names a class. The words *joy, love, hate, jealousy, sorrow*, on the other hand, name a particular emotion. Study the following sentences.

Those animals are very hungry.
Those lions and tigers are very hungry.

Most students who applied for that position were well educated.
Most of the graduate students who applied for the teaching assistantship were working for their doctorate.

In the yard were some trees and many flowers.

In the back yard were an oak tree, a towering pine, and three chestnut trees. There were also several planters of geraniums and three beds of violets.

Word choice is vitally important to effective writing. Word choice should fit the purpose and the subject. The beginning writer, therefore, should choose his words wisely in order to achieve effective and stimulating communication of his ideas.

The subject of the two descriptive selections which follow is the same, "The Stars." Write a paragraph or two discussing the different treatment, especially the word choice and emotional mood of each.

The stars are suns. Some of the stars are bigger and brighter than our own sun, and some are smaller and fainter. Our sun seems so much brighter and larger than all other stars simply because it is much nearer to us than any of the rest. Our sun is only about 93 million miles away. Yet it is far enough away that a rocket from earth, traveling 25,000 miles an hour, or 7 miles a second, would take 152 days and 8 hours, or about five months, to reach the sun. But the nearest star except for our sun is so far away that our 7-miles-a-second rocket would take almost 115,000 years to reach it. Even this star is a close neighbor, as stars go. Others are millions of times farther away.

We see two kinds of starlike objects in the sky. One is the stars themselves. The other is the sun's "family" of planets that circle the sun as the earth does. [21]

A few stars are known which are hardly bigger than the earth, but the majority are so large that hundreds of thousands of earths could be packed inside each and leave room to spare; here and there we come upon a giant star large enough to contain millions of millions of earths. And the total number of stars in the universe is probably something like the total number of grains of sand on all the sea-shores of the world. Such is the littleness of our home in space when measured up against the total substance of the universe.

This vast multitude of stars are wandering about in space. A few form groups which journey in company, but the majority are solitary travellers. And they travel through a universe so spacious that it is an event of almost unimaginable rarity for a star to come anywhere near to another star. For the most part each voyages in

[21] From *The World Book Encyclopedia.* © 1967 Field Enterprises Educational Corporation.

splendid isolation, like a ship on an empty ocean. In a scale model in which stars are ships, the average ship will be well over a million miles from its nearest neighbor, whence it is easy to understand why a ship seldom finds another within hailing distance. [22]

Images and figurative language

"The etymologist," writes Emerson, "finds the deadest word to have been once a brilliant picture. Language is fossil poetry. As the limestone of the continent consists of infinite masses of the shells of animalcules, so language is made up of images or tropes (figures of speech), which now, in their secondary use, have long ceased to remind us of their poetic origin."

Images, as defined for our purposes, are rhetorical and literary devices that evoke in the reader mental and visual pictures of something not actually present. Images can be effective rhetorical and poetic devices because they evoke emotions, give a freshness and vividness to writing and meaning to things that otherwise would be difficult for the writer to understand. Observe the series of images in the passages which follow.

[1]The lieutenant of the youth's company was shot in the hand. He began to swear so wondrously that a nervous laugh went along the regimental line. The officer's profanity sounded conventional. It relieved the tightened senses of the new men. It was as if he had hit his fingers with a tack hammer at home.

[2]He held the wounded member carefully away from his side so that the blood would not drip upon his trousers.

[3]The captain of the company, tucking his sword under his arm, produced a handkerchief and began to bind with it the lieutenant's wound. And they disputed as to how the binding should be done.

[4]The battle flag in the distance jerked about madly. It seemed to be struggling to free itself from an agony. The billowing smoke was filled with horizontal flashes.

[5]Men running swiftly emerged from it. They grew in numbers until it was seen that the whole command was fleeing. The flag suddenly sank down as if dying. Its motion as it fell was a gesture of despair.

[6]Wild yells came from behind the walls of smoke. A sketch in gray and red dissolved into a moblike body of men who galloped like wild horses.

[7]The veteran regiments on the right and left of the 304th immediately began to jeer. With the passionate song of the bullets and the banshee shrieks of shells were mingled loud catcalls and bits

of facetious advice concerning places of safety.

[8] But the new regiment was breathless with horror. "Gawd! Saunders's got crushed!" whispered the man at the youth's elbow. They shrank back and crouched as if compelled to await a flood. [23]

Crane creates a series of impressionistic pictures of the battle by skillful and deliberate word choice. He uses literal terms and figurative language to convey his factual and emotional description of the battle. The result is a memorable reading experience.

Commenting on the use of imagery in *The Red Badge of Courage,* Modecai and Erin Marcus write:

There is extensive use of animal imagery in Stephen Crane's *The Red Badge of Courage.* This imagery largely takes the form of similes and metaphors. Excluding all of the numerous sunken metaphors which imply animal-like action, this short novel contains at least eighty figures of speech employing animals or their characteristics. These images occur in the narrative itself, in the dialogue, and in the thoughts of the central character. However unaware Crane may have been of the abundance and patterning of this imagery, the consistency with which it is used often furthers his characterization and presentation of ideas, and constitutes a significant method of communicating meaning.

The imagery employs domestic, wild, and imaginary animals, and also makes reference to undefined animal-like characteristics. References to domestic animals occur most frequently. With very few exceptions they are applied to people rather than to things, and they always refer to the enlisted men rather than to the officers. Wild animals, on the other hand, are used to describe things as well as individuals. Imaginary animals and vague animal comparisons tend to be used to describe groups of men. [24]

Figurative language (figures of speech), for the most part, is the expression of emotions and ideas by comparing and identifying one thing with something else more familiar to the reader or listener. It is a language conveying meaning beyond the literal meaning of words. It evokes emotions, makes vivid sensory experiences, and elicits images. On many occasions, figurative language enables a writer to communicate experiences which he would find very difficult or even impossible to do in literal terms. It enables a writer also to accomplish in a few words much that he would find impossible to accomplish in many words. When Crane wanted to make clear and vivid the fears of the young soldier as he stood facing an unknown and unseen enemy, he identifies the enemy with a "composite monster"; therefore, he writes, "The composite monster which had caused the other troops to flee had not appeared . . . ." A few pages later he uses the same metaphor and develops the animal imagery more fully.

To the youth it was an onslaught of redoubtable dragons. He became like the man who has lost his legs at the approach of the red and green monster. He waited in a sort of a horrified, listening attitude. He seemed to shut his eyes and wait to be gobbled.

When William Wordsworth wished to describe the beauty and solitariness of Lucy, a young girl who is the subject of several of his poems, he expressed those qualities in the following poetic words:

A violet by a mossy stone
Half hidden from the eyes!
Fair as a Star, when only one
Is shining in the sky.

The most common kinds of figurative language (figures of speech) are simile, metaphor, personification, and allusion. A *simile* is a directly stated comparison introduced by the word *like* or *as*. A well-written simile is effective because it is vivid and evocative. It enables a writer to express meaning far beyond literal terms. Crane compares the feelings of the youth to those of a man who has "lost his legs at the approach of the red and green monster." Wordsworth's Lucy is not just beautiful and solitary; she is "fair as a Star, when only one is shining in the sky." Study the following similes; observe the things compared, the evocative effect, the enrichment of meaning.

But my body was like a harp and her words and gestures like fingers running upon wires. [25]

Pepe's wrist flicked like the head of a snake. [26]

The lazy geese, like snow cloud
Dripping their snow on the green grass . . . . [27]

Cigars were becoming as old fashioned as chin whiskers. [28]

Weighed down with its heavy load, the plane felt clumsy, like a duck with clipped wings. [29]

The squat ferryboats below plowed across our wake, and great flat barges carrying rectangular mounds of different colored earth like spools of gold and tawny silk. [30]

The present life of man, O king, seems to me, in comparison to that time which is unknown to us, like to the swift flight of a sparrow through the room wherein you sit at supper in winter with your commanders and ministers, and a good fire in the midst, whilst the storms of rain and snow prevail abroad; the sparrow, flying in at one door, and immediately out at another, whilst he is within, is safe from the wintry storm; but after a short space of fair weather, he immediately vanishes out of your sight, into the dark winter from which he had emerged. So this life of man appears for a short space, but of what went before, or what is to follow, we are utterly ignorant. If, therefore, this new doctrine [Christianity] contains something more certain, it seems justly to deserve to be followed. [31]

The asteroids occur as a single swarm. [32]

A *metaphor* is an implied comparison without the introductory word *like* or *as*. Like the simile, the metaphor identifies one object with another and makes meaning clear and vivid by similarities — usually the second partner of the comparison is more familiar and more evocative.

In ten years of studied undercover work they have rolled back the tide of public distaste . . . . [33]

That time of year thou mayst in me behold
When yellow leaves, or none, or few, do hang
Upon these boughs, which shake against the cold,
Bare ruined choirs, where late the sweet birds sang. [34]

Yet the diaphragm is the bellows that blows the fire of life into your speech and adds oomph to your personality. [35]

The moon was a ghostly galleon tossed upon cloudy seas . . . [36]

No man is an island, entire of itself; every man is a piece of the continent, a part of man . . . . [37]

It [the sea] is a silent jungle. [38]

Personification is a figure of speech endowing animals, ideas, abstractions, and inanimate objects with human characteristics. Such common expressions as "the lonely hills," "the tired mountains," "the peaceful ocean," "a restful hamlet" are examples of personification.

Time's cruel hand. [39]

The forests, somber and dull, stood motionless and silent on each side of the broad stream. [40]

A plaintive murmur rose in the night, a murmur saddening and startling, as if the great solitudes of the surrounding woods had tried to whisper into his ear the wisdom of their immense and lofty indifference. [41]

An *allusion* is a reference to famous people and events in history, literature (including the Bible), and mythology.

We of these later days, living in the narrow temperate zone surrounding our sun and peering into the far future, see an ice age of a different kind threatening us. Just as Tantalus, standing in a lake so deep that he only just escaped drowning, was yet destined to die of thirst, so it is the tragedy of our race that it is probably destined to die of cold, while the greater part of the substance of the universe still remains too hot for life to obtain a footing. [42]

Also Ulysses once — that other war.
  (Is it because we find his scrawl
  Today on every privy door
  That we forget his ancient role?)
Also was there — he did it for wages —
When a Cathay-drunk Genoese set sail.
Whenever "longen folk to goon on pilgrimages,"
Kilroy is there;
    he tells The Miller's Tale. [43]

EXERCISES

9. Word power

Read the list of words below. Alongside any word that you consider vague or general in meaning, place a (V); alongside any word that you consider concrete or specific in meaning, place a (C).

1. thing	6. stone	11. air	16. vehicle
2. cute	7. truth	12. clothes	17. man
3. place	8. animal	13. John Smith	18. chair
4. box	9. dog	14. element	19. fence
5. wood	10. baseball	15. automobile	20. trousers

10. Word power

Read the list of phrases and expressions below. If you consider the word group to be fresh and original, place (F) alongside it. If you consider the word group to be stale and worn out, place (W) alongside it.

1. slept like a log	11. roar like a lion
2. sweet as sugar	12. helpful looking bottles
3. purrs like a kitten	13. heart of gold
4. jolly chins clustered	14. innocent as a baby
5. hands, dimpled at every joint	15. constant creeping water
6. in rich profusion	16. the spray sluiced
7. sly as a fox	17. each pounding spank
8. slender slicing knife	18. the day's grind
9. plump chickens dangled their necks	19. pretty as a picture
10. a diamond in the rough	20. a silent jungle

11. Power of words

Study the language in the passage below. Is it dominantly literal or figurative? Give reasons for your choice.

Captain Madwell rose to his feet and drew his sword from the scabbard. He passed the fingers of his left hand along the edge from hilt to point. He held it out straight before him, as if to test his nerves. There was no visible tremor of the blade; the ray of bleak skylight that it reflected was steady and true. He stooped and with his left hand tore away the dying man's shirt, rose and placed the point of the sword just over the heart. This time he did not withdraw his eyes. Grasping the hilt with both hands, he thrust downward with all his strength and weight. The blade sank into the man's body — through his body into the earth; Captain Madwell came near falling forward upon his work. The dying man drew up his knees and at the same time threw his right arm across his breast and grasped the steel so tightly that the knuckles of the hand visibly whitened. By a violent but vain effort to withdraw the blade the wound was enlarged; a rill of blood escaped, running sinuously down into the deranged clothing. At that moment three men stepped silently forward from behind the clump of young trees which had concealed their approach. Two were hospital attendants and carried a stretcher. [44]

12. *Power of words*

Study the language in the passage below. Is it dominantly literal or figurative? Give reasons for your choice.

Spring had come. Streams of water hurried gurgling between the frozen dung-heaps in the wet streets of the town. The people moving to and fro were gayly dressed and gayly chattering. Behind the fences of the little gardens the buds on the trees were swelling, and their branches rustled faintly in the fresh breeze. Everywhere there was a running and a dripping of clear drops .... The sparrows chattered incoherently, and fluttered to and fro on their little wings. On the sunny side, on fences, trees, and houses, all was movement. There was youth and gladness in the sky and on the earth and in the heart of man. In one of the principal streets there was straw lying in front of a large house; in the house lay the dying woman who had been hastening abroad. [45]

13. *Power of words*

Read the poem below. Observe the poet's effective use of figures of speech. Identify eight figures of speech and write down the line number and the type of each figure.

The sea is calm to-night.
The tide is full, the moon lies fair
Upon the straits; — on the French coast the light
Gleams and is gone; the cliffs of England stand,
Glimmering and vast, out in the tranquil bay.
Come to the window, sweet is the night-air!
Only, from the long line of spray
Where the sea meets the moon-blanch'd land,
Listen! you hear the grating roar
Of pebbles which the waves draw back, and fling,
At their return, up the high strand,
Begin, and cease, and then again begin,
With tremulous cadence slow, and bring
The eternal note of sadness in.

Sophocles long ago
Heard it on the Aegean, and it brought
Into his mind the turbid ebb and flow
Of human misery; we
Find also in the sound a thought,
Hearing it by this distant northern sea.

The Sea of Faith
Was once, too, at the full, and round earth's shore
Lay like the folds of a bright girdle furl'd.
But now I only hear
Its melancholy, long, withdrawing roar,
Retreating, to the breath
Of the night-wind, down the vast edges drear
And naked shingles of the world.

Ah, love, let us be true
To one another! for the world, which seems
To lie before us like a land of dreams,
So various, so beautiful, so new,
Hath really neither joy, nor love, nor light,
Nor certitude, nor peace, nor help for pain;
And we are here as on a darkling plain
Swept with confused alarms of struggle and flight,
Where ignorant armies clash by night. [46]

ASSIGNMENTS

8. *Power of words*
    Write the poem "Dover Beach" in prose.

9. *Power of words*
    Write a paragraph commenting on the effectiveness
of the language of "Dover Beach."

10. *Power of words*
    Write a paragraph comparing your prose version of
"Dover Beach" with the original poem.

Informative or objective description
    To write effective description, as does Mark Twain
in the model (p. 172), you must first establish clearly in your own
mind your purpose. If your intent is to inform the reader about the
subject, you will write informative or objective description. Your

purpose will be to reproduce as faithfully as possible your subject. To write this kind of description, you must be objective and impersonal. If it is to be a true representation of what you see, you must not become involved emotionally with the subject. Instead of evocative words and impressionistic feelings, you must rely on precise words, factual details, and selective specifics that will enable the reader to complete the picture accurately from your report. In informative description, then, your task is to create with words a faithful image of the subject you are seeing.

Read again Mark Twain's description of a Missouri farm (p. 159). Observe in your study of the paragraph his objectivity, his precise and concrete word choices, his skilled movement through space. In writing this informative description, Mark Twain relies heavily on the concrete and specific to make true his picture of the farm. He does not write, "the farmhouse stood in the yard," "the yard was fenced with rails and palings," "in the front yard were a dozen or more tall trees." Instead, he writes, "the farmhouse stood in the *middle* of a *very large* yard," "the yard was fenced on *three* sides with *rails* and on the *rear* side with *high palings,*" "in a *corner* of the *front* yard were a *dozen lofty hickory* trees and a *dozen black walnuts.*"

Mark Twain does not jump aimlessly from one salient aspect of the whole scene to another. He moves in a natural order from the farmhouse — the dominant impression — to the less important aspects: the fences, orchard, fields, quarters, trees.

In addition, he does not overload his description with excessive details and specifics. Even the keenest observer cannot hope to perceive a thing as it really exists. A writer of description, therefore, must select skillfully those aspects which will enable the reader to create the images. Mark Twain does not generalize; on the other hand, he does not carry his concreteness to extremes; for example, he writes a "very large yard," "high palings," "corner of the front yard," "lofty hickory trees." He does not detail each image by citing feet and inches for yard area or tree height. With this kind of selectivity, he permits the reader to complete the total picture.

Emotional or subjective description

If your purpose is to communicate your feeling about a subject rather than to inform, you will write *emotional* or *subjective* description. In this kind of description, you focus on the emotion the subject arouses in you, not the way the subject looks. Your task is to translate into words the evocative experience so the reader may share it with you. In the following description, Mark Twain is again recalling memories of past days. This description, however, is different from his recollection of the Missouri farm.

I can call back the solemn twilight and mystery of the deep woods, the earthy smells, the faint odors of the wild flowers, the sheen of rain-washed foliage, the rattling clatter of drops when the wind shook the trees, the far-off hammering of woodpeckers and the muffled drumming of wood-pheasants in the remoteness of the forest, the snapshot glimpses of disturbed wild creatures scurrying through the grass — I can call it all back and make it as real as it ever was, and as blessed. I can call back the prairie, and its loneliness and peace, and a vast hawk hanging motionless in the sky with his wings spread wide and the blue of the vault showing through the fringe of their endfeathers. I can see the woods in their autumn dress, the oaks purple, the hickories washed with gold, the maples and the sumachs luminous with crimson fires, and I can hear the rustle made by the fallen leaves as we plowed through them. I can see the blue clusters of wild grapes hanging amongst the foliage of the saplings, and I remember the taste of them and the smell. I know how the wild blackberries looked and how they tasted; and the same with the pawpaws, the hazelnuts, and the persimmons; and I can feel the thumping rain upon my head of hickory-nuts and walnuts when we were out in the frosty dawn to scramble for them with the pigs, and the gusts of wind loosed them and sent them down. I know the stain of blackberries and how pretty it is, and I know the stain of walnut hulls and how little it minds soap and water, also what grudged experience it had of either of them. I know the taste of maple sap and when to gather it, and how to arrange the troughs and the delivery tubes, and how to boil down the juice, and how to hook the sugar after it is made; also how much better hooked sugar tastes than any that is honestly come by, let bigots say what they will. [47]

DISCUSSION

How different is this subjective description from Mark Twain's objective picture of his Missouri farm! In this description, the general, not the specific, the subjective, not the objective, the connotative word and the abstract, not the concrete word and phrase, and feelings about the subject, not its appearance, dominate. In this description, Mark Twain wants his reader to share with him those memorable experiences of by-gone days.

Point of view

After you have your purpose clearly in mind, you begin to organize the material. Point of view will dictate to a large extent the kind of development. In informative description, point of view is the position in space from which you view the subject. In emotional description, point of view is your mental attitude, feelings, or mood which the subject evokes in you.

You may view the subject, for example, from a fixed physical position in space, such as from the top of a hill, the foothills of a towering mountain range, from a bridge high above a turbulent river, from the dock as a ship departs, from the rear of a spacious banquet hall, or from the shore of a lake out onto the lake. From whatever fixed position you take, you then describe your subject in some kind of natural and logical order. You may decide to move from the most distant point to the nearest point, or from the nearest point to the most distant point, from top to bottom or from bottom to top, from right to left or from left to right, from inside to outside or from outside to inside, from front to back or from back to front. You may wish to focus on a single dominant impression and move to the less important aspects or from the less important aspects to the dominant impression; for example, a snow-capped mountain peak in a rugged mountain range, the large red nose of a melancholy clown, the deep lines in the tired face of a great man, or the loneliness of a solitary figure standing in a large stadium after the big game.

You may wish to describe your subject from a shifting point of view. You may be moving through a crowd in order to describe individual reactions to a crime, an accident, a holocaust. You may wish to describe various rooms in a famous building, such as the White House. You may be describing a battlefield, a natural wonder of the world, or a lonely seashore as you fly over it. The possibilities are, of course, almost limitless.

In the paragraph which follows, the writer stands at the entrance of the public room after he and his readers (he uses the pronoun "you" to bring the reader into the scene) have crossed the "dusky entry" and moved on through "yon low-arched way." His eyes and the reader's eyes notice first the dim interior, then the high beams above and the old wrinkled planks of the floor underneath. He takes his reader next to one side of the room where stands a long, low, shelflike table. Finally, he moves to the further angle of the room to a bar made from the vast arched bone of a whale's jaw in which stands Jonah, the bartender — the dominant impression of the whole description.

Crossing this dusky entry, and on through yon low-arched way — cut through what in old times must have been a great central chimney with fireplaces all round — you enter the public room. A still duskier place is this, with such low ponderous beams above, and such old wrinkled planks beneath, that you would almost fancy you trod some old craft's cockpits, especially of such a howling night, when this corner-anchored old ark rocked so furiously. On one side stood a long, low, shelflike table covered with cracked glass cases, filled with dusty rarities gathered from this wide world's remotest nooks. Projecting from the further angle of the room stands a dark-looking den — the bar — a rude attempt at a right whale's head. Be that how it may, there stands the vast arched bone of the whale's jaw, so wide, a coach might almost drive beneath it. Within are shabby shelves, ranged round with old decanters, bottles, flasks; and in those jaws of swift destruction, like another cursed Jonah (by which name indeed they called him), bustles a little withered old man, who, for their money, dearly sells the sailors deliriums and death.

Abominable are the tumblers into which he pours his poison. Though true cylinders without — within, the villainous green goggling glasses deceitfuly tapered downward to a cheating bottom. Parallel meridians rudely pecked into the glass, surround these footpads' goblets. Fill to *this* mark, and your charge is but a penny; to *this* a penny more; and so on to the full glass — the Cape Horn measure, which you may gulp down for a shilling. [48]

In the description above, the point of view does not change throughout the description. Study the following example of description from a fixed physical point of view. Hardy, the writer of this description, first identifies his subject: the beautiful Vale of Blakemore or Blackmoor. Next, he tells the reader that his point of view will be from "the summits of the hills that surround it."

[1]The village of Marlott lay amid the north-eastern undulations of the beautiful Vale of Blakemore or Blackmoor aforesaid, an engirdled and secluded region, for the most part untrodden

as yet by tourist or landscape-painter, though within a four hours' journey from London.

[2]It is a vale whose acquaintance is best made by viewing it from the summits of the hills that surround it — except perhaps during the droughts of summer. An unguided ramble into its recesses in bad weather is apt to engender dissatisfaction with its narrow, torturous, and miry ways.

[3]This fertile and sheltered tract of country, in which the fields are never brown and the springs never dry, is bounded on the south by the bold chalk ridge that embraces the prominences of Hambledon Hill, Bulbarrow, Nettlecombe-Tout, Dogbury, High Stoy, and Bubb Down. The traveller from the coast, who, after plodding northward for a score of miles over calcareous downs and corn-lands, suddenly reaches the verge of one of these escarpments, is surprised and delighted to behold, extended like a map beneath him, a country differing absolutely from that which he has passed through. Behind him the hills are open, the sun blazes down upon fields so large as to give an unenclosed character to the landscape, the lanes are white, the hedges low and plashed, the atmosphere colourless. Here, in the valley, the world seems to be constructed upon a smaller and more delicate scale; the fields are mere paddocks, so reduced that from this height their hedgerows appear a network of dark green threads overspreading the paler green of the grass. The atmosphere beneath is languorous, and is so tinged with azure that what artists call the middle distance partakes also of that hue, while the horizon beyond is of the deepest ultramarine. Arable lands are few and limited; with but slight exceptions the prospect is a broad rich mass of grass and trees, mantling minor hills and dales within the major. Such is the Vale of Blackmoor. [49]

By describing a subject from a fixed physical position, a writer, of course, limits his view. He can describe only what he sees from that position. Sometimes, writers describe a subject from a shifting point of view. A writer may be in a moving airplane, a automobile, a ship. He may be moving in a crowd of people, walking in a park, a museum, an old house. He may be climbing a hill, a mountain, up the stairs from one floor of a house to another. As he moves along he describes what he sees, feels, tastes, hears, and touches. Stephen Crane presents this kind of movement in the selection that follows. Henry Fleming, the youthful hero of *The Red Badge of Courage,* runs away from the fighting in his first battle. Crane creates a series of impressions as he describes the flight of the youth.

¹He ran like a blind man. Two or three times he fell down. Once he knocked his shoulder so heavily against a tree that he went headlong.

²Since he had turned his back upon the fight his fears had been wondrously magnified. Death about to thrust him between the shoulder blades was far more dreadful than death about to smite him between the eyes. When he thought of it later, he conceived the impression that it is better to view the appalling than to be merely within hearing. The noises of the battle were like stones; he believed himself liable to be crushed.

³As he ran on he mingled with others. He dimly saw men on his right and on his left, and he heard footsteps behind him. He thought that all the regiment was fleeing, pursued by these ominous crashes.

⁴In his flight the sound of these following footsteps gave him his one meager relief. He felt vaguely that death must make a first choice of the men who were nearest; the initial morsels for the dragons would be then those who were following him. So he displayed the zeal of an insane sprinter in his purpose to keep them in the rear. There was a race.

⁵As he, leading, went across a little field, he found himself in a region of shells. They hurtled over his head with long wild screams. As he listened he imagined them to have rows of cruel teeth that grinned at him. Once one lit before him and the livid lightning of the explosion effectually barred the way in his chosen direction. He groveled on the ground and then springing up went careering off through some bushes.

⁶He experienced a thrill of amazement when he came within view of a battery in action. The men there seemed to be in conventional moods, altogether unaware of the impending annihilation. The battery was disputing with a distant antagonist and the gunners were wrapped in admiration of their shooting. They were continually bending in coaxing postures over the guns. They seemed to be patting them on the back and encouraging them with words. The guns, *stolid and undaunted,* spoke with dogged valor. [50]

Narration and description

Description seldom appears as a pure form. You are more likely to find it as part of narration, exposition — even argumentation. Moreover, you will find that seldom is description entirely informative or entirely emotional. It is more likely to lie somewhere between these two extremes. Writer's intent determines the kind of writing or the kind of description which will dominate. In the model paragraphs which follow, description plays a significant role. Herman Melville tells what happened to some small whaling boats caught in a squall, especially what happened to the boat that contained Starbuck, the narrator of *Moby Dick,* and Queequeg, two important characters in the novel. He relies heavily on descriptive details to make the telling of the incident vivid and interesting; yet the account of the incident is the focus of his attention. Though his approach is to a certain extent subjective and informative, he translates powerfully into words his feelings of despair and hopelessness with many words, phrases, and sentences, such as "in vain," "There, then, he sat, the sign and symbol of a man without faith, hopelessly holding up hope in the midst of despair."

[1]The wind increased to a howl; the waves dashed their bucklers together; the whole squall roared, forked, and crackled around us like a white fire upon the prairie, in which unconsumed, we were burning; immortal in these jaws of death! In vain we hailed the other boats; as well roar to the live coals down the chimney of a flaming furnace as hail those boats in that storm. Meanwhile the driving scud, rack, and mist, grew darker with the shadows of night; no sign of the ship could be seen. The rising sea forbade all attempts to bale out the boat. The oars were useless as propellers, performing now the office of life preservers. So, cutting the lashing of the water-proof match keg, after many failures Starbuck contrived to ignite the lamp in the lantern; then stretching it on a waif pole, handed it to Queequeg as the standard-bearer of this forlorn hope. There, then, he sat, holding up that imbecile candle in the heart of that almighty forlornness. There, then, he sat, the sign and symbol of a man without faith, hopelessly holding up hope in the midst of despair.

[2]Wet, drenched through, and shivering cold, despairing of ship or boat, we lifted up our eyes as the dawn came on. The mist still spread over the sea, the empty lantern lay crushed in the bottom of the boat. Suddenly Queequeg started to his feet, hollowing his hand to his ear. We all heard a faint creaking as of ropes and yards hitherto muffled by the storm. The sound came nearer and nearer; the thick mists were dimly parted by a huge, vague form. Affrighted, we all sprang into the sea as the ship at last loomed into view, bearing right down upon us within a distance of not much more than its length.

[3]Floating on the waves we saw the abandoned boat, as for one instant it tossed and gaped beneath the ship's bows like a chip at the base of a cataract; and then the vast hull rolled over it, and it was seen no more till it came up weltering astern. Again we

swam for it, were dashed against it by the seas, and were at last taken up and safely landed on board. Ere the squall came close to, the other boats had cut loose from their fish and returned to the ship in good time. The ship had given us up, but was still cruising, if haply it might light upon some token of our perishing — an oar or a lance pole. [51]

Study the model which follows. Observe the way the writer uses description in the narration of "Rip Van Winkle."

[1]In a long ramble of the kind on a fine autumnal day, Rip had unconsciously scrambled to one of the highest parts of the Kaatskill mountains. He was after his favorite sport of squirrel-shooting, and the still solitudes had echoed and re-echoed with the reports of his gun. Panting and fatigued, he threw himself, late in the afternoon, on a green knoll, covered with mountain herbage, that crowned the brow of a precipice. From an opening between the trees he could overlook all the lower country for many a mile of rich woodland. He saw at a distance the lordly Hudson, far, far below him, moving on its silent but majestic course, with the reflection of a purple cloud, or the sail of a lagging bark, here and there sleeping on its glassy bosom, and at last losing itself in the blue highlands.

[2]On the other side he looked down into a deep mountain glen, wild, lonely, and shagged, the bottom filled with fragments from the impending cliffs, and scarcely lighted by the reflected rays of the setting sun. For some time Rip lay musing on this scene; evening was gradually advancing; the mountains began to throw their long blue shadows over the valleys; he saw that it would be dark long before he could reach the village, and he heaved a heavy sigh when he thought of encountering the terrors of Dame Van Winkle.

[3]As he was about to descend, he heard a voice from a distance, hallooing, "Rip Van Winkle, Rip Van Winkle!" He looked round, but could see nothing but a crow winging its solitary flight across the mountain. He thought his fancy must have deceived him, and turned again to descend, when he heard the same cry ring through the still evening air: "Rip Van Winkle! Rip Van Winkle!" — at the same time Wolf bristled up his back, and giving a low growl, skulked to his master's side, looking fearfully down into the glen. Rip now felt a vague apprehension stealing over him; he looked anxiously in the same direction, and perceived a strange figure slowly toiling up the rocks, and bending under the weight of something he carried on his back. He was surprised to see any human being in this lonely and unfrequented place; but supposing it to be some

one of the neighborhood in need of his assistance, he hastened down to yield it. [52]

EXERCISE

14. *Description*
Read the model descriptive paragraph below. Answer the questions that follow it.

During the whole of a dull, dark, and soundless day in the autumn of the year, when the clouds hung oppressively low in the heavens, I had been passing alone, on horseback, through a singularly dreary tract of country; and at length found myself, as the shades of the evening drew on, within view of the melancholy House of Usher. I know not how it was — but, with the first glimpse of the building, a sense of insufferable gloom pervaded my spirit. I say insufferable; for the feeling was unrelieved by any of that half-pleasurable, because poetic, sentiment, with which the mind usually receives even the sternest natural images of the desolate or terrible. I looked upon the scene before me — upon the mere house, and the simple landscape features of the domain — upon the bleak walls — upon the vacant, eye-like windows — upon a few rank sedges — and upon a few white trunks of decayed trees — with an utter depression of soul which I can compare to no earthly sensation more properly than to the after-dream of the reveler upon opium — the bitter lapse into everyday life — the hideous dropping off of the veil. There was an iciness, a sinking, a sickening of the heart — an unredeemed dreariness of thought which no goading of the imagination could torture into aught of the sublime. What was it — I paused to think — what was it that so unnerved me in the contemplation of the House of Usher? It was a mystery all insoluble; nor could I grapple with the shadowy fancies that crowded upon me as I pondered. I was forced to fall back upon the unsatisfactory conclusion that while, beyond doubt, there *are* combinations of very simple natural objects which have the power of thus affecting us, still the analysis of this power lies among considerations beyond our depth. It was possible, I reflected, that a mere different arrangement of the particulars of the scene, of the details of the picture, would be sufficient to modify, or perhaps to annihilate its capacity for sorrowful impression; and, acting upon this idea, I reined my horse to the precipitous brink of a black and lurid tarn that lay in unruffled lustre by the dwelling, and gazed down — but with a shudder even more thrilling than before — upon the remodeled and inverted images of the gray sedge, and the ghastly tree-stems, and the vacant and eye-like windows. [53]

    1. What type of description does the writer use?
    2. List fifteen words or phrases that enable the writer
       to fulfill his purpose.
    3. What dominant mood does the writer create?

ASSIGNMENT

11. Description

Rewrite the description of the House of Usher as objective description.

EXERCISES

15. Description

Read the model descriptive paragraph below. Answer the questions that follow it.

On the summit of one of the heights of the Odenwald, a wild and romantic tract of Upper Germany, that lies not far from the confluence of the Main and the Rhine, there stood, many, many years since, the Castle of the Baron Von Landshort. It is now quite fallen to decay, and almost buried among beech-trees and dark firs; above which, however, its old watchtower may still be seen, struggling, like the former possessor I have mentioned, to carry a high head, and look down upon the neighboring country. [54]

    1. What feature dominates this description?
    2. What is the figure of speech in the last two lines?
       Is it effective? Why? or Why not?

16. Description

Read the model descriptive paragraph below. Answer the question that follows it.

It was a crisp and spicy morning in early October. The lilacs and laburnums, lit with the glory fires of autumn, hung burning and flashing in the upper air, a fairy bridge provided by kind Nature for the wingless wild things that have their home in the tree tops and would visit together; the larch and the pomegranate flung their purple and yellow flames in brilliant broad splashes along the slanting sweep of the woodland; the sensuous fragrance of innumerable deciduous flowers rose upon the swooning atmosphere; far in the empty sky a solitary oesophagus slept upon motionless wing; everywhere brooded stillness, serenity, and the peace of God. [55]

1. In an English handbook or rhetoric, look up the meaning of the term "Fine Language." Now comment on the language of the selection that you have just read.

17. Description

Read the model descriptive paragraph below. Answer the questions that follow it.

The first thing to see, looking away over the water, was a kind of dull line — that was the woods on t'other side; you couldn't make nothing else out; then a pale place in the sky; then more paleness spreading around; then the river softened up away off, and warn't black any more, but gray; you could see little dark spots drifting along ever so far away — trading-scows, and such things; and long black streaks — rafts; sometimes you could hear a sweep screaking; or jumbled-up voices, it was so still, and sounds come so far; and by and by you could see a streak on the water which you know by the look of the streak that there's a snag there in a swift current which breaks on it and makes that streak look that way; and you see the mist curl up off of the water, and the east reddens up, and the river, and you make out a log cabin in the edge of the woods, away on the bank on t'other side of the river, being a wood-yard, likely, and piled by them cheats so you can throw a dog through it anywheres; then the nice breeze springs up, and comes fanning you from over there, so cool and fresh and sweet to smell on account of the woods and the flowers; but sometimes not that way, because they've left dead fish laying around, gars and such, and they do get pretty rank; and next you've got the full day, and everything smiling in the sun, and the song-birds just going it! [56]

1. Is this an informational or emotional description?
2. From what point of view does the writer describe the scene?
3. What are some adjectives, verbs, participles (-*ing* words) that make the description effective? Underline them in the selection.

18. Description

Read the model descriptive paragraph below. Answer the questions that follow it.

The first sparrow of spring! The year beginning with younger hope than ever! The faint silvery warblings heard over the

partially bare and moist fields from the bluebird, the song sparrow, and the red-wing, as if the last flakes of winter tinkled as they fell! What at such a time are histories, chronologies, traditions, and all written revelations? The brooks sing carols and glees to the spring. The marsh hawk, sailing low over the meadow, is already seeking the first slimy life that awakes. The sinking sound of melting snow is heard in all dells, and the ice dissolves apace in the ponds. The grass flames up on the hillsides like a spring fire, — "et primitus oritur herba imbribus primoribus evocata," — as if the earth sent forth an inward heat to greet the returning sun; not yellow but green is the color of its flame; — the symbol of perpetual youth, the grass-blade, like a long green ribbon, streams from the sod into the summer, checked indeed by the frost, but anon pushing on again, lifting its spear of last year's hay with the fresh life below. It grows as steadily as the rill oozes out of the ground. It is almost identical with that, for in the growing days of June, when the rills are dry, the grass-blades are their channels, and from year to year the herds drink at this perennial green stream, and the mower draws from it betimes still puts forth its green blade to eternity. [57]
their winter supply. So our human life but dies down to its root, and

1. Is this informational or emotional description?
2. Mention some figures of speech the writer uses?
3. Underline some effective modifiers and verbs.
4. Does the paragraph have a main idea that would support a view that this is an example of expository description?

ASSIGNMENTS

12. Description

Write an objective description of approximately 300 words on one of the following subjects.

1. A classroom
2. A cabin in the mountains or a cottage on a lake
3. Your room
4. Sounds, smells, sights in a factory, bakery, restaurant, etc.
5. Describe some place or thing from a position above it; for example New York city from the Empire State Building

13. Description

Write an emotional description of approximately 300 words on one of the following subjects.
1. A cemetery
2. A historic shrine
3. A sunset
4. The last game
5. Graduation
6. A scenic view

14. Narration and description

Write a narration of approximately 500 words in which description plays a significant role.

THE TURTLE
by John Steinbeck

[1] The concrete highway was edged with a mat of tangled, broken, dry grass, and the grass heads were heavy with oat beards to catch on a dog's coat, and fox-tails to tangle in a horse's fetlocks, and clover burrs to fasten in sheep's wool; sleeping life waiting to be spread and dispersed, every seed armed with an appliance of dispersal, twisting darts and parachutes for the wind, little spears and balls of tiny thorns, and all waiting for animals and for the wind, for a man's trouser cuff or the hem of a woman's skirt, all passive but armed with appliances of activity, still, but each possessed of the anlage of movement.

[2] The sun lay on the grass and warmed it, and in the shade under the grass the insects moved, ants and ant lions to set traps for them, grasshoppers to jump into the air and flick their yellow wings for a second, sow bugs like little armadillos, plodding restlessly on many tender feet. And over the grass at the roadside a land turtle crawled, turning aside for nothing, dragging his high-domed shell over the grass. His hard legs and yellow-nailed feet threshed slowly through the grass, not really walking, but boosting and dragging his shell along. The barley beards slid off his shell, and the clover burrs fell on him and rolled to the ground. His horny beak was partly open, and his fierce, humorous eyes, under brows like fingernails, stared straight ahead. He came over the grass leaving a beaten trail behind him, and the hill, which was the highway embankment, reared up ahead of him. For a moment he stopped, his head held high. He blinked and looked up and down. At last he started to climb the embankment. Front clawed feet reached forward but did not touch. The hind feet kicked his shell along, and it scraped on the

grass, and on the gravel. As the embankment grew steeper and steeper, the more frantic were the efforts of the land turtle. Pushing hind legs strained and slipped, boosting the shell along, and the horny head protruded as far as the neck could stretch. Little by little the shell slid up the embankment until at last a parapet cut straight across its line of march, the shoulder of the road, a concrete wall four inches high. As though they worked independently the hind legs pushed the shell against the wall. The head upraised and peered over the wall to the broad smooth plain of cement. Now the hands, braced on top of the wall, strained and lifted, and the shell came slowly up and rested its front end on the wall. For a moment the turtle rested. A red ant ran into the shell, into the soft skin inside the shell, and suddenly head and legs snapped in, and the armored tail clamped in sideways. The red ant was crushed between body and legs. And one head of wild oats was clamped into the shell by a front leg. For a long moment the turtle lay still, and then the neck crept out and the old humorous frowning eyes looked about and the legs and tail came out. The back legs went to work, straining like elephant legs, and the shell tipped to an angle so that the front legs could not reach the level cement plain. But higher and higher the hind legs boosted it, until at last the center of balance was reached, the front tipped down, the front legs scratched at the pavement, and it was up. But the head of wild oats was held by its stem around the front legs.

[3] Now the going was easy, and all the legs worked, and the shell boosted along, waggling from side to side. A sedan driven by a forty-year old woman approached. She saw the turtle and swung to the right, off the highway, the wheels screamed and a cloud of dust boiled up. Two wheels lifted for a moment and then settled. The car skidded back onto the road, and went on, but more slowly. The turtle had jerked into its shell, but now it hurried on, for the highway was burning hot.

[4] And now a light truck approached, and as it came near, the driver saw the turtle and swerved to hit it. His front wheel struck the edge of the shell, flipped the turtle like a tiddly-wink, spun it like a coin, and rolled it off the highway. The truck went back to its course along the right side. Lying on its back, the turtle was tight in its shell for a long time. But at last its legs waved in the air, reaching for something to pull it over. Its front foot caught a piece of quartz and little by little the shell pulled over and flopped upright. The wild oat head fell out and three of the spearhead seeds stuck in the ground. And as the turtle crawled on down the embankment, its shell dragged dirt over the seeds. The turtle entered a dust road and jerked itself along, drawing a wavy shallow trench in the dust with its shell. The old humorous eyes looked ahead, and the horny beak opened a little. His yellow toe nails slipped a fraction in the dust. [58]

CHAPTER FIVE *References*

1. Reprinted with the permission of Charles Scribner's Sons from The Introduction by Malcolm Cowley to *The Short Stories of F. Scott Fitzgerald*. Copyright 1951 Charles Scribner's Sons.
2. From "Lessons of the Past" by Edith Hamilton, in *The Saturday Evening Post*. Reprinted by permission of Doris Fielding Reid.
3. From "Undergraduates on Apron Strings" by Howard Mumford Jones, in *The Atlantic Monthly*. Reprinted by permission of the author.
4. From *The Age of Aristocracy 1688 to 1830* by William B. Willcox. Copyright © 1960 by D. C. Heath and Company.
5. From *This Realm of England* by Lacey Baldwin Smith. Copyright © 1966 by D. C. Heath and Company.
6. From *Life on the Mississippi* by Mark Twain.
7. From "Rip Van Winkle" by Washington Irving.
8. From *Walden* by Henry David Thoreau.
9. "Night Watch," by Roy Popkin, as condensed in the September, 1965, *Reader's Digest*. Reprinted by permission of *The National Observer*.
10. "Five Missed Chances at Pearl Harbor," by Walter Lord, as condensed in the December, 1957, *Reader's Digest*. Copyright 1957 by The Reader's Digest Association, Inc. Reprinted with permission from *Reader's Digest* and The Sterling Lord Agency.
11. From "Rip Van Winkle" by Washington Irving.
12. From "How to Ski" by Strand Mikkelsen. Reprinted courtesy of *Popular Science Monthly*. © 1930, by Popular Science Publishing Company, Inc.
13. From *Make the Team in Basketball* by Clair Bee. Copyright © 1961 by Grosset & Dunlap, Inc., by permission of the publisher, Grosset & Dunlap, Inc.
14. From *How to Communicate Orally* by Glenn R. Capp. © 1961. Reprinted by permission of Prentice-Hall, Inc., Englewood Cliffs, New Jersey.
15. From *How to Read Better and Faster* by Norman Lewis, copyright 1951. Published by Thomas Y. Crowell Company.
16. Reprinted from "Design With June Flowers" by Adrienne Green, in the June, 1967, issue of *Family Circle* Magazine. © The Family Circle, Inc. 1967.
17. From *The Sea Around Us* by Rachel L. Carson. Copyright © 1950, 1951 by Rachel L. Carson. Reprinted by permission of The Oxford University Press, Inc.
18. From *The Sea Around Us* by Rachel L. Carson. Cf. 17.
19. From "The Sea," in *Life Nature Library* by Leonard Engel, and the Editors of *Life*. Copyright © 1961 by Time, Inc. Reprinted by permission of Time-Life, Inc.
20. From *Mark Twain's Autobiography*. Copyright, 1924 by Clara Gabrilowitsch; renewed 1952 by Clara Clemens Samossoud. Reprinted by permission of Harper & Row, Publishers.
21. From "The Star" in *The World Book Encyclopedia*.
22. From *The Mysterious Universe* by Sir James Jeans. Reprinted by permission of the publisher, The Cambridge University Press.
23. From *The Red Badge of Courage* by Stephen Crane.
24. From "Animal Imagery in *The Red Badge of Courage*," by Modecai and Erin Marcus, in *Modern Language Notes* (February, 1959). Reprinted by permission of The Johns Hopkins Press.

25. From "Araby" by James Joyce.
26. From "Flight" by John Steinbeck.
27. From "Bells for John Whiteside's Daughter." Copyright © 1924 by Alfred A. Knopf, Inc., renewed 1952 by John Crowe Ransom. Reprinted from *Selected Poems* by John Crowe Ransom by permission of the publisher.
28. From "They Made the Cigar Respectable" by Keith Monroe.
29. From *North to the Orient* by Anne Morrow Lindbergh.
30. Cf. 29.
31. From *Ecclesiastical History of the English Nation* by Bede.
32. From *The Universe Around Us* by Sir James Jeans.
33. From "They Made the Cigar Respectable" by Keith Monroe.
34. William Shakespeare.
35. From "Put Your Best Foot Forward" by Stephen S. Price.
36. From "The Highwayman" by Alfred Noyes.
37. From "Meditation, XVII" by John Donne.
38. From *The Silent World* by J. Y. Cousteau.
39. William Shakespeare.
40. From "The Lagoon" by Joseph Conrad.
41. Cf. 40.
42. From *The Mysterious Universe* by Sir James Jeans. cf. 22.
43. From "Kilroy" by Peter Viereck. Reprinted with permission of the author and copyright owner, Peter Viereck, from his book, *New and Selected Poems*, Bobbs Merrill Company, New York, 1967; first appeared in *The Atlantic Monthly*.
44. From "The Coup de Grâce" by Ambrose Bierce.
45. Leo Tolstoy.
46. From "Dover Beach" by Matthew Arnold.
47. From *Mark Twain's Autobiography*. Cf. 20.
48. From *Moby Dick* by Herman Melville.
49. From *Tess of the d'Ubervilles* by Thomas Hardy.
50. From *The Red Badge of Courage* by Stephen Crane.
51. From *Moby Dick* by Herman Melville.
52. From "Rip Van Winkle" by Washington Irving.
53. From "The Fall of the House of Usher" by Edgar Allan Poe.
54. From "The Spectre Bridegroom" by Washington Irving.
55. From "A Double-Barreled Detective Story" by Samuel L. Clemens.
56. From *Adventures of Huckleberry Finn* by Mark Twain.
57. From *Walden* by Henry David Thoreau.
58. "The Turtle," from *The Grapes of Wrath* by John Steinbeck. Copyright 1939, copyright © renewed 1967 by John Steinbeck. Reprinted by permission of The Viking Press, Inc.

Comparing and contrasting

In the previous chapter, you learned to organize and develop thought into paragraphs by skillful arrangement of sentences. These orders of organization and development may serve also as the framework within which the more complex orders of structuring thought may be developed. Within the general to particular, particular to general, and question to answer patterns, you can structure more complex thought by comparison, contrast, analogy, comparison and contrast, analysis, definition, and any combination of methods.

Comparison and contrast

In writing comparison and contrast, you clarify and explain your subject by showing likenesses and unlikenesses between two or more persons, places, things, ideas, or situations. You use comparisons and contrasts every day since they are the most natural methods of organizing thought. You may compare two vacuum cleaners, two electric razors, toothpastes, automobiles, or lawn mowers as to price, performance, and durability before buying one. You may wish to point out to a friend how two or more leaders, teams, colleges, courses, newspapers are alike; therefore you compare them in order to stress similarities. You may, on the other hand, wish to show that socialism differs from capitalism and communism, high school from college, water skiing from snow skiing, an American from an Indian, or ancient Greece from ancient Rome; therefore, you compare the two or more subjects stressing differences (contrast). Beginning writers, however, are cautioned to master the techniques of comparing or contrasting two subjects before moving on to three or more subjects — a more difficult process.

Comparison

Comparison is a method of organizing and developing thought to show similarities between persons, places, things, ideas, or situations. Contrast is a method of organizing and developing thought to show differences between persons, places, things, ideas, situations. In writing comparison and contrast, some of the methods of structuring ideas are essentially the same. First, define clearly your purpose. You may want simply to show the likenesses or differences between two subjects, for example, a schoolteacher and a salesman, New York and Los Angeles, the Chinese and the Hindu. With this kind of purpose, you create interest usually by selecting subjects with which your reader is not familiar or which your reader would not logically expect to possess like or unlike characteristics. Thus, you are able to hold his interest and, at the same time, fulfill your purpose of presenting information about the two subjects. You may, on the other hand, compare or contrast two subjects in order to inform your reader about something the two subjects themselves explain, clarify, or establish. You might compare two religions, for instance, to show that they are basically alike or ancient Greece with ancient Rome to emphasize the importance of the "Greek way."

Second, select two subjects that are comparable, that is, from the same group or class. You can compare two nationalities, Americans and Indians; two kinds of education, specific and general; two countries, ancient Greece and ancient Rome; two leaders, Hitler and Mussolini; two forms of government, monarchy and aristocracy; and two economic systems, socialism and capitalism; they are of the same class and possess sufficient similar characteristics to be comparable. You would probably find it difficult to effectively compare Americans with socialists, communism with dictatorship, athletes with politicians, Danish education with American education because they do not have sufficient like characteristics to be comparable and because they are not really subjects for comparison. An individual, for example, could be an American and also a socialist; communism for many years has functioned under a form of dictatorship; an athlete could be also a politician; Danish education is so different from American education in size, philosophy, and goals that a really meaningful comparison or contrast between the two systems would be impossible.

Third, list as many points of comparison or contrast as possible. In this step, you can make good use of a preliminary plan much like the one suggested below. Suppose, for example, you were comparing the United States and India.

Preliminary plan

Purpose: To show the similarities between the United States and India

1. federations
2. problems of federal-state relationships
3. a written constitution
4. supreme court
5. judiciary independent of executive
6. variety of religions *
7. many poor people *
8. belief in the rule of law and civil liberties
9. class systems *
10. law a respected profession
11. burden of proof on the prosecution
12. "sacredness of individual" *
13. no man guilty unless proved so

Fourth, eliminate any irrelevant or less important points of comparison. The points marked with the asterisk were eliminated.

Fifth, prepare a topic or sentence outline before writing the comparison; for example:

The United States and India

Thesis Statement: To show the similarities between the United States and India

I. Similarities between the United States and India
    A. Federations
    B. Problems of federal-state relationships
    C. A written constitution
    D. A supreme court
    E. An independent judiciary
    F. Belief in the rule of law and civil liberties
    G. Law a respected profession
    H. Burden of proof on prosecution
    I. No man guilty unless proved so

this: A sentence outline for the comparison might look like

The United States and India

Statement of the Thesis: To show how the United States and India are alike in many respects.

I. The United States and India are alike in many respects.
    A. Both nations are federations.
    B. Both are concerned with the ticklish problems of federal-state relationships.
    C. Both have a written constitution.
    D. Both have a supreme court that often has to be its official interpreter.
    E. In both countries, the judiciary is independent of the executive branch.
    F. Both are pledged to maintain the rule of law and all civil liberties including the right to freedom of discussion and freedom of assembly.
    G. In both countries the law is a respected profession.
    H. Both believe that the burden of proof is on the prosecution.
    I. In both countries, no man is guilty until he is legally proved so.

Read now the original paragraph on which the preliminary plan and the outlines were based. Observe the use of the transitional word *both* and the clear presentation of the various points of comparison. Notice also an occasional contrasting point.

Both nations are federations, and the ticklish problems of federal-state relationships often give anxious moments to their governments and peoples. Both have a written constitution and a supreme court that often has to be its official interpreter, though in India the constitution is more detailed, and thus the court's scope for interpretation is more limited. The judiciary is independent of the executive in both countries. Both are pledged to maintain the rule of law and all civil liberties, including the right to freedom of discussion and freedom of assembly. Indeed, so close is the resemblance in this matter that there is hardly any issue of the fortnightly publication of the Indian Civil Liberties Union that does not note and summarize relevant judgments of the American Supreme Court, often comparing the view taken in like circumstances by the Indian courts, pointing out the development of certain doctrines in the United

States, and sometimes urging the acceptance of the same view in India. The law is a respected profession in both countries. Complaints about the delays and costs of legal procedure are not unknown in the United States, though they are not so common as in India. Observance of the rule that the burden of proof is on the prosecution, and that no man is guilty until he is legally proved so, is equally strict in the two countries. [1]

Study the model comparison which follows:

In the plant world the road runner's opposite number is certainly the cactus. To most people — and quite properly — it is the desert plant par excellence. Many kinds are, like the road runner, at home in the desert and nowhere else. Like the road runner also they belong to a family of pioneers which moved into arid America and changed itself radically to meet the new conditions. Most of the cuckoo tribe live by following other habits in other environments. The relatives of the desert cacti do the same. [2]

DISCUSSION

Joseph Wood Krutch compares a cactus to a road runner. He announces the comparison with the topic sentence: "In the plant world the road runner's opposite number is certainly the cactus." Yet, he stresses the similarities:

1. The cactus and road runner are at home in the desert and nowhere else.
2. Both belong to a family of pioneers which moved into arid America.
3. Both changed radically to meet the new conditions.
4. Most of the cuckoo tribe live by following other habits in other environments. The relatives of the desert cacti do the same.

Joseph Wood Krutch uses the words "like" and "same" to indicate the points of similarity.

Study the following model comparison. The writer begins with a rather generalized statement and ends with a specific statement of the comparison between New England and the Southwest. And though he notes contrast between a New England summer and one in the Southwest, he is mainly interested in pointing out similarities between the two regions.

This world, for all its caressing warmth, does not teem. It can be brilliantly colorful but it is never, as a New England summer often is, lush. And like New England at every season except summer, it has its own special kind of austerity, one which has, again like New England, its origin in a climatic severity. Long-continued cold in the one case, long-continued drought in the other, teaches the inhabitants of both regions an art of endurance which gives to each region what many find a part of its charm; and a New Englander might reasonably be expected, for that very reason, to learn more easily to love this land than those natives to climates in every way softer could be expected to love it. "Damn braces; bless relaxes" said Blake, and drought and cold are the "damns" which brace, respectively, New England and the Southwest. [3]

EXERCISES

1. Comparison

   Read the model comparison below. Make a complete sentence outline of its organizational structure. Answer the questions below.

   The experiences of the Chinese and the Hindus have marked similarities, but the tragic experience of the Hebrews is unique. China and India have each known an almost changeless civilization during two thousand years, securely based on a national religion and an ethical code that reflect a national soul at peace with itself. Even the challenge of foreign religions — Buddhism in China and Mohammedanism in India — has not upset the basic pattern. Both nations have lived self-contained lives with little curiosity about the lands beyond their borders, except in commerce, but both have been exploited for the past four hundred years by more aggressive peoples from the West. Both hold immense lands which are still too small to support their vast populations. As a result both face bewildering problems of adjustment in the twentieth century. [4]

   1. What is the topic sentence? Does it announce the comparison?
   2. List the guide words that aid coherence.
   3. How many points of comparison are there?

2. Comparison

   Read the model comparison below. Answer the questions which follow it.

There remains little critical disagreement with respect to the eminence of *Benito Cereno* and *Billy Budd* in American literature. Both are supremely representative of Melville and both attest to the great originating power of the American mind in art. Both are capable of providing abundantly the simple pleasure of first encounter, without respect to their great variety and complexity in significance. As works inviting studious exploration, they are among the richest in the literature of the English-speaking nations. Each encompasses history in its endless paradox; each unfolds in the symbolism that has been traced here. [5]

    1. What is the function of the opening sentence?
    2. What are the guide words?
    3. How many points of comparison are there?
    4. What are the subjects being compared?

3. Comparison

Read the model comparison below. Make a topic outline of its organizational pattern. Answer the questions which follow it.

Perhaps the best way for us to appreciate Poe's nightmare vision of what it is like to be without an identity, or to have one and lose it, is to compare his narrators with two modern and more fully developed fictional characters in the same predicament. A number of parallels exist, for instance, between Poe's composite criminal-victim and Joe Christmas in William Faulkner's *Light in August* (1932). Of uncertain parentage, brought up by foster parents whom he leaves hurriedly for fear he may have killed his foster father, Christmas looks like "a phantom, a spirit, strayed out of its own world and lost." An old Negro gardener tells him: "'You don't know what you are. And more than that, you won't never know. You'll live and you'll die and you won't never know.'" As a child at the orphanage, Christmas is, like the narrator of "The Tell-Tale Heart," constantly under the surveillance of an old man, who turns out to be his grandfather. "If the child had been older he would perhaps have thought *He hates me and fears me. So much so that he cannot let me out of his sight.*" As might be expected, Joe Christmas develops into a man who seeks to hurt and be hurt, assailing those who love him and in the end passively and peacefully accepting the violence of those who hate him.

There are resemblances, too, between Poe's tales of terror and Ralph Ellison's *Invisible Man* (1952). Ellison's hero, like the "I" of "MS. Found in a Bottle" is invisible and nameless, existing in a world where dream and reality fade into each other. He undergoes a number of initiatory experiences, each of them disillusioning. One scene places the hero in an electrified glass box where he is to receive shock treatment. Dimly reminiscent of "The Pit and the Pendulum," with physicians replacing the Inquisitors, the episode is superficially comic, but really appalling. At the end of the novel the hero inadvertently goes underground. Chased by two white men, he falls into an open manhole. Lost in the darkness, he burns various identification papers to light his way out but discovers that there is no exit. There is some hope that he will eventually emerge from this womb-tomb, his identity affirmed. [6]

1. What is the function of the topic sentence in paragraph one?
2. What are the two subjects being compared in the first paragraph? In the second paragraph?
3. List the guide words in both paragraphs.
4. What is the function of the opening sentence in the second paragraph?
5. What is the central thought that links both paragraphs?

ASSIGNMENT

1. Comparison

Write a paragraph of 100 to 150 words developed by comparison on one of the following topics.

1. Luxury and necessity
2. Family: today and yesterday
3. College and high school: teachers (courses, facilities, etc.)
4. Dating and going steady
5. Movies and television
6. Two famous men or women
7. Two generations of college students
8. Two American automobiles
9. Two magazines (newspapers)
10. Two vacation spots

At this time, review the transitional words and expressions which will help you to move your reader smoothly and logically through your developing comparisons and contrasts.

COMPARISON	CONTRAST
both	but
each	in contrast
like	however
respectively	yet
likewise	on the contrary
similarly	on the other hand
also	opposite
and	difference

Contrast

In writing contrast, you structure thought differently from comparison since you must consider contrasting points. A preliminary plan and outline, therefore, are even more essential in order to determine true and relevant points of contrast and to effectively present them. Suppose, for example, you were given the assignment to contrast Mussolini and Hitler. Your first step would be to list as many points as possible, making sure that for every point under Subject A, Mussolini, you have a comparable contrasting point under Subject B, Hitler. Your preliminary plan might look something like this one:

Preliminary plan

Purpose: To show the differences between Mussolini and Hitler

Subject A (Mussolini)	Subject B (Hitler)
1. a short fat man with a round face and bald head	1. a short, thin man with piercing eyes and a strange hair cut
2. moderate and progressive thinker	2. believed in a weird, irrational ideology
3. constantly changed views according to political climate	3. held firm to his beliefs to the end
4. never regarded Fascist docrine as a permanent thing	4. held to a narrow, rigid doctrine and policy
5. followed a temperate course regarding war	5. prepared for and welcomed war
6. killed by his own people	6. killed himself
7. no strong racial feelings	7. persecuted the Jews
8. strutted and talked a great deal but didn't mean everything he said	8. a fanatic who believed everything he said

Eliminate any irrelevant or less important points of contrast.

Next, decide on a pattern of organization and development which will best fulfill your purpose and suit your material. If you wish to keep each subject in its entirety before the reader, organize and develop by "wholes" — a subject-at-a-time contrast. If you wish to emphasize the points of the contrast, develop and organize point by point (alternating pattern).

In the subject-at-a-time pattern, you can begin your contrast with a topic sentence, clarifying your purpose and announcing your contrast. For example, "The two top Fascists, Hitler and Mussolini, were eventually lumped together as twin Fascist dictators, but it is important to understand that there was a great deal of difference between the two men and the two regimes." You then present a complete picture of Subject A in the remainder of the same paragraph or in only the first part of that paragraph. In the second paragraph or in the second part of the first paragraph, you present a complete picture of Subject B, discussing comparable contrasting points. You may find it necessary to clarify, explain, or elaborate on each point in making clear the contrasts. Thus, in this kind of development, you obtain completeness by adequately supporting the contrast between the two or more subjects.

You can modify this pattern slightly by beginning at once with the points of contrast and concluding with a statement of the main idea (particular to general order). In organizing and developing contrast, you must keep both sides before the reader by firmly establishing true points of contrast and maintaining them in logical order throughout the development. A skillfully prepared preliminary plan will help you establish true points of contrast. In addition, a well-structured outline will aid you in organizing the material before you begin to write. Study the sentence outline for the contrast between Mussolini and Hitler, the subject of the preliminary plan on page 195.

Mussolini and Hitler

Statement of Thesis: To show the differences between the two top Fascists, Mussolini and Hitler.

I.   There were many differences between Mussolini and Hitler.
    A. Mussolini was a pragmatic and moderate Fascist.
    B. No racial doctrine in Italian Fascist ideology.

    C. Mussolini changed views constantly.

    D. He followed a temperate course regarding war.

II. Hitler was very different.

    A. He was an irrational and fanatical Fascist leader.

    B. He slaughtered over five million Jews.

    C. He followed an unswerving and weird ideology.

    D. He welcomed war.

Read now the model paragraphs used for discussion purposes.

    The two top Fascists, Hitler and Mussolini, were eventually lumped together as twin Fascist dictators, but it is important to understand that there was a great deal of difference between the two men and between their two regimes. Mussolini was, at least until toward the end of his career, more pragmatic and moderate. There was, for example, no racial doctrine in Italian Fascist ideology. Mussolini had founded the Fascist movement without any overpowering preconceptions; he constantly changed tack according to the political climate and never regarded Fascist doctrine or policy as a fixed entity. He was always ready to add or subtract or go off in a new direction. Though Mussolini talked of the glories of war and the need for a militaristic policy, he followed a more temperate course in practice and kept the peace for thirteen years, knowing full well that Italy would gain nothing by a major war.

    Hitler was very different. He carved out a weird, irrational ideology near the beginning of his career and adhered to it unswervingly. Though he had a fine sense of political tactics and timing, he was no pragmatist like Mussolini, but was bent on certain fixed, narrow ends. His mind betrayed the marks of severe emotional instability, conceiving irrational hatreds and enthusiasms of a thoroughly demonic nature which he was determined to see through to the end. Hitler's thirst for power and domination ultimately knew no bounds. Mussolini merely talked and strutted, but Hitler meant every bit of his bellicosity. He was prepared for war, should it come, for he was willing to wage the most frightful war of all time. When he said the Jewish curse had to be eliminated once and for all, it led to the slaughter of five million people. Italian fascism was comparatively quiescent until the Nazi example spurred it to new activity; the dynamic pace of Hitler hardly flagged from January 1933 to April 1945. In the process, anti-Semitism, the concentration camps, and slave labor produced a febrile and sadistic nightmare without any parallel in the Italian experience. [7]

The subject-at-a-time pattern works best in short papers since the reader can keep the points of contrast related to each subject more easily in mind than in a rather long paper.

If you wish to stress individual points of contrast instead of the "wholes" or if you are writing a rather long paper containing many points of contrast and clarifying material with each point, you organize and develop the contrast *point by point* or in *alternating pattern*. In structuring this pattern, you may announce the contrast and the main idea in an opening topic sentence or conclude with the main idea. Then you present first one point concerning Subject A, and follow immediately with a comparable and contrasting point concerning Subject B. You continue onward in the same way until you have exhausted all the points. You should, of course, structure a preliminary plan and an outline to assist you in organizing this pattern. Study the model point by point contrast which follows.

Yet there are differences too. The Hindu is an extreme mystic, the Chinese an intensely practical thinker. The Hindu's caste system has long supported the aristocratic principle in Indian society, whereas the democratic tradition has always been strong in China, even through centuries of monarchy. Of all peoples the Hindus are most lacking in a sense of time, so that even the major events in Indian history are sometimes difficult to date. The Chinese, on the other hand, have a meticulous interest in chronology and consider history the most honorable form of literature. The greatest Indian poetry is narrative, especially epic; the Chinese poets have best expressed themselves in lyrics. [8]

Consider now a preliminary plan for the above paragraph.

Preliminary plan

Purpose: To show the differences between the Hindu and the Chinese

Differences between the Hindu and the Chinese

1. Hindu — a mystic	1. Chinese — a practical thinker
2. caste system	2. democratic system
3. Hindu — no sense of time	3. meticulous concerning time
4. narrative poetry	4. lyrical poetry

A sentence outline for the same model might look something like the following:

Contrast between the Hindu and the Chinese

Statement of Thesis: To show the differences between the Hindu and the Chinese.

I. There are also differences between the Hindu and the Chinese.
   A. The Hindu is an extreme mystic.
   B. The Chinese is a practical thinker.
   C. The caste system has been an important part of Indian society.
   D. The democratic system has been very strong in China.
   E. The Hindu is lacking in a sense of time.
   F. The Chinese is very concerned with time.
   G. Indian poetry is narrative.
   H. Chinese poetry is lyrical.

Study the model point by point contrast which follows. Observe that the writer considers one point concerning astrology in China in the first part of the second sentence and follows at once with a contrasting point concerning Babylonian astrology in the second half of the same sentence. He then develops point by point in separate sentences. Notice also that he closes the discussion with a comment of his own.

Babylonian astrology became a second celestial religion; but it was quite unlike the first, that of ancient China. In China the stars became gods; in Babylon the gods became stars. To the Chinese the mysteries of the cosmos were so sublime that they degraded their traditional popular divinities to demons and created a cult of the stars without priests, myths, or dogmas. The Babylonians, on the other hand, placed their native divinities one after another in the heavens, and transferred the mythic traits of these divinities to the stars. Here was an amazing evolution: for the first and only time a civilized religion rendered the divine beings visible and calculable by identifying them with the seven wandering stars. [9]

DISCUSSION

A sentence outline best reveals the structural organization of this alternating pattern.

Babylonian and Chinese Astrology

Statement of Thesis: To show the differences between Babylonian and Chinese astrology.

I. Babylonian astrology became a second celestial religion; but it was quite unlike the first, that of ancient China.
    A. In China the stars became gods.
    B. In Babylon the gods became stars.
    C. To the Chinese the mysteries of the cosmos were so sublime that they degraded their traditional popular divinities to demons and created a cult of the stars without priests, myths, or dogmas.
    D. The Babylonians, on the other hand, placed their native divinities one after another in the heavens, and transferred the mystic traits of these divinities to the stars.
    E. Concluding statement: Here was an amazing evolution: for the first and only time a civilized religion rendered the divine beings visible and calculable by identifying them with the seven wandering stars.

EXERCISES

4. Contrast

Read the model contrast below. Answer the questions which follow it.

The way of the desert and the way of the jungle represent the two opposite methods of reaching stability at two extremes of density. In the jungle there is plenty of everything life needs except mere space, and it is not for want of anything else that individuals die or that races have any limit set to their proliferation. Everything is on top of everything else; there is no cranny which is not both occupied and disputed. At every moment, war to the death rages fiercely. The place left vacant by any creature that dies is seized almost instantly by another, and life seems to suffer from nothing except too favorable an environment. In the desert, on the other hand, it is the environment itself which serves as the limiting factor. To some extent the struggle of creature against creature is mitigated, though it is of course not abolished even in the vegetable kingdom. For the plant which is in the one place would be strangled to death by its neighbor dies a thirsty seedling in the desert because that same neighbor has drawn the scant moisture from the spot of earth out of which it was attempting to spring. [10]

1. What is the function of the first sentence?
2. Is the contrast developed by an alternating pattern or by a subject-at-a-time pattern?
3. What transitional words signal a change in the direction of the writer's thought and emphasize the contrast?
4. What is the chief point of contrast? Are there other contrasting points or could this material be considered as support?
5. Does the writer also discuss a situation common to both the desert and the jungle?

5. Contrast

Read the model contrast below. Answer the questions that follow it.

To come from India to China is like waking from a dream. Often in India I felt that I was in an enchanted land. Melancholy, monotony, austerity; a sense as of perennial frost, spite of the light and heat; a lost region peopled with visionary forms; a purgatory of souls doing penance till the hour of deliverance shall strike; a limbo, lovely but phantasmal, unearthly, over-earthly — that is the kind of impression India left on my mind. I reach China, awake, and rub my eyes. This, of course, is the real world. This is every-day. Good temper, industry, intelligence. Nothing abnormal or over-strained. The natural man, working, marrying, begetting and rearing children, growing middle-aged, growing old, dying — and that is all. Here it is broad daylight; but in India, moon or stars, or a subtler gleam from some higher heaven. Recall, for example, Benares — the fantastic buildings rising and falling like a sea, the stairs running up to infinity, the sacred river, the sages meditating on its banks, the sacrificial ablutions, the squealing temple-pipes, and, in the midst of this, columns of smoke, as the body returns to the elements and the soul to God. This way of disposing of the dead, when the first shock is over, lingers in the mind as something eminently religious. Death and dissolution take place in the midst of life, for death is no more a mystery than life. In the open air, in the press of men, the soul takes flight. She is no stranger, for everything is soul — houses, trees, men, the elements into which the body is resolved. Death is not annihilation, it is change of form; and through all changes of form the essence persists. [11]

1. What is the function of the first sentence?
2. What is the pattern of development?

3. What point of contrast does the writer develop extensively? Why?

6. Contrast

Read the model contrast below. Answer the questions that follow it.

Thus the Puritan was made up of two different men, the one all self-abasement, penitence, gratitude, passion, the other proud, calm, inflexible, sagacious. He prostrated himself in the dust before his Maker: but he set his foot on the neck of his king. In his devotional retirement, he prayed with convulsions, and groans, and tears. He was half-maddened by glorious or terrible illusions. He heard the lyres of angels or the tempting whispers of fiends. He caught a gleam of the Beatific Vision, or woke screaming from dreams of everlasting fire. Like Vane, he thought himself intrusted with the sceptre of the millennial year. Like Fleetwood, he cried in the bitterness of his soul that God had hid his face from him. But when he took his seat in the council, or girt on his sword for war, these tempestuous workings of the soul had left no perceptible trace behind them. People who saw nothing of the godly but their uncouth visages, and heard nothing from them but their groans and their whining hymns, might laugh at them. But those had little reason to laugh who encountered them in the hall of debate or in the field of battle. These fanatics brought to civil and military affairs a coolness of judgement and an immutability of purpose which some writers have thought inconsistent with their religious zeal, but which were in fact the necessary effects of it. The intensity of their feelings on one subject made them tranquil on every other. One overpowering sentiment had subjected to itself pity and hatred, ambition and fear. Death had lost its terrors and pleasure its charms. They had their smiles and their tears, their raptures and their sorrows, but not for the things of this world. Enthusiasm had made them Stoics, had cleared their minds from every vulgar passion and prejudice, and raised them above the influence of danger and of corruption. It sometimes might lead them to pursue unwise ends, but never to choose unwise means. They went through the world, like Sir Artegal's iron man Talus with his flail, crushing and trampling down oppressors, mingling with human beings, but having neither part nor lot in human infirmities, insensible to fatigue, to pleasure, and to pain, not to be pierced by any weapon, not to be withstood by any barrier. [12]

1. Write a good title for this selection.
2. What is the method of development used to make clear the contrast?

3. To what two men is the Puritan compared?
4. In what way does the writer conclude his contrast?
5. Would the allusion to Talus likely be effective if this piece of writing were written today?

7. Contrast

Read the model contrast below. Answer the questions that follow it.

I have lived by the sea-shore and by the mountains. — No, I am not going to say which is best. The one where your place is is the best for you. But this difference there is: you can domesticate mountains, but the sea is *feræ naturæ.* You may have a hut, or know the owner of one, on the mountain-side; you see a light half-way up its ascent in the evening, and you know there is a home, and you might share it. You have noted certain trees, perhaps; you know the particular zone where the hemlocks look so black in October when the maples and beeches have faded. All the reliefs and intaglios have electrotyped themselves in the medallions that hang round the walls of your memory's chamber. — The sea remembers nothing. It is feline. It licks your feet, — its huge flanks purr very pleasantly for you; but it will crack your bones and eat you, for all that, and wipe the crimsoned foam from its jaws as if nothing had happened. The mountains give their lost children berries and water; the sea mocks their thirst and lets them die. The mountains have a grand, stupid, lovable tranquility; the sea has a fascinating, treacherous intelligence. The mountains lie about like huge ruminants, their broad backs awful to look upon, but safe to handle. The sea smooths its silver scales until you cannot see their joints — but their shining is that of a snake's belly, after all. — In deeper suggestiveness I find as great a difference. The mountains dwarf mankind and foreshorten the procession of its long generations. The sea drowns out humanity and time; it has no sympathy with either; for it belongs to eternity, and of that it sings its monotonous song forever and ever. [13]

1. Does the writer announce his contrast?
2. By what pattern of development does the writer make clear the contrast?
3. Look up the meaning of the word *personification* if you do not already know it. Does a knowledge of its meaning help in appreciating this contrast?
4. Compare the language in this contrast with the language in the model contrast in Exercise 4.

5. The writer contrasts, compares, and contrasts the sea in one part of this selection. Explain this statement.

8. Contrast

Read the model contrast below. Answer the questions that follow it.

When I was a college senior in 1939, we used to sing a plaintive song about going out into the "cold, cold world." It wasn't really so very cold then, but we did enjoy meditating on the fraughtness of it all. It was a big break we were facing, we told ourselves, and those of us who were going to try our luck in the commercial world could be patronizing toward those who were going on to graduate work or to academic life. We were taking the leap.

Seniors still sing the song, but somehow the old note of portent is gone. There is no leap left to take. The union between the world of organization and the college has been so cemented that today's seniors can see a continuity between the college and the life thereafter that we never did. Come graduation, they do not go outside to a hostile world; they transfer. [14]

1. Write a good title for this selection.
2. Are the points of contrast as clearly delineated in this model as in others that you have studied?
3. Do you consider this an effective contrast? Why? Why not?

Though the subject-at-a-time and the point by point are the most common methods of organizing and developing comparisons and contrasts, writers modify these basic orders in certain ways. In the model contrast below, the subject-at-a-time pattern is slightly modified. Study the model; then, in a sentence or two explain the modification.

[1] The difference between the two can be seen most clearly in the great art of each type. Mozart is a typical composer of the classic school. His music is calm, restrained, reasonable, the melodies and harmonies are clear and perfect. The emotions are subordinated to the forms used. Beethoven followed Mozart in his early works; and his early symphonies, notably the second and the fourth, are classic. But his more characteristic symphonies, such as the fifth and the ninth, are romantic. The music is personal and emotional; it expresses the struggles of the composer as he sought

to find peace and calm. It is not contained and perfect, but exuberant, exultant, and free.

[2] The difference, again, is clearly demonstrated if we take two pieces of sculpture, the Greek *Hegeso Stele* and the American *Adams Memorial* by Saint-Gaudens. Both are tombstones. The Greek stele shows us Hegeso with her servant; both are intently watching as Hegeso lifts some jewel from the box. It is a simple scene of every-day life, quiet and impersonal in its treatment. On the other hand, the Adams monument wraps us at once in mystery and questioning. A robed and hooded figure is seated before a severe granite slab. Is it man or woman? What does it Mean? Is it supposed to symbolize Death? Or Grief? Moreover, our attention no longer ends with the object, as it did with the stele of Hegeso; the object now serves as a point of departure for our emotions and questionings.

[3] The Greek temple is classic and the medieval cathedral is romantic. Both are religious edifices, but they show a difference in the attitudes that created them, a difference far deeper than the dissimilarities of construction and mechanics. The Greek temple is hard, bright, exact, calm and complete; the walls and the columns are no higher than will stand of their own strength; the lintels and the roof are simple, sane, and sensible. Nothing more is attempted than can be accomplished, and the result is a perfect building, finished and finite. Anyone can understand its main construction at a glance.

[4] The Gothic cathedral, on the other hand, is built on the principle of balance. The openings are not made with lintels but are arched. One stone is held in place only by its relation to the other stones. The walls will not stand alone; they must be buttressed. As the walls go higher the arches become more pointed, the roof becomes steeper, and the buttresses are strengthened with pinnacles and flying buttresses, the whole so carefully and cleverly balanced that a fault in one stone might cause a wall or even the entire building to collapse. The whole cannot be grasped at a glance; one is conscious only of its great complexity, its infinite variety, its striving upward and beyond.

[5] The Greek temple might be as solid as a statue, for all the feeling we have of its interior; the inside does not matter; it has no more character than the inside of a box. But with the Gothic cathedral, on the other hand, the outside sends us inevitably within. The inside is equally as complicated and diverse as the outside, with its aisles and arches, and the light coming in through stained-glass windows. One can never see the whole, but vistas like that corner of Chartres open up, and these are always changing as the

light changes. It is a mystery in light and dark, an experience of un-
limited space, and it is the essence of romanticism. [15]

Study the model which follows. Observe the space
allotted to the developing of the point concerning the American
Southwest. Notice also the emphatic final sentence.

In New England the struggle for existence is visibly the
struggle of plant with plant, each battling his neighbor for sunlight
and for the spot of ground which, so far as moisture and nourish-
ment are concerned, would support them all. Here, in the American
Southwest, the contest is not so much of plant against plant as of
plant against inanimate nature. The limiting factor is not the neighbor
but water; and I wonder if that is, perhaps, one of the things which
makes this country seem to enjoy a kind of peace one does not find
elsewhere. The struggle of living thing against living thing can be
distressing in a way that a mere battle with the elements is not. If
some clump of cactus dies this summer it will be because the cactus
has grown beyond the capacity of its roots to get water, not because
one green fellow creature has bested it in some limb-to-limb struggle.
In my more familiar East the crowding of the countryside seems almost to parallel the crowding of the cities. Out here there is, even in
nature, no congestion. [16]

Combining comparison and contrast
        In the following two models, observe the combination
of comparison and contrast.

Model 1
        Between Hobbes and John Locke (1632–1704) there
existed very little agreement and much contrast of opinion. They
concurred upon the tendency of man to be perverse and predatory
and agreed that government was necessary to prevent anarchy.
They also agreed that a government which does not bring about
public benefit should be deposed. Beyond these points they differed completely. Locke was a Whig who, unlike Hobbes, detested
the Stuarts and looked upon their reign as having neither legal
nor moral justification. After the deposition of the last Stuart king
in 1688, Locke was free to publish his political views in *Two Treatises
of Government* (1690). In these essays he intended largely to justify
the Glorious Revolution and uphold the new parliamentary government, but in so doing he achieved still more lasting importance by
unwittingly laying the groundwork for the Constitution of the United
States. [17]

Model 2

[1]When Hawthorne began writing, American literature as such hardly existed. Like Irving, with whom he must always be compared, Hawthorne was determined to create it. Both turned to the past of their regions, both hoped to transmute history into legend when genuine folk legend was lacking, both lamented the thinness of the American scene as material for art. But Hawthorne was not much, or for long, interested in the picturesque for its own sake, and as his insights were deeper than Irving's, so his achievement was greater. For Hawthorne, the past was chiefly interesting as a means of discovering *permanent* truth, including the reality of the present.

[2]A more revealing comparison may be made with Poe. if Hawthorne had written "The Masque of the Red Death," we may be sure he would have shaped it to embody a moral meaning. The action of the nobility in shutting themselves up in the castle and locking the gate that commoners might not share the supposed safety of their refuge Hawthorne would have seen not only as a breaking of the second Great Commandment, to "love thy neighbor as thyself," but as a self-imposed isolation, a breaking out of the "magic circle" of humanity, which would inevitably entail its proper doom. Poe's meaning is only, at last, that man cannot avoid death. Hawthorne, no less aware of man's mortality, would have explored the moral meanings of the attempt to do so.

[3]Both Poe and Hawthorne responded to "the power of blackness," both had "haunted" minds, both were Gothic — anti-realist — writers, and both are related to the Symbolist movement of the later century and of our own time. But Melville, another writer in the dark tradition, is closer than Poe to Hawthorne in the handling of symbols. Like Hawthorne, he sometimes wrote in the old tradition of allegory, working from abstractions toward emblematic characters and situations. Hawthorne's allegories spring from his moral imagination by way of Spenser and Bunyan. But both Hawthorne and Melville move, when their imaginations are most deeply aroused, into a kind of symbolic writing that is about half way between traditional allegory and the practice of contemporary symbolists like Faulkner. In Hawthorne's best fiction there is still a lack of realism, in the sense of detailed representation, a lack of that cetological ballast that makes *Moby Dick* a realistic study of whaling as well as a symbolic romance on the theme of Job; but to balance the lack there is a quality of imaginative control, of thoroughly created, shaped and molded, embodied meaning, the quality of the finished, the fully imagined work of art. If such completeness of control of meaning brings its limitations, it also offers its rewards. On this matter Hawthorne's work stands in sharp contrast to that of Melville and Faulkner. Here he is closer to Eliot. [18]

In his book *Pattern and Purpose in Writing* (Holt, Rinehart and Winston, 1963), Lavoisier Lamar points out an interesting variation of the contrast pattern by citing the following passage by S. I. Hayakawa. Hayakawa uses comparison to heighten the contrast. Observe how the similarities between poetry and advertising actually stress the differences.

[1] One does not often mention poetry and advertising in the same breath. Poetry is universally conceded to be the loftiest attainment of the verbal arts; its merits are attested to by the wise of all ages. Advertising, on the other hand, is not even an autonomous art; it is the handmaiden of commercial motives; its name carries connotations (well earned, one might add) of half-truths, deceptions, and outright fraud, of appeals to vanity, fear, snobbery, and false pride, of radio programs hideous with wheedling voices.

[2] Tthere are many more contrasts. The best poetry seems to be fully appreciated only by the few and to be beyond the comprehension of the many. Advertising, however, is considered best when it is laughed over, thought about, and acted upon by multitudes. Poetry is, in the general apprehension, something special to be studied in schools, to be enjoyed by cultivated people who have time for that sort of thing, to be read on solemn or momentous occasions. Advertising is a part of everyday life.

[3] But poetry and advertising have much in common. They both make every possible use of rhyme and rhythm, of words chosen for their connotative rather than their denotative values, of ambiguities that strike the level of unconscious responses as well as the conscious. Furthermore, they both strive to give meaning and overtones to the innumerable data of everyday experience; they both attempt to make the objects of experience symbolic of something beyond themselves. A primrose by the river's brim ceases to be "nothing more" because the poet invests it with meanings; it comes to symbolize the insensitiveness of Peter Bell, the benevolence of God, or anything else he wants it to symbolize. The advertiser is concerned with the primrose only if it happens to be for sale. Once it is on the national market, the advertiser can increase its saleability by making it thrillingly reminiscent of gaiety, romance, and aristocratic elegance, or symbolic of solid, traditional American virtues, or suggestive of glowing health and youth, depending upon his whim. This is what the writer of advertising does with breakfast food, toothpaste, laxatives, whisky, perfume, toilet bowl cleaners. Indeed almost all advertising directed to the general public is the *poeticizing of consumer goods.*

⁴Poetry and advertising are similar too in that they invite the reader to put himself in a role other than his own. In reading poetry we identify ourselves with the characters that a poet creates or with the poet himself. In the course of the experiences that a poet puts us through during these identifications, we feel as others have felt, we see as others have seen, we discover new ways of looking upon ourselves in our relationships with fellow human beings. Advertisers also invite us to make identifications of ourselves in new roles, although the roles are simpler, pleasanter, and more easily within reach. Readers are invited to look upon themselves as "smart housewives and hostesses" (who serve Spam), as "men of distinction" (who drink Calvert's), as responsible and prudent fathers (who protect their dependents with Metropolitan insurance policies), as well-regulated families (who take Ex-Lax). [19]

Points to remember

1. Define clearly your purpose.
2. Select comparable subjects from the same class or group.
3. List as many points of comparison or contrast as possible.
4. Eliminate less important and irrelevant points.
5. Prepare a preliminary plan.
6. Decide on a pattern of organization and development.
7. Structure a partial outline or a complete outline of the paper before writing.
8. Use transitional words and expressions to indicate comparisons and contrasts and aid in the flow of thought.

ASSIGNMENT

2. Contrast

Write a short theme of 300 to 500 words developed by contrast on one of the following topics.

1. Two famous persons (authors, generals, actors, actresses)
2. A foreign compact car and an American compact car
3. Two sports (football and rugby, perhaps)
4. Two philosophies, religions, ideologies
5. College and high school

6. Snow skiing and water skiing
7. London and Paris (any other cities)
8. Living at college and living at home
9. Small college and large college
10. Fraternities; high school and college
11. Two customs
12. Two dates
13. Weapons: yesterday and today
14. Christmas: yesterday and today
15. Dating and going steady

Study now these longer pieces of writing.

"THEY" AND "WE"
by Malcolm Cowley

[1] It was in the Working Girls' Home that I first became conscious of the difference between two generations. There were two sorts of people here: those who had lived in the Village before 1917 and those who had just arrived from France or college. For the first time I came to think of them as "they" and "we."

[2] They wore funny clothes: it was the first thing that struck you about them. The women had evolved a regional costume, then widely cartooned in the magazines: hair cut in a Dutch bob, hat carried in the hand, a smock of some light fabric (often embroidered Russian linen), a skirt rather shorter than the fashion of the day, gray cotton stockings and sandals. With heels set firmly on the ground and abdomens protruding a little — since they wore no corsets and dieting hadn't become popular — they had a look of unexampled solidity; it was terrifying to be advanced upon by six of them in close formation. But this costume wasn't universal. Some women preferred tight-fitting tailored suits with Buster Brown collars; one had a five-gallon hat which she wore on all occasions, and there was a girl who always appeared in riding boots, swinging a crop, as if she had galloped down Sixth Avenue, watered her horse, and tied him to a pillar of the Elevated; I called her Yoicks. The men, as a rule, were more conventional, but tweedy and unpressed. They did not let their hair grow over their collars, but they had a good deal more of it than was permitted by fashion. There were a few Russian blouses among them, a few of the authentic Windsor ties that marked the bohemians of the 1890's.

[3] "They" tried to be individual, but there is a moment when individualism becomes a uniform in spite of itself. "We" were accustomed to uniforms and content to wear that of the American middle classes. We dressed inconspicuously, as well as we were able.

⁴"They" were older, and this simple fact continued to impress me long after I ceased to notice their clothes. Their ages ran from sixty down to twenty-three; at one end of the scale there was hardly any difference. But the Village had a pervading atmosphere of middle-agedness. To stay in New York during the war was a greater moral strain than to enter the army; there were more decisions to be made and uneasily justified; also there were defeats to be concealed. The Village in 1919 was like a conquered country. Its inhabitants were discouraged and drank joylessly. "We" came among them with an unexpended store of energy: we had left our youth at home, and for two years it had been accumulating at compound interest; now we were eager to lavish it even on trivial objects.

⁵And what did the older Villagers think of us? We had fresh faces and a fresh store of jokes and filthy songs collected in the army; we were nice to take on parties, to be amused by and to lecture. Sometimes they gave us advice which was never taken because it was obviously a form of boasting. I don't believe they thought much about us at all.

⁶But these differences in costume, age and mood were only the symbols of another difference. Though our paths had momentarily converged, they were not the same. "We" had followed the highroad; "they" had revolted and tried to break new trails.

⁷"They" had once been rebels, political, moral, artistic or religious — in any case they had paid the price of their rebellion. They had separated themselves from parents, husbands, wives; they had slammed doors like Nora in *A Doll's House*; they never got letters from home. "We," on the other hand, had never broken with our parents, never walked stormily out of church, never been expelled from school for writing essays on anarchism. We had avoided issues and got what we wanted in a quiet way, simply by taking it. During the ten years that preceded the war something had happened to the relations between parents and children. The older Villagers had been so close to their fathers and mothers that, in a way, they had been forced to quarrel and reject them. "We" had been placed at a greater distance from our elders; we liked and even loved them without in the least respecting their opinions; we said, "Yes, sir," if we were Southerners, "All right," if we lived in a Northern city, and did what we pleased.

⁸"They" had been rebels: they wanted to change the world, be leaders in the fight for justice and art, help to create a society in which individuals could express themselves. "We" were convinced at the time that society could never be changed by an effort of the will.

⁹"They" had been rebels, full of proud illusions. They made demands on life itself, that it furnish them with beautiful

adventures, honest friendships, love freely given and returned in an appropriate setting. Now, with illusions shattered, they were cynics. "We," on the contrary, were greatly humble and did not ask of Nature that she gild our happy moments or wildly reecho our passions. We did not feel that our arguments on aesthetics should take place in aesthetic surroundings: we were content to sit in the kitchen, two or three young men with our feet on the bare table, discussing the problem of abstract beauty while we rolled Bull Durham into cigarettes and let the flakes sift down into our laps. We had lost our ideals at a very early age, and painlessly. If any of them survived the war, they had disappeared in the midst of the bickerings at Versailles, or later with the steel strike, the Palmer Raids, the Ventralia massacre. But they did not leave us bitter. We believed that we had fought for an empty cause, that the Germans were no worse than the Allies, no better, that the world consisted of fools and scoundrels ruled by scoundrels and fools, that everybody was selfish and could be bought for a price, that we were as bad as the others — all this we took for granted. But it was fun all the same. We were content to build our modest happiness in the wreck of "their" lost illusions, a cottage in the ruins of a palace. [20]

MRS. KING & MRS. KENNEDY
by Mrs. Medgar Evers

[1] Listening to the final services for the Rev. Dr. Martin Luther King Jr., surrounded by faces as familiar as the morning papers, I sat with my daughter, Rena, thirteen, hearing the sounds of old, much-loved hymns, feeling myself pulled back five years to the time when we had gone through it ourselves.

[2] Seeing Coretta King with her four children, I knew what she had been through that morning: the hushed atmosphere in her home, the helpful hands laying out the unfamiliar black dress, the last-minute checking of each child's appearance, the fighting back of tears, knowing you must not let down until it is all, finally, over. Watching the photographers focus on her during the services, I felt again the emptiness in the pit of my stomach I had felt at Medgar's funeral, the hurtful knowledge that when you have shared your husband with all of his people, you cannot, even in your grief at his death, have privacy.

[3] It was too familiar, too painful, too much like what had happened to me for me to be able to separate myself from it. Beside me, as he had been at Medgar's funeral, was Medgar's brother, Charles. Nearby were friends who had stood at the graveside in Arlington National Cemetery as the guns were fired in the final salute.

I thanked God that today there would be no guns to remind Coretta King, as they had reminded me, of how the end had come.

⁴It was then that I remembered Jacqueline Kennedy and, rising, went to her. I murmured my name, and she gasped, "Oh, my goodness!" and took my hand. We stood like that for a moment, and I thought I could see in her eyes what I knew must be in my own: the sense that we, who had both been through this before, were here together seeing a third woman stricken in the same way.

⁵My daughter, Rena, had pleaded to fly with me to the funeral in Atlanta, and at the last minute I had decided to bring her. Seeing Yolanda, the Kings' oldest child, just her own age, Rena had wanted to go to her and comfort her, knowing what it was like.

⁶Now, Rena stood by me looking up at Mrs. Kennedy, and I became aware of a strange kinship of three young girls: Caroline Kennedy, Yolanda King, and my own Rena.

⁷They had all lost their fathers in the whirlwind of hate and violence. Three times, three Americans, mad with the belief that by killing a leader you can stop a movement, had found their targets in telescopic sights and squeezed a trigger in the insane hope of ending an era. Would these three girls have to raise their children in the shadow of the same hate that had blighted their youths?

⁸In the march from the church to Morehouse College, Dr. King's alma mater, nearly 200,000 Americans quietly demonstrated their mutual commitment to the struggle for justice that has already taken such a frightening toll. I saw old friends, people I had not seen for years. We all greeted each other silently; there was no need for words. We were marching beside each other still in the same march that had begun so long ago.

⁹When the service was over, Charles sat weeping, unable to move, exactly as he had five years before outside Fort Myer Chapel at Arlington, and I recalled what Bishop Stephen Gill Spottswood had said in that chapel service: "I hope that Medgar Evers will be the last black American to give his life in the struggle to make the Constitution come alive." He was not, of course, and I wondered now, with the death of Martin Luther King, how many, many more fine men must die before we achieve in America a community in which race is irrelevant.

¹⁰As Charles shook with sobs, Senator Robert F. Kennedy, who had also lost a brother to an assassin's bullet, came to sit beside him and comfort him. They sat, side by side, two men joined in bereavement, one black, one white, weeping for their lost brothers and for the man who had spent the last dozen years of his life trying to make us all brothers.

¹¹And that, more than anything, gave me hope for the future. Coretta King, Jacqueline Kennedy, and I, brought together by this latest tragedy, were linked not only by hideous coincidences

of the past. Here, on the same day, we were joined as well in our determination to be counted among those Americans who will continue to march toward the dream of Martin Luther King Jr. [21]

THE AMERICAN SICKNESS
by Stewart Alsop

[1] Something odd and new and interesting is beginning to happen in this jungle-city. Riot-wracked Newark, in which Negroes are now a majority of the population, may well be the prototype city of the American future. So this odd, new, and interesting phenomenon is worth describing.

[2] The convenient symbols of the phenomenon are LeRoi Jones and Tony Imperiale. LeRoi Jones is a poet, an intellectual, a Moslem, and a leading Negro militant and Whitey-baiter. Tony Imperiale is a karate instructor, a devout Catholic, and the leader of the North Ward Citizens' Committee. The members of his "committee" — Imperiale claims 1,500 in Newark and another 3,500 in allied committees in nearby towns — patrol the streets of the predominantly white North Ward, riding in cars with two-way radios, and wearing black-painted helmet liners. They are said to have an arsenal of at least 1,000 rifles. Their purpose is to protect the North Ward against what Imperiale has called "black radical animals."

[3] It is quite genuinely impossible to imagine two human beings more unlike in most ways than Jones and Imperiale. And yet there are certain ways in which LeRoi and Tony (they call each other by their first names) are oddly alike.

[4] Tony, a second-generation Italian-American, is a great granite block of a man. His arms are great, meaty bunches of muscle, and looking at his sledgehammer fists, you can believe the stories about how a karate expert can split a thick block of wood with a single blow.

[5] LeRoi Jones is a small, bearded man, with delicate, eloquent hands and dark, angry, wounded eyes. He has been convicted of carrying concealed weapons — two revolvers — during the 1967 Newark riot, and he is appealing the conviction. There is at least reason to suspect that he was convicted as much for his obscene and violently anti-white verse, which was read in court, as for the part he played in the riot.

[6] Tony Imperiale's English is of the "dem-dese-dose" variety, and he has no intellectual pretensions whatever. LeRoi Jones talks the English of the intellectuals, and talks it well. "Essentially what we are fighting for," he says, "is the power to define our lives. Newark is a city where black people are in the majority, and we mean to be masters of our own space."

[7] Despite such differences, there are those odd similarities all the same. Tony and his men like to dress up, in their black helmet liners and — until they were forbidden by the authorities — in olive-green fatigues. LeRoi Jones and his men like to dress up too — in tarbooshes, brightly colored turtleneck sweaters and red vests.

[8] Headquarters for Imperiale's Citizens' Committee is the one-story cinderblock building where Tony teaches karate. The helmet liners are hung on one wall of the meeting room, and tacked on another wall are such samples of black militant propaganda as a pamphlet on *How to Make Molotov Cocktails* and a flyer titled *The Wops Want Race War.*

[9] LeRoi Jones operates out of the Spirit House, a decaying clapboard house in the heart of the black slums of the Central Ward. The walls of the main meeting room are lined with oil paintings, some good, some very bad. Among the worst — artistically, at least — is a picture of a terrified, praying white man, being strangled by two black hands.

[10] Both Imperiale and LeRoi Jones are tireless talkers, and both are sick with the American sickness — an obsession with physical violence. Imperiale makes much of the fact that his "committee" disciplines white as well as black offenders against "law and order." "We found some young white punks pushing pills," he said, "and we pulled up alongside them in a patrol of six cars, and I said, 'You getthehell outta here, and if you come back we'll break your kneecaps and throw you in the sewer.' Sometimes you gotta talk a little rough to these punks."

[11] LeRoi Jones's verbal violence is reserved for "honkies," but he too thinks and dreams and writes in terms of the pain men can inflict on other men. One of his poems is a paean in praise of the pleasures of "smashing at jelly-white faces."

[12] There are other ways in which Imperiale and his people and Jones and his people think much alike. Both detest what seems to them the condescending and corrupt paternalism of the local and federal authorities. Both dismiss the poverty program as a farce, and both hate the public-housing program.

[13] Brother Kamil, "chief of security" for LeRoi Jones's Spirit House, took this reporter on a Cook's tour of black Newark. His Exhibit A was one of the high-rise, rent-subsidized, prison-like apartment buildings, still showing the scars inflicted by .50 caliber machine-gun bullets during the riot. "The people were trapped in there like rats," he said.

[14] On a similar tour of the North Ward, Imperiale used the same words. He pointed to a Negro-occupied high-rise in the edge of his ward. "That's where a lot of the trouble comes from," he said. "But what the hell did they expect? The people in there are trapped

like rats. They have nowhere to go and nothing to do."

[15]Imperiale feels nothing but contempt for the liberal-minded suburban ladies who descend on the black slums to prettify them by day, and retire to their split-levels by night. "That's a insult," says Imperiale, "painting their railings or cleaning up their messes, like they're dirty kids. We got more respect for them than that."

[16]His contempt for the liberalism of white suburbia is shared by LeRoi Jones. "At least," Jones says, "Tony Imperiale is an authentic spokesman for his people."

[17]"LeRoi and I don't love each other, that's for sure," says Imperiale, "but we respect each other."

[18]This mutual respect is born of a mutual predicament. Much has been written of the predicament of LeRoi Jones and his people — the poverty, the entrapment in the slums, the chasm that separates them from affluent white America. Very little has been written about the predicament of Tony Imperiale and his people.

[19]As in many other "core cities," there is no white middle class at all left in Newark. The poor whites who remain are there because they are poor. Threatened by violence and by an engulfing Negro tide, they feel themselves trapped and abandoned, and as alienated from affluent America as the Negroes.

[20]This mutuality has found physical expression in the "hot line" — a private telephone connection between Imperiale's karate house and LeRoi Jones's Spirit House. "Say we get a rumor a bunch of black punks is moving on the North Ward, or they get a rumor our guys are moving on the Central Ward," Imperiale explains. "Without the hot line — boom, we're at each other's throats. This way I can pick up the phone and check right away with LeRoi or Kamil, and they can check with me."

[21]The hot line suggests what is so odd, new, and interesting in Newark. For it reflects a kind of balance of terror, based on the mutually recognized territorial imperatives of the divided and tortured city. The balance is certainly unstable — even more unstable than the global balance of terror. But at least it exists. And if the mutuality of interest on which it is based is ever explicitly recognized by both LeRoi's people and Tony's people, a truly revolutionary situation will then exist. Then the comfortable whites in their comfortable suburbs may really have something to worry about. [22]

Analogy

Analogy is a method of organizing and developing thought by comparison. In structuring thought by analogy, a writer explains or clarifies an unfamiliar subject by likening it to a familiar subject. Writers use analogy to make the new, different, complex, difficult more understandable for the reader. Analogy, therefore, explains, clarifies, illustrates, simplifies; it does not prove anything.

In the model analogy below, Emerson compares society to a wave. Most analogies like this model are part of a larger piece of writing.

> Society is a wave. The wave moves onward, but the water of which it is composed does not. The same particle does not rise from the valley to the ridge. Its unity is only phenomenal. The persons who make up a nation to-day, next year die, and their experience dies with them. [23]

Writers will usually announce the analogy and then develop it. In addition, analogies, as a rule, rise spontaneously from the material as the writer's thoughts flow onward. Study the following model. Notice that the writer announces the comparison in the first sentence. To make the meaning clear, he compares the atmosphere of the earth to any window.

> The atmosphere of Earth acts like any window in serving two very important functions. It lets light in and it permits us to look out. It also serves as a shield to keep out dangerous or uncomfortable things. A normal glazed window lets us keep our houses warm by keeping out cold air, and it prevents rain, dirt, and unwelcome insects and animals from coming in. As we have already seen, Earth's atmospheric window also helps to keep our planet at a comfortable temperature by holding back radiated heat and protecting us from dangerous levels of ultraviolet light.
>
> Lately, we have discovered that space is full of a great many very dangerous things against which our atmosphere guards us. It is not a perfect shield, and sometimes one of these dangerous objects does get through. There is even some evidence that a few of these messengers from space contain life, though this has by no means been proved yet. [24]

In the model analogy that follows, decide which subject is the familiar and which subject is the unfamiliar one. Observe also that again the writer announces his analogy.

> We can perhaps form some sort of a picture of the nature of these spontaneous disintegrations or jumps, by comparing the atom to a party of four card-players who agree to break up as soon

as a hand is dealt in which each player receives just one complete suit. A room containing millions of such parties may be taken to represent a mass of radio-active substance. Then it can be shown that the number of card-parties will decrease according to the exact law of radio-active decay on one condition — *that the cards are well shuffled between each deal.* If there is adequate shuffling of the cards, the passage of time and the past will mean nothing to the card-players, for the situation is born afresh each time the cards are shuffled. Thus the death-rate per thousand will be constant, as with atoms of radium. But if the cards are merely taken up after each deal, without shuffling, each deal follows inevitably from the preceding, and we have the analogue of the old law of causation. Here the rate of diminution in the number of players would be different from that actually observed in radio-active disintegration. We can only reproduce this by supposing the cards to be continually shuffled, and the shuffler is he whom we have called fate. [25]

In the model which follows, the analogy is not formally announced; it is nevertheless very effective.

It is too often overlooked that we can only discuss these questions in terms of probabilities. The man of science is accustomed to the reproach that he changes his views all the time, with the accompanying implication that what he says need not be taken too seriously. It is no true reproach that in exploring the river of knowledge he occasionally goes down a backwater instead of continuing along the main stream; no explorer can be sure that a backwater is such, and nothing more, until he has been down it. What is more serious, and beyond the control of the explorer, is that the river is a winding one, flowing now east, now west. At one moment the explorer says: "I am going downstream, and, as I am going towards the west, the ocean which is reality seems most likely to lie in the westerly direction." And later, when the river has turned east, he says: "It now looks as though reality is in the east." No scientist who has lived through the last thirty years is likely to be too dogmatic either to the future course of the stream or as to the direction in which reality lies: he knows from his own experience how the river not only for ever broadens but also repeatedly winds, and, after many disappointments, he has given up thinking at every turn that he is at last in the presence of the

murmurs and scents of the infinite sea.

With this caution in mind, it seems at least safe to say that the river of knowledge has made a sharp bend in the last few years. [26]

Models of effective analogies

Model 1

The sea is old, old almost beyond imagining. And the earth itself is still older. To give some idea of just how old, we might try setting the ages of geologic time against the span of our own 12-month year. By that comparison, if we say the earth was formed about February, then the primeval ocean came into being perhaps as early as March, certainly no later than June. By the same yardstick, we would say that the first life appeared in August and the earliest fossils in November, dinosaurs had their day about mid-December and the age of man did not begin until the last day of the last week of the year — in fact, his real ascent from animals did not start until about 10:30 p.m. on the 365th day. [27]

Model 2

An analogy might help us to remember the principle of diffusion. Suppose we had a hundred blindfolded people tightly bunched in one corner of a large gymnasium and held in this corner by a surrounding rope. These people could move to a certain extent, but would be so crowded that they could not move freely about with one another. These we might compare to the crystal of dye with its molecules in the solid state. Now suppose that the rope was cut and the people were told to walk and keep walking. Those at the outer edge of the bunch could not move inward, but they could begin walking outward. As they moved out those farther in could begin walking. There would be frequent collisions at first among the congestion of the newly loosed people, but each time they collided they would turn and move in a different direction. Those that moved outward from the greater concentration of people would travel farther without collisions. When they hit the walls they would turn and go in a different direction. In the course of time there would be a gradual dispersion of people until they would be about equally spaced in the room and would remain that way even though they continued walking and bumping. If we think of the particles of a dissolved substance in place of the people and the energy of heat as the force which keeps them moving, we have a rough impression of what happens in diffusion. [28]

Model 3

We are in a strange position today. We have seen across billions of light-years to other universes. We have looked closely into all the nooks and crannies of our neighbor galaxies. And we have not been able to see much of our home galaxy, except by guessing and inferring. We do not have nearly as much solid information about the shape and character of the Milky Way as we do about a spiral galaxy called NCG 5149. (It is not a pretty name, but man cannot find a pretty title for every star and nebula found by now. It is a rather pretty galaxy, however, and we shall see it as if we were directly above it.

It is as if we had moved into a house and then found we were shut off from the rooms. If we want to know what we have, we have to go about the neighborhood, snooping busily into all the other houses that look like ours and may have been built from the same general plan. [29]

Model 4

What is the education which can do this? What is the furniture which makes the only place belonging absolutely to each of us, the world within, a place where we like to go? I wish I could answer that question. I wish I could produce a perfect decorator's design warranted to make any interior lovely and interesting and stimulating; but, even if I could, sooner or later we would certainly try different designs. My point is only that while we must and should change furniture, we ought to throw away old furniture very cautiously. It may turn out to be irreplaceable. A great deal was thrown away in the last generation or so, long enough to show some results. Furniture which had for centuries been foremost, we lightly, in a few years, discarded. The classics almost vanished from our field of education. That was a great change. There is a marked difference between the writers of the past and the writers of today who have been educated without the benefit of Greek and Latin. Is this a matter of cause and effect? People will decide for themselves, but I do not think anyone will question the statement that clear thinking is not the characteristic which distinguishes our literature today. We are more and more caught up by the unintelligible. People like it. This argues an inability to think, or, almost as bad, a disinclination to think. [30]

Model 5

Teaching may be compared to selling commodities. No one can sell unless someone buys. We should ridicule a merchant who said that he had sold a great many goods although no one had bought any. But perhaps there are teachers who think that they have done a good day's teaching irrespective of what pupils have learned. There is the same exact equation between teaching and learning that there is between selling and buying. The only way to increase the learning of pupils is to augment the quantity and quality of real teaching. Since learning is something that the pupil has to do himself and for himself, the initiative lies with the learner. The teacher is a guide and director; he steers the boat, but the energy that propels it must come from those who are learning. The more a teacher is aware of the past experiences of students, of their hopes, desires, chief interests, the better will he understand the forces at work that need to be directed and utilized for the formation of reflective habits. The number and quality of these factors vary from person to person. They cannot therefore be categorically enumerated in a book. But there are some tendencies and forces that operate in every normal individual, forces that must be appealed to and utilized if the best methods for the development of good habits of thought are to be employed. [31]

ASSIGNMENT

3. *Analogy*

Keeping in mind that an analogy is useful in explaining the unfamiliar to the reader, write an analogy on one of the following topics.

1. Jealousy is like an uncontrolled fire.
2. Hatred is like a cancer.
3. Common sense is like a compass.
4. Good study-habits are like a well-trained staff.
5. Maturing is like mountain climbing.
6. Education is like a safari.
7. Ignorance is like blindness.
8. Reading is like a voyage of discovery.
9. Prejudice is like a narrow skirt; one can walk neither very far nor very fast.
10. Constant nagging wears away the most solid rock of contentment.

CHAPTER SIX *References*

1. From *As Others See Us,* by A. D. Gorwala, copyright 1959 by Princeton University Press. Reprinted by permission of Princeton University Press.
2. From *The Voice of the Desert* by Joseph Wood Krutch.

Reprinted by permission of William Morrow and Company, Inc. Copyright © 1954 by Joseph Wood Krutch.

3. From *The Desert Year* by Joseph Wood Krutch. Reprinted by permission of William Morrow and Company, Inc. Copyright © 1952 by Joseph Wood Krutch.

4. Reprinted from *The World in Literature,* Volume I by Robert Warnock and George Anderson. Copyright 1950 by Scott, Foresman and Company, and reprinted with their permission.

5. From *American Literary Masters,* Volume I, edited by Charles R. Anderson. Copyright © 1965 by Holt, Rinehart and Winston, and reprinted with their permission.

6. From *American Literary Masters,* Volume I, edited by Charles R. Anderson. Cf. 5.

7. From *A History of the Western World: 1715 to the Present* by Clough, et al. Copyright © 1964 by D. C. Heath and Company, and reprinted with their permission.

8. Reprinted from *The World in Literature,* Volume I, by Robert Warnock and George Anderson. Cf. 4.

9. From *And There Was Light* by Rudolf Thiel, translated by Richard and Clara Winston. Copyright © 1957 by Alfred A. Knopf, Inc., and reprinted with their permission.

10. From *The Desert Year* by Joseph Wood Krutch. Cf. 3.

11. From *Appearances* by G. Lowes Dickinson. Copyright 1914. By permission of Withers, Nicholl, Manisty & Co., London.

12. From "The Puritans" by Thomas Babington Macaulay.

13. From "The Sea-shore and the Mountains" by Oliver Wendell Holmes.

14. From *The Organizational Man* by William H. Whyte, Jr. Copyright © 1956 by William H. Whyte, Jr. By permission of Simon & Schuster, Inc.

15. From *The Humanities* by Louise Dudley and Austin Faricy. Copyright © 1940 and 1951 by McGraw-Hill Book Company, Inc. By permission.

16. From *The Desert Year* by Joseph Wood Krutch. Cf. 3.

17. From *Backgrounds of American Literary Thought,* Second Edition, by Rod W. Horton and Herbert W. Edwards. Copyright © 1967 by Meredith Publishing Company. Reprinted by permission of Appleton-Century-Crofts, Inc.

18. From *American Literary Masters,* edited by Charles Anderson. Cf. 5.

19. From "Poetry and Advertising" by S. I. Hayakawa. Originally appeared in *Poetry*; copyright 1946 by The Modern Poetry Association. Reprinted by permission of the Editor of *Poetry* and the author.

20. From *Exile's Return* by Malcolm Cowley. Copyright 1934, 1935, 1941, 1951, copyright © renewed 1962, 1963 by Malcolm Cowley. Reprinted by permission of The Viking Press, Inc.

21. "Mrs. King and Mrs. Kennedy," by Mrs. Medgar Evers, in *The Ladies' Home Journal* (June, 1968). Copyright © 1968 by The Curtis Publishing Company. Reprinted by permission of Curtis Brown, Inc.

22. "The American Sickness" by Stewart Alsop, in *The Saturday Evening Post* (July 13, 1968). Reprinted by permission of the author.

23. From "Self-Reliance" by Ralph Waldo Emerson.

24. From *The Mysterious Sky* by Lester del Rey. Copyright © 1964 by Lester del Rey. Reprinted by permission of Chilton Book Company.

25. From *The Mysterious Universe* by Sir James Jeans. Reprinted by permission of the publisher, The Cambridge University Press.

26. From *The Mysterious Universe* by Sir James Jeans. Cf. 25.

27. From "The Sea" in *Life Nature Library,* by Leonard Engel and the Editors of *Life.* Copyright © 1961 by Time, Inc. Reprinted by permission of Time-Life, Inc.

28. From *Biology and Its Relation to Mankind* by A. M. Winchester. Copyright 1964, D. Van Nostrand and Company, Inc., Princeton, New Jersey.

29. From *The Mysterious Sky* by Lester del Rey. Cf. 24.

30. From "Lessons of the Past" by Edith Hamilton, in *The Saturday Evening Post* (September 27, 1958). Reprinted by permission of Doris Fielding Reid.

31. From *How We Think* by John Dewey. Copyright D. C. Heath and Company, and reprinted with their permission.

SEVEN
Breaking down a subject

Analysis is a method of organizing and developing thought by breaking down a subject into its component parts in order to convey a discovery about it to the reader. By breaking down the "whole" into its parts, a writer can treat each part separately, making its relationship to the whole and the other parts clearer. In this book, analysis is broken down into three methods of organizing and developing thought: (1) by classification, (2) by division, and (3) by cause and effect or effect and causes.

Since all analysis is a method of thought by which the "whole" is broken down, you might assume that confusion could result by such arbitrary divisions of the process. Such need not be the case. You will find some of the methods distinctly different. In others the intent of the writer serves as a guide to the dominant kind of development.

Classification

In developing thought with analysis by classification, you break down a subject into groups or classes in order to give order and meaning to a number of persons, places, things, events, or ideas. With a clearly defined purpose in mind, you group or classify on the basis of distinctive characteristics, traits or qualities. You might wish, for example, to inform the people in your town that you are attending a college that rates high in academic circles. You write an article for the home town newspaper which includes sections developed by classification: the faculty broken down on the basis of degrees, stressing the large number of doctorates, the student body broken down into categories on the basis of grades and high scholarship. As a member of student government, you might find it necessary to break down the student body into groups on the basis of age, marital status, political, religious, or social affiliations, or into those students who are employed full-time, part-time, or who do not work while going to school.

Many classifications are already part of your experience. You may have given order to a collection of books, rocks, coins, Indian arrows or stamps by placing them into readily identifiable groups. You have probably become aware of classifications in your schooling: kinds of plants and animals, races of men, types of clouds, volcanoes, glaciers, and storms. Whatever the classification, the purpose is clear: to give order and meaning to a seemingly disorganized mass of persons, places, things, happenings, or ideas.

When you break down a subject into major classes, you are structuring what is known as a *simple system of classification*. You are already familiar with many simple systems of classification; for example, races, sports, automobiles, clouds, rocks, animals, plants, clothes, political parties, governments. The model classification which follows, though somewhat mechanical in structure, illustrates the simple system of classification. The writer breaks down motives into five classes on the basis of needs underlying the motives.

Maslow's classification of motives. A more comprehensive classification of motives has been formulated by Maslow. He has proposed a theory of motivation in which motives are classified according to the basic needs underlying the motives. Needs are classified into five groups or levels and arranged in a hierarchy of pre-potency. This arrangement means that "the appearance of one need usually rests on the prior satisfaction of another, more prepotent need." The five groups of needs, listed in descending order of their pre-potency, are as follows:

1. *Physiological needs.* This group includes the need for food, for water, for oxygen, for constant temperature, etc.
2. *Safety needs.* These needs are concerned with seeking safety and avoiding pain, threats, and danger.
3. *Love needs.* These needs give rise to the desire to belong, to be wanted, to be loved by friends, relatives, and family.

4. *Esteem needs.* These needs give rise to the desire for self-respect, strength, achievement, adequacy, prestige, attention, and appreciation.
5. *Self-actualization needs.* This group is characterized by saying that one must do what he can do. [1]

A chart showing this classification looks like this:

Basis for classification: according to needs underlying the motives.

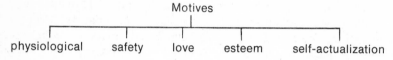

Further dividing of a subject into subdivisions is known as a *complex system of classification.* A very familiar example of this system is the classifying of words as parts of speech.

Basis for classification: the way a word is used in a sentence.

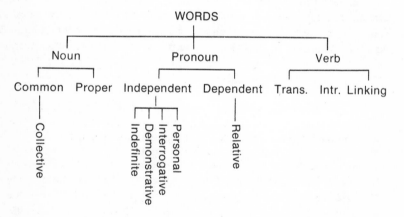

Study the model which follows. Notice the first sentence announcing the classification. Is this a simple or complex system of classification?

Most of these meteorites are of two kinds. One is stony in nature, like a piece of rock from the sky. The largest of these that we have yet found is at Norton, Kansas, and it is estimated to weigh 1 ton. The other kind is composed of an alloy of nickel and iron, similar to what is believed to make up the interior of the Earth. The largest known nickel-iron meteorite is in Grootfontein, in Africa. Its weight is probably more than 60 tons. [2]

How do you organize and develop analysis by classification? First, you decide on a basis of classifying that will fulfill your purpose. Thus purpose determines the basis for the classification. If you are interested in the number of male and female teachers in a department or school, you classify on the basis of sex. If you were anxious to defend the faculty, you might classify teachers on the basis of experience, stressing the large number of teachers who have been at the school ten or more years. Once you have decided on a basis for classifying, you must maintain it throughout the classification.

Study the model classification below. It is the introductory paragraph to a classification of modern economic systems. This selection is interesting since it explains the problem of selecting a basis for classifying. After discussing the difficulty of finding a valid basis for classifying economic systems, the writer divides economic systems into five types on the basis of economic activity and governmental control.

Modern economic systems can be classified in several ways. Because each system has many attributes, there are many possible classifications. Thus, economic systems can be classified on the basis of the amount of government control, on the basis of the importance attached to economic activity, on the basis of complexity, or on almost any other basis. An exhaustive treatment of classifications would involve a series of books. Within the brief scope of this book it will be possible to focus major attention on only one of these differences, namely, the relation between economic activity and government control. Five types stand out in this classification: capitalism, regulated capitalism, socialism, fascism, and communism. [3]

In classifying, you are answering the questions: "What is this a sort of, or what are sorts of this?" [4] Then by comparing and contrasting, you place persons, places, things, ideas into groups or classes on the basis of significant characteristics. In the complex system of classification which follows, the writer divides glaciers into three main classes: (1) mountain or valley glaciers, (2) confluent or piedmont glaciers, and (3) continental or ice sheet glaciers (also called ice caps). Within the types, the writer points out subtypes, such as a *reconstructed glacier,* a *cliff* or *hanging glacier, polar* or *high-latitude,* and the *tidewater* or *tidal glacier.*

[1]As glacial ice spreads or flows from the place where it was formed, it assumes various shapes that are molded to a considerable extent by the surface over which the ice flows. On the basis of their mode of occurrence, all glaciers may be classified as follows: (1) mountain, or valley, glaciers, which descend from high peaks and occur along the flanks of mountain ranges; (2) confluent, or piedmont, glaciers, which are the joined extrusions of several alpine glaciers; and (3) continental, or ice-sheet, glaciers (also called icecaps), which cover vast areas.

[2]Although all glaciers may be included conveniently within these types, several subtypes are often recognized. Some of these, which are probably special cases of the alpine, or valley, type, have certain peculiarities that have suggested their names. Thus a *reconstructed* glacier is one that cascades down a steep slope or projects from a hanging valley, breaks off, and falls in the form of blocks, or chunks, which pressure and freezing reunite at the base of the plunge. Perched on the upper part of a cliff, often at the head of a steep, blunt-ended valley, there may be a broad, snow-capped mass of clear ice, often crescent-shaped; this is called a *cliff* glacier, or *hanging* glacier. The *polar,* or *high-latitude,* glacier of northern Greenland is a steep-sided, blunt-ended tongue of ice extending down a valley from the plateau on which the ice sheet is located. The *tidewater,* or *tidal,* glacier though basically a valley type, extends out into the sea, where its outer end, usually rising and falling with the tide, periodically breaks off in great chunks, or blocks, which float away as *icebergs.*

[3]The term icecap may be regarded as synonymous with continental glacier, or ice sheet, but the term has been used also in a more limited way to designate the smaller patches or remnants of ice that spread or move out from a center. Those still present on Iceland are excellent examples. [5]

In the classification which follows the writer places literature into three basic types: drama, epic, and lyric. The writer then states clearly the characteristics by which each type may be grouped and also differentiated: formal traits, general structure, tone, kind and source of subject, and the relation of the narrator to the action.

¹To cut through the seemingly impenetrable tangle of genre classification, we might begin by considering the oldest grouping, which has come down from classical antiquity. It consists of three basic literary types: drama, epic, and lyric. These three can be differentiated in a number of ways: according to rather obvious formal traits, general structure, tone, kind and source of subject, and, finally, relation of the narrator to the action.

²The drama, first of all, comes to the spectators through the combined actions and speeches of characters as they move about on a stage. Northrop Frye, in his *Anatomy of Criticism,* describes it as words that are acted out in front of the audience. Furthermore, drama tends to be a concentrated form, in which action leads rather rapidly to a climax and denouement, usually without time to introduce wholly unrelated material. As for the subject matter, it ranges from that of tragedy — often the historical or legendary exploits of noble figures who may seem to be larger than life — to that of comedy — usually invented, fictitious versions of everyday life and the actions of more or less exaggerated people who tend to be ordinary rather than heroic. Finally, in drama the writer seems to be hidden behind the action, letting his characters do the acting and speaking, so that even when one of them is virtually a mouthpiece for the playwright's ideas, as Tanner in Shaw's *Man and Superman* and Undershaft in the same author's *Major Barbara* appear to be, that fact is qualified by the speaker's still being a dramatic person with a limited point of view.

³The epic, being a long narrative poem, is more purely a form of speech. This is especially true of the older epics such as the *Iliad*, the *Odyssey,* and *Beowulf*, which were intended to be chanted by a *rhapsode* or *scop* before a group of listeners. The epic is also much longer than the drama; at the Pan-Athenaic festivals in the fifth century B.C. the rhapsodes had to take turns chanting the *Iliad* or *Odyssey,* since the task was too much for any one man. Being longer, the epic tends to have a less tight structure than the drama, sometimes even becoming episodic: presenting, that is, a series of loosely related incidents, as in the *Odyssey*. It is clear that in Virgil's *Aeneid* tightly and loosely constructed books are presented alternately, as if on the analogy of the *Iliad* on the one hand and the *Odyssey* on the other. Epic subject matter consists of the exploits of heroic figures, men of great stature and even gods; these exploits are given vast significance, affecting whole civilizations in the work of Homer and Virgil, and, finally, in Milton's *Paradise Lost,* affecting the whole of mankind. Like tragedy, the epic is likely to draw its subjects from history and myth instead of inventing new tales. As for the relation of the narrator to the action, he may intervene in his own voice to invoke a muse, to ask the traditional epic question — as

Homer asks what god has brought about a quarrel between Agamem-
non and Achilles — or, like Milton, to make moral comments on the
action described. In this the epic poet is unlike the dramatist.

⁴As the very name suggests, the lyric was originally
intended to be sung, to the accompaniment of a lyre. It is usually
much shorter than either the drama or the epic, taking only a matter
of minutes to speak or to read. Being so much shorter, it tends to be
more tightly constructed; in fact, it usually has great unity and may
be restricted to exploring a single mood. Its subject matter consists
of personal emotions, such as love or grief, or public emotions, such
as the patriotic admiration of national heroes or reverence for the
gods or God. The tone may be either serious or light. For the most
part, the lyric makes use of neither historical and legendary nor
fictitious material. It draws mainly on the immediate experience or
mood of the poet, whether as a personal or a public individual.
The lyric poet, finally, seems to speak purely as himself, in his own
voice: he presents himself as being closely related to the objects and
actions described, whether they are his mistress in her silks, the
daffodils beside the lake, or his dead friend whom he mourns. As
Professor Frye has observed, in this form the audience seems to be
concealed from the poet, whereas in drama the poet seems to be
concealed from the audience. [6]

In classifying glaciers, the writer is answering the question: "What is this a sort of?" — that is, "when granular snow or
the massive ice results from its recrystallization accumulates to
a great thickness, it begins to move, or flow, outward under its
own weight and thus forms a glacier." [7] Thus, mountain, piedmont, and continental ice masses are glaciers because they are
masses of granular snow or the massive ice resulting from its
recrystallization. Yet each of these glaciers represents a distinct
class because each one possesses distinctive characteristics which
are different from the others. Any new ice mass, therefore, would
be placed into one of these classes on the basis of its characteristics.

In classifying literature, the writers indicate that the
classes can be differentiated in a number of ways: according to
formal traits, general structure, tone, kind and source of subject,
and relation of the narrator to the action. Read the paragraphs
again. Notice the way the writers show how one class differs in
the previously mentioned characteristics from another. In classifying works of prose and poetry, then, these writers are asking

and answering two questions: "What is this a sort of?" These works are works of literature. Yet, because they possess distinctive different characteristics, they must be divided into groups or classes: drama, epic, and lyric. In this analysis, the writers answer the question "What are sorts of this?" In other words, works that possess similar characteristics to those of the drama, epic, or lyric would be appropriately placed into the proper class.

Read the classification which follows. Answer the following questions.

1. What is the writer sorting out?
2. What is the basis for classifying?
3. Into how many classes does the writer break down his subject?
4. Is this a simple or complex system of classification?

Scientific findings when stated in words are usually classified into *laws, theories,* and *hypotheses.* If the evidence indicates that the finding is clearly established, and can be stated definitely without too many "ifs, ands and provideds," then it is called a "law." Examples are the "Law of Falling Bodies" in physics, "Boyle's Law" in chemistry, the "Law of Diminishing Returns" in economics. Discoveries which are probably true, but for which the evidence is not quite so conclusive, are usually called "theories." It is necessary to emphasize, however, that a theory is not a guess, it is not "a notion spun out of thin air" but is a truth for which there exists considerable but not final and conclusive evidence. Finally, there are "hypotheses." A hypothesis is an idea about which we are not yet sufficiently certain to permit us to call it a law or a theory, but there is, nevertheless, some evidence to support it. An idea usually does not remain a hypothesis very long. It is usually soon tested and if found true becomes a theory or a law, if found to be false is discarded. This may, of course, take a long time. [8]

DISCUSSION
The writer classifies scientific findings into three important classes: laws, theories, and hypotheses on the basis of "evidence." He develops the classification by defining the terms *laws, theories,* and *hypotheses.* His supporting material consists of examples and explanations. A chart for this classification looks something like the following:

Scientific findings

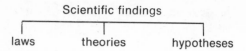

Classifications to be effective must be fully developed. If you do not firmly establish a class that has several traits in common, and if you do not clearly differentiate one class from another, the reader will not easily grasp the analysis. You may develop classification in the same way as comparison and contrast. You may, for example, begin with a topic sentence announcing the classification. Then, you could develop the classification by contrasting and differentiating one class from others like it. In the model classification which follows, the writer structures his classification in this way:

[1] Generally speaking, we can classify the ways in which people use the language: (1) standard English, (2) colloquial English, and (3) illiterate English. Each of these levels has its own trademarks. Standard is that English spoken and written by educated people in formal situations. It is void of slang, profanity, and provincialisms (word or expressions common to a particular group or location). In addition, standard English does not contain errors in grammar. In writing, it is free from errors in punctuation. It is not the type of English used when a coach gives a pep talk at halftime; it is not the type of English used when playing golf, writing a letter to a personal friend, or hitting your thumb with a hammer.

[2] Colloquial English is that level of language used by many well-educated people in informal situations. In it we find some slang expressions and idioms, a rather liberal use of grammar, and a vocabulary marked by simplicity. We hear or read this level of language on radio and television, in informal speeches, and in many newspaper and magazine articles. It is, in most cases, the language of the workaday world.

[3] The illiterate level of language is not acceptable in any formal or informal situation. It should be avoided entirely in an academic atmosphere. Usually, it is spoken by people who are not educated; however, it is often used by individuals who have had some formal education but who still rely on the illiterate level because it is so thoroughly etched in their language patterns. It is marked by incorrect grammar (ain't, he done, they brung), a limited vocabulary, poor pronunciation, and a tremendous variety of constructions familiar only to a particular group of people. It is not appropriate in any case for the college student in his written work (an exception

here would be in a work of fiction where the writer would use illiterate English for character identification). Again, in educated groups, illiterate English is just unacceptable. As college students, you should correct any errors in speech and writing that fall within this level of usage. [9]

The writer breaks down the English language on the basis of the way people use it, into three levels: standard English, colloquial English, and illiterate English. He announces the classification in the first sentence of the first paragraph. He indicates the traits for the distinctive classes in the second sentence: "Each of these levels has its own trademarks." He then presents the trademarks (characteristics) common to standard English in the rest of the paragraph. In the second paragraph he presents comparable contrasting points to show that colloquial English is a distinctive class. In the third paragraph, he again presents the same points to show that illiterate English differs from the other two levels; therefore, it too must be a separate class.

A sentence outline of the previous model shows its structural organization more clearly.

Levels of English

Statement of Thesis: To show the way people use the language.

I. Generally speaking, we can classify the ways in which people use the language: (1) standard English, (2) colloquial English, (3) illiterate English. Each of these levels has its own trademarks. Standard is that English spoken and written by educated people in formal situations.
    A. It is void of slang, profanity, and provincialisms.
    B. Standard English does not contain errors in grammar.
    C. In writing, it is free from errors in punctuation.
    D. Standard English is not used in informal situations: pep talks, playing golf, personal letters, hitting a thumb with a hammer.
II. Colloquial English is that level of language used by many well-educated people in informal situations.
    A. In it we find some slang expressions and idioms.
    B. A liberal use of grammar and a simple use of vocabulary are common.

    C. Colloquial English is essentially a spoken language.

    D. Colloquial English is the language of the workaday world.

III. The illiterate language is not acceptable in any formal or informal situation.

    A. It is the language of the uneducated.

    B. It is marked by incorrect grammar.

    C. Illiterate English is marked also by limited vocabulary, poor pronunciation, and a variety of constructions familiar only to a particular group.

    D. Illiterate English is not appropriate for college students in their written work. In educated groups, illiterate English is unacceptable.

The next model classification illustrates development point by point. Observe that the writer relies heavily on contrast in establishing his styles (classes): classicism and romanticism. His purpose, however, is not merely to contrast classicism and romanticism; his intent is to establish the two classes by sorting out on the basis of "qualities that characterize classicism," such as "clarity, simplicity, restraint, objectivity, and balance," and contrasting with qualities "that characterize romanticism," such as "love of the remote and indefinite, escape from reality, lack of restraint in form and emotions, preference for picturesque or grandeur or passion."

The qualities that characterize classicism are clarity, simplicity, restraint, objectivity, and balance. The qualities that characterize romanticism are love of the remote and the indefinite, escape from reality, lack of restraint in form and emotions, preference for picturesqueness or grandeur or passion. Classicism and romanticism are fundamentally in opposition; what is classic is not romantic, and what is romantic is not classic. The classic is restrained; the romantic is not restrained. The classic is finished, perfect; it has great beauty of form; the romantic is unfinished, imperfect, and it is often careless of form. The classic is simple, the romantic is complex; the classic is objective, the romantic is subjective; the classic is finite, concerned only with projects that can be realized and accomplished; the romantic is infinite, concerned with plans that can never be realized, affecting "thoughts co-equal with the clouds." [10]

Study now this excellent model of the complex as well as simple system of classification. Construct classification charts to illustrate both systems.

[1]Musical instruments may be classified roughly according to the way the vibrator is set in motion, by bowing, blowing, or beating. Those in which the sound is made by beating are called the *instruments of percussion*: drum, xylophone, cymbals. Those in which the sound is made by blowing are *wind instruments*: horn, trumpet, flute. Those in which the sound is made by bowing are stringed instruments: violin, cello. The last name is the least satisfactory because certain of the stringed instruments, the harp, for example, are not bowed. Therefore, they are called stringed instruments, not *bowed instruments*. This is the usual classification of instruments: percussion, wind, strings. It is supposed that instruments of percussion came first, then wind instruments, and last, strings. A child follows this order in his natural development; at first he likes rattles and other toys that make noise by beating. Later he learns to whistle, and he likes the wind instruments, pipes of all kinds. Still later he begins to play on the strings, violin or cello.

[2]Wind instruments are further subdivided into *wood winds:* piccolo, flute, oboe, clarinet, English horn, and bassoon; and *brasses*: trumpet, horn, trombone, and tuba. The names originally corresponded to the materials of which the instruments were made; most of the instruments of the brass family are still made of brass, but the name *wood winds* has stuck though the flute and piccolo are now always made of metal.

[3]Thus we have four families of instruments:

1. Strings.
2. Wood winds.
3. Brasses.
4. Percussion.

For obvious reasons the human voice, the organ, and the piano are not usually classed in one of these groups but are put in a separate section by themselves.

[4]The instruments of percussion include all those in which the vibrator is struck or hit. These can be divided into two classes: those of indefinite pitch and those of definite pitch. Instruments of indefinite pitch include rattles, gongs, triangles, cymbals, tambourines, and castanets. Rattles are often gourds in which are placed pebbles and gravel to make sound when they are shaken. The tambourine is a small drum with metal disks or bangles in the rim. Gongs, cymbals, and triangles are metal pieces that sound when struck. Castanets, which are much used by Spanish dancers, are small, spoonshaped shells of hardwood or ivory; usually a pair is used in each hand. The drum has a piece of tightly stretched skin as its vibrator. All drums are of indefinite pitch except the timpani or kettle-

drums, which can be tuned. Other instruments of definite pitch are the
xylophone, marimba, orchestral bells, and celesta. In these instruments small bars of metal or wood are hit with wooden hammers.
In the xylophone and the marimba the bars are of wood; they are
struck by two hammers held in the hands of the performer. In the
orchestral bells and the celesta the bars are of metal and are struck
by hammers which are manipulated from a keyboard.

[5] The brasses are so named because the instruments are
of brass. In the brass family the lips are the vibrators. A simple illustration of the lips as vibrators is found in whistling. In a brass
instrument the lips are pressed tightly against the mouthpiece,
and the sound is made as the air is blown through them. To the group
of brasses belong the various members of the horn family: trumpet,
French horn, trombone, and tuba.

[6] In the wood-wind family there are two types of vibrator:
air and reed. Of the air as vibrator one may have a very simple example by blowing across the top of a bottle or jug. If he uses bottles
of different sizes he can get different sounds and, as the various jug
bands have demonstrated, can play a tune by blowing first on one
bottle and then on another. The sound is made because the air is
set vibrating, and the stream of air thus becomes the vibrator. Instruments in which air is the vibrator are the flute and the piccolo,
which is a small flute.

[7] The principle of the reed as vibrator is demonstrated
by the small boy who whistles by blowing on a leaf or blade of grass
held tightly across his mouth. The reed, which is a very elastic tongue
of wood or metal, is placed in or upon an opening through which the
air passes; the player, by blowing, sets the reed to vibrating and
produces sound. Reeds may be single or double. In the single-reed
instruments, the clarinet and saxophone, a single reed flutters back
and forth between the air in the player's mouth and the air in the
instrument. In the double-reed instruments, the oboe, English horn
(contralto oboe), and bassoon, the air passes between two reeds,
causing them to vibrate. [11]

Keep these points in mind about classification:

1. Classification is a method of giving order to developing thought by sorting out persons, places, things, ideas, situations and placing them into classes or groups.

2. There are two systems of classification: the simple
system (main divisions of a subject) and the complex system
(main divisions and subdivisions of a subject).

3. In classifying, a writer answers the questions:
"What is this a sort of, or what are sorts of this?"

4. A writer must have a purpose for classifying.

5. In preparing a classification, list as many characteristics under each class as possible; then eliminate any that are irrelevant or less important.

6. Make a chart of the classification.

7. Prepare a topic or sentence outline before writing the classification.

8. Classify exhaustively enough to make clear the purpose.

9. By comparing and contrasting on the basis of significant characteristics, you can establish the classes.

10. Writers will often announce the classification and its basis in the early sentences.

11. Classifications may be organized and developed in a variety of ways; by subject-at-a-time, point by point, and by making the class clear with examples and illustrative material are common methods of development.

EXERCISES

1. Classification

Read the model paragraph below. Answer the questions that follow it.

Listeners can be classified into four groups: (1) Some do not listen; they "tune the speaker out" and think of matters foreign to the speaker's subject. They get little from a speech. (2) Some only half-listen; their spasmodic listening fluctuates all the way from careful attention to no attention. They understand fragments of the speech but they do not see the idea as a whole. (3) Some listen with passive acceptance; they accept all the speaker says without question. Because of their lack of discrimination, they add little to what the speaker says from their own experiences. (4) Some listen with discrimination; this critical type of listener gets the most from a speech. If you adopt the following measures you will soon find yourself a member of this group. [12]

1. What does the last sentence tell you about the function of this paragraph?
2. What subject does the writer break down into groups?
3. What serves as the basis for the classification?

2. Classification

Read the model paragraphs below. Answer the questions that follow.

Two groups of needs are recognized: viscerogenic and psychogenic. Viscerogenic needs are grounded in the physiological systems of the organism. They may be highly specific, as the needs for sleep and breathing, or relatively specific, as the need for food. The object most appropriate for the satisfaction of a drive (and its subsequent cathexis) is seldom absolutely specific. This does not mean, however, that the range of variability is limitless. Bark from a tree regularly fed to a baby can hardly be expected to satisfy his nutritional requirements; on the other hand, he does not absolutely require milk, either from the mother's breast or from a bottle.

In addition to the viserogenic needs, there are what we are calling psychogenic needs. These needs grow out of social relationships — interactions with other personalities. But whether such needs have the same status initially as the viscerogenic needs, or whether they are derivative in their origin (that is, growing out of situations in which drives are satisfied) is not known. At any rate they acquire autonomy as the individual develops. It is generally agreed that most, if not all, of the psychogenic needs are derived through social experience. [13]

1. What is the basis for the classification?
2. Is the development point by point, subject-at-a-time, or some other method?
3. Does the writer announce the classification?
4. Mention some specific characteristics that distinguish one group from the other.

3. Classification

Read the model paragraphs below. Answer the questions that follow.

The kinds and varieties of human relationships are almost countless, and so various categories have been devised for classifying the most frequent forms. By organizing and classifying similar phenomena, the student can make greater progress in his study of human relationships. One such category, known as *sociology,* attempts to describe, classify, and explain the elemental forms of behavior and the principles which govern group living. Another category, called *economics,* limits itself to those relationships which result from man's quest for goods. Another category, known as *civics* or *political science*, specializes in those relationships which result from official governmental control. Still another category, *geography*, limits itself to the relationships between man and the earth and between men in their attempts to meet the problems of the natural environment. One inclusive, over-all subject, *history*, undertakes to make a record of man's cooperative successes and failures. While other subjects concerned with human relationships exist and might well constitute part of the curriculum, these five are the ones which receive major attention.

In recent years the term *behavioral sciences* has been used to designate a broad area of study that encompasses psychology and parts of the natural and social sciences. It draws its materials especially from sociology, social psychology, cultural anthropology, psychology, psychiatry, and the medical sciences. It focuses its attention on a study of factors that influence, condition, or determine man's behavior as a member of a social group. [14]

1. What is the writer classifying?
2. Into how many groups (subjects) does he break down the subject?
3. List some of the guide words that aid the flow of thought?

ASSIGNMENT

1. Classification

The following selection was taken from a geology textbook. Rewrite it in less formal style.

[1] Dunes may take several forms, depending on the supply of sand, the lay of the land, the restricting vegetation, and the steadiness of the direction of the winds. The principal types are (1) lee dunes (sand drifts), (2) crag-and-tail dunes, (3) other longitudinal dunes, (4) barchans, (5) seifs, (6) transverse dunes, and (7) complex dunes.

[2] *Lee dunes.* Lee dunes, or sand drifts, are longitudinal dunes which develop as long, narrow sand ridges in the shape of the wind shadow behind a rocky ledge or behind clumps of vegetation, or as sloping embankments of sand blown over a cliff.

[3] *Crag-and-tail dunes.* Crag-and-tail dunes tail out behind a crag. These deposits, and lee dunes, are fixed in position, but, with the addition of great quantities of sand, typical migratory dunes may form and move away from the outer tips of the sand drifts.

[4] *Other longitudinal dunes.* Longitudinal dunes are elongated in the direction of the effective winds, generally where strong

winds blow across areas of scanty sand or where winds have to contest against the holding effect of grass or small shrubs. Occasionally
oblique winds are seemingly needed to "shepherd" the sand into
ridges. These fluted dunes grade into other forms. Some are blown
up the slopes of valley walls.

⁵ *Barchans.* Barchans form in open areas, unrestricted
by topographic or vegetational barriers, where the wind direction
is fairly constant and the sand supply is limited, particularly over a
solid rock base. A typical barchan is crescent-shaped, with the
gentle windward slope on the outer curve and with the points, or
wings, of the crescent drawn out with the wind on the leeward side,
in a streamlined form.

⁶ *Seifs.* A seif is a longitudinal dune considerably modified by quartering winds. One simple variety resembles, in plan
outline, an Arabian sword. It is associated with barchans, and con-
versions of barchans to seifs, and vice versa, are said to occur.
Another variety is essentially a lee dune with a knife-edge crest between one rounded windward side and a steeper slip face on the
other. A third variety is a huge Saharan sand ridge with a sharp,
broadly wavy crest. The forms of seifs, especially their crests, frequently change when the wind shifts from the prevailing direction.
Seifs are especially well developed in Arabia, the Libyan Desert,
the French Sahara, and the Australian desert.

⁷ *Transverse dunes.* Transverse dunes form where the
sand supply is copious and the dry-weather wind direction is constant, as along many seacoasts. The great bulk of sand in such a
setting piles up a ridge or a series of ridges across the wind. Their
crests generally are sinuous and uneven, partly from unequal accumulation and partly from wind-swept channels between high
points on their summits. Large patches of transverse dunes seem
to advance in multiple ranks.

⁸ *Complex dunes.* Complex dunes, lacking clean-cut
forms, develop where wind directions are variable, sand is abundant,
and, perhaps, vegetation interferes. Barchans, seifs, or transverse
dunes locally become crowded and hence overlap, thus losing their
characteristic shapes in a confused welter of diverse slopes.

⁹ *Blowouts.* On a grass-covered dune or other area of
sand, a break in the sod may become the location of a blowout,
where the sand moved out by the wind is formed into a curved,
parabolic dune around the margin of the hollowed-out area. The
dune embracing the blowout is usually horseshoe-shaped, with the
concavity, or open end, to windward. The cavity excavated may be
very irregular, but the slope out of it is more or less continuous
with the windward slope of the associated dune, and the rounded
front on the outside is the slip face. Blowouts also occur in and

among crowded dunes wherever a sag develops that allows air currents to funnel through the sand surface. By this blowout process the complexity of transverse sand ridges and other closely grouped dunes may be increased. [15]

IDOLS OF THE MIND
by Francis Bacon

[1] The idols and false notions which are now in possession of the human understanding, and have taken deep root therein, not only so beset men's minds that truth can hardly find entrance, but even after entrance obtained, they will again in the very instauration of the sciences meet and trouble us, unless men being forewarned of the danger fortify themselves as far as may be against their assaults.

[2] There are four classes of Idols which beset men's minds. To these for distinction's sake I have assigned names, — calling the first class *Idols of the Tribe;* the second, *Idols of the Cave;* the third, *Idols of the Marketplace;* the fourth, *Idols of the Theatre.*

[3] The formation of ideas and axioms by true induction is no doubt the proper remedy to be applied for the keeping off and clearing away of idols. To point them out, however, is of great use; for the doctrine of Idols is to the Interpretation of Nature what the doctrine of the refutation of Sophisms is to common Logic.

[4] The Idols of the Tribe have their foundation in human nature itself, and in the tribe or race of men. For it is a false assertion that the sense of man is the measure of things. On the contrary, all perceptions as well of the sense as of the mind are according to the measure of the individual and not according to the measure of the universe. And the human understanding is like a false mirror, which, receiving rays irregularly, distorts and discolours the nature of things by mingling its own nature with it.

[5] The Idols of the Cave are the idols of the individual man. For every one (besides the errors common to human nature in general) has a cave or den of his own, which refracts and discolours the light of nature; owing either to his own proper and peculiar nature; or to his education and conversation with others; or to the reading of books, and the authority of those whom he esteems and admires; or to the differences of impressions, accordingly as they take place in a mind preoccupied and predisposed or in a mind indifferent and settled; or the like: So that the spirit of man (according as it is meted out to different individuals) is in fact a thing variable and full of perturbation, and governed as it were by chance. Whence it was well observed by Heraclitus that men look for sciences in their own lesser worlds, and not in the greater or common world.

[6]There are also Idols formed by the intercourse and association of men with each other, which I call Idols of the Marketplace, on account of the commerce and consort of men there. For it is by discourse that men associate; and words are imposed according to the apprehension of the vulgar. And therefore the ill and unfit choice of words wonderfully obstructs the understanding. Nor do the definitions or explanations wherewith in some things learned men are wont to guard and defend themselves, by any means set the matter right. But words plainly force and overrule the understanding, and throw all into confusion, and lead men away into numberless empty controversies and idle fancies.

[7]Lastly, there are Idols which have immigrated into men's minds from the various dogmas of philosophies, and also from wrong laws of demonstration. These I call Idols of the Theatre; because in my judgment all the received systems are but so many stage-plays, representing worlds of their own creation after an unreal and scenic fashion. Nor is it only of the systems now in vogue, or only of the ancient sects and philosophies, that I speak; for many more plays of the same kind may yet be composed and in like artificial manner set forth; seeing that errors the most widely different have nevertheless causes for the most part alike. Neither again do I mean this only of entire systems, but also of many principles and axioms in science, which by tradition, credulity, and negligence have come to be received . . . . [16]

CLASSIFICATION OF CLOUDS
by Paul E. Lehr, Will Burnett, and Herbert S. Zim

[1]Clouds are classified according to how they are formed. There are two basic types: (1) Clouds formed by rising air currents. These are piled up and puffy. They are called "cumulus," which means piled up or accumulated. (2) Clouds formed when a layer of air is cooled below the saturation point without vertical movement. These are in sheets or foglike layers. They are called "stratus," meaning sheetlike or layered.

[2]Clouds are further classified by altitude into four families: high clouds, middle clouds, low clouds, and towering clouds. The bases of the latter may be as low as the typical low clouds, but the tops may be at or above 75,000 feet.

[3]High clouds are composed almost entirely of tiny ice crystals. Their bases average about 20,000 feet above the earth. Three types exist: Cirrus clouds, thin, wispy, and feathery, are composed entirely of ice crystals. Cirrus clouds usually form at 25,000 feet and above, where the temperature is always far below freezing. These clouds are frequently blown about into feathery strands called

"mares' tails." Cirrocumulus clouds, generally forming at 20,000 to 25,000 feet, are rarely seen. These thin, patchy clouds often form wavelike patterns. These are the true mackerel sky, not to be confused with altocumulus rolls. They are often rippled and always too thin to show shadows. Cirrostratus clouds form at the same altitudes as cirrocumulus. These are thin sheets that look like fine veils or torn, wind-blown patches of gauze. Because they are made of ice crystals, cirrostratus clouds form large halos, or luminous circles, around sun and moon.

[4] Middle clouds are basically stratus or cumulus. Their bases average about 10,000 feet above the earth. Altostratus are dense veils or sheets of gray or blue. They often appear fibrous or lightly striped. The sun or moon does not form a halo, as with higher, ice-crystal cirrostratus, but appears as if seen through frosted glass. Altocumulus are patches or layers of puffy or roll-like clouds, gray or whitish. They resemble cirrocumulus, but the puffs or rolls are larger and made of water droplets, not ice crystals. Through altocumulus the sun often produces a corona, or disk, generally pale blue or yellow inside, reddish outside. The corona's color and spread distinguish it from the cirrostratus halo — a larger ring, covering much more of the sky.

[5] Low clouds have bases that range in height from near the earth's surface to 6,500 feet. There are three main kinds: Stratus is a low, quite uniform sheet, like fog, with the base above the ground. Dull-gray stratus clouds often make a heavy, leaden sky. Only fine drizzle can fall from true stratus clouds, because there is little or no vertical movement in them. Nimbostratus are the true rain clouds. Darker than ordinary stratus, they have a wet look, and streaks of rain often extend to the ground. They often are accompanied by low scud clouds (fractostratus) when the wind is strong. Stratocumulus are irregular masses of clouds spread out in a rolling or puffy layer. Gray with darker shading, stratocumulus do not produce rain but sometimes change into nimbostratus, which do. The rolls or masses then fuse together and the lower surface becomes indistinct with rain.

[6] Cumulonimbus are the familiar thunderheads. Bases may almost touch the ground; violent updrafts may carry the tops to 75,000 feet. Winds aloft often mold the tops into a flat anvil-like form. In their most violent form these clouds produce tornadoes. Cumulus are puffy, cauliflowerlike. Shapes constantly change. Over land, cumulus usually form by day in rising warm air, and disappear at night. They mean fair weather unless they pile up into cumulonimbus. Cumulus and cumulonimbus are both clouds of vertical development, unlike the layered clouds described previously. Clouds of the cumulus type result from strong vertical currents.

They form at almost any altitude, with bases sometimes as high as 14,000 feet. [17]

ASSIGNMENT

2. *Classification*
Write a classification theme of approximately 500 words. Listed below are some subject areas that may be helpful in your selecting a topic.

1. Intelligence	5. Governments	9. Marriages	12. Teachers
2. Drives	6. Dates	10. Weapons	13. Students
3. Rulers	7. Friends	11. Penal	14. Races
4. Dates	8. Families	Institutions	15. Customers

Partition
Analysis by partition is a method of organizing and developing thought by breaking down a subject into its aspects or component parts. Partitioning is similar to classification (they are frequently used in combination) in that a writer has a basis for partitioning and maintains that basis throughout the process. You might, for example, break down the campaign of John F. Kennedy for the Presidency into six phases in order to show Kennedy's political astuteness. Another student might present in chronological order a series of events or happenings to emphasize the bloody rise of modern communism. Still another writer might divide the ocean by spatial patterning into three realms for informative purposes or a carburetor into its various parts to stress its complexity.
Analysis by partition enables a writer (1) to discuss individual parts separately, and (2) to show the importance and the relationship of each part to the whole. In partitioning, a writer focuses on the "Whole"; he helps his reader to discover something about the individual parts in order that he might understand the whole more completely.

Physical partition
A writer, for example, may divide the human ear into three parts to show that the ear is an amazing organ. This kind of partition is called a *physical partition;* it involves breaking down something tangible into parts. The basis in most physical partitions is obvious: the individual units. The ear consists of (1)

the outer ear which is further divided into the auricle and the external auditory canal; (2) the middle ear made up of the ear drum and the auditory ossicles (the three small bones known as the hammer, anvil, and stirrup); and the inner ear consisting of the vestibule, the semicircular canals, and the chochlea.

In the physical partition that follows, the writer breaks down a typical wave into its physical characteristics.

Before constructing an imaginary life history of a typical wave, we need to become familiar with some of its physical characteristics. A wave has height, from trough to crest. It has length, the distance from its crest to that of the following wave. The period of the wave refers to the time required for succeeding crests to pass a fixed point. None of these dimensions is static; all change, but bear definite relations to the wind, the depth of the water, and many other matters. Furthermore, the water that composes a wave does not advance with it across the sea; each water particle describes a circular or elliptical orbit with the passage of the wave form, but returns very nearly to its original position. And it is fortunate that this is so, for if the huge masses of water that comprise a wave actually moved across the sea, navigation would be impossible. Those who deal professionally in the lore of waves make frequent use of a picturesque expression — the 'length of fetch.' The 'fetch' is the distance that the waves have run, under the drive of a wind blowing in a constant direction, without obstruction. The greater the fetch, the higher the waves. Really large waves cannot be generated within the confined space of a bay or a small sea. A fetch of perhaps 600 to 800 miles, with winds of gale velocity, is required to get up the largest ocean waves. [18]

Study the following physical partition. Answer the questions which follow it.

The national seashore does have two spectacular features. One is the magnificent wall of cliffs, 60 to 70 feet high, where the Cape's tablelands meet the Atlantic. The first panoramic glimpse of the great outer beach from these cliffs — as from Truro Lighthouse — has been called "one of the most memorable experiences in America." People tell tall tales about the winds here blowing back pieces of wood cast over the bank, and Thoreau once recorded that boys and men "amuse themselves by running and trying to jump off the bank with their jackets spread, and being blown back." North of these impressive cliffs are eight square miles of some of the most spectacular dunes on our Atlantic coast. The build-

ing material came from the highlands to the south — gnawed out of
the cliffs by wind and wave, carried for miles by ocean currents,
then picked up, shaped, shifted and reshaped by centuries of winds.
People who have braved this wilderness during the winter, when the
northwest winds blow, report that you can see dunes change shape in
an hour. Some are free-moving, others stabilized with beach grass
and low-growing dwarf-like trees. [19]

QUESTIONS

1. What is the subject?
2. Into what aspects of the "whole" is the subject divided?
3. By what methods of development does the writer present his
   partition?
4. Does the writer announce the partition?

Conceptual partition

In the model partition which follows, the writer explains the rather complex process of reasoning. This kind of
partitioning is known as a *conceptual partition* since the writer
breaks down a concept into its parts or aspects in order to give it
meaning.

A complete act of reasoning according to Dewey (2)
can be broken into five steps as follows: (1) a problem or felt difficulty;
(2) definition of the difficulty; (3) the suggestion of possible solutions; (4) an examination of the suggested solutions and the bearing
of the suggestions on the problem; and (5) observations and experi-
ments leading to the acceptance or rejection of each suggestion.
Every act of reasoning does not necessarily involve all of these steps.
An individual confronted with a problem may not take time to define
it or state it in the form of an answerable question. If he does, he may
take the first suggestion as a solution without testing it mentally
(step 4) to see how it bears on the problem. Quite obviously the individual is not engaging in a complete act of reasoning though he
insists that he is reasoning. Let us examine the steps in more detail. [20]

DISCUSSION

In order to explain a complete act of reasoning, the
writer breaks it down into five steps. He follows this introductory
paragraph with a more detailed examination of each step.

In the *conceptual partition,* a writer must arbitrarily impose on his subject some basis for partitioning. In the following model conceptual partition, the writer explains why some city streets are safe and some are not. She announces her purpose, basis for partition, and the organization pattern with the words "A city street equipped to make a safety asset out of the presence of strangers, as successful city neighborhoods always do, must have three main qualities . . . ."

[1]Everyone knows that a well-used city street is apt to be safe. A deserted one is apt to be unsafe. But how does this work, really? And what makes a city street well used or shunned? Why is the inner sidewalk mall in Washington Houses — which is supposed to be an attraction — shunned when the sidewalks of the old city just to its west are not? What about streets that are busy part of the time and then empty abruptly? A city street equipped to make a safety asset out of the presence of strangers, as successful city neighborhoods always do, must have three main qualities:

[2]First, there must be a clear demarcation between public and private spaces. They cannot ooze into each other as they do typically in housing projects where streets, walks, and play areas may seem at first glance to be open to the public but in effect are special preserves. (The fate of Washington Houses' large Christmas tree is a classic example of what happens when the distinction between public and private space is blurred, and the area which should be under public surveillance has no clear practicable limits.)

[3]Second, there must be *eyes* upon the street, eyes belonging to what we might call its natural proprietors. To insure the safety of both residents and strangers, the buildings on a street must be oriented to it. They cannot turn their backs or blank sides on it and leave it blind.

[4]And third, the sidewalk must have users on it fairly continuously, both to add more effective eyes and to induce plenty of people in buildings along the street to watch the sidewalks. Nobody enjoys sitting on a stoop or looking out a window at an empty street. But large numbers of people entertain themselves, off and on, by watching street activity. [21]

DISCUSSION

The structural organizational pattern of this partition is simple and effective. In order to explain why some city streets are safe and some are not, Jane Jacobs, the writer, states that a safe city street must have three main qualities. Her development is clear and effective. She introduces the subject with a series of questions and states her partition. Then, she develops each quality for safety in a separate paragraph indicated by the transitional words: first, second, and third.

You can now readily see that partition differs from classification. In analyzing by classification, you break a subject down into groups or classes and focus the reader's attention on the class divisions. You show classes of clouds, volcanoes, types of teachers, books etc., so that other persons, places, things, ideas which the reader may meet in future studies may be conveniently grouped. In partitioning, you break the subject down into its component parts to focus the reader's attention on their relationship to the "whole." You ask the question: "How can I treat each part so that I make my discovery about the 'whole' clear and meaningful?" You break down a wave into its physical characteristics, for example, in order to make the reader more familiar with it; America's priceless seashore into two spectacular features so that the reader will help you save national seashores, the complete act of reasoning into five steps so that the reader will understand the complex process more easily, and safety of streets into three qualities so that the reader will learn what can be done to insure such safety.

Organizing and developing the physical or conceptual partition is a relatively simple process. A writer usually announces his partition and the reasons for the analysis in the opening sentence or paragraph. He then treats each part or aspect of the whole, stressing its importance to his purpose and its relationship to the subject. Writers will frequently indicate the divisions by guide words or figures, such as the ordinal numbers one, two, three, four, and the transitional expressions: first, second, third, finally, and the figures (1), (2), (3), (4).

Study the model partition which follows. The writer's subject is the objective method. His purpose is to show the advantages of the method — an arbitrary basis for partitioning. He could have partitioned to show the steps in the method, the complexity of the method, or in some other way depending upon his purpose.

Objective observation. The objective method allows one person to observe what another does, not what he thinks or feels.

Its first great advantage is that (1) the observations can be verified. The environment in which the act is performed may be standardized in detail or may be systematically described, so that it can be duplicated or recognized by another worker, or by the same worker at a later date. The behavior itself is also described in detail, complicated apparatus often being used to get graphic records of the subject's behavior, records which can be analyzed by several psychologists. Another great advantage is that (2) it permits study of animals, children, the feebleminded, and the insane, and even the normal subject need not be specially trained in self-observation. [22]

Observe the development in the following model. The writer announces the partition in the opening sentence; he then treats the first aspect (factor) in the rest of that paragraph. In the second paragraph, he considers the second factor: the salt content of deep-ocean water.

It is known that the movements of deep-ocean water are governed by two main factors — its temperature and its salt content. At the surface, the ocean's temperature can range from a high of 86 degrees Fahrenheit in the Persian Gulf to a low of 31 degrees Fahrenheit or even lower in the Arctic and Antarctic. The reason this very cold water does not freeze is its salt content. Along the 40th parallel, the latitude of Philadelphia, surface temperature in the Atlantic can go from a shivery 50 degrees Fahrenheit in winter to a comfortable 70 degrees Fahrenheit in summer. But these variations in temperature are only skin-deep. A more accurate guide to true oceanic temperatures is found in a zone, or layer, beginning 100 to 600 feet below the surface and extending down to about 3,000 feet. In this zone, water temperatures gradually drop, even in warm parts of the world. Below it, the temperature of the water is almost uniform, hovering very close to the freezing point the year round. We have already noted that cold water is heavier than warm and tends to sink. Salt can make water heavy, too. On the whole, the saltiness of the open sea stays close to 3.5 per cent. Near melting polar ice, however, it tends to be less salty because the ice that is melting is nearly fresh. By contrast, the water near freezing ice will have more than an average amount of salt since the ice that is in the process of freezing leaves extra salt behind in the water. This kind of water — both cold and salty — will sink the deepest. At the very bottom of the sea is found its heaviest water. This water is loaded with salt from beneath the Antarctic ice shelf. It rides the ocean floor all the way to the equator and across it into the Northern Hemisphere. [23]

EXERCISES

4. Partition

Read the model paragraph below. Answer the questions that follow it.

The life of the ocean is divided into distinct realms, each with its own group of creatures that feed upon each other and depend on each other in different ways. There is, first of all, the tidal zone, where land and sea meet. Then comes the realm of the shallow seas around the continents, which goes down to about 500 feet. It is in these two zones that the vast majority of marine life occurs. The deep ocean adds two regions, the zone of light and the zone of perpetual darkness. In the clear waters of the western Pacific, light could still be seen at a depth of 1,000 feet through the portholes of the *Trieste* on its seven-mile dive. But for practical purposes the zone of light ends at about 600 feet. Below that level there is too little light to support the growth of the "grass" of the sea — the tiny, single-celled green plants whose ability to form sugar and starch with the aid of sunlight makes them the base of the great food pyramid of the ocean. [24]

1. Into how many distinct realms is the life of the ocean divided?
2. Is the development spatially? chronologically? some other kind?
3. Does the topic sentence announce clearly the partitioning?
4. List some of the guide words the writers use.
5. Write a title for this passage.

5. Partition

Read the selection below. Make a topic outline of its structural organization. What would be a good title for the material?

The war gave Britain two new opportunities to use her resources. One was commercial. The collapse of the Bourbon regime at Madrid loosened the hold that Spain had had on her American empire and began its rapid disintegration. Her colonists, hungry for manufactured goods, opened their ports to Britain and so gave her, at the moment when Napoleon's blockade was beginning to produce serious economic repercussions at home, the market that her merchants had coveted for a century. It was too limited a market to end her difficulties, but it did help to tide her over the most critical phase. Her other opportunity was strategic. After years of landing expeditionary forces on the Continent and having them chased back into the sea, she had the chance to use her army effectively. Naval control of the coast enabled her to strike where she pleased, supply her troops, and evacuate them if need be; the Spaniards' hatred of the French gave her a base of popular support. Her redcoats alone, or the Spanish irregulars alone, might have been crushed, but not the two in conjunction. The French could not concentrate against the former without opening their communications to the latter, or disperse over the countryside to hunt down guerrillas without exposing their detachments to the British army. For the first time since 1793 that army was able to prove itself. [25]

Title

Statement of the thesis: To show how the war gave Great Britain an opportunity to use her resources.

I.

    A.

    B.

II.

    A.

    B.

    C.

6. *Partition*

Read the model paragraphs below. Answer the questions that follow them.

The two interpretations of American history that have largely shaped our evaluation of the past have been those of Frederick Jackson Turner and Charles A. Beard. According to the former, the greatest single factor in determining the character of American life has been the democratizing effect of a continually expanding frontier. The prospect of opportunity for all caused the United States to drive westward, and this expansion brought the pioneer into contact with a primitive environment which, while encouraging individualism, at the same time had a levelling effect which tended to erase distinctions of birth, social status, and education.

On the other hand, the interpretation of Charles A. Beard stresses the almost inexorable pressure of economic self-interest in determining the course of our history from its very inception.

To Beard, the motives of the original colonists, of the Revolutionary leaders, and even of the framers of the Constitution were predominantly those of economic opportunism rather than of religious and democratic conviction, and he believed that this spirit of self-seeking perpetuated itself through all the subsequent problems of the young nation. [26]

> 1. What is the subject?
> 2. Is this subject developed by contrast or partition? Which method is used to develop the other one?
> 3. What is the main idea of the selections? Does each paragraph have a stated main idea?

7. *Partition*

Read the model selection below. Answer the questions that follow it.

[1] Let your first principle be — learn the facts, then speak. Recognize that you have an obligation as well as a right in speaking. Make sure that the information you give to your listeners is true-to-fact.

[2] In his writings on rhetoric, Aristotle treats three factors important to this standard: (1) the ethical factors residing in the speaker, (2) his emotional appeal, and (3) the argument itself or the logical appeal. A good speech has an element of all three of these means of proof, but it will not center too largely on one to the exclusion of the others. The easiest way to evoke an immediate response from an audience is through an excess of emotional appeal. Almost any experienced speaker can work up an audience to an emotional state conducive to irrational action. Unfortunately, the quality of such impulsive decisions is low. A sensational revival preacher aroused his audience to such an emotional pitch over the use of tobacco that members of the audience marched down to the front and deposited their pipes, cigarettes, and cigars in containers, amidst firm resolves never to smoke again. Within a week after the close of the revival, the local stores reported sales of tobacco unparalleled in the history of the small community.

[3] A defense lawyer went on such an emotional binge in a sensational criminal case that the jury recorded an eleven-to-one vote for acquittal within the first hour of their deliberations. Six hours later they brought in a unanimous vote for conviction, thanks to one juror who kept his head. After time for more mature deliberation, a person emotionally induced to take a particular stand may waiver or repudiate his impulsive decision. Excessively emotionalized

speaking may accustom listeners to depend on emotional stimulation for decision. Thus, one may tend to forsake rational grounds in making decisions. [4] Logic depends primarily on evidence and reasoning. Evidence consists of the facts used to support ideas; and reasoning, the process of drawing inferences from the facts. Examples of illogical reasoning consist of such devices as quoting unqualified authorities, presenting unrepresentative examples, citing limited statistics, drawing sweeping conclusions from meager evidence, making inferences from negative instances, and drawing conclusions by comparing objects not comparable. A good speaker avoids such fallacies as he makes his basic appeal to logic. [27]

1. What subject is being partitioned?
2. Into how many parts does the writer break down his subject?
3. Which part is developed most fully?
4. What is the function of paragraph 1?
5. What is the function of paragraph 2?
6. Does the writer break down his subject into three distinct parts? Does he discuss fully each part? Why not?

WHAT DO YOU KNOW ABOUT VIOLENCE?
by Mrs. Medgar Evers

[1] Last fall, after their fourth summer away at camps in New England, my two older children returned home with their first questions about the riots in Negro ghettos that have disturbed the peace of recent American summers. The explosions of previous years had passed unremarked, most likely because of their camps' insulation from the news. This time, though, word of the awful upheavals in Newark and Detroit seeped through.

[2] Their reactions — and those of other Negro children they know — have differed strikingly from each other. Some are deeply disturbed at the shooting of unarmed Negroes by police and National Guardsmen. Some are simply horrified by the violence. A third group is embarrassed that Negroes should riot at all. Tearfully, one young girl asked me why they couldn't get out and work to improve their conditions.

[3] Hearing her question, I was pulled back to a time when the now frightening words *long, hot summer* meant for me simply the torrid, oppressive humidity of August in the low, flat Mississippi Delta. My husband, Medgar, was alive then, and young, just starting

out as an insurance salesman, and filled with smoldering anger at the conditions of the impoverished Delta Negro sharecroppers and tenants he called on. In an anguish of frustration at what he saw, he began to think about a Mississippi Mau Mau whose campaign of terror against white oppressors might alert the nation to these new and degrading forms of near-slavery.

⁴Over and over during those months, Medgar had asked: Why don't Negroes rise up and rebel? Now, years later, a young girl was asking me the opposite question: Why do they?

⁵The depression of some youngsters was, I think, a reflection of that terrible sense of futility all Negroes feel when it is borne in on them still one more time that to be black in America is to be, in some degree, helpless in the face of white hostility. Reading recently of the battle plans, the riot training of police and National Guard troops, the stockpiling of new weapons in city after city in readiness for this summer's expected riots, I have myself felt much the same thing.

⁶As a Negro, I feel these preparations are directed at me, for I know that when it comes to the treatment Negroes receive because they are Negroes, I, too, am indistinguishably black. Caught driving through a Negro ghetto as it explodes, I will be seen by whites as just another black woman. Race war — of the mind or in the streets — divides solely on the basis of color. No one will ask who I am, where I live, what I believe.

⁷And so the summer riots and my children's reactions to them have forced me to take a long, hard look at my feelings about racial violence. It has not been pleasant; nor am I sure I can convey these feelings precisely — to white Americans in particular. For Negro Americans have always lived closer to violence than their white compatriots, though they have more often been its victims than its perpetrators. And living close to violence, while it does not confer expertise, does give one a different perspective.

⁸You cannot grow up as a Negro in the South and not know the uses of violence and the threat of violence. They are, of course, the ultimate means of oppression. They are in the very air you breathe, though one can, with luck, live for years without feeling them directed against one personally. I began to feel the threat of violence personally after I married Medgar and learned that, unlike most Mississippi Negroes, he was not cowed by it. From that point on, until I heard the rifle shot that killed him, I lived in growing fear of it.

⁹*A rifle at the bedside.* Medgar, in spite of his months of toying with the idea of a Mississippi Mau Mau, eventually rejected violence as a means of fighting injustice and oppression. He chose,

instead, to work for freedom with freedom's tools: the law, the courts, the vote, the press. Yet he knew, as I did, that the choice of peaceful means did not assure peaceful opposition, and he never rejected violence as a defense against violence. At the same time when he taught our children to drop to the floor of the house at any unaccustomed sound in the night, he slept with a loaded rifle at our bedside. He would have used it to defend himself and us if he had been compelled.

[10]So when I brought the children to Southern California after his murder, I came with a strong sense that violence was a white tool that must be fought against. I wanted my children to grow up in a better world than we had left, but I wanted them to grow up with their father's courage and commitment to fight back if necessary. And then — just a year after we had settled in the small college town that was to be our new home — the Negro ghetto of Watts, in nearby Los Angeles, exploded.

[11]This was a new kind of violence. For the first time on such a scale, black hands set the fires, black arms threw the missiles. Yet if the fires and missiles were directed at something vaguely seen as white America, as I believe they were, they were only rarely and almost incidentally aimed at individual white Americans. It was their own ghetto prison, not forbidden white neighborhoods, that the rioters destroyed. To call it a race riot — as some did — was to miss this crucial point completely.

[12]At the height of the Watts upheaval, white people in my adopted city, 30 miles away, wanted to know my feelings about it. And, though we were one of only four Negro families in town, one white woman asked fearfully if I thought there would be a riot here. I wondered, with a flash of anger, if she thought we four Negro families might suddenly burn down our own houses. I felt pity for her fear, but I was angered by her apparent belief that I, because I was a Negro, would understand violence because it, too, was Negro. I wanted to tell her that it was a white man who murdered my husband in the dead of the night.

[13]The Watts riot occurred at a time when I was driving each day to Los Angeles to attend the national convention of my sorority, Delta Sigma Theta. Many of the Negro women attending the convention were staying with relatives or friends in Watts. When the area was suddenly sealed off, some were trapped inside. Others, at the convention, could not get back to Watts, and told of receiving telephone reports from relatives and friends inside the police lines. My heart went out to the people trapped in the furies they described, for I knew that the vast majority of Negroes in Watts were locked in their houses praying for the riot to end.

[14]Driving home each night, I took a freeway that skirts Watts, hearing on my radio reports that snipers were shooting at cars along my route, my hands freezing on the wheel in sudden fear of being picked off in the dark. Finally, at home with the TV turned on, I watched in horror the endless scenes of violence.

[15]I felt what I saw on television on two distinct levels. As a Negro, I experienced fear, a desire to hide, to run from the white-helmeted police and the troops with fixed bayonets. Simultaneously, I felt the coverage was an incitement to whites to arm themselves against all Negroes. It seemed to me it was deliberately being presented that way.

[16]Much as I hated violence, sure as I was that the riot would solve nothing, I understood what had driven these people to it. It was the same utter frustration that had driven Medgar to nightmarish dreams of a Mississippi Mau Mau. And there were moments, I admit, during those hours of watching television, when I almost wished they would succeed in burning the ghetto to the ground.

[17]Ironically, it was a news flash of a white policeman killed in line of duty that brought me to my senses — and to tears. For the announcement said that he had a wife and children. Hearing that, I was suddenly back in Jackson, Mississippi, on the floor of our carport, holding my own dying husband in my arms.

[18]*How it all began.* Both deaths were caused, in the final analysis, by the hate that separates whites and Negroes in America. We speak of violence in the Negro ghettos of the North, and we think of Negroes burning and looting white-owned stores. We talk of violence in the rural counties of the South, and we visualize a white mob attacking a Negro. What we tend to forget is that both pictures are joined by a common history, a record of violence and brutality that dates at least from the days when ships with white masters carried cargoes of black slaves.

[19]And we have all of us, I think, spent far too much time separating Northern experience from Southern experience and far too little examining the threads that connect them. One of those threads is white fear of Negroes. Originally Southern, this fear has become almost tangible in the North since the ghetto riots began. I feel it wherever I go. It is apparently a universal truth that you cannot hold a people down without fearing they will someday rise up and smite you.

[20]Today most Northerners know that in the six American cities with the largest Negro population — all of them in the North — half of the Negroes were born in the South. And these, too, are threads, millions of them, weaving the familiar Southernness that blankets much of Negro life in the North. It is a Southernness that

transcends accents and "soul food," that has colored everything from attitudes toward police to feelings about white institutions.

[21] *Riots are contagious.* As long as the Negroes of the Northern ghettos behaved in familiar Southern ways — fearing the police, submissive to white institutions — their intolerable conditions could be safely ignored by white society. The description of the typical rioter in the recent report of the National Advisory Commission on Civil Disorders indicates why this is no longer so: "The typical rioter was a teen-ager or young adult, a lifelong resident of the city in which he rioted, a high-school dropout . . . somewhat better educated than his nonrioting Negro neighbor . . . usually underemployed or employed in a menial job. He was proud of his race, extremely hostile to both whites and middle-class Negroes and, although informed about politics, highly distrustful of the political system."

[22] The contagious quality of the riots — within a single ghetto and from city to city — suggests that more and more of these angry young Negroes are rejecting the threat-induced submissiveness of their parents' Southern past. Born and bred on city streets, they are demanding in violent and inarticulate ways to be part of a Northern future. Their methods are wrong and destructive of their goals, but their message is clear. Their misguided energies cry out for constructive leadership. I do not see it in the Stokely Carmichaels and Rap Browns that the press increasingly insists are their leaders. Nor do I believe for a minute that such men have any important following.

[23] I want my two sons to be angry young men. I don't want them to forget what it is like to be a Negro in America. But I want them to use their anger in more constructive ways than rioting. Their father was a good example.

[24] Medgar was murdered specifically because his message and his methods were working in the fight for equal justice and opportunity. If his life proved anything, it was that not even the racist climate of a Mississippi could prevent him from becoming a man in the fullest sense of the word. [28]

THE COMMUNITY COLLEGE
by Sigurd Rislov

[1] Since the turn of the century, a new educational institution has appeared in America. During the past twenty years, it has grown at an accelerated pace and there are reasons for believing that it will become standard equipment in the nation's public school program.

[2] This institution is the public two-year college, sometimes called a junior college, a community college, or just plain

college. The typical community college is a local organization, either district or county. Nine tenths of its students live within a 35-mile radius. There are no fraternities or sororities and usually no dormitories. It boasts small classes, emphasis on teaching, a comprehensive advisory and counseling program for its students, and a personal student-teacher relationship. It undertakes three major functions.

[3] First and paramount is its program of lower-division, freshman-sophomore, courses paralleling the state university and other senior institutions. Students planning to specialize in any of the regular or academic professional areas, such as law, medicine, dentistry, engineering, teaching, business, psychology, physics, chemistry, botany, can begin college in their own community and transfer with comparable advanced standing to senior institutions for completion of their training without loss of time or credits. About 35 per cent of the full-time students in community colleges complete advanced work at a senior institution.

[4] Second, it provides terminal training for students who are not going to be baccalaureate candidates but who want and need more education than high school provides. For these there are such alternatives as trade courses in airframe and aircraft engine mechanics, auto mechanics, radio and television servicing, metal shop, machine shop, or courses for the semiprofessional technician in the various branches of engineering or in laboratories. Some terminal students take business courses, secretarial training, or agriculture. Others take regular lower-division college courses in order to be more knowledgeable persons with broader intellectual and emotional horizons, whatever their occupations.

[5] Besides these two services for the college-age population, the community college attempts to be an educational and cultural reservoir for the adult population of the area. This is its third function and it does this in several ways. One is by providing evening courses for people already employed or in business. The content of such courses is determined by the nature of the group for which they are operated and by interests and wants of the population. There may be classes in modern world problems, history, psychology, philosophy, economics, or whatever interest and facilities warrant. Many of the adults in these classes are college graduates who either want to take those courses which their degree requirements excluded, or want to retake some they once had in order to renew acquaintance with an area of worth to them. Others are without academic degrees, but wish to drink deeper at the Pierian spring.

[6] Another primarily adult service of the community college is to act as a focal point for cultural activities. Do those with musical ability wish to cultivate their talents? The college organizes

a chorus, an orchestra, or produces an opera with a local cast. Are there people willing to put forth a concerted effort to make better sense out of current affairs? A college-community forum is organized and leading figures in contemporary problems are brought in to present their views and discuss possible solutions. Comparable assistance can be given to amateur thespians, writers, artists, both in performance and appreciation.

[7] This triadic obligation — to the university-bound student, to the terminal student, and to the adult — is, of course, not assumed by every two-year college. Some have a highly specialized objective to which all else is legitimately subordinate. What has been described is what appears to be the emerging pattern for the typical public two-year college. [29]

PHILOSOPHICAL METHOD OF THE AMERICANS
by Alexis De Tocqueville

[1] The philosophical method of the eighteenth century, then, is not only French, but democratic, and this explains why it was so readily admitted throughout Europe, where it has contributed so powerfully to change the face of society. It is not because the French have changed their former opinions and altered their former manners that they have convulsed the world, but because they were the first to generalize and bring to light a philosophical method by the aid of which it became easy to attack all that was old and to open a path to all that was new.

[2] If it be asked why at the present day this same method is more rigorously followed and more frequently applied by the French than by the Americans, although the principle of equality is no less complete and of more ancient date among the latter people, the fact may be attributed to two circumstances, which it is first essential to have clearly understood.

[3] It must never be forgotten that religion gave birth to Anglo-American society. In the United States, religion is therefore mingled with all the habits of the nation and all the feelings of patriotism, whence it derives a peculiar force. To this reason another of no less power may be added: in America religion has, as it were, laid down its own limits. Religious institutions have remained wholly distinct from political institutions, so that former laws have been easily changed while former belief has remained unshaken. Christianity has therefore retained a strong hold on the public mind in America; and I would more particularly remark that its sway is not only that of a philosophical doctrine which has been adopted upon inquiry, but of a religion which is believed without discussion. In

the United States, Christian sects are infinitely diversified and per-
petually modified; but Christianity itself is an established and ir-
resistible fact, which no one undertakes either to attack or to defend.
The Americans, having admitted the principal doctrines of the Christian religion without inquiry, are obliged to accept in like manner
a great number of moral truths originating in it and connected with
it. Hence the activity of individual analysis is restrained within narrow
limits, and many of the most important of human opinions are removed from its influence.

⁴The second circumstance to which I have alluded is that
the social condition and the Constitution of the Americans are
democratic, but they have not had a democratic revolution. They
arrived on the soil they occupy in nearly the condition in which we
see them at the present day; and this is of considerable importance.

⁵There are no revolutions that do not shake existing
belief, enervate authority, and throw doubts over commonly received ideas. Every revolution has more or less the effect of releasing
men to their own conduct and of opening before the mind of each
one of them an almost limitless perspective. When equality of conditions succeeds a protracted conflict between the different classes
of which the elder society was composed, envy, hatred, and unchar-
itableness, pride and exaggerated self-confidence seize upon the
human heart, and plant their sway in it for a time. This, independently of equality itself, tends powerfully to divide men, to lead
them to mistrust the judgment of one another, and to seek the light
of truth nowhere but in themselves. Everyone then attempts to
be his own sufficient guide and makes it his boast to form his own
opinions on all subjects. Men are no longer bound together by ideas,
but by interests; and it would seem as if human opinions were reduced to a sort of intellectual dust, scattered on every side, unable
to collect, unable to cohere.

⁶Thus that independence of mind which equality sup-
poses to exist is never so great, never appears so excessive, as
at the time when equality is beginning to establish itself and in the
course of that painful labor by which it is established. That sort of
intellectual freedom which equality may give ought, therefore, to be
very carefully distinguished from the anarchy which revolution brings.
Each of these two things must be separately considered in order not
to conceive exaggerated hopes or fears of the future.

⁷I believe that the men who will live under the new forms
of society will make frequent use of their private judgment, but I
am far from thinking that they will often abuse it. This is attributable
to a cause which is more generally applicable to democratic countries, and which, in the long run, must restrain, within fixed and
sometimes narrow limits, individual freedom of thought. [30]

ASSIGNMENTS

3. Partition

Write a partition theme about some physical object in order to show one or any combination of the following:

1. Its value	5. Pleasure it gives
2. Complexity	6. Harm it causes
3. Simplicity	7. Problems it creates
4. Cost	8. Organizational structure

4. Partition

Write a conceptual partition of approximately 500 words on one of the following subjects:

1. The nature of something, such as democracy, socialism, school spirit, history, etc.
2. Athletics
3. Hunting
4. Marriage or divorce
5. Movie idols
6. A typical date (weekend, college, teen-ager, etc.)
7. My town, (campus, church, coach, teacher, etc.)
8. Ways to appreciate music, art, sports, etc.

Cause and effect

A writer develops thought by breaking down a subject into causes and effect or effect and causes in order to explain how an event, happening, or result occurred or to predict a future happening — the result of a given set of circumstances or conditions. In writing analysis by cause and effect, a writer answers the questions: "What conditions or circumstances cause this?" "Given a set of conditions or circumstances, what will be the effect?"

Cause and effect relationships are common in our daily lives. Helen refuses to go to the dance with Bob. At once Bob begins to seek the reasons for her refusal. The basketball team loses six games in a row after winning the first ten games. Everyone, especially the coach, is asking: "What are the reasons for the defeats?" Bill, the president of the student council, points out to his colleagues on the council what he believes will be some of the effects of the recent tuition raise. Jane, another council member, speaks of some possible results of the new dress code. Jim explains the results of the recent changes in the constitution.

What are the causes of increased crime? alcoholism? increased divorces? drug addiction? juvenile delinquency? What effects? What are the causes and effects of the Civil War, World War I, World War II? Why are there so many accidents? people unemployed? school drop-outs? earthquakes? suicides? What effects do these happenings have? Events such as these can be understood and solved only if the causes are found. Cause and effect relationships, then, are a very important as well as a common aspect of everyday living.

In the model paragraphs which follow, observe the introductory question and the answer developed by causes.

. . . But most laymen do not ask the next questions: Why is Grand Canyon unique, or why are such canyons, even on a smaller scale, rare? And the answer to those questions is that a set of very special conditions was necessary.

First there must be a thick series of rock strata slowly rising as a considerable river flows over it. Second, that considerable river must carry an unusual amount of hard sand or stone fragments in suspension so that it will be able to cut downward at least as rapidly as the rock over which it flows is rising. Third, that considerable river must be flowing through very arid country. Otherwise rain, washing over the edges of the cut, will widen it at the top as the cut goes deeper. That is why broad valleys are characteristic of regions with normal rainfall; canyons, large and small, of arid country. [31]

DISCUSSION

The structural organization and development of these two paragraphs is simple. Joseph Wood Crutch states his purpose, announcing the causal relationship in the first two sentences. He poses a question and answers it with "a set of very special conditions." In explaining the formation of canyons, he cites three conditions. Within a question to answer framework, then, the writer develops by stating three causes. He uses the guide words: first, second, and third to give distinctiveness to each condition.

Study the following model:

The vagaries of currents may have disastrous effects on life. The Humboldt Current, that mighty draught of frigid water that runs up the west coast of South America, shifts unexpectedly

seaward at times. The result, for fish, for fowl and for men who make
their living from its waters, is catastrophic. As it moves along the
coast, the Humboldt Current carries with it a rich load of nutrients.
A southerly wind stirs up eddies and off-shoots on the shoreward side
of the current, causing upwelling of water so full of phosphates and
other fertilizing minerals that it nourishes one of the richest populations of marine life in the world. The current supports an extensive
Peruvian fishing fleet. It also supports tens of millions of birds, whose
droppings — guano harvested from offshore rocks — are the basis
of a big fertilizer industry. Every few years, however, the southerly
wind falls, the upwelling ceases, warm water moves in and the fish
vanish. Millions of birds starve, and catastrophe overtakes the fishing
and fertilizer industries. [32]

DISCUSSION
          In the first sentence the writer announces the causal
relationship: "the vagaries (wild, capricious or fantastic actions)
of currents have disastrous effects on life." The development is
with a pattern of general through specifics (deduction). When the
southerly wind falls, "the upwelling ceases, warm water moves in
and the fish vanish. Millions of birds starve, and catastrophe overtakes the fishing and fertilizer industries." Yet the Humboldt
moving along the coast brings much good when a southerly wind
"stirs up eddies and off-shoots on the opposite side of the current, causing upwelling of water . . . ."

          Most cause and effect writing is simply organized.
Within the general to particular framework (deduction) or particular to general framework (induction), a writer will develop
by time, by climax, by citing conditions or circumstances. To make
each cause or effect distinct, writers will use transitional words
and phrases. Among the most common transitional expressions
are the following:

EFFECT:	result	consequence	outcome	outgrowth
	effect			
CAUSE:	because	due to	factors	reasons
	bring about	basis	sources	give rise to

Induction (movement from causes to effect) and deduction
(movement from effect through causes) are natural orders for
developing causal relationships.

Observe the simple and effective pattern of the model paragraph which follows:

What caused the economic miracle which Erhard has so brilliantly brought to pass? (1) Germans are a notoriously industrious people; they work hard, and are thrifty. Despair ruled the nation in 1946; hard work was not merely something expected of every citizen, but salvation — a way out of a stultifying blind alley. (2) Much of the prewar German industrial plant was destroyed by Allied bombing, or dismantled by the French and British after the war; hence most German factories are comparatively new, built from scratch, and highly modern and efficient. (3) Marshall Plan aid poured roughly three billion dollars into the country. (4) The massive stream of refugees from East Germany and expellees from beyond the Oder-Neisse provided an almost inexhaustible labor market. Even today unemployment scarcely exists; in fact, labor shortage is acute. (5) Until comparatively recently Germany was disarmed and, like Japan, did not have to allocate a large percentage of its budget to armament. [33]

As with many of the other patterns of organization and development of thought, you should plan carefully before writing. In planning, follow these suggestions:

1. Have your purpose clearly in mind.

2. Be sure that you have sufficient knowledge of the subject to develop it.

3. Distinguish clearly between causes and effects. A preliminary listing of causes and effects can be helpful in this step.

4. Distinguish between remote causes and immediate causes. Select those causes and effects that best develop your main idea.

5. Don't forget that a writer's special interest in a happening can play a significant part in his selection of conditions; for example: A juvenile drug addict is arrested for stealing drugs. The causes of the crime and his addiction might be different when viewed through the eyes of (1) the drug addict, (2) his parents, (3) the arresting officer, (4) the judge, (5) the family doctor, (6) the defense attorney, (7) the attorney for the prosecution, (8) the parole officer, (9) the owner of the store who was brutally beaten, (10) the family of the store owner.

6. A complex situation or happening usually consists of several conditions or circumstances; some of these conditions are important and relevant; some unimportant; some incidental.

7. Do not consider something to be a cause that is not truly a cause *(Non Causa pro Causa)*; for instance: John received a brain concussion in the final game of the season. In the next few months his grades went steadily down. At the end of the semester, he left school. Many students assumed that the injury was the cause of his poor grades and his leaving school. When he returned in the fall, they learned that the real reasons were his worry over his father's prolonged illness and the financial condition of the family. He left school to help the family until his father could return to his work.

8. Avoid making the *post hoc* fallacy. The words *post hoc, ergo propter hoc* mean "after this, therefore because of this." Many people assume that because event B follows event A closely in time that event A caused event B. This fallacy is the source of many superstitions: a black cat crosses our path, spilling salt, breaking a mirror, souring of milk by a clap of thunder, thirteen at a table, and opening an umbrella in the house — to mention only a few.

Remember that an event which follows another event can be a clue to a causal relationship. It does not definitely establish one.

9. Keep in mind the possibility of chain causes and effects. One cause can be an effect leading to another result. Think of the chain of causes and effects set in motion by the assassination of President Kennedy.

EXERCISES

8. Cause and Effect

Study the model paragraph below. Answer the questions that follow.

And the Grand Canyon is the grandest of all canyons because at that particular place all the necessary conditions were fulfilled more exuberantly than at any other place in the whole world. The Colorado River carries water from a relatively wet country through a dry one, it bears with it a fantastic amount of abrasive material, the rock over which it flows has been slowly rising during several millions of years, and too little rain falls to widen very rapidly the gash which it cuts. Thus in desert country everything from the color of a mouse or the shape of a leaf up to the largest features of the mountains themselves is more likely than not to have the same explanation: dryness. [34]

1. Does the writer establish the relationship of causes and effects with the opening sentence?
2. How many conditions are responsible for the Grand Canyon?
3. What conditions does the writer emphasize? How?
4. Where is the topic sentence?

9. Cause and Effect

Read the model paragraph below. Complete the sentence outline that follows it.

An arsenic-contaminated environment affects not only man but animals as well. A report of great interest came from Germany in 1936. In the area about Freiberg, Saxony, smelters for silver and lead poured arsenic fumes into the air, to drift out over the surrounding countryside and settle down upon the vegetation. According to Dr. Hueper, horses, cows, goats, and pigs, which of course fed on this vegetation, showed loss of hair and thickening of the skin. Deer inhabiting nearby forests sometimes had abnormal pigment spots and precancerous warts. One had a definitely cancerous lesion. Both domestic and wild animals were affected by "arsenical enteritis, gastric ulcers, and cirrhosis of the liver." Sheep kept near the smelters developed cancers of the nasal sinus; at their death arsenic was found in the brain, liver, and tumors. In the area there was also "an extraordinary mortality among insects, especially bees. After rainfalls which washed the arsenical dust from the leaves and carried it along into the water of brooks and pools, a great many fish died." [35]

Title

I. An arsenic-contaminated environment affects not only man but animals as well. (Next sentence elaborates on this idea.)
  A.
  B.
  C.
    1.
    2.
    3.

10. *Cause and Effect*
Read the model paragraph below. Answer the questions that follow it.

The effects of World War II on Britain were manifold. 357,000 Britons had been killed (30,000 of them merchant seamen, 60,000 of them civilian air raid victims) and 600,000 more had been disabled. If the Second World War proved for Britain only one third as deadly as the first, it was because British troops had not had to undergo four years and more of continuous full-scale land fighting. The Sommes, Passchendaeles, and Verduns, of the First World War were called Leningrad, Moscow, and Stalingrad in the Second. Yet Britain's cities had been destroyed in a manner for which the earlier war provided no precedent. Her port facilities and her railways had deteriorated. She had a national indebtedness of twenty-five billion pounds and for the first time since the seventeenth century was, in terms of her total international accounts, a debtor country. She was still dependent upon the import of food and raw materials; yet most of the export industries with which she balanced accounts had been converted to military purposes, and the merchant marine which gained her "invisible earnings" was 30 per cent smaller than it had been in 1938. The ghost of the Pax Britannica had been laid and naval supremacy conceded to the United States. [36]

1. What is the main idea of this paragraph?
2. What are the various methods used to develop the writer's thought?
3. If you eliminate the first sentence and make the last sentence the opening topic sentence, what kind of development would you have: from cause to effect or effect to causes?

Read now these longer selections.

[1] The *facts* of urban growth, as we have seen, are reasonably clear. To determine *why* the growth has occurred is not as easy a task as might be thought. Sometimes it is held that people have moved from farms to cities "because they like city life" or because of the attractiveness of the real or imagined higher wages paid in the city. This seems not to be the whole truth, however, because during the years of great urban growth there had also been occurring an unprecedented depression in American agriculture. Therefore, we do not know whether the migration to the cities was due to the

greater attractiveness of the cities or because rural living had become so economically unattractive that many people were left no real choice. Probably both factors reinforced one another. Assuming that the migrants preferred to move to the city, we still do not know whether they preferred the urban mode of living or were merely willing to endure it for the sake of the somewhat higher wages which they would receive, or thought they would receive, in the cities.

²It is possible to approach the reasons for the growth of cities from a less personal angle. Cities grew because there was a sufficient demand for labor in the cities to enable people to make a living there. That fact is fundamental, although one must not assume that everyone who lives in the city actually makes a living there. Numerous persons in the city are supported in whole or in part by philanthropy, not only in depression periods but in normal times as well. The point, however, is that the city-dominated economic systems must be economically able to support not only those gainfully employed there, but also those who are directly or indirectly supported by those gainfully employed. Cities have been able to support their large populations because of the presence of the great basic employing units — factories. It would be a mistake to assume, however, that the production of goods is the sole or even major type of urban employment. Cities are also the centers of the great service institutions: colleges and universities, hospitals, banks, insurance companies, and recreational services of all kinds, to mention a few of the more obvious ones. The affairs of government, moreover, are employing a greater and greater proportion of the population, particularly since the services of government are constantly expanding. These centers of government are, of course, all located in urban centers. In short, *our society has produced a culture which emphasizes the kind of values and activities which we seem best to carry out when functioning in large,* sometimes tremendous, *cities.* [37]

QUESTIONS

1. What is the purpose of the first paragraph?
2. Is the main idea stated in the second paragraph?
3. Is the movement of thought by induction, deduction, some other order?
4. What are some of the guide words that indicate causes and effects?

Read the next model. Study the analysis which follows:

[1]"The campus is serving as a graveyard for most of the robins that attempt to take up residence in the spring," said Dr. Wallace. But why? At first he suspected some disease of the nervous system, but soon it became evident that "in spite of the assurances of the insecticide people that their sprays were 'harmless to birds' the robins were really dying of insecticidal poisoning; they exhibited the well-known symptoms of loss of balance, followed by tremors, convulsions, and death."

[2]Several facts suggested that the robins were being poisoned, not so much by direct contact with the insecticides as indirectly, by eating earthworms. Campus earthworms had been fed inadvertently to crayfish in a research project and all the crayfish had promptly died. A snake kept in a laboratory cage had gone into violent tremors after being fed such worms. And earthworms are the principal food of robins in the spring.

[3]A key piece in the jigsaw puzzle of the doomed robins was soon to be supplied by Dr. Roy Barker of the Illinois Natural History Survey at Urbana. Dr. Barker's work, published in 1958, traced the intricate cycle of events by which the robins' fate is linked to the elm trees by way of the earthworms. The trees are sprayed in the spring (usually at the rate of 2 to 5 pounds of DDT per 50-foot tree, which may be the equivalent of as much as *23 pounds per acre* where elms are numerous) and often again in July, at about half this concentration. Powerful sprayers direct a stream of poison to all parts of the tallest trees, killing directly not only the target organism, the bark beetle, but other insects, including pollinating species and predatory spiders and beetles. The poison forms a tenacious film over the leaves and bark. Rains do not wash it away. In the autumn the leaves fall to the ground, accumulate in sodden layers, and begin the slow process of becoming one with the soil. In this they are aided by the toil of the earthworms, who feed in the leaf litter, for elm leaves are among their favorite foods. In feeding on the leaves the worms also swallow the insecticide, accumulating and concentrating it in their bodies. Dr. Barker found deposits of DDT throughout the digestive tracts of the worms, their blood vessels, nerves, and body wall. Undoubtedly some of the earthworms themselves succumb, but others survive to become "biological magnifiers" of the poison. In the spring the robins return to provide another link in the cycle. As few as 11 large earthworms can transfer a lethal dose of DDT to a robin. And 11 worms form a small part of a day's rations to a bird that eats 10 to 12 earthworms in as many minutes.

[4]Not all robins receive a lethal dose, but another consequence may lead to the extinction of their kind as surely as fatal poisoning. The shadow of sterility lies over all the bird studies and

indeed lengthens to include all living things within its potential range. There are now only two or three dozen robins to be found each spring on the entire 185-acre campus of Michigan State University, compared with a conservatively estimated 370 adults in this area before spraying. In 1954 every robin nest under observation by Mehner produced young. Toward the end of June, 1957, when at least 370 young birds (the normal replacement of the adult population) would have been foraging over the campus in the years before spraying began, Mehner could find *only one young robin.* A year later Dr. Wallace was to report: "At no time during the spring or summer [of 1958] did I see a fledgling robin anywhere on the main campus, and so far I have failed to find anyone else who has seen one there."

[5]Part of this failure to produce young is due, of course, to the fact that one or more of a pair of robins dies before the nesting cycle is completed. But Wallace has significant records which point to something more sinister — the actual destruction of the birds' capacity to reproduce. He has, for example, "records of robins and other birds building nests but laying no eggs, and others laying eggs and incubating them but not hatching them. We have one record of a robin that sat on its eggs faithfully for 21 days and they did not hatch. The normal incubation period is 13 days . . . Our analyses are showing high concentrations of DDT in the testes and ovaries of breeding birds," he told a congressional committee in 1960. "Ten males had amounts ranging from 30 to 109 parts per million in the testes, and two females had 151 and 211 parts per million respectively in the egg follicles in their ovaries." [38]

DISCUSSION

The writer begins with a generalization: "The campus is serving as a graveyard for most of the robins . . . ." She then indicates the kind of development with the words "But why?" She answers the question in the same paragraph with the words "the robins were really dying of insecticidal poisoning . . . ." Her next paragraph discusses chain causes: the earthworms eat the spray; the robins eat the earthworms; the robins die. In the next paragraph, she traces an even more intricate pattern of circumstances: elm trees are sprayed in the spring; the poison forms on the leaves and bark; the leaves fall to the ground; the earthworms feed on the leaves and swallow the insecticide; the robins eat the earthworms and die.

In paragraphs 4 and 5 Rachel Carson discusses another consequence that may lead to the extinction of robins: the shadow of sterility.

Study the model which follows. Notice the shift in the direction of thought.

[1]Jacksonian democracy was, in essence, a revival of Jeffersonian principles in a society already committed unconsciously but irrevocably to Hamiltonian policy. It was a shortlived movement which interrupted and modified, but did not materially alter our economic course. It opened the gates for populist politics and made democratic principles indispensable ever afterward in political campaigns. More important, it left a residue of democratic idealism that this nation must have if it is to achieve its true destiny. But, in the immediate sense, Jacksonian democracy failed for two reasons. First, the people at large had not yet reached that stage of experience and education that Jefferson understood was necessary in order to have a responsible electorate. Jackson was a man of principle and integrity; many of his followers were not. In letting down the bars of the political arena to all comers, Jacksonian democracy admitted a shocking number of those political hooligans whose ward-heeling tactics have ever since become a standard disgrace to our political life on both a local and a national level; in justifying the spoils system of political appointments, the movement altered much of our political activity from a debate of principles to a mere seeking of the fruits of victory. The election of 1828 acted as a healthy check to the development of a one-sided economy but it also indicated that the people of the United States were not yet ready for a constructive and responsible democratic movement.

[2]The second reason for Jackson's failure to reconstitute Jeffersonian agrarianism was that, in the final analysis, industrialism promised the successful far greater rewards than did farming. Having once tasted the potential rewards of the American System, the average man was not willing to exchange its vast possibilities for the "healthy mediocrity" of agrarianism. Individual dignity, security, contented self-sufficiency were all very fine to him, but the other branch of the road, though leading through a rough and uncertain jungle that threatened to swallow many a traveller, still promised to lead to an opulent and shining land. It was not greed alone that caused young America to choose the second road. Rather, it was the healthy optimism of a virile, pioneering society that led it along a course it considered to be the upward way. To have stopped with the simple security of Jeffersonian mediocrity would have seemed mere sloth; to have concurred with Jackson's distrust of the fruits of capitalism would have been economic sabotage. To the nineteenth-century mind our way as a nation led to the El Dorado of material magnificence in which happy state the spirit of agrarian democracy remained only a faint but ineradicable echo of the past. [39]

DISCUSSION

This writing illustrates a modified reversal pattern within the general to particular (deduction) pattern. The writer begins with an apparent topic sentence: "it (Jacksonian democracy) was a short-lived movement which interrupted and modified, but did not materially alter our economic course." He then supports this generalization with three results arranged in order of increasing importance (climax): (1) it opened the gates for populist politics, (2) it made democratic principles indispensable ever afterward in political campaigns, and (3) it left a residue of democratic idealism. With the transitional word *but*, he shifts the direction of his thought to the failures of the Jacksonian democracy. He devotes the remainder of that paragraph and the whole of paragraph 2 to citing the two reasons (causes) for that failure.

ASSIGNMENTS

5. *Causes*

Write a theme of approximately 500 words on one of the following topics:

1. Why persons leave a church
2. Why young people leave home
3. Why I like (surfing, football, etc.)
4. Why I believe in God
5. Major causes of crime
6. Major causes of broken homes
7. Reasons for dropouts
8. Why somen work
9. Why I support some (cause, political candidate, plan)
10. Why I welcome (change, vacations, new ideas, the new season in television or other subject)
11. Why I consider burial customs uncivilized
12. Why persons drink too much
13. Why I like going steady
14. Why certain customs are ridiculous
15. Causes of some (war, accidents at home, etc.)

6. *Effects*

Write a theme of approximately 500 words showing the effect or effects of some situation, happening, action.

7. Causes and effects

Write a theme of approximately 500 words developed by causes and effects along with other methods.

8. Partition

Write a paragraph criticizing the model student theme that follows.

CUSTOM OF MONETARY EXCHANGE

by R. A. Bandurraga

[1] Money is undoubtedly the most popular of all ancient conveniences. Whether we consider it to be the root of all evil or the source of all that is jolly and good, there's no denying the advantages that money has over earlier systems of swapping and bartering. Anyone who has ever attempted to pay a fifty-cent taxi fare, as I have, with a twenty dollar bill can readily imagine the difficulties that might arise in trying to get the same cab driver to make change for an ox; to say nothing of having to give a tip in terms of broccoli and carrots.

[2] Applied to modern living, such a system could not be controlled and would be ridiculous; but no more ridiculous than some of the peculiar forms of money that men have been known to hoard or fight about: shells, feathers, beads, stones, whale's teeth, beetle's legs, iron bars, and human scalps.

[3] Our own money seems to be based somewhat more sensibly, and has its origins in such age-old desirable objects as gold, silver, women, and cows.

[4] The words "capital" and "chattel" are derived from the same word as "cattle". Our monetary interests were derived from the word "pecus", the Latin term for cows. Today's "fee" stems from the ancient Scandinavian word Fe, meaning cattle. Besides, our modern coins have "heads" and "tails".

[5] Copper ingots found in a Bronze Age palace on the island of Crete are in the shape of oxen, and the Homeric Greeks computed prices in terms of the ox standard. As a prize for a wrestling match, Achilles offered the winner "a large tripod to stand on the fire, which the spectators valued at twelve oxen. For the loser, he brought out a woman well skilled in women's work, valued at only four oxen." Hard was the struggle for that fine tripod, leaving me to believe that the woman was no bargain, even at four oxen (things haven't changed much).

[6] While the early Greeks regulated the price of slave girls in terms of cattle currency, the ancient Irish figured the price of cattle and everything else in terms of slave girls, or "kumals".

⁷Though gold and silver ornaments were often used as money, the "kumal" was so popular of a currency that she was considered both "legal and tender" as late as the Middle Ages. Easily the liveliest loot of all time, the "kumal" was valued at three cows, with sheep, heifers, and bags of grain serving as small change.

⁸Grain was also a common currency in Ancient Egypt. Taxes were paid in cereals and graineries served as banks, upon which the privileged and wealthy could draw checks against their own deposits (first banking system). Gold was mined mainly for export, and was measured in "grains" that corresponded to the weight of a grain of wheat, just as later it was measured in "carats" to the weight of a carrot seed.

⁹In a similar manner, the Babylonian "shekel" was one hundred and eighty grains of Barley, and offered a uniform standard by which to weigh a lump of silver in 3000 B.C. Although the Lydians are credited with minting the first small coins in the seventh century B.C., the earlier Babylonians issued silver ingots stamped with the images of gods, who supposedly guaranteed the weight and purity of the metal. Gold and silver were stored in temples, where they would receive divine protection, and in Judea, Greece, and Rome, coins were minted in temples.

¹⁰The word money comes from the Latin word "Moneta", a surname of June, in whose temple at Rome money was coined.

¹¹From here, it is a big jump through history of the usage of coins for purchasing items to the use of paper money in the U.S. in 1812. The main problem with paper currency was that the only limitation was the availability of printing presses and the ink (things still haven't changed much).

¹²As I look at a one dollar bill, I must laugh. It simply states "This note is legal tender for all debts public and private." It says nothing about being redeemable in lawful monies, gold and silver. To me this piece of paper is worthless. I have reverted back to "X" number of years, B.C.; all I have to do is exchange this piece of paper for a "piece of paper's worth of merchandise".

¹³As opposed to the present cold war with the Soviet Union, just imagine an all-out economic cold war. It would seem that the strategic use of gold could be every bit as decisive as the strategic use of nuclear weapons in a war that was military and hot. The stockpiling of both gold and weapons would invite speculation that bombs and bullion may be more alike than we had reason to suspect. In view of this similarity and previously noted instance of weapons evolving in harmless currency, this writer is prompted to offer the suggestion that a nuclear war might be avoided by simply switching the international monetary base from gold to H-bombs. Since nations are notably reluctant to part with their money, the new nuclear wealth

would be considered too precious to waste on waging war. H-bombs would be kept in vaults, and cherished, as gold is cherished today, while money values might be measured in H-bombs, which are redeemable in the joys of peace.

[14]The more immediate question though, is not whether dollars and rubles will ever be based on a nuclear standard but whether the whole idea of money might not be on the way out. With the growing popularity of credit cards and the advent of automated accounting, the writer can see the possibility and practicability of currency being replaced by a vast system of credit.

WHO KILLED BENNY PARET?

by Norman Cousins

[1]Sometime about 1935 or 1936 I had an interview with Mike Jacobs, the prize-fight promoter. I was a fledgling reporter at that time; my beat was education but during the vacation season I found myself on varied assignments, all the way from ship news to sports reporting. In this way I found myself sitting opposite the most powerful figure in the boxing world.

[2]There was nothing spectacular in Mr. Jacobs' manner or appearance; but when he spoke about prize fights, he was no longer a bland little man but a colossus who sounded the way Napoleon must have sounded when he reviewed a battle. You knew you were listening to Number One. His saying something made it true.

[3]We discussed what to him was the only important element in successful promoting — how to please the crowd. So far as he was concerned, there was no mystery to it. You put killers in the ring and the people filled your arena. You hire boxing artists — men who are adroit at feinting, parrying, weaving, jabbing, and dancing, but who don't pack dynamite in their fists — and you wind up counting your empty seats. So you searched for the killers and sluggers and maulers — fellows who could hit with the force of a baseball bat.

[4]I asked Mr. Jacobs if he was speaking literally when he said people came out to see the killer.

[5]"They don't come out to see a tea party," he said evenly. "They come out to see the knockout. They come out to see a man hurt. If they think anything else, they're kidding themselves."

[6]Recently, a young man by the name of Benny Paret was killed in the ring. The killing was seen by millions; it was on television. In the twelfth round, he was hit hard in the head several times, went down, was counted out, and never came out of the coma.

[7]The Paret fight produced a flurry of investigations. Governor Rockefeller was shocked by what happened and appointed

a committee to assess the responsibility. The New York State Boxing Commission decided to find out what was wrong. The District Attorney's office expressed its concern. One question that was solemnly studied in all three probes concerned the action of the referee. Did he act in time to stop the fight? Another question had to do with the role of the examining doctors who certified the physical fitness of the fighters before the bout. Still another question involved Mr. Paret's manager; did he rush his boy into the fight without adequate time to recuperate from the previous one?

[8]In short, the investigators looked into every possible cause except the real one. Benny Paret was killed because the human fist delivers enough impact, when directed against the head, to produce a massive hemorrhage in the brain. The human brain is the most delicate and complex mechanism in all creation. It has a lacework of millions of highly fragile nerve connections. Nature attempts to protect this exquisitely intricate machinery by encasing it in a hard shell. Fortunately, the shell is thick enough to withstand a great deal of pounding. Nature, however, can protect man against everything except man himself. Not every blow to the head will kill a man — but there is always the risk of concussion and damage to the brain. A prize fighter may be able to survive even repeated brain concussions and go on fighting, but the damage to his brain may be permanent.

[9]In any event, it is futile to investigate the referee's role and seek to determine whether he should have intervened to stop the fight earlier. That is not where the primary responsibility lies. The primary responsibility lies with the people who pay to see a man hurt. The referee who stops a fight too soon from the crowd's viewpoint can expect to be booed. The crowd wants the knockout; it wants to see a man stretched out on the canvas. This is the supreme moment in boxing. It is nonsense to talk about prize fighting as a test of boxing skills. No crowd was ever brought to its feet screaming and cheering at the sight of two men beautifully dodging and weaving out of each other's jabs. The time the crowd comes alive is when a man is hit hard over the heart or the head, when his mouthpiece flies out, when the blood squirts out of his nose or eyes, when he wobbles under the attack and his pursuer continues to smash at him with pole-axe impact.

[10]Don't blame it on the referee. Don't even blame it on the fight managers. Put the blame where it belongs — on the prevailing mores that regard prize fighting as a perfectly proper enterprise and vehicle of entertainment. No one doubts that many people enjoy prize fighting and will miss it if it should be thrown out. And that is precisely the point. [40]

CHAPTER SEVEN *References*

1. From *Introduction to General Psychology* by Frederick B. Knight. Copyright © 1953 by D. C. Heath and Company. By permission.

2. From *The Mysterious Sky* by Lester del Rey. Copyright © 1964 by Lester del Rey. Reprinted by permission of Chilton Book Company.

3. From *Sociology* by John Cuber. Copyright © 1963 by Appleton-Century-Crofts, Inc. Reprinted by permission of the publisher.

4. From *Design for Thinking*, by Albert Upton. By permission of the Stanford University Press.

5. From *Geology: Principles and Processes*, Fifth Edition, by William H. Emmons, et. al. Copyright © 1960 by Mc-Graw-Hill Book Company, and reprinted with their permission.

6. From *Introduction to Literary Criticism* by Marlies K. Danziger and W. Stacey Johnson. Copyright © 1961 by D. C. Heath and Company. By permission.

7. From *Geology: Principles and Processes*, Fifth Edition, by William H. Emmons et. al. Cf. 5.

8. From *Sociology* by John Cuber. Cf. 3.

9. From *Rhetoric: A Handbook for Writers* by J. William Johnson. Copyright 1967 by Wadsworth Publishing Company. By permission.

10. From *The Humanities* by Louise Dudley and Austin Faricy. Copyright © 1940, 1951 by McGraw-Hill Book Company, Inc., and reprinted with their permission.

11. From *The Humanities* by Louise Dudley and Austin Faricy. Cf. 10.

12. From *How to Communicate Orally* by Glenn R. Capp, © 1961. Reprinted by permission of Prentice-Hall, Inc., Englewood Cliffs, New Jersey.

13. From *Personality and Social Interaction* by Robert H. Dalton. Copyright © 1961 by D. C. Heath and Company. By permission.

14. From *Teaching Social Studies in the High School* by Edgar

B. Wesley and Stanley P. Wronski. Copyright © 1964 by
D. C. Heath and Company. By permission.

15. From *Geology: Principles and Processes,* Fifth Edition, by
William H. Emmons, et. al. Cf. 5.

16. "Idols of the Mind" by Francis Bacon.

17. From *Weather* by Paul E. Lehr, R. Will Burnett, and Herbert
S. Zim. Copyright © 1957 by The Golden Press, Inc. and
reprinted with their permission.

18. From *The Sea Around Us* by Rachel L. Carson. Copyright
© 1950, 1951 by Rachel L. Carson. Reprinted by permission
of the Oxford University Press, Inc.

19. From "They're Saving America's Priceless Seashore," by
Don Wharton. Reprinted with permission from the August,
1966, *Reader's Digest.* Copyright 1966 by the Reader's
Digest Association, Inc.

20. From *Introduction to General Psychology* by Frederick B.
Knight. Cf. 1.

21. From *The Death and Life of Great American Cities* by Jane
Jacobs. Copyright © 1961 by Jane Jacobs. Reprinted by
permission of Random House, Inc.

22. From *Psychology and Life,* copyright D. C. Heath and
Company. By permission.

23. From "The Sea" in *Life Nature Library,* by Leonard Engel
and the Editors of *Life.* Copyright © 1961 by Time, Inc.
Reprinted by permission of Time-Life, Inc.

24. From "The Sea" in *Life Nature Library,* by Leonard Engel
and the Editors of *Life.* Cf. 23.

25. From *The Age of Aristocracy 1688 to 1830* by William B.
Willcox. Copyright © 1966 by D. C. Heath and Company.
By permission.

26. From *Backgrounds of American Literary Thought,* Second
Edition, by Rod W. Horton and Herbert W. Edwards. Copyright © 1967 by The Meredith Publishing Company. Reprinted by permission of Appleton-Century-Crofts, Inc.

27. From *How to Communicate Orally,* by Glenn R. Capp.
Cf. 12.

28. "What Do You Know About Violence," by Mrs. Medgar
Evers, in *The Ladies' Home Journal* (July, 1968). Copyright © 1968 by The Curtis Publishing Company. Reprinted
by permission of Curtis Brown, Inc.

29. "The Community College," by Sigurd Rislov, in *The Atlantic Monthly* (June, 1957). Copyright © 1957 by The Atlantic Monthly Company, and reprinted with their permission and the author's.
30. From "Philosophical Method of the Americans" by Alexis De Tocqueville.
31. From *The Voice of the Desert* by Joseph Wood Krutch. Reprinted by permission of William Morrow and Company, Inc. Copyright © 1954, 1955 by Joseph Wood Krutch.
32. From "The Sea" in *Life Nature Library* by Leonard Engel and the Editors of *Life*. Cf. 23.
33. From *Inside Europe Today* by John Gunther (Harper, 1961). Reprinted by permission of Harper & Row, Publishers.
34. From *The Desert Year* by Joseph Wood Krutch. Reprinted by permission of William Morrow and Company, Inc. Copyright © 1952 by Joseph Wood Krutch.
35. From *Silent Spring* by Rachel L. Carson. Copyright 1962. By permission of the publisher, Houghton Mifflin Company.
36. From *Britain Yesterday and Today* by Walter L. Arnstein. Copyright © 1966 by D. C. Heath and Company. By permission.
37. From *Sociology* by John Cuber. Cf. 3.
38. From *Silent Spring* by Rachel L. Carson. Cf. 35.
39. From *Backgrounds of American Literary Thought* by Rod W. Horton and Herbert W. Edwards. Cf. 26.
40. "Who Killed Benny Paret?" by Norman Cousins. Copyright 1962 Saturday Review, Inc. By permission.

EIGHT
Defining and combining various orders

Definition

Definition is a method of identifying and making clear the meaning of a word or term. By defining, a writer answers the question, "What is the meaning of this?" In addition, he puts limits on the word or term in the form of characteristics that distinguish it from other entities. In the example definition sentence that follows, the writer defines the word *incursion*.

The Spanish *incursion*, a sudden hostile invasion into Aztec territory, was the beginning of the end for Montezuma and the Aztec nation.

In addition to defining the word *incursion*, the writer places limits on its use by characterizing it as a movement that is sudden and hostile. An incursion, therefore, is a certain kind of movement into another's territory; it differs from a visit, a migration to settle land, an invasion that is not sudden and in some cases, not hostile.

Simple definition

Most definitions, like the one in the example sentence above, are short, usually a word-synonym, a phrase, or a sentence. Some definitions, however, are a paragraph or an entire essay running on for several pages. The short definition is called a *simple definition;* the longer ones are known as *extended definitions.* You have probably had many occasions in speaking and writing to use the simple definition. You are aware, therefore, of its problems. It must be worked smoothly and unobtrusively into the flowing thought which develops the main idea. Most dictionary entries, like the example which follows, are too mechanical for this purpose. Yet, from studying a dictionary entry at this time, you can learn some things which will help in defining. Study the entry for the underlined word in the sentence below:

That kind of cactus is <u>indigenous</u> to the Mohave Desert.

in·dig·e·nous \in-'dij-ə-nəs\ *adj* [LL *indigenus*, fr. L *indigena*, n., native, fr. OL *indu, endo* in, within (akin to L *in* and to L *de* down) + L *gignere* to beget] **1 :** produced, growing, or living naturally in a particular region or environment **2 :** INBORN, INNATE **syn** see NATIVE — in·dig·e·nous·ly *adv* — in·dig·e·nous·ness *n* [1]

Answer the following questions:
1. How many meanings are given for the word?
2. What are some possible synonyms [words with nearly the same meaning]?
3. Which meaning will fit best in the context of the example sentence?
4. What does the sign "syn see *native*" mean?

Your answers should be an indication of the problems of working with a dictionary entry. This kind of definition is obviously too mechanical for smooth incorporation into writing. In addition, a dictionary entry presents multiple meanings of a word; some of these meanings are more general than the original; some are more confusing. Moreover, the entry points out the difficulty of working with word synonyms. The word *native* fits very well. Are *inborn* and *innate* as satisfactory?

When you follow the directions given by the sign "syn see *native*," under the entry *native*, you will find the following information:

ına·tive \'nāt-iv\ *adj* [ME *natif*, fr. MF, fr. L *nativus*, fr. *natus*, pp. of *nasci* to be born — more at NATION] **1 :** INBORN, INNATE **2 :** belonging to a particular place by birth **3** *archaic* **:** closely related **4 :** belonging to or associated with one by birth **5 :** NATURAL, NORMAL **6 a :** grown, produced, or originating in a particular place or in the vicinity **:** LOCAL **b :** INDIGENOUS **7 :** SIMPLE, UNAFFECTED **8 a :** constituting the original substance or source **b :** found in nature esp. in an unadulterated form **9** *chiefly Austral* **:** having a usu. superficial resemblance to a specified English plant or animal — na·tive·ly *adv* — na·tive·ness *n*
syn NATIVE, INDIGENOUS, ENDEMIC, ABORIGINAL mean belonging to a locality. NATIVE implies birth or origin in a place or region and may suggest compatibility with it; INDIGENOUS applies to species or races and adds to NATIVE the implication of not having been introduced from elsewhere; ENDEMIC implies being peculiar to a region; ABORIGINAL implies having no known race preceding in occupancy of the region [2]

In the synonyms at the close of the entry, did you observe the various shades of meaning, especially the meaning of *indigenous* and *native*? The dictionary, though an invaluable aid to definition, must be used with discernment.

How can you work simple definitions smoothly into your developing thought? Several methods have worked successfully for experienced writers. The first way is by the synonym, allowing for the limitations mentioned in the discussion above.

He lacked the *incentive* or *stimulus* to begin the onerous task. More than a sport, baseball is an environment, a condition of our warm-weather existence. [3]

Most of all, perhaps, he longs for the screwballs — the weird and hilarious assortment of real eccentrics and simple extroverts who used to be drawn to the game and who are the subjects of most of the baseball yarns which the fan treasures. [4]

Second, by direct explanation:

This spontaneous and loyal support of our preconception — this process of finding "good" reasons to justify our routine beliefs — is known to modern psychologists as "rationalizing" — clearly a new name for a very ancient thing. [5]

Henry Jones was more than an instructor; he was a *choreographer* — a true master in the art of designing the dance.

By indirect explanation:

Trance is a similar abnormality in our society. Even a mild mystic is *aberrant* in Western civilization. [6]

John was a *voracious* reader with an insatiable appetite for westerns.

By the simile:

He was a *stolid*, unimaginative man, in appearance and intelligence much like a dumb ox.

The island was as *inaccessible* as a medieval fortress.

By an analytic or formal definition:

In using this method, a writer defines by placing the word or term in a class (*genus*) and then identifying it with characteristics that show how it differs from other members of the same class.

Term ――――――→ class ――――→ differentiae

A dog is a carniverous domesticated animal (*Canis familiaris*).

A fox is a flesh-eating mammal of the dog family, smaller than wolves and noted for craftiness.

A wolf is a large doglike carnivorous mammal of the *genus canis,* yellowish or brownish gray with coarse fur, erect, pointed ears and a bushy tail.

A republic is a form of government in which the power resides in the people (the electorate).

An aristocracy is a form of government in which the power resides in the hands of the best individuals or a small privileged class.

In organizing the simple definition, avoid the following mistakes:

(1) Do not use the expressions "is where" and "is when" in beginning the main part of the definition. The verb *is* (a linking verb) should be followed by a noun, pronoun, or an adjective, not by an adverbial clause introduced by "where" or "when."

A stadium *is where* they hold sport spectaculars.
A stadium is a structure in which sport spectaculars are held.

Socialism *is when* the ownership and operation of the means of production and distribution is vested in the community as a whole.
Socialism is a theory or system of social organization which advocates the vesting of the ownership and control of the means of production capital, land, etc., in the community as a whole. [7]

(2) Do not use the "circular definition" — a practice of defining a term with the term itself.

Dictation is the act of dictating.

Communism is an economic system practiced by communists.

An aristocracy is a form of government ruled by aristocrats.

A depository is where something valuable is deposited.

(3) Define a word or term in simpler language than the original.

The word *surreptitious* as a synonym for *clandestine* isn't really too much help; *secret* is a simpler synonym.

The words *servile, obsequious, sycophantic* are not very helpful in explaining the meaning of *subservient; fawning, cringing,* and *slavish* are better.

The following explanation of the term *dialectical materialism* seems to be somewhat complicated:

The theory of reality affirming continuous transformation of matter and dynamic interconnectedness of things and concepts, and implying social transformation through socialism toward a classless society, which was advanced by Karl Marx and Friedrich Engels and adopted as the official Soviet philosophy. [8]

(4) In using the analytic or formal definition, follow these few suggestions:

(a) Make the class broad enough to include all the members.
Sports is broad enough to include all the activities in that group: football, tennis, baseball, and so forth.

Literature is a broad enough class to include both poetry and prose works; *poetry* or *prose* is not broad enough.

(b) Do not make the class too broad.
Entertainment is too broad a classification in which to place an individual sport; there are too many kinds of entertainments which are not sports: motion pictures, musicals, plays.

(c) Make sure to differentiate the members of different classes.
Biology is a science.
Biology is a science which treats of living organisms.

A sheriff is a law enforcement officer.

A sheriff is the chief executive officer of a state or county who is responsible for law enforcement in those areas.

(5) Remember that examples are excellent for clarification in the process of defining; they are not definitions.

The *gill fungi* include many species such as *mushrooms* and *toadstools*.

Political conservatives are men like Barry Goldwater and William Buckley, Jr.

EXERCISES

1. Simple definition*

What method of defining has been used in these sentences? Choose from the methods listed below.

a. by synonym
b. by direct explanation
c. by indirect explanation

d. by simile
e. by historical method
f. by formal definition

1. Helen was an ultraconservative. She resisted violently any kind of change.
2. The incident was as bizarre as any from *The Arabian Nights.*
3. A panegyric is an oration, a writing in praise of a person, an eulogy.
4. A ducat is any one of various coins formerly issued in various parts of Europe, especially, that first issued in Venice in 1284.
5. His panegyric, a beautiful tribute to the late President, was published in the literary magazine.
6. Obdurate means obstinate, stubborn, unbending.
7. Euphuism is an affected style in imitation of that of Lyly, fashionable in England about the end of the sixteenth century, characterized by long series of antitheses, frequent similes relating to fabulous natural history, alliteration, and so forth.

** The Random House Dictionary of the English Language College Edition,
Copyright (c) 1968 by Random House, Inc., served as the source for definitions
used in this exercise.*

8. The recreant Benedict Arnold paid the price that most traitors pay for disloyalty.
9. Was it merely a sanctimonious action or a true display of deep religious devotion?
10. His sanctimonious, hypocritical display of respect for the fallen leader was not missed by the grief-stricken followers.
11. An oligarchy is a form of government in which the power is vested in a few persons.
12. Jane was a recalcitrant person, opposing any form of authority.
13. The pills could be as lethal as suicide.
14. A mongoose is a slender, ferretlike carnivore that feeds on rodents, birds, eggs.
15. To recapitulate is to represent ideally or to typify.

2. Simple definition

What kind of error in defining is illustrated in each statement below?

1. To extrapolate is to conjecture.
2. Provincial means belonging to a particular province.
3. Slothfulness is when a person is indolent or lazy.
4. An athlete is a person who plays football.
5. Prolix means verbose.
6. A turnpike is where they have a high-speed highway maintained by tolls.
7. Socialism is an economic system practiced by socialists.
8. Dross is a factory dumping its waste into a river.
9. Neurology is a branch of medicine.
10. Athletics can be a highly competitive form of entertainment.
11. Poetry is a form of literature.
12. Neurology is a form of medicine practiced by neurologists.
13. A catastrophe is the San Francisco earthquake.
14. A soloist is a person who sings a hymn in a choir.
15. Deciduous means transitory.

Extended definition

An extended definition is the organization and development of the meaning of a word or term beyond the limits of the simple definition. It may be a paragraph or two or even an entire essay in length. Writers develop meanings of words and terms more extensively because the devices effective in the simple definition are not adequate for making the meaning of many terms and words in our language clear. Words and terms like socialism, school spirit, democracy, love, literature, personality, objectivity, symbolism, transcendentalism, ethnocentrism, dualism, affluent society cannot be defined adequately with a word-synonym or a few lines of explanation. In addition, many writers feel that accepted definitions do not define the word or term as they are using it; therefore, they write definitions of their own. In the following model, the writer discards the traditional definition of *literary criticism* for the broader interpretation commonly accepted in our own time.

Literary criticism is traditionally defined as the art of judicious condemnation or praise: Samuel Johnson, for instance, describes the critic as "a man able to distinguish the faults and beauties of writing." But in our own time, the term has taken on wider significance, to include the analysis, elucidation, and interpretation of literature. With his awareness of how complex the literary work is, the modern critic usually recognizes that he may have to give close attention to detail, consider some of the relevant historical background, and even reinterpret the essential meaning of a piece of writing before he can pass judgment upon it. [9]

DISCUSSION

The organization and development of this paragraph is simple. The writer presents the traditional definition "as the art of judicious condemnation or praise." He then cites the definition of literary criticism by Samuel Johnson as an example. Next, he explains that the term in our time "has taken on wider significance, to include the analysis, elucidation, and the interpretation of literature." He closes with a discussion of the concerns of the modern critic.

Except for the extended formal definition, you may organize and develop definitions by any one or any combination of the methods that you have studied. You will find the question to answer method a natural one for definition.

What exactly is a tornado? The general picture is familiar enough. The phenomenon is usually brewed on a hot, sticky day with south winds and an ominous sky. From the base of a thundercloud a funnel-shaped cloud extends a violently twisting spout toward the earth. As it sucks in matter in its path, the twister may turn black, brown or occasionally even white (over snow). The moving cloud shows an almost continuous display of sheet lightning. It lurches along in a meandering path, usually northeastward, at 25 to 40 miles per hour. Sometimes it picks up its finger from the earth for a short distance and then plants it down again. The funnel is very slender: its wake of violence generally averages no more than 400 yards wide. As the tornado approaches, it is heralded by a roar as of hundreds of jet planes or thousands of railroad cars. Its path is a path of total destruction. Buildings literally explode as they are sucked by the tornado's low-pressure vortex (where the pressure drop is as much as 10 per cent) and by its powerful whirling winds (estimated at up to 500 miles per hour). The amount of damage depends mainly on whether the storm happens to hit populated areas. The worst tornado on record in the U.S. was one that ripped across Missouri, lower Illinois and Indiana in three hours on March 18, 1925, and killed 689 people.

The tornado's lifetime is as brief as it is violent. Within a few tens of miles (average: about 16 miles) it spends its force and suddenly disappears. [10]

In the model paragraphs which follow, Thomas Henry Huxley uses analogy effectively in defining "A Liberal Education."

[1]What is education? Above all things, what is our ideal of thoroughly liberal education — of that education which, if we could begin life again, we would give ourselves — of that education which, if we could mould the fates to our own will, we would give our children? Well, I know not what may be your conceptions upon this matter, but I will tell you mine, and I hope I shall find that our views are not very discrepant.

[2]Suppose it were perfectly certain that the life and fortune of every one of us would, one day or other, depend upon his winning or losing a game of chess. Don't you think that we should

all consider it to be a primary duty to learn at least the names and the moves of the pieces; to have a notion of a gambit, and a keen eye for all the means of giving and getting out of check? Do you not think that we should look with a disapprobation amounting to scorn, upon the father who allowed his son, or the state which allowed its members, to grow up without knowing a pawn from a knight?

³Yet it is a very plain and elementary truth, that the life, the fortune, and the happiness of every one of us, and, more or less, of those who are connected with us, do depend upon our knowing something of the rules of a game infinitely more difficult and complicated than chess. It is a game which has been played for untold ages, every man and woman of us being one of the two players in a game of his or her own. The chessboard is the world, the pieces are the phenomena of the universe, the rules of the game are what we call the laws of Nature. The player on the other side is hidden from us. We know that his play is always fair, just, and patient. But also we know, to our cost, that he never overlooks a mistake, or makes the smallest allowance for ignorance. To the man who plays well, the highest stakes are paid, with that sort of overflowing generosity with which the strong shows delight in strength. And one who plays ill is checkmated — without haste, but without remorse.

⁴My metaphor will remind some of you of the famous picture in which Retzsch has depicted Satan playing at chess with man for his soul. Substitute for the mocking fiend in that picture a calm, strong angel who is playing for love, as we say, and would rather lose than win — and I should accept it as an image of human life.

⁵Well, what I mean by Education is learning the rules of this mighty game. In other words, education is the instruction of the intellect in the law of Nature, under which name I include not merely things and their forces, but men and their ways; and the fashioning of the affections and of the will into an earnest and loving desire to move in harmony with those laws. For me, education means neither more nor less than this. Anything which professes to call itself education must be tried by this standard, and if it fails to stand the test, I will not call it education, whatever may be the force of authority, or of numbers, upon the other side. [11]

ASSIGNMENT

1. Definition

Read the selection that follows. Write a paragraph discussing its structural organization. Stress its various kinds of development.

RADICALISM AND CONSERVATISM
by Arthur M. Schlesinger

[1] What do the terms "conservative" and "radical" mean? Popular usage has tended to rob these expressions of exact meaning and to convert them into epithets of opprobrium and adulation which are used as the bias or interest of the person may dictate. The conservative, having mapped out the confines of truth to his own satisfaction, judges the depravity and errors of the radical by the extent of his departure from the boundaries thus established. Likewise the radical, from his vantage-point of truth, measures the knavery and infirmities of his opponents by the distance they have yet to travel to reach his goal. Neither conservative nor radical regards the other with judicial calm or "sweet reasonableness." Neither is willing to admit that the other has a useful function to perform in the progress of society. Each regards the other with deep feeling as the enemy of everything that is fundamentally good in government and society.

[2] In seeking a workable definition of these terms, the philosophic insight of Thomas Jefferson is a beacon light to the inquirer. When Jefferson withdrew from active political life at the close of his presidency in 1809, he left behind him the heat and smoke of partisan strife and retired to a contemplative life on his Virginia estate, where his fellow-countrymen learned to revere him as the "Sage of Monticello." The voluminous correspondence of these twilight years of his life is full of instruction for the student of history and politics. His tremendous curiosity caused him to find an unfailing source of speculation in the proclivity of mankind to separate into contrasting schools of opinion. In one luminous passage, representative of the bent of his thought, he declared: "Men, according to their constitutions, and the circumstances in which they are placed, differ honestly in opinion. Some are Whigs, Liberals, Democrats, call them what you please. Others are Tories, Serviles, Aristocrats, etc. The latter fear the people, and wish to transfer all power to the higher classes of society; the former consider the people as the safest depository of power in the last resort; they cherish them, therefore, and wish to leave in them all the powers to the exercise of which they are competent."

[3] In this passage Jefferson does not use the expressions "conservative" and "radical" — indeed, those words had no place in the American political vocabulary until Civil War times — but his penetrating analysis throws a flood of light on the significance of those terms nevertheless. The Tory who fears the people and the Whig who trusts them are equivalent to our own categories of "conservative" and "radical." Thus Jefferson finds the vital distinction between the two schools of opinion in their respective attitudes toward popular government.

⁴ But before accepting Jefferson's classification as correct, what shall we do with the common notion that the conservative is a person who opposes change and that the earmark of the radical is his liking for innovation? This does not seem to be a fundamental distinction. If a difference of opinion concerning the need of change were the basic difference between the two, then Americans who advocate a limitation of the suffrage to male property-owners may properly be regarded as radicals, for they advocate an alteration in the established order; and French patriots of today opposing the reestablishment of the Orleanist monarchy are to be classed as conservatives, for they would keep things unchanged. Few people would be willing to follow the logic of their premises to such conclusions. On the other hand, it cannot be denied that history has generally shown the radical in the role of an active proponent of change and has cast the conservative for the part of the stalwart defender of things as they are. Is such evidence to be dismissed as a coincidence oft-repeated, or has there been behind the actions of both radical and conservative some self-interested purpose which has determined their respective attitudes toward the established order?

⁵ The very question perhaps suggests the answer. Broadly speaking, all history has been an intermittent contest on the part of the more numerous section of society to wrest power and privilege from the minority which had hitherto possessed it. The group which at any period favored broader popular rights and liberties was therefore likely to find itself as a contender for the new and untried, leaving to its antagonists the comfortable repute of being the conservators of the *status quo* and the foes of change. But, though the historical conditions influenced the character of the contest, such conditions were, after all, merely the stage setting of the struggle. Advocacy of change should, under such circumstances, be regarded merely as the means employed to attain an end and, in no sense, as an end in itself. Recurring now to Jefferson's definition, the goal sought by each group — whether it be in the direction of greater or less democracy — would appear to constitute the real difference between the two. [12]

In addition to organization and development by the various methods with which you are already familiar, such as comparison, contrast, classification, process, cause and effect, analogy, writers also develop definitions by presenting (1) the historical meanings, (2) the etymology, and (3) the negative meaning of a word or term. The following model stresses the historical and etymological meanings of the word *personality*.

Historically, the term *personality* has many meanings, ranging from the popular phrase "she has personality" to the profound theological usage found in the expression "personality of God" as expounded in the doctrine of the Trinity. Personality, thus, has come to have a great variety of connotations. When we examine the word etymologically we see that our confusion is only increased; for the Latin word *persona*, from which our term personality comes, as it has been translated into various languages, may signify nobody or no one when used with a verb in the French language, or it may mean a representative of a great body, as *parson* in English. These varieties of usage only emphasize the fact that personality is a generic term which has no specific meaning, universally accepted. Even animals are referred to as "having personality"; here the connotation is characteristic individuality.

Of writers on the subject of personality, Allport (1937) has done the most adequate and comprehensive job of reviewing the historical meanings derived from the Latin *persona.* He distinguished fifty different definitions or meanings. Yet, as MacKinnon (1944) has pointed out, two opposed meanings stand out from the earliest to the latest of these definitions. On the one hand, personality is thought of as a mask, a mere shield of outward and usually superficial appearance; on the other hand, it is conceived as the inner nature, the substance of a man. [13]

DISCUSSION

The writer begins by showing the historical meaning of the word *personality*. From this analysis, he arrives at the conclusion that the word "has come to have a great variety of connotations. He points out that an etymological examination of the word will only add to the confusion. Next, he mentions the fifty different definitions of the word accumulated by Allport. Finally, he states the two opposing definitions.

In the following definition, the writer points out the several meanings of the word *literature*. He then presents a broad definition of the word. In the second paragraph, the writer discusses the etymology of the word and speaks about important oral traditions. In the final sentence, he repeats the definition; he will consider "literature broadly as a verbal art, leaving open the question of whether the words are written or spoken."

What, we may begin by asking, *is* literature, and how can we best define it? The answer is not at all self-evident, for the term can be used in several different senses. It can mean anything written in verse or in prose. It can mean only those works which have a certain distinction. Or it can refer to mere verbiage: "all the rest is literature." For our purposes, it may be best to start by defining it in as broad and neutral a way as possible, simply as a verbal art; that is, literature belongs traditionally to the arts as opposed to the sciences or to practical knowledge, and its medium is the word, as opposed to the visual signs of painting and sculpture or the tones of music.

When we say that its medium is the word, we are going beyond the root meaning of *literature,* which is derived from the Latin *littera,* "letter," and therefore seems to refer primarily to the written or printed word. But many civilizations, from the ancient Greek to the Scandinavian, French, and English, have produced important oral traditions. Even such lengthy narrative poems as Homer's *Iliad* and *Odyssey,* the Icelandic sagas, and the Old English *Beowulf* were presumably sung or chanted by professional bards centuries before they were written down. In order to include these and other oral works, it is useful to consider literature broadly as a verbal art, leaving open the question of whether the words are written or spoken. [14]

In defining, writers will frequently say what the word or term is not; then they will follow with the definition. Study the model which follows. Mr. Krutch defines "his Lower Sonoran Desert" by telling his reader what it is not; then he describes what it is.

"Desert" is an unfortunate word all around and most of its usual associations are inaccurate as well as unfavorable. In the first place the word doesn't even mean "dry," but simply uninhabited or deserted — like Robinson Crusoe's island. In that sense, the expanse about me is far from being a desert, for it is teeming with live things very glad indeed to be right there. Even in its secondary meaning, "desert," suggests to most people the rolling sand dunes of the Sahara. Something like that one may find in Death Valley; perhaps in parts of the Majave; and especially, with an added weirdness, in the hundreds of square miles of New Mexico's White Sands, where the great dunes of glistening gypsum drift like snowbanks, one can hardly believe they are not. Most of my Lower Sonoran Desert, however, is not at all like that. The sandy soil is firm and hard-packed; it supports life, less crowded than in wetter regions but pleasantly flourishing. Nature does not frown here. She smiles invitingly. [15]

FINK
by William Gillis

[1] A word popular among undergraduates these days is "fink." If I trace its etymology correctly, it may be more appropriate on the campus than students realize. Originally in America the word belonged to underworld and to labor slang. Gang members use it to denote a person disloyal to the gang, while to union men the word means "strikebreaker," a definition not far from that of the underworld.

[2] In the language of students a "fink" is a person inclined toward antisocial behavior or one whose actions place him on the outside of student society. He is "out of it." It is not difficult to see how its earlier usage is reflected in this definition.

[3] I could not find a suitable etymology for the word in any of the standard sources, but usage of the American word bears a strong resemblance to slang use of the German word *Fink*, "finch." To German students it designates *"ein Student ohne Verbindung,"* i.e., a student without organizational connections. If the word did migrate from Germany, it has moved into its proper orbit, student talk.

[4] But how could German student slang enter the language of American union men? The slang usage of *Fink*, as far as I can tell, is either obsolete or not widespread today. Possibly connected with it, however, are the common colloquial words *Schmutzfink* and *Dreckfink,* "a dirty person." "Fink" is more likely directly traceable to these words, our word being a shortened form. [16]

WHAT IS A VOLCANO?
by Fred Bullard

[1] "What is a volcano?" is a familiar question. An oft-given answer is that "a volcano is a burning mountain from the top of which issue smoke and fire." Such a statement, although it does express the popular idea of a volcano, held even today, contains few elements of truth. In the first place, no "burning" in the sense of combustion, such as the burning of wood, occurs in a volcano; moreover, volcanoes are not necessarily mountains; furthermore, the activity takes place not always at the summit but more commonly on the sides or flanks; and finally the "smoke" is not smoke but condensed steam, mixed, frequently, with dust particles until it is dark in color, and the "fire" is the reflection of the red-hot material on the vapor clouds above the volcano.

[2] The great cloud of gases, vapor, and ash particles is the most conspicuous feature of the explosive eruption of a volcano. The eruption cloud may be luminous or dark depending on whether the material is incandescent and whether it contains a small or large amount of ash particles. The "fiery" and "smoky" appearances, together with the red glow reflected from the lava in the crater be-

neath, are responsible for the popular idea that volcanoes are "burning mountains." Apparently supporting this fallacy, the material that falls from the eruption cloud (known to the geologist as "pyroclastics" from the Greek *pyro*, meaning "fire," plus *clastic*, meaning "broken") often resembles ash and cinders, by which names they are still known. Although there is intense heat in a volcano, actual burning plays only a minor role in volcanic activity and is confined to almost imperceptible flames from certain combustible gases such as hydrogen.

³To describe what a volcano is *not* is much easier than to give a concise definition of what it *is*. A volcano is a vent or chimney which connects a reservoir of molten matter known as "magma," in the depths of the crust of the earth, with the surface of the earth. The material ejected through the vent frequently accumulates around the opening, building up a cone, called the "volcanic edifice." The loftiest mountains on earth are volcanic edifices. The material ejected consists of liquid lava and broken fragments of partially or completely solidified rock (pyroclastic debris), as well as great quantities of gases. The gases are the motivating force and the most important factor in volcanic action. Some authors have maintained that the only feature common to all volcanoes is the channel through which the molten or gaseous material reaches the surface, and therefore a volcano should be defined as "the vent through which this material is erupted." This, however, leaves us in the difficult position of trying to explain that Vesuvius is not really a volcano but merely a mountain built around one! As now used, the term *volcano* includes both the vent and the accumulation (cone) around it. [17]

ASSIGNMENTS

2. *Definition*
     In a paragraph from 100 to 150 words, define one of the following words:
assassin   precocious   adversity   prestidigitation   clairvoyant

3. *Definition*
     Write a theme of approximately 500 words on any one of the following subjects:

myth	Ivory Tower	husbandry
coup d'etat	sportsmanship	manners
Common Market	colonialism	etiquette
cartel	chivalry	customers
Habeas Corpus	totem pole	ownership
delinquency	climate	ruthlessness
friendship	combustion	school spirit
integrity	parity	courage

"THE SILENT GENERATION"

by Thornton Wilder

[1] A younger generation has been calling attention to itself again. These crises in the public appraisal of the young used to occur at longer intervals; now, with the acceleration of social changes, they appear with increasing frequency. Some of us remember the Jazz Age; this was followed by the Lost Generation; now we are in a state of alarm about the Silent Generation.

[2] I have been given an article on "The Younger Generation" which appeared in *Time* magazine on November 5, 1951, and have been asked to comment on it. There I read that these young people "do not issue manifestoes, make speeches, or carry posters . . . do not want to go into the Army. . . . Their ambitions have shrunk. . . . They want a good secure job . . . either through fear, passivity, or conviction, they are ready to conform. . . . They are looking for a faith."

[3] All this I recognize. I propose that we read the manifestations differently.

[4] The Jazz Age preceded and accompanied the first world war. There was a breaking of windows and great scandal. It made evident to all that the American home or the patriarchal pattern had come to an end. The young people won the latchkey. Then the young men went off to the war. That made them heroes. As heroes they acquired more liberties than they had seized as rebellious bad boys. The Lost Generation was the generation that did not know what to do with its new liberties. The younger generation of today is facing the too-long delayed task of consolidating its liberty and of impressing upon it a design, a meaning, and a focus. No wonder they strike us as silent.

[5] An even greater task rests on their shoulders. They are fashioning the Twentieth Century Man. They are called upon to illustrate what the Germans call a "life-style" for our times. This work is usually done by men and women of middle age, but in the accelerated tempo of these war-punctuated years a man or woman of forty-five is out of date. He does not respect or despise the same institutions as an intelligent person in the middle twenties, does not read the same books, admire the same art, nor agree on the same social or cultural premises. The Silent Generation (loquacious enough among its contemporaries) holds its tongue because it cannot both explore itself and explain itself.

[6] The first charge against these young people is apathy. They do not fling themselves into causes; they are not easily moved to enthusiasm; the expression on their faces is impassive, is "dead pan."

[7] But I know where they learned this impassivity. They

learned it at home, as adolescents, guarding themselves against their parents. Guardedness is not apathy. In all my reading I have discovered no age in which there was so great a gulf between parent and child. A seismic disturbance has taken place in the home. Within forty years America has ceased to be a patriarchy; it is moving toward a matriarchy but has not yet recognized and confirmed it. There is nothing wrong with a matriarchy; it does not connote any emasculation of men; it is merely a shift of balance. What is woeful for all parties is the time of transition. These young people grew up in the fluctuating tides of indeterminate authority. A father was no longer held to be, *ex officio,* wise and unanswerable. The mother had not yet learned the rules of supporting and circumscribing her new authority. Father, mother, and children have had daily to improvise their roles. This led to a constant emotional racket in the air. The child either learned a silent self-containment or fell into neurosis.

⁸The second charge is that they "aim low" — they want a good secure job. The article in *Time* says that, as far as their domestic life is concerned, they look forward to a "suburban idyll."

⁹What they want, at all cost, is not to find themselves in "false situations." Life is full of false situations, especially American life today. The most frequent and glaring of them is incompetence in high places. My generation saw a great deal of this in government, in the Army, in culture, and in education. We exercised our wit upon it, but we were ourselves (not yet free of patriarchal influence) still vaguely respectful of rank and office and status. This generation is not impressed by any vested authority whatever. And their freedom to judge authority is accompanied by their willingness to be judged. Their caution reposes upon their unwillingness to exercise any authority or responsibility for which they do not feel themselves to be solidly prepared and adequate. They hate the false and they shrink from those conspicuous roles which all but inevitably require a certain amount of it. I find this trait very promising. Plato was the first to say that high place is best in the hands of those who are reluctant to assume it.

¹⁰I have said that the Silent Generation is fashioning the Twentieth Century Man. It is not only suffering and bearing forward a time of transition, it is figuring forth a new mentality.

¹¹In the first place, these young people will be the first truly international men and women. At last it has ceased to be a mere phrase that the world is one. Compared to them my generation was parochial. Their experience and their reading — their newspapers as well as their textbooks — have impressed upon them that the things which all men hold in common are more important and more productive than the things which separate them. In the Twenties and

Thirties one felt oneself to be one among millions; these young people feel themselves to be one among billions. They know it not as a fact learned, but as a self-evident condition; they know it in their bones. On the one hand the individual has shrunk; on the other, the individual has been driven to probe more deeply within himself to find the basis for a legitimate assertion of the claim of self. This conviction is new and its consequences are far-reaching — in international relations, in religion, in social reform, in art, and in the personal life.

[12] For instance, we went to war against and among "foreigners" and "enemies." That attitude was narrow; henceforward all wars are civil wars. This generation goes forward not to punish and destroy, but to liberate oppressed and misguided brothers. The Army authorities go into anxious huddles over the unabashed candor with which young men can be heard exploring ways of avoiding military service. The Army — like the church, like the university — is an echoing gallery of out-dated attitudes and sentiments. It still thinks soldiers can be coerced and it still thinks that the primary qualifications of a soldier are courage and obedience. In a machine warfare, the soldier is a kind of engineer; his primary virtue is technical skill and his function is co-operation, not obedience.

[13] Most of us were Protestants; the beliefs held by others were the objects of our all but condescending anthropological curiosity. Today these young people are interested in the nature of belief itself. Some of us in the previous generations hurled ourselves into social reform and social revolution; we did it with a personal passion that left little room for deliberation and long-time planning. To correct one abuse we were ready to upset many a benefit. It was of such crusaders that the Sidney Webbs were finally driven to say, "We hate moral indignation." The emerging International Man will move less feverishly in his enlarged thought-world. This generation is silent because these changes call not for argument but for rumination. The mistakes of the previous generations are writ large over the public prints.

[14] These young people are setting new patterns for the relation of the individual to the society about him. The condition of being unimpressed by authorities and elders has thrown them back more resolutely on themselves. They are similarly unimpressed by time-honored conventions. For instance, young married couples today make few concessions to the more superficial aspects of social life. In my generation young brides suffered if their street address was not "right" and if their table silver was not distinguished. Young men were very conscious of influential connections, commissions in the Army, membership in good clubs. Members of this generation exhibit a singular insistence on wishing to be appraised for them-

selves alone. How often I have known them to conceal sedulously the fact that they come of privileged family. This insistence on being accepted as an individual produces an unprecedented candor. A college girl said to me: "You know I've always been an awful liar. I'm trying to get over it." A veteran, in the presence of his stricken parents, informed a mixed company that he had been a "psycho" for six months after the war. Such expressions reveal the consolidations of a liberty — the liberty of belonging to oneself and not to a social fiction.

[15] These paragraphs have been part description, part explanation, part testimony of faith. Faith is in constant correspondence with doubt. It may be that these young people have been injured by the forces which have been sweeping across the world in their formative years. It may be that what I have called their self-containment is rather a cautious withdrawal from the demands of life. It may be that they lack passion and the constructive imagination. My faith returns, however, with each new encounter. I have just crossed the ocean with a boatload of choice young "Fulbrights" (all hail to the Senator!). The traits I have been describing reappear constantly. They have two orientations well in hand, to themselves and to the larger ranges of experience. It is toward those middle relationships that they are indifferent — current opinion and social usage and the imperatives of traditional religion, patriotism, and morality. Their parents wring their hands over them; their professors find them lukewarm or cool; the Army grows anxious; we older friends are often exasperated. These impatiences are provoked by the fact that they wish to live correctly by their lights and not by ours. In proportion as we are free we must accord them that. [18]

STEVENSON — TRAGEDY AND GREATNESS
by Hans J. Morgenthau
[1] Adlai Stevenson has been praised and buried. His wit and eloquence have been duly noted; his honesty and his disappointments commented on. Yet these qualities do not explain the impact his death has made upon the people. After all, there have been other witty, eloquent, honest and disappointed candidates for the Presidency whom men have not mourned as they mourn Adlai Stevenson. What sets Adlai Stevenson apart from all the other seekers after high office of his time, successful or unsuccessful? What is the gift which only he has brought to American life, which made the vanquished shine more brightly than the victor? The answer is both simple and complex: It is the quality of greatness tinged with tragedy. The man in the street felt that tragic greatness without being able to define its substance. Everybody knew that here was a unique political figure, different from all others and in an undefinable, almost mys-

terious sense superior to them. Everybody also sensed that this
political figure, in all his uniqueness, was more like ourselves than the
common run of politicians (this is what we mean when we say that
he was "more human" than they) and that his tragic failure was in
some way the tragedy of all of us writ large. Adlai Stevenson was indeed political Everyman. His promise was ours, and so was his
failure, and the tears we shed for him we shed for ourselves.

[2]Wherein did Adlai Stevenson's greatness consist?
Wherein does any man's greatness consist? It consists in his ability
to push the human potential for achievement in a particular respect
to its outer limits, or beyond them if they are defined in terms of what
can be expected in the ordinary course of events. Thus we speak of
great painters and great writers, great liars and great lovers, great
statesmen and great merchants, great saints and great crooks. We
call them great because they have done what others may do well,
indifferently or badly, with a measure of excellence that at least
intimates perfection.

[3]Adlai Stevenson was great in his relationship to power.
He was not a great statesman because he did not have the chance
to use power for the purposes of the state. He was not a great politician because he did not choose to be a politician. But he was a
great seeker after power, and it was his very greatness in the pursuit
of power that was, as we shall see, responsible for the tragedy of
his failure.

[4]In order to understand the substance of Stevenson's
greatness, we must remind ourselves that there are two ways in which
to be great in the pursuit of power. The search for power ordinarily
entails, at least in a certain measure, the sacrifice of the intellectual
and moral virtues. It is in the nature of the struggle for power that the
competitors must deceive themselves as they deceive others. Those
who have chosen power as the ultimate aim in life must use truth
and virtue as means to their chosen end and discard them when they
do not serve that end. The prototype of this power seeker is endowed
with what Russell Kirk in a contemporary reference has called "a
canine appetite for personal power." He is a Borgia or a Stalin, the
Machiavellian prince, who will stop at nothing to gain and hold the
power he seeks. He will sacrifice all other values for the sake of power.
His greatness consists in that single-minded, ruthless pursuit of
power, of which lesser — and better — men are incapable. They stop
at some point on the road to power, distracted and restrained by the
common virtues of intellect and ethics.

[5]Man is capable of another kind of greatness in the
pursuit of power, which owes less to Machiavelli than to Plato's
postulate of the philosopher-king and to the Hebrew-Christian

ideal of the wise and good ruler. That greatness consists not in the single-minded pursuit of power but in the ability to subordinate the pursuit of power to transcendent intellectual and moral values. Rather than being possessed by power, those men possess it; rather than being devoured by it, they tame it. History has indeed known few rulers of this kind. But they have, as far as I can see, all been secure in the possession of power, generally by virtue of the automatic character of monarchical succession. Those who had to fight for gaining and keeping power, which is of course the normal situation in a democracy, have generally been precluded by this ever-present concern from attaining that greatness. The best they have been able to achieve has been an uneasy *modus vivendi*, a compromise between the demands of power and the requirements of the intellectual and moral virtues, with power having an excellent chance of prevailing when the chips are down. Of those who could not take power for granted but had to fight for it, I know only one who has attained that greatness: Abraham Lincoln. And it is indeed impossible to think of the substance of Stevenson's greatness without reflecting on the greatness of Lincoln. What they have in common explains their greatness; in what they differ accounts for the triumph of the one and the failure of the other.

[6]What Lincoln and Stevenson have in common is a high degree of freedom from illusion, to which politicians — as all men — are prey, about themselves, about their actions, and about the world. What took the place of these illusions was a lucid awareness, both intellectual and moral, of the nature of the political act, of their involvement in it, and of the consequences of that involvement for themselves and for the world. That awareness gave them the intellectual distinction and moral sensitivity, which set them apart from the common run of politicians. It gave their actions the appearance of indecisiveness and the reality of moral force. It accounts for their personal qualities of eloquence, wit and sadness.

[7]Lincoln and Stevenson knew both the moral risks and the practical hazards inseparable from the political act. They knew that to act politically was to take a jump into the dark. Innocent people would suffer, and the outcome was uncertain. Moral absolution could not be bought with good intentions nor could success be vouchsafed through ingenuity. The actor on the political stage takes his fate into his hands. Try as he may, he cannot escape the risks and hazards of his acts. If he is of the run of the mill, he will consult the flight of the birds, the constellation of the stars, or their modern equivalent, the public opinion polls, and receive the illusion of that certainty which the facts of experience refuse him. If he is great in the manner of Lincoln and Stevenson, he cannot help but face the risks and

hazards of his acts, to weigh them against the risks and hazards of alternative acts, to shudder at what he must do — and do it as though those risks and hazards did not exist. He acts in awareness, and in spite of, these risks and hazards. Here is the measure of the heroic dimension of Lincoln's actions.

[8] What the actor's mind knows, his action is ignorant of. It can afford to be determined and bold because the mind has done its task of knowing, weighing, and judging. It is for that very same reason that the act carries within itself the conviction of justice in the sense of being appropriate to the end to be achieved. What needs to be done will be done, but nothing more, is the message the act seems to convey. Here is the core of the moral force of Lincoln's policies.

[9] That contrast and tension between what the actor knows and what he must do accounts for his eloquence, his wit and his sadness. In both Lincoln and Stevenson, eloquence is more than a mere matter of rhetoric and literary skill; wit is more than a mere matter of fleetness of brain and quickness of tongue; and sadness is more than a mere matter of mood and nerves. They are the qualities of souls that have been formed by their awareness of what the political act implies, and by the burden of having to act nevertheless.

[10] Lincoln and Stevenson share the gift of eloquence and wit with other great political figures. One thinks of Bismarck, Churchill, and Adenauer. The quality of sadness is theirs alone. It is the function of an intellectual and moral sensitivity in the face of power which, so it seems, is peculiarly American. It gives immunity against that ultimate illusion to which even the intellectually aware and morally sensitive political actor is apt to succumb. His heroism makes him act; his intellect makes him explain himself; his wit makes him transcend the incongruities of his political existence at least in thought. And so he may delude himself into believing that now he has mastered the political world. Lincoln and Stevenson were incapable of that ultimate illusion. They knew that, when all is said and done, they were still faced, without remedy or escape, with the moral ambiguities and practical pitfalls of the political act. Knowing what they knew about themselves, their actions, and the world, they could not but be sad. Their sadness denotes the resigned acceptance of the moral and intellectual imperfections of the political world and of their precarious place within it.

[11] It is hardly necessary to point out that these qualities of greatness are more fully developed in Lincoln than they are in Stevenson. They were not clearly visible before Lincoln entered the White House; it was the pain of great decisions that brought them to the fore. Thus they have a grave and somber aura which Stevenson's qualities are lacking. Stevenson's greatness was not

the result of an ineluctable confrontation between personality and fate: The only great decision he had to face, it is true three times, was whether or not to seek the nomination. Rather it was the spontaneous expression of a great personality in intellectual anticipation of the fateful decisions he might have to make. Hence the peculiar quality of playfulness, of the aimless intellectual exercise, which is alien to Lincoln.

[12]What is the relevance of this difference between Lincoln and Stevenson for the latter's failure to gain political power after his initial success in Illinois? The answer to that question is obscured and rendered speculative by the intrinsic hopelessness of the 1952 and 1956 campaigns and by his failure to win the nomination in 1960. But why did he pursue the aspiration, foredoomed to failure, of becoming Secretary of State? And why did he silently suffer for four and a half years the humiliation of being Ambassador to the United Nations? Can these questions be explained away as accidents of history? Or do these persistent failures point to a fatal flaw, a tragic defect in Stevenson's greatness, which barred his way to power, but which might not have barred him from making great use of it had he been able to achieve it? I think indeed that there was such a flaw. In order to understand its nature, let us return for a moment to Lincoln.

[13]Abraham Lincoln, we have said, revealed his greatness only after he had reached the highest office. He made his way to that office as a politician competing with other politicians, seeking power in the manner of politicians, always tough and sometimes ruthless and devious. Lincoln made no bones about wanting power, and the people gave it to him. It was only after he had reached it that he also achieved that awareness of, and detachment from it in which we found the key to his greatness.

[14]Stevenson showed his awareness of, and detachment from, power from the very outset. No doubt, he wanted power. When it eluded him in 1952, he said that he envied one man, the Governor of Illinois. When as Ambassador to the United Nations and nominal member of the cabinet he had the trappings of power without its substance, he complained about the "disadvantage in being anywhere other than the seat of power." He never forgave himself for his indecision in 1960. He wanted power, but he wanted it only with intellectual and moral reservations openly revealed. He wanted power, but not with that "canine appetite," with that single-minded animal ferocity which carried his competitors in the Democratic Party to success. He wanted power, but he did not want it badly enough. His was a civilized pursuit of power in a barely civilized political world. Yet the people want their politicians to be wholehearted and uncomplicated in their pursuit of power. By being so,

the politicians give a token that they can hold and use power when they have it. It was this distance between the core of Stevenson's person and the pursuit of power and the interplay between the two, articulated by him and sensed by the people, that fascinated the masses and gained him their admiration but not their confidence.

[15] It was that very same distance that saved the defeated Stevenson from the disintegration which is the common lot of the frustrated seekers of great power. They hate or drink themselves to death. Stevenson in defeat could fall back upon that moral and intellectual core of his person that remained unaffected by the lust for power. He remained what he had been: eloquent, witty, and sad, but now he was so in a peculiarly purposeless way. The desire for power, too, remained; yet surviving the possibility of its satisfaction, it became patently futile and carried within itself a measure of humiliation.

[16] Stevenson wanted to be Secretary of State, and I suggested him in 1960 to the President-elect for that position; for I thought then, as I think now, that he was far better qualified than his competitors. But it should have been obvious to him — and to me — that politically the appointment was impossible; for the victor did not owe him that much and, more importantly, he could not be expected to countenance the star of Foggy Bottom to shine brighter than the sun of the White House.

[17] Stevenson's acceptance of the ambassadorship to the United Nations, to which I was opposed from the outset, and his unwillingness to relinquish it reveal most poignantly the desperation of his pursuit of power. The services he rendered to the country in that position could have been performed as well by lesser men, and they do not compensate for the personal diminution he suffered as a mouthpiece for policies on which he had no influence and was but rarely consulted.

[18] Had Stevenson been more unrestrained a seeker of power, he might have disintegrated in defeat. Had he been less addicted to the pursuit of power, he might have given it up in defeat altogether and become one of the great reflective men of the nation. He did neither. What could already be discerned in 1952, 1956, and 1960 now became almost pathetically obvious: the conflict between intellectual and moral awareness and the pursuit of power, spoiling both. [19]

Combination of methods

Most paragraphs and longer pieces of writing, as was mentioned earlier, are organized and developed by a combination of the methods discussed in some detail in this book. This fact has probably become obvious to you by this time, especially from your studying some of the model selections in chapters 7 and 8, since they illustrated development by other methods besides analysis and definition. A writer's intent, therefore, indicates which form dominates.

Read again Hans J. Morgenthau's definition essay in which he defines the tragic greatness of Adlai Stevenson. As you read Morgenthau's words, study the various methods of development he uses to make his intent meaningful. Use the following questions as a guide to your analysis of the article.

1. What questions does he ask in the first paragraph?
2. Does he answer the questions? Do his answers help the reader understand the intent of the writer and establish the dominant method of development?
3. State the basic definition in paragraph 2.
4. How does he emphasize his definition in paragraph 3?
5. In what way does the transitional phrase *two ways* (paragraph 4) indicate the development that follows? What kind of development does the writer use in paragraphs 4 and 5?
6. What methods of development does the writer use to develop the thought in paragraphs 6 through 10?
7. Is the analogy effective in paragraphs 7 and 8? Read the final sentence of paragraph 8. Does the analogy give it meaning?
8. Cite evidence of parallelism in paragraph 9? Does it give emphasis to the thought?
9. What is the method of development in paragraphs 11 through 13? How can we relate this thought to the thought in paragraphs 6 through 10?
10. In what paragraphs does the writer voice personal opinions?
11. Is the final paragraph an effective conclusion? Why? Why not?
12. Who is Yorick? Does the touch of irony in the final paragraph help the meaning the writer wishes to convey? In what way?

In the short selection that follows, David Brinkley analyzes the film "The Graduate" and uses this analysis to make clear his viewpoint concerning the classic conflict between parents and children summed up in the phrase "The Generation Gap."

To develop this central idea, he partitions, contrasts, and makes good use of examples and specific details. In addition, his essay is simply but effectively organized. He varies the introduction–middle–conclusion pattern slightly by six brief introductory paragraphs about the film "The Graduate"; then, in paragraphs 7 and 8, he makes clear the thesis: "The enduring conflicts between parents and children have now, suddenly, been phrase-mongered into something called The Generation Gap." He shows the differences between the two groups by point by point contrasts and closes this discussion with a main idea in the form of a question: "How could they ever understand each other?" He closes with a cogent restatement of the thesis: "All that is new about The Generation Gap is the phrase itself" relating this idea again to the film.

In addition to skillfully organizing and developing his central thought, Brinkley also gives that thought variety and emphasis with several brief well-written sentences that serve as single sentence paragraphs. In these single-sentence paragraphs, Brinkley places his most important ideas. He uses other kinds of variety and emphasis, such as varying the beginnings, the kinds of sentences, and the internal structure of sentences. Observe, in particular the use of parallelism in paragraph 9.

WHAT'S WRONG WITH "THE GRADUATE"
by David Brinkley

[1] One night at our house my son and several of his college-age friends found themselves in heated agreement. They thought *The Graduate* was absolutely the best movie they ever saw, and so I went to see it to find out what they liked so much.

[2] Well, it was far from the best movie I ever saw and, except for a few minutes at the beginning, I thought it was pretty bad. But it seemed they liked it because it said about parents and elders what *they* would have said about us if they had made the movie themselves — that we are self-centered and materialistic, that we are licentious and deeply hypocritical about it, that we try to make them into walking advertisements for our own affluence, our own vanities draped around their necks like garlands of rancid marigolds.

[3] These are harsh judgments. I wonder how often they are true.

[4] In the movie, a boy named Benjamin comes home from college to find his parents have invited friends — their friends, not

his — to a party where he is to be put on display and congratulated for his academic and athletic triumphs. It turns out these upper-middle-class, lower-middle-age friends, in their forced and alcoholic cheer, don't even know what his triumphs were, and are vastly interested in themselves and in him hardly at all.

[5]There is a scene where the father, with unknowing brutality, *uses* Benjamin, browbeating him into a hideously embarrassing little performance, forcing him to come out to the swimming pool in a new skin-diving outfit, its price loudly announced, and then to make him flounder into the pool for the raucous amusement of the father's guests.

[6]These episodes are shrewdly and effectively developed, and even though the picture thereafter stumbles into confusion, it persuades a college-age audience that Benjamin's furies are their furies.

[7]With our black arts of communications and phrase-mongering, yet another musty commonplace has now been made to appear a glittering discovery because it is impaled on the point of a vivid phrase.

[8]The enduring conflicts between parents and children have now, suddenly, been phrasemongered into something called The Generation Gap.

[9]A parent and a child are of two different orders of being. The age difference is only the least of it. One gives, one gets. One is independent, one dependent. One is experienced, one is not. One is looking toward finishing his work, one has yet to begin. One has many responsibilities, one has none. One grew up in depression and war, one in vast prosperity and mainly in peace. One grew up with Franklin Roosevelt and Benny Goodman, the other with Eisenhower, Kennedy and The Beatles. How could they ever understand each other?

[10]We knew all this before we knew the new phrase and before *The Graduate* put up there on the screen a caricature of this classic conflict.

[11]Parents as phony and cruel as these would never get, nor even deserve, a son's understanding; and a son coming out of college as dumb, awkward and inarticulately self-pitying as Benjamin would have trouble holding theirs.

[12]All that is new about The Generation Gap is the phrase itself. And, in spite of the enthusiasm for it among the young, it seems to me *The Graduate* only makes a few exaggerated points about familiar facts of life and then slides off into the kind of frantic nonsense Mack Sennett would have made if he had had the money. [20]

ASSIGNMENTS

4. Combination of methods

Read the following selection. Answer the questions that follow.

**WHY THE DEVIL DON'T YOU
TEACH FRESHMEN TO WRITE?**

by Edwin R. Clapp

[1] Despite all the outcry and accusation in recent years, despite the growing mass and competence of professional assaults upon the problem, it seems that Johnny still "can't write." One reason is, I think, a misunderstanding, both lay and learned, of what writing means. When the man next to me in the Chicago plane discovers that I teach English, he mumbles something about watching his grammar. When Dr. Stackblower, associate professor of anthropology, bears down on me roaring, "Why the devil don't you teach the freshmen to write?" I know that he has just read some paper rich in orthographical mayhem. If Johnny makes a gross blunder in usage or spelling, both businessman and academic are shocked by his "English." But if Johnny scrambles the logic of his argument, or drifts into irrelevance, or dishes out bland generalizations innocent of support, or winds up in Timbuktu when he set out for Oshkosh — the man in the plane (or the street) is unlikely to be aware of error. And if Dr. Stackblower is, he will charge it to incompetence in anthropology. That "English" is implicated never crosses either of their minds.

[2] I think we need to be clearer about what writing involves, what we want of Johnny, and what in practice we are willing to do to get it. Though "Johnny" may stand for any of his avatars from the elementary to the graduate school, let our Johnny be a college undergraduate, while "we" are all those charged with his education. In this context, let us look at him and at writing and at ourselves.

[3] Writing has two dimensions: literacy and competence. Literacy involves what is often called "correctness" or "mechanics" — the ability to spell, to punctuate, to follow accepted conventions of grammar and usage, to employ everyday words in their common meanings. Such ability is certainly necessary. Writing in which it is lacking is at best irritating and distracting, at worst incomprehensible. As a description of writing, however, literacy is incomplete, external, and negative; it represents the capacity not to make mistakes. But it is an easy definition. The capacity it represents is clearly visible within the framework of the sentence. It lends itself to measure. Misspellings and grammatical errors can be counted. Tests based

upon them can be devised and used as indices of verbal skill. Spelling above all — both to Professor Stackblower and the man in the plane for Chicago — is the great sign and symbol of the command of language. Be thou as chaste as ice, as pure as snow — and misspell "cat" — thou shalt not escape calumny. By and large the great world, lay and learned, equates "good English" with literacy, and particularly with spelling.

[4]In contrast with literacy, competence means the ability to control language as the vehicle of thought and feeling, to recognize a subject and its boundaries, to order and support ideas, to conduct an argument or define a quality, to distinguish what is relevant from what is not, to express with precision differences of mood and force and meaning. Usually it is consistent with and inclusive of literacy as a substructure above and beyond which it grows, but this is not always true. Otherwise competent writers may, for instance, spell badly. Competence is manifested in the substance, organization, and texture of discourse in its larger units as well as in the sentence. Subtler and more complex than literacy, it is not hard to recognize but does not lend itself to counting. And when recognized, competence may by its very nature be thought of less as mastery of expression than as an aspect of the thing expressed. Thus it may go undervalued or even unnoted when Johnny's writing is assessed. And yet, competence — far more than literacy — is the true goal, both for Johnny and for all of us.

[5]If we fret over Johnny's English, we must be clear what we are asking of him. We have confused literacy and competence, as definitions of ability and as desired ends. We have demanded literacy, when we *ought* to demand competence — not as a flat alternative, which it is not, but as an ability of greater value that in the fullness of its attainment will bring literacy with it, if only as a kind of by-product. Spelling we must make a special case. It is as much a matter of social decorum as an essential of communication; and when a genuine problem, it must be attacked as a distinctive one, often in terms of both psychology and language. (Ihope not to be misunderstood; I want Johnny to spell. But spelling has come to occupy a place in the public mind out of all proportion to its significance, and thus to obscure more important issues.) We can have more of competence and literacy (*and* better spelling) than we now have; we can have it tomorrow in the college and the day after in the schools, but only at the price of looking harder at ourselves as well as at Johnny. We shall need more dollars in some places, and — as competence in writing is inextricably involved with competence in reading, and this with thought — perhaps more sweat and tears. But to begin with, more light.

⁶*Why* is the ability to write well seemingly attained so seldom, so incompletely, and with such difficulty? A full answer would require a book. It would involve the nature of language and our understanding of language, the character of American society and education, and the whole fabric of the modern world — all interwoven and all changing. I can attempt here only a sketch of some chapters.

⁷First, Johnny's failures are sometimes more apparent than real; or, more accurately, they are of differing orders of magnitude. Demanding literacy as we do, we may overlook genuine if partial competence. I have struggled with more than one Johnny whose knowledge and insight were matched by his command of expression in everything save spelling, but whose feats in this department so occupied the foreground of attention as to obscure his real merits. Professor Stackblower naturally writes him down as another example of the inadequacies of the English Department. But to make due allowance for such anomalies is no more than to nibble off an edge of the problem.

⁸Second, the teaching of "English," particularly but not only in the elementary and secondary school, has often meant a formally conceived literacy of labels and categories abstracted from the communicative and expressive functions of language, a literacy operating with equally external tools and devices — rote memory, workbooks, rigid and sometimes quite wrong grammatical dicta divorced from the plain facts of usage, the taxonomy of discourse. There is no doubt an element of necessity in all this. Much remains to be learned about the teaching of the language skills. But much is a product of confused aims, ignorance, and acceptance of the easy way, and for this the institution that educates the teacher bears a substantial responsibility.

⁹Third, in the schools the basic relationships (differences as well as similarities) between spoken and written language, reading and writing, bread-and-butter prose and imaginative literature, and their implications for teaching have remained relatively undeveloped. In particular, the coupled reading and writing of expository prose, the prose of thought, seems to have been neglected; and this coupling is crucial for competence. There are all sorts of reasons: the overloaded teacher struggling with too many and too large classes (one place where more dollars are needed), the resultant impossibility of an adequate amount of critical attention to an adequate amount of student writing, the nice questions of the kinds of reading appropriate to the several stages of Johnny's development and of how best to explore with him the processes of the mind expressed in an ordered world of prose — plus the brute fact that thought is hard.

¹⁰Fourth, the universality of English as the language of all the disciplines has had mixed consequences for the teaching and

learning of reading and writing. Successful expression everywhere involves the same elements: precision, clarity, order, relevance. But this very commonalty, this fact that he takes the vehicle of language for granted, gives the teacher of biology or history or economics an option between meaningful exploitation of reading and writing in *his* area and buck passing, between opportunity and escape. He may consider English, construed as literacy, strictly the business of the English teacher, and ignore the shared world of competence. With honorable exceptions, lip service, if that, has for the most part been given the idea that every teacher has a responsibility for how his students write; and the idea that he has a vested interest, let alone a responsibility, in how they read has not even been suggested — even though to distinguish reading and writing from thinking and knowing is almost an exercise in tautology. Nor does this situation represent merely inertia or indifference, or one more expression of that academic tribalism to which the departmentalization of learning gives rise — though all these may contribute.

[11] A fifth consideration, closely related to the last but more basic, is the nature of language itself. If "all art constantly aspires to the condition of music," because in music content and form are one, in language the separation of the thing said from the way of saying, the what from the how, is in some partial and superficial sense possible. Thus "English" comes to be considered the garment of thought, discrete from the substance, which alone is biology or history or economics. One can detach the conventions, the mechanics, the "rules" of punctuation, grammar, usage (and of course spelling!) from fact and idea, keep the latter for oneself, and relegate the former to the exclusive custody of the English teacher, who thus becomes essentially a glorified proofreader. This is no fancy. I have been approached more than once by a professor of, let us say, engineering, who wanted me to find him a colleague to attend to the English of a report writing course while *his* staff took care of the engineering. Now, it is certainly true that the instructor in English is not *per se* qualified in engineering. It is just as true that the engineer really qualified as engineer ought also to be qualified in the world of discourse that engineering shares. We have returned to, perhaps in part accounted for, the dichotomy between literacy and competence. If the teacher of whatever subject thinks of English as only literacy, incidental or alien to the subject itself, the student is to be forgiven if *he* comes to regard English as a garb to be put on primarily or exclusively for the eccentrics who teach it. And his indignation is to be understood, if not pardoned, when he is confronted by the instructor in biology or history or economics or engineering who insists that thought and expression are facets of the same thing and that

the student is accountable to him for both. Fortunately, this instructor is as little a figure of fiction as Professor Stackblower; unfortunately, there are not so many of him.

[12] A last reason for Johnny's parlous condition is that in school and out "good English," whether construed as literacy or competence, is in our time and society an artefact and a minority attainment. Very likely *good* English or French or Greek has always been a mark of education. For language itself is speech and usage, but popular and educated speech and usage are not identical, and *written* language (that which is read and composed to be read) is not identical with either, although closer to and largely governed by the standards of the latter. We expect educated speech to be in appropriate ways literate; we expect educated writing to be competent as well. We Americans are a democratic and heterogeneous society, divided by region and sometimes by origin; mobile, often in a significant sense homeless; quite variously schooled; instructed to a degree by sound and picture (as in popular conversation, radio, television); often lacking in bookish background and tradition; in tastes and ideals much drawn to the immediate and physical, the practical and technological. Should we be surprised that in such a context literacy in terms of upper-middle-class usage (not to mention competence in a form of discourse reaching toward art) is imperfectly attained by our young through the limited process of formal education? If this sketch gives something like a true picture of the reasons why "English" is the way it is, what is to be done about Johnny?

[13] Education, like politics, is an art of the possible. The beginning of wisdom is, in the cant phrase, to "take the student where he is." Where is Johnny? He is, you will recall, a college undergraduate, let's say a freshman. He has typically been exposed to a number of years of drill founded on a traditional and dubious grammar; he has done some writing of quite variable amount and character; he has read a few standard works of literature and probably a slender but startling miscellany of contemporary fare; he doesn't know how to pursue an idea through a piece of prose that has one; he concocts what *he* considers English for his English teacher and is shocked if anybody else expects this odd behavior of him; and, as there is no guarantee that he spells correctly, Professor Stackblower is quite likely to be displeased with him. He has grown up believing that English means literacy because this is what he has been taught, and if it hasn't taken very well he is rather apologetic about it. Probably nobody has had time, strength, or inclination to help him very far toward competence. But, perhaps just because he is now eighteen or thereabouts, he can be helped toward competence and, if necessary, literacy into the bargain.

[14] The initial help must come from the English Department. "Freshman composition" has, of course, been taught in a fantastic variety of ways, and I have no pet formula to peddle, certainly no panacea. The essentials are, negatively, not to rehash the conventions of grammar again *seriatim et ad nauseam;* positively, to read a certain amount of serious well-fabricated exposition in order to discover the subject, its parts, their ordonnance and function — in short what it says and how and why; and to do some writing of the same kind and in the same spirit. Johnny is to discover, if he hasn't, that reading, writing, and thinking are a kind of three-wheeler which will take him down a number of roads. *En route,* he is firmly reminded that literacy is expected of him (spelling, too). He may find the going tough, but all the roads will take him toward competence, whatever incidental signs they bear. They are long roads, and he may not get all the way.

[15] He will not — any more often than he does now — unless what happens to him in his English class is reinforced by what happens to him elsewhere. Johnny must come to believe that how he writes matters, not just to his English instructor, but to everybody else. He *won't* believe this unless in the first place he writes — instead of filling in boxes in multiple-choice tests. He won't, unless in the second place his instructor in history or biology or economics also believes it, and shows Johnny that he does. Even Professor Stackblower, if he would trouble only to circle Johnny's misspellings in a paper or two and give Johnny to understand that his grades have taken a shocking turn for the worse because of them, might be surprised by Johnny's improvement. I have seen it happen. Strangely enough, this simple step does not always occur to Stackblower.

[16] To some it will seem platitudinous, and to others (especially battle-hardened academicians) utopian, to propose that college faculties take reasonable responsibility for whatever standards of literacy and/or competence they profess. The grounds for misgiving were succinctly put by the dean of a school of business administration who had requested the English Department to provide additional discipline in writing for his students. When I asked why his faculty shouldn't undertake this task themselves, he lowered his voice and said, "Frankly, I don't think they know enough — and besides, it's too hard work!" It may well be that Professor Kitzhaber is right in doubting (in his useful little book *Themes, Theories, and Therapy*) that any general and sustained faculty acceptance of "reasonable responsibility" is forthcoming. If so, in my opinion Johnny will stay where he is.

[17] But mine is a genuinely modest proposal. By "reasonable responsibility" I mean that when in any course in any de-

partment student writing is demanded, the judgment of this writing should be consistent with accepted institutional standards applicable to the occasion, and that this judgment should be reflected in grades. I don't ask that all members of a faculty set themselves up as grammarians or rhetoricians, or that as readers they devote the time and energy to style and structure one expects of the instructor in English. I ask that the faculty member who professes to be scandalized by misspelling and other gross errors at the level of literacy make known his displeasure in terms Johnny will understand. Neither great *expertise* nor effort would be required merely to check these off, particularly if some institution-wide code were adopted. As to competence, it is this that the faculty member who is baffled and offended by vagueness, confusion, and general impenetrability is seeking, although he may not consciously set out to demand clarity, order, or even evidence. One recalls the astonished delight with which M. Jourdain discovered that he was talking prose. I wish my colleagues to become aware that prose on the level of competence, the prose of written discourse, is what they really want of students. I think that they can get it, or get more of it than they have. Johnny is capable of writing better than he does — on demand. Such a demand would be far more potent than any addition to the standard formal requirements in English.

[18] We have been talking about Johnny — and Joanne — simply as undergraduates. They may be destined for business, or the professions, or government service, or housewifery. If they come, however painfully, to understand that "English" means something more and other than literacy, this is a gain not only today for them as individuals and for the microcosm of the college, but also tomorrow for their children and the macrocosm of society and the schools. Faculty responsibility means much more than merely pacifying Professor Stackblower.

[19] But to say "tomorrow" brings us back to my colleagues in English. If Johnny and Joanne are headed for careers as *English* teachers, they ought to be better equipped than their predecessors. I have been saying that undergraduate Johnny, whether in spite of or because of his experience in the schools, can be got to write. His teachers can be educated to do more for him, to help him further and earlier up the ladder of literacy and competency. I can attempt no blueprint here, but let my colleagues read and take to themselves Dr. Conant's description of typical faculty attitudes in *The Education of American Teachers*. We in college English need to accept responsibility for educating the public-school teacher, as we do the graduate student. We need to make a larger place in our curricula for language and writing alongside literature (which is what everybody, including

me, yearns to teach). If we can — and I think we can — get Johnny to put whatever brains he has into learning *really* to read and *really* to write, we shall have done our whole duty as teachers of English, including our duty to literature. Perhaps it is the first duty of all teachers. [21]

1. What is the function of paragraphs 1 and 2?
2. Does the writer definitely state a thesis sentence in the early paragraphs?
3. For the purposes of analysis, the writer breaks down writing into two dimensions. What are they?
4. Paragraphs 3 and 4 are developed chiefly by analysis (partition). What two other methods does the writer use?
5. List some transitional words and expressions that indicate the direction of the flow of thought in the first five paragraphs.
6. What is the chief function of paragraph 6?
7. By what methods does the writer answer the question asked in paragraph 6?
8. By what method or methods does the writer develop the thought of the cant phrase (paragraph 13) "to take the student where he is"?
9. How does defining help the writer's modest proposal for solving the problem?
10. In what ways does the thought of the last two paragraphs relate to his introductory paragraphs?
11. Is the true thesis of the essay revealed in paragraph 14? If so, write it.
12. Who is Stackblower? Is the name wisely selected for the writer's purpose? Why?

5. *Combination of methods*

Read the following selection. Answer the questions that follow it.

THE CASE AGAINST WOMEN
by James Thurber

[1] A bright-eyed woman, whose sparkle was rather more of eagerness than of intelligence, approached me at a party one afternoon and said, "Why do you hate women, Mr. Thurberg?" I quickly adjusted my fixed grin and denied that I hated women; I

said I did not hate women at all. But the question remained with me, and I discovered when I went to bed that night that I had been subconsciously listing a number of reasons I do hate women. It might be interesting — at least it will help pass the time — to set down these reasons, just as they came up out of my subconscious.

[2] In the first place, I hate women because they always know where things are. At first blush, you might think that a perverse and merely churlish reason for hating women, but it is not. Naturally, every man enjoys having a woman around the house who knows where his shirt studs and his briefcase are, and things like that, but he detests having a woman around who knows where *everything* is, even things that are of no importance at all, such as, say, the snapshots her husband took three years ago at Elbow Beach. The husband has never known where these snapshots were since the day they were developed and printed; he hopes, in a vague way, if he thinks about them at all, that after three years they have been thrown out. But his wife knows where they are, and so do his mother, his grandmother, his great-grandmother, his daughter, and the maid. They could put their fingers on them in a moment, with that quiet air of superior knowledge which makes a man feel that he is out of touch with all the things that count in life.

[3] A man's interest in old snapshots, unless they are snapshots of himself in action with a gun, a fishing rod, or a tennis racquet, languishes in about two hours. A woman's interest in old snapshots, particularly of groups of people, never languishes; it is always there, as the years roll on, as strong and vivid as it was right at the start. She remembers the snapshots when people come to call, and just as the husband, having mixed drinks for everybody, sits down to sip his own, she will say, "George, I wish you would go and get those snapshots we took at Elbow Beach and show them to the Murphys." The husband, as I have said, doesn't know where the snapshots are; all he knows is that Harry Murphy doesn't want to see them; Harry Murphy wants to talk, just as he himself wants to talk. But Grace Murphy says that she wants to see the pictures; she is crazy to see the pictures; for one thing, the wife, who has brought the subject up, wants Mrs. Murphy to see the photo of a certain costume that the wife wore at Elbow Beach in 1933. The husband finally puts down his drink and snarls, "Well, where are they, then?" The wife, depending on her mood, gives him either the look she reserves for spoiled children or the one she reserves for drunken workmen, and tells him he knows perfectly well where they are. It turns out, after a lot of give and take, the slightly bitter edge of which is covered by forced laughs, that the snapshots are in the upper right-hand drawer of a certain desk, and the husband

goes out of the room to get them. He comes back in three minutes with the news that the snapshots are not in the upper right-hand drawer of the certain desk. Without stirring from her chair, the wife favors her husband with a faint smile (the one that annoys him most of all her smiles) and reiterates that the snapshots *are* in the upper right-hand drawer of the desk. He simply didn't look, that's all. The husband knows that he looked; he knows that he prodded and dug and excavated in that drawer and that the snapshots simply are not there. The wife tells him to go look again and he will find them. The husband goes back and looks again — the guests can hear him growling and cursing and rattling papers. Then he shouts out from the next room. "They are *not* in this *drawer,* just as I told you, Ruth!" The wife quietly excuses herself and leaves the guests and goes into the room where her husband stands, hot, miserable, and defiant — and with a certain nameless fear in his heart. He has pulled the desk drawer out so far that it is about to fall on the floor, and he points at the disarray of the drawer with bitter triumph (still mixed with that nameless fear). "Look for yourself!" he snarls. The wife does not look. She says with quiet coldness, "What is that you have in your hand?" What he has in his hand turns out to be an insurance policy and an old bankbook — and the snapshots. The wife gets off the old line about what it would have done if it had been a snake, and the husband is upset for the rest of the evening; in some cases he cannot keep anything on his stomach for twenty-four hours.

⁴Another reason I hate women (and I am speaking, I believe, for the American male generally) is that in almost every case where there is a sign reading "Please have exact change ready," a woman never has anything smaller than a ten-dollar bill. She gives ten-dollar bills to bus conductors and change men in subways and other such persons who deal in nickels and dimes and quarters. Recently, in Bermuda, I saw a woman hand the conductor on the little railway there a bill of such huge denomination that I was utterly unfamiliar with it. I was sitting too far away to see exactly what it was, but I had the feeling that it was a five-hundred-dollar bill. The conductor merely ignored it and stood there waiting — the fare was just one shilling. Eventually, scrabbling around in her handbag, the woman found a shilling. All the men on the train who witnessed the transaction tightened up inside; that's what a woman with a ten-dollar bill or a twenty or a five-hundred does to a man in such situations — she tightens him up inside. The episode gives him the feeling that some monstrous triviality is threatening the whole structure of civilization. It is difficult to analyze this feeling, but there it is.

⁵Another spectacle that depresses the male and makes him fear women, and therefore hate them, is that of a woman looking

another woman up and down, to see what she is wearing. The cold, flat look that comes into a woman's eyes when she does this, the swift coarsening of her countenance, and the immediate evaporation from it of all humane quality make the male shudder. He is likely to go to his stateroom or his den or his private office and lock himself in for hours. I know one man who surprised that look in his wife's eyes and never afterward would let her come near him. If she started toward him, he would dodge behind a table or a sofa, as if he were engaging in some unholy game of tag. That look, I believe, is one reason men disappear, and turn up in Tahiti or the Arctic or the United States Navy.

⁶I (to quit hiding behind the generalization of "the male") hate women because they almost never get anything exactly right. They say, "I have been faithful to thee, Cynara, after my fashion" instead of "in my fashion." They will bet you that Alfred Smith's middle name is Aloysius, instead of Emanuel. They will tell you to take the 2:57 train, on a day that the 2:57 does not run, or, if it does run, does not stop at the station where you are supposed to get off. Many men, separated from a woman by this particular form of imprecision, have never showed up in her life again. Nothing so embitters a man as to end up in Bridgeport when he was supposed to get off at Westport.

⁷I hate women because they have brought into the currency of our language such expressions as "all righty" and "yes indeedy" and hundreds of others. I hate women because they throw baseballs (or plates or vases) with the wrong foot advanced. I marvel that more of them have not broken their backs. I marvel that women, who coordinate so well in languorous motion, look uglier and sillier than a goose-stepper when they attempt any form of violent activity.

⁸I had a lot of other notes jotted down about why I hate women, but I seem to have lost them all, except one. That one is to the effect that I hate women because, while they never lose old snapshots or anything of that sort, they invariably lose one glove. I believe that I have never gone anywhere with any woman in my whole life who did not lose one glove. I have searched for single gloves under tables in crowded restaurants and under the feet of people in darkened movie theatres. I have spent some part of every day or night hunting for a woman's glove. If there were no other reason in the world for hating women, that one would be enough. In fact, you can leave all the others out. [22]

1. What is the function of paragraph 1?
2. What form of development dominates this essay?

3. What is the main idea that paragraphs 2 and 3 develop?
4. How many reasons does Thurber give for hating women?
5. How many clearly stated topic sentences are there in the essay?
6. What is the chief reason the writer gives for hating women?
7. What is the tone of this writing: serious, tragic, humorous, objective? Explain how tone plays an important part in a reader's understanding the writer's intent?
8. How do transitional words and expressions aid the writer's flow of thought?

6. Combination of methods

Write a serious theme of approximately 500 words on "Why I Dislike (something) ——————."

Read the model selections that follow. Study the structural organization of each selection. Write a theme of approximately 500 words on some subject of your own choosing.

SLANG AND CRIME
by Paul Roberts

[1] Criminals have always been prolific producers of slang because they are so obviously marked off from respectable society. They deliberately widen the gulf by multiplying language differences, and they often use the differences for practical purposes: to recognize one another, to shield their conversation from hostile ears. Criminal groups of the seventeenth and eighteenth centuries in England developed large vocabularies of slang — or *cant,* as it was then called — which rendered their talk almost meaningless to an outsider.

[2] Much of the slang in common use today comes ultimately from characters on the other side of the law. This will be recognizable, for example, in words relating to American money. For "money" in general we have such terms as *dough, lettuce,* the *green* or the *big green, folding stuff,* and various others. The different denominations all have their slang terms: *singles* or *fish* for one dollar bills; *fin* for a five; *sawbuck* for a ten and *double sawbuck* for a twenty; *C-note* or *century* for a hundred; *grand* for a thousand. All of these are old, well-weathered terms and are familiar to many

people who wouldn't dream of holding up a drugstore. But it is clear that they have their highest frequency in those districts where policemen would prefer to go in pairs.

[3]In games slang is common everywhere, but it is most prolific in those games which are more or less disreputable. Bridge and golf have their slang terms, but gambling games have more, and roulette, for which the participants may wear evening clothes, has fewer than craps or poker, for which they usually do not. Poker has a wide variety of slang terms — or at least had when the writer had the game explained to him by an obliging friend. Thus in addition to the general names for the cards — *ace, deuce, king* — another set of slang terms are, or were, in use: *bull* or *bullet* for "ace," *cowboy* for "king," a *pair of ducks* for "a pair of deuces." Two aces and two eights are a *dead man's hand,* three tens are *thirty miles* or *thirty miles of railroad,* a flush of any sort is *all blue.*

[4]Dice, even more disreputable than poker, has a correspondingly higher incidence of slang terms.

[5]The connection between slang and the criminal element is seen again in the dope racket, the terms of which have been made more or less generally familiar by the movies and television. The word *dope* itself is originally slang, but it is now in more general use than *narcotics.* Within the racket, terms abound. The words *marijuana* and *heroin* seem scarcely to occur among users or peddlers of the drugs, as is suggested by the fact that addicts speaking of heroin on a television program pronounced it to rhyme with *groin.* Usually, apparently, they say *H* or *big H* or *horse* or *caballito* (a Spanish word meaning "little horse" or "horsey.") Marijuana is referred to by several slang terms, of which *hay* seems to be most enduring. An injection of a narcotic is a *fix.* To inject it in the vein is to *mainline.* A salesman or peddler is a *pusher.* An addict is a *junkie.* To rid oneself of an addiction is to *kick the habit.* It will be seen that a narcotics addict can discuss his troubles at some length without being understood by anyone outside the circle. [23]

WHAT TO DO WHEN CHILDREN CHEAT
by Orville Palmer

[1]Our daughter came home from high school one afternoon recently, upset and angry. Several of her classmates had cheated on a test; and she felt it was unfair to the students who had studied hard that those who had cheated would get high grades without having worked honestly to earn high marks.

[2]"You're right," we said. "Why don't you tell your teacher about it tomorrow. We're sure he won't stand for cheating in his classroom."

³ But although the cheating had upset our daughter, she didn't want to report it. Her reluctance to "tell," and her outrage, expressed her personal dilemma and the dilemma faced by teachers and parents: what to do about cheating.

⁴ Cheating, as any principal or teacher knows, has always existed. But many people believe that it is now more widespread and more serious than it used to be. In schools and colleges across the land, cheating has become a major concern.

⁵ If, indeed, cheating is on the rise, it may well be because there is so much pressure put on youngsters today to get top grades. For cheating is frequently caused by the desire of students to please their parents, and by their need to get better marks so they can get into the "right" college.

⁶ Parents may not realize how much they contribute to their youngsters' dishonest behavior. For one thing, more and more parents virtually do their children's homework for them, without stopping to consider if such help really helps the student. Some parents are scrupulously honest themselves, and refrain from actually doing their children's work for them, but they may place the youngsters under such heavy pressure to excel in school that they turn to cheating in order to get the grades they couldn't otherwise make.

⁷ If parents become almost panic-stricken at the prospect of their children's academic shortcomings, the youngsters may respond in one of several ways. Some react by working harder and do improve their grades, but others become so anxious that they do even more poorly, practically ceasing to function, and some children cheat.

⁸ A good deal of cheating, therefore — but not all — is done to get good grades. There are also the "anything for kicks" youngsters who cheat for somewhat the same reasons that they drag race cars, shoplift, or wreck property — because they have nothing more constructive they want to do or can do, and because such flouting of rules is considered smart by their friends. Generally, those who consider it smart to cheat will voice as a defense, "Everybody does it, why shouldn't I?"

⁹ Young people who subscribe to this morality have somehow failed to develop a working sense of right and wrong. Yet long before a child reaches school age, he has learned a great deal about what his parents consider "good" behavior. In subtle and direct ways he learns about trust, kindness, honesty as he sees his parents live out these same qualities in their relationships with him. A child who is eventually to understand what the right things are to do or say under various circumstances must first feel right about himself. He must know that his parents value him for what he is. He must be given reasonable discipline which in turn can lead to self-

discipline. He must see a pattern of consistency in what his parents say and do. A father, for example, who preaches honesty and then boasts about how he cheated the income tax collector does not help his youngsters to look upon cheating as wrong.

[10]To prevent the kind of borderline cheating which is all too prevalent, it's up to parents to see that ethical values are transmitted to their children. For cheating includes not just flagrant dishonesty but also such deceptions as collaborating on assigned work without permission or copying material by changing it only slightly. Unless parents take their principles seriously and don't make a practice of small deceits, they can't expect their children to have high standards.

[11]Some teachers are also partly responsible for children's cheating. There are teachers who rightly encourage the use of reference books but foolishly neglect to explain the difference between the proper use of source materials and plagiarism, or the difference between legitimate and illegitimate paraphrasing.

[12]Some schools do fairly well in insisting on honesty and fair play. These schools have absolutely clear regulations and fair procedures for handling violations of the rules. In most large urban high schools, the problem of cheating is partially handled by having the teachers take maximum precautions against it. Tests are carefully proctored and all reports and papers are scrutinized. The opportunities for cheating are kept to a minimum, the penalties to a maximum.

[13]Another often successful method of cutting down on cheating is a student honor system.

[14]A typical honor system is the one at Princeton University. No examination is proctored. Upon completing a test the student states on his paper that he has neither given nor received assistance. Anyone convicted of cheating is recommended for expulsion by a student honors committee. Such an honor system works, Princeton students and officials say, because students respect it; because they have learned to place a higher value on honesty — and on their obligation to the college and to their fellow students — than on grades.

[15]In colleges, an honor system can be introduced easily. In most secondary schools an honor system would probably work best if it were first set up with selected groups of the older, brighter students. Then other groups might be given a chance to indicate by secret ballot if they wished to accept the system.

[16]Many schools already employ an honor system in some classes. They place these classes on their honor by not monitoring exams, by leaving the students alone in a classroom for indeterminate

periods of time, and by allowing the students to take home examinations (frequently open-book tests) to complete overnight. Knowing that they are trusted makes most students proud to remain trustworthy.

[17] To be effective, an honor system must also take into account the loyalty which students feel toward one another. As the experience with our daughter shows, you can't ask adolescents to betray their classmates. Even if a friend has done something they consider morally wrong, it would disturb them to be responsible for his possible disgrace or expulsion from school. Besides, many youngsters are apt to regard the detection of cheating as the teacher's job, not theirs.

[18] To minimize cheating, schools can also place less emphasis on grades. Grades are not a true gauge of knowledge, and good marks should not be the main or sole goal of education.

[19] Evaluation techniques can be changed, or improved, so that tests would not be regarded by so many students as frightening. Examinations should be fair and reasonable, and there should be other measures of a student's ability, so that one end-term test, for example, would never be the only basis for determining a grade.

[20] Finally, cheating should be discussed openly and frankly in the classroom: why the cheater ultimately cheats himself. At all times, the teacher's views on cheating, and other violations of school regulations, should be made perfectly clear.

[21] Parents should work with the schools, perhaps through parent-teacher groups, to discuss the problem of cheating, to probe the possibility of setting up an honor system, and to impress on their children the importance of ethical behavior.

[22] If a child needs help with his homework, his parents should consult with his teacher to determine the kind of assistance they can give him at home, without actually doing the work for him. Most important, parents must resist putting unfair pressure on their youngsters to achieve higher grades than they may be capable of.

[23] In short, I believe that the widespread problem of cheating can be solved with a threefold attack: the establishment of sounder, enlightened testing practices along with a lessening of the importance of grades; the setting up of honor systems at schools and absolutely clear rules about cheating; a greater effort by parents and teachers to transmit their moral standards to their children.

[24] With schools and parents working together, youngsters can be helped to understand that cheating means cheating themselves of one of the most precious possessions a person can have — self-esteem. Eventually, it is self-esteem, rather than marks, which will help them make the grade. [24]

THE CORROSIVENESS OF PREJUDICE
by McGeorge Bundy

[1] The most deep-seated and destructive of all the causes of the Negro problem is still the prejudice of the white man. This is not a new proposition — it was Myrdal's central finding a generation ago, and Styron has just reaffirmed it in a major work of art. The social scientist and the artist do not say that prejudice is the only source of our trouble, and neither do I: the catalog of such sources is very long, and provides much opportunity for fierce self-criticism to whites who do *not* have prejudice and indeed to Negroes themselves. Still it is the white man's fears and hates that must have first place . . .

[2] Prejudice is a subtle and insidious vice. It can consume those who think themselves immune to it. It can masquerade as kindness, sympathy, and even support. The cause of the American Negro has nourished the self-righteousness of generations of white men who never troubled to understand how destructive it can be to make the uplifting of others the means of one's own self-esteem.

[3] Prejudice, of course, is not a novelty among Americans. We have managed to be narrow-minded about one another since 1607 in the South and 1620 in the North. The combination of fear and contempt has exercised its potent charms on one social group after another; it is no respecter of religion or race. But I think we make a mistake when we attempt to compare the white/black relation with those between the Yankees and the Irish, or the WASPs and the Jews, or any other of the dozens of conflict-laden relations that have marked our social history. This one is so much deeper and bigger that it has a different order of meaning.

[4] Yet the answer has to be the same here as in every other case: that prejudice must be overcome. Men *are* brothers, with all that brotherhood implies in terms of rights and claims. And if I do not feel that way, then I am guilty of an offense against the fundamental principles of the open society; in this sense there is no right to prejudice.

[5] This first commandment is harder for some among us than for others. No man is the best judge of his own behavior in such matters, and reasonable men should be wary of hasty judgment on others. Yet the deep corrosiveness of white prejudice requires honest recognition, for as long as it persists it will be the most powerful single enemy of the very Negro progress which will in the end do most to end it.

[6] A dialogue has developed between some Negroes and some whites in these last years on "black nationalism" as against "integration." I do not hold with those who suppose that it is for the Negro alone to discuss his own purposes: no group in our society can properly claim such immunity from outside comments.

[7] Yet in offering these comments I recognize that Negroes have the same rights as the rest of us to make their own decisions about what they will do and with whom they will associate. That much said, it seems to me the plainest of facts that the destiny of the Negro in America is to be both Negro and American, and that as he makes progress he is likely to do what the rest of us do: he will take pride in his particular group at the same time that he insists on full membership in the society as a whole.

[8] There can be paradox and even conflict in this double assertion, but the black man, like white groups before him, will make it just the same. How can he not? Can he really give up all that attaches him to his kind of people on his kind of terms? Who can deny the right of young black students to have a part of their lives kept black? And who can be surprised that many of them exercise that right?

[9] Yet apartness will not be enough. The drive toward integration is at least equally authentic, and the individual who deliberately limits his associations to "his own kind" — for whatever reason — limits his life as an individual. Moreover the Negro, like everyone else, has a right — an obligation — to play his part in the society as a whole, and in that wider society the great opportunities can never be reserved for one kind only. Much too slowly still, but with steadily increasing speed, American Negroes will take their share of leadership in the general institutions of society. They will not thereby cease to be black, and not for a long time will any proud Negro forget the need to serve his people's cause along with his own individual interests. But none of us who are white should suppose that Negroes will really choose to stand aside from American life as a whole. They will insist, instead, on integration. There is only one bar and bench, only one system of government, only one national marketplace, and only one community of scholars. Our great general institutions — unions and universities, businesses and bureaucracies — will have to be open to all.

[10] Where Negroes take public power — as they will, more and more — they will face the same tension between the interest of their own people and the interest of all that other leaders from minority groups have faced in their first moments of victory. The choices thus forced will inevitably cause some resentment on both sides. For a Negro to prefer a Negro, or to refuse to prefer him, can each cause trouble; it has been so in cases where the heritage of bitterness was less. Such public tension will parallel the internal tension that Negroes will experience at the intersecting edges of their need for apartness and their need for membership in the whole. There is no reason to believe that Negroes will be less fair than others as they come to make such choices.

[11] The American Negro will have to have much more economic and political power than he has today before the rest of us will have any reason to believe that he has more than his fair share. (As it has for the rest of us, equality for the Negro will mean a share of privilege as well as a share of power.)

[12] Our society is going to solve this problem. The white man will outgrow his prejudices and the Negro will strengthen both his sense of identity and his membership in the whole of society. This is the only possible final outcome. All the rest is temporary. It is a colossal task, of course, because the inheritance of neglect and injustice is enormous. But it will happen. No one can tell how long it will take, and it will happen faster in some parts of our land and life than in others.

[13] Already there is less prejudice than there was; in spite of noisy rejections at each extreme, black men and white men are learning to know each other better and to work together more honestly than before. Abrasions at the edges of this process should not blind us to the fact that the national direction is right, though the pace is badly wrong. There is more self-respect and determination among Negroes and more awareness among whites than we would have found in earlier decades . . . .

[14] Progress against prejudice will grow in speed as the next generation moves on stage. I believe that before the present college generation begins to lose patience with its college-age children this problem will be more behind us than ahead. For I believe the young today, both white and black, are learning to regard as natural the equality which many of the rest of us see only as logical. What we see as a legal right they tend to see as a human reality. They have begun to live on the far side of prejudice, and they will decide.

[15] From the three conclusions I have outlined above I draw a fourth: that the preachers of hate who seem so much the men of the moment are in fact merely spume on the wave of the past. They sometimes seem to dominate the television screens, and that is not altogether the fault of the broadcasters. Throughout our history we have given excessive attention to wild men, taking them too readily at their own valuation, and assuming too easily that the few who really do intend to live by hate are the real leaders. Yet no one who has dealt honestly with legitimately militant black leaders will confuse their properly angry words with any conspiracy to commit general violence, and no one who loves this country can believe that the ultimate instinct of its white majority is that of the backlash. Certainly we have been, at times, a violent people, but we have never made a religion of violence, or even a politics. The country of Abraham Lincoln is not going to become a no man's land for an apocalyptic

contest between white and black fanatics. It is inevitably going to right these ancient wrongs, and this time by peaceful means.

[16] The mode by which the inevitable comes to pass is effort. There is nothing automatic about any part of the American Dream. Those of us who want peaceful progress toward equality will have to work for it. All Americans, black and white, North and South, must show new initiative, and accept new responsibility. [25]

SPOOFING AND SCHTIK
by Pauline Kael

[1] "I trust ya', Honey — but cut the cards"

[2] Advertising experts look to the future and find — a new breed of sophisticates that will not be so easy to convince.

[3] They're coming. The new generation of young adults. Wise, hip, skeptical — unlike any audience businesses and advertisers have ever known before. A new breed of sophisticates who have been deluged by advertising since they were 3. Bred to new wisdom at television's knee. Able to "tune out" automatically at the first sign of advertising puffery. Promising advertisers no problem so great as that of sophisticated disbelief.

[4] Purveyors of the advertising scene see this coming. The simplest social analysis of the highly educated, worldly American society now emerging indicates it.

[5] This is an almost-full-page ad in the New York *Times*, May 11 and June 16.

[6] And what is the ad for? *Good Housekeeping* and its Consumers' Guaranty Seal. The ad closes with "Seeing it in Good Housekeeping is believing."

[7] The basic flattery of the customer is familiar, but the *kind* of flattery is new. Advertising, TV commercials, movies are trying to outwit disbelief by including it in the sell.

[8] Are those who no longer "believe" the advertising they hear and see really "a new breed of sophisticates," part of "the highly educated, worldly American society now emerging"? If disbelief were the result of knowledge, every New York cabdriver would be an educated man. What this generation was bred to at television's knee was not wisdom but cynicism: it is an indication of how self-important and self-congratulatory advertising men have become that they equate the cynical indifference of those wised up to *their* methods with wisdom.

[9] Our society is disastrously utilitarian. We can no longer distinguish the ad from the entertainment, the front cover of the national magazine, in which an actor poses to plug his film, from the

back cover, in which an actor sells cigarettes and indirectly also plugs a film. Television shows with groups of celebrities are a series of plugs (for books, records, nightclub appearances, movies) interrupted by commercials. Movies are constructed with product tie-ins worked into their structure: mattresses, stoves, toothpaste, airlines, whiskey, all with their brand names shining. The companies so advertised in turn feature the movie in *their* ads. Even without product tie-ins, modern-dress movies look just like ads and sell the advertising way of life. This is one of the reasons why our movies seem so slickly unreal: they look like the TV commercials that nobody "believes."

[10] The acceleration in the standardization of mass culture since the end of World War II means that we are all hit by the same commodities, personalities, ideas, forces, fashions at the same time, and hit increasingly hard. If you drive across the country you'll find the same movies playing in every town and city, *Fanny Hill* and *Candy* on sale in every drugstore, pop and op in the bank and shop. At roadside restaurants you'll hear the same semi-parodistic songs coming out of jukeboxes; at a motel in the middle of nowhere you'll see the same TV shows, the same commercials you saw at home. The motel itself may be an exact reproduction of other motels, and you'll drive past supermarkets and housing developments that you could swear you'd already passed. The people in the small towns smell, look, read, react like the people in the big cities; there are no sticks anymore.

[11] Only "schtik" — the fraudulent uniqueness that sells when real individuality or difference is risky. Schtik is the special bit, the magic gimmick that makes the old look new, the stale seem fresh; it is what will "grab" the public. It is the desperate hope of an easy solution when the sellers cannot predict what the public, satiated increasingly fast, will buy.

[12] What stories will seem believable, what themes will involve modern audiences, what will interest people? The problem that the "purveyors of the advertising scene" analyze is also being doublefaced by the slick magazines and by Hollywood. Like the *Mademoiselle* editor explaining why a piece of Jean Harlow fiction was being printed, "We thought it would be sort of campy and fun," they clutch at any little schtik.

[13] They're afraid they can't do the same old stuff anymore — not straight, anyway — so they do it "tongue-in-cheek." They pretend they're superior to it. There is a story told about Tennessee Williams at the opening of *The Rose Tattoo*. When a stagehand said in consternation, "Why, Mr. Williams, they're laughing." Williams is supposed to have replied, "If they laugh, it's a comedy." People all over the country were bored with or laughing at advertising, commercials, magazines, movies, so the purveyors found a face-saving device. Now

advertising kids advertising, TV commercials kid TV commercials, movies kid movies. They go "way-out," become "send-ups"; they nudge us that what they're doing is just a "put-on." It's as embarrassed and halfhearted a strategy as that of the fat man who makes himself a buffoon so you can't make more fun of him than he has already.

[14]Spoofing has become the safety net for those who are unsure of their footing. Unlike satire, spoofing has no serious objectives: it doesn't attack anything that anyone could take seriously; it has no cleansing power. It's just a technique of ingratiation: the spoof apologizes for its existence, assures us that it is harmless, that it isn't aiming for beauty or expressiveness or meaning or even relevance. To many in the advertising business and to those young artists who often seem to be in the same business, it is a way of life — or, rather, a time killer on the way to the grave.

[15]Still, the purveyors are full of anxieties. In screening rooms, the publicity men and critics can be heard asking nervously, "Will audiences outside the big cities get the joke?" Is it perhaps that they're uncertain whether *they* get it either? What *is* the point? Who is being put-on? Way-out where? Send-up what?

[16]We're sending ourselves up. We are reaching the point at which the purveyors don't care about anything but how to sell and the buyers buy because they don't give a damn. When there is no respect on either side, commerce is a dirty word.

[17]But not all the new generation is buying. Many of them don't just " 'tune out' automatically at the first sign of advertising puffery" because they know there's no place to tune in again. They're surrounded by selling, and they tune out, period. They want some meaning, some honesty, some deeper experience, and they try to find them in romantic ideas of rejection and revolution based on their moral revulsion from the situation in the South, in folk music, in underground movies, in narcotics.

[18]Even the worst underground movies — the most chaotic, confused, and boring, the most amateurish — may still look more "real," more "sincere" than industrial products like *The Sandpiper* or *Harlow,* which you can't believe, or gigantic spoofs like *The Great Race,* which you're not supposed to believe. But though the desire, the need, the clamor, among college students particularly, for underground movies grows out of important kinds of rejection, the underground movement is infected by what the students are trying to escape.

[19]The underground cinema is largely a fabrication of publicity: the students are "put-on" by *Film Culture* and the *Village Voice,* and then they're fobbed off with parodies of Maria Montez movies, Andy Warhol spoofs of experimentation, and underground

variants of exploitation films. And if these films often spoof old movies, new big movies are already an imitation of the underground. *What's New, Pussycat?* has the kind of jokes associated with underground movies; *The Knack* is already a fashionable, professionally "youthful" treatment of underground attitudes.

[20] A movie that looks amateurish is not necessarily an answer to commercialism — it may be an innocent or a very shrewd form of commercialism; and commercial movies can all too easily imitate the amateurish look. Thus far, underground movies are too easy an answer: they're an illusory solution to a real problem — a commercialized society that nobody believes in. [26]

WHERE ARE WE?
by Carl Becker

[1] I was interested in the letter of Five Bewildered Freshmen, and in the discussion it gave rise to. The freshmen say they have been engaged in the intellectual life for more than two months and don't know what it's all about. This is bad, but who is to blame? Some say the students are to blame, and some say the professors. What is to be done about it? You suggest a foundation or an orientation course such as is given in other universities.

[2] For my part I don't blame anyone — not the freshmen, certainly. It's not especially the student's fault if he doesn't know what it's all about. If he did, he wouldn't need to come to college. That's why, I have always supposed, young people come to college — to get some notion, even if only a glimmering, of what it's about. They come to get "oriented." But why expect to be oriented in two months, or a year? The whole four-years college course is a course in orientation. It isn't a very satisfactory one, indeed. Four years isn't enough. Life itself is scarcely long enough to enable one to find out what it's all about.

[3] Neither do I blame the professors — not particularly. Many people appear to think that professors possess some secret of knowledge and wisdom which would set the students right as to the meaning of things if they would only impart it. This, I do assure you, is an illusion. I could write you a letter on behalf of Five Bewildered Professors which would make the five bewildered freshmen appear cocksure by comparison. The professors are in the same boat. They don't know either what it's all about. They tried to find out when in college, and they have been trying ever since. Most of them, if they are wise, don't expect ever to find out, not really. But still they will, if they are wise, keep on trying. That is, indeed, just what the intellectual life is — a continuous adventure of the mind in which something is being discovered possessing whatever meaning the adventurer can find in it.

⁴This effort to find out what it's all about is, in our time, more difficult than ever before. The reason is that the old foundations of assured faith and familiar custom are crumbling under our feet. For four hundred years the world of education and knowledge rested securely on two fundamentals which were rarely questioned. These were *Christian philosophy* and *Classical learning*. For the better part of a century Christian faith has been going by the board, and Classical learning into the discard. To replace these we have as yet no foundations, no certainties. We live in a world dominated by machines, a world of incredibly rapid change, a world of naturalistic science and of physico-chemico-libido psychology. There are no longer any certainties either in life or in thought. Everywhere confusion. Everywhere questions. Where are we? Where did we come from? Where do we go from here? What is it all about? The freshmen are asking, and they may well ask. Everyone is asking. No one knows; and those who profess with most confidence to know are most likely to be mistaken. Professors could reorganize the College of Arts if they knew what a College of Arts should be. They could give students a "general education" if they knew what a general education was, or would be good for if one had it. Professors are not especially to blame because the world has lost all certainty about these things.

⁵One of the sure signs that the intellectual world is bewildered is that everywhere, in colleges and out, people are asking for "Orientation" courses which will tell the freshmen straight off what it is all about. If we were oriented we shouldn't need such courses. This does not mean that I am opposed to an orientation course for freshmen. I would like an orientation course for freshmen. I would like one for seniors. I would like one for professors and trustees. I would like one for President Farrand and President Butler. Only, who is to give it? And what is it to consist of? I asked Professor Hayes, "What about your orientation course at Columbia?" He said, "It's a good thing for the instructors who give it." I asked a man whose son had taken the course, "What did he get out of it?" The reply was, "He read three books in three unrelated fields of knowledge and got a kick out of one of them." Who knows the "background" or the "general field of knowledge"? If the course is given by many professors the student will be taking several courses as one course instead of several courses as separate courses. If one man gives it what will it be? It will be as good as the man is. If we could get a really top-notch man to give a course, no matter what, and call it an orientation course, I should welcome it. H. G. Wells might give such a course, and it would be a good course. I doubt if it would orient any one or settle anything, but it would stir the students up and make them think. That would be its great merit. That is the chief merit of

any course — that it unsettles students, makes them ask questions.
[6]The Five Bewildered Freshmen have got more out of their course than they know. It has made them ask a question — What is it all about? That is a pertinent question. I have been asking it for thirty-five years, and I am still as bewildered as they are. [27]

THE PLACE OF INTERCOLLEGIATE ATHLETICS IN HIGHER EDUCATION: HOLD THAT TIGER!

by Frank N. Gardner

[1]College and university presidents, faculty representatives, athletic directors, coaches — all those who have anything whatsoever to do with intercollegiate athletics — are keenly aware of the fact that they have a tiger by the tail. They are afraid to hold on to it, and they are afraid to let it go. My own judgment is that we should hold on to the tail but get more control of the whole tiger.

[2]With this positive affirmation about intercollegiate athletics, I have probably lost approximately one-third of my readers. I base this estimate upon my own experience of faculties. Roughly one-third of any faculty has either a congenital or an experiential aversion to intercollegiate athletics, and tends to view the whole subject with alarm. For the remaining two-thirds, the plan of this article is to discuss briefly (1) values in intercollegiate athletics, (2) present abuses, (3) corrective measures in the recent past, (4) present trends, and (5) steps which need to be taken in the future.

[3]As an ex-athlete who also participated in intercollegiate debate and student religious activities, sang second tenor in the college male quartet, played a not-so-hot trombone in the college band and orchestra, and engaged in more strictly academic co-operative enterprises, I can testify that there were some things I learned faster and better as a participant in intercollegiate athletics than in any other way. These things were co-operation; striving for individual excellence; self-discipline; the subordination of self, if necessary for the good of the group; achieving and winning if at all possible; and best of all, winning within the rules. Quite readily I will grant that these values may be learned in other ways and in other activities. Yet I must state that, for me, they came chiefly through intercollegiate athletics. Hundreds of other ex-athletes will make the same assertion. Unfortunately, the opportunity of acquiring these values is not extended to larger numbers of young men because of concentration upon the "senior varsity." Why should the values I gained from participation in athletics be limited in football to men like myself — simply because I weighed 215 pounds, stood 6 feet 2 inches, and possessed a sturdy frame? More teams (junior varsity, B-squads, "150-pound" football teams, "five foot eight inch" basketball teams) need to be financed.

⁴Then, too, it seems to me that intercollegiate athletics serves better than any other activity as a rallying point for student and alumni interest and loyalty. For years I have observed that the concerts of the Drake-Des Moines Philharmonic Orchestra or the Drake University Theatre's presentations do not quite engender the kind of personal involvement which takes place when my university plays St. Louis University in basketball. Some may deplore this, but it remains a fact. The important thing is to utilize the fact wisely.

⁵The values of participation in intercollegiate athletics led to an awakening of interest on the part of college administrators, and when college presidents discovered that people would actually pay money to see burly young men throw a leather-covered ball through the air or through a hoop — often committing athletic mayhem in the excitement of the game — interest waxed hot indeed! Intercollegiate athletics grew rapidly. As the turnstiles clicked and ticket-takers tore admission tickets in half, huge stadiums were built, and later tremendous field houses. Profits at many institutions were great enough to finance the construction of laboratories, dormitories, chapels, and other buildings. Gains from a good football team were sufficient to support not only the whole intercollegiate athletic program but also intramural sports and other activities.

⁶As time passed, coaches, administrators, and boards of trustees learned to their sorrow that the American public demands a winner for its money. A state-university president found it relatively easy to get an appropriation from the state legislature following victory in a bowl game. A winning coach soon received a salary almost as large as that of the university president (sometimes even larger). A losing coach usually found himself consigned to Gehenna in short order! The pressures in some areas for a winning team are almost unbelievable. They are exerted by the American public, and no facet of intercollegiate athletics is free from them.

⁷To win, as the football coaches say, you "have to have the horses." No Percheron ever won the Kentucky Derby. And no conference-football championship was ever won without top-grade athletic material. The best athletes are commonly referred to as the blue chips (a strange phrase for a theologian such as I to grasp immediately). How does one get them? He goes after them! And now we have arrived at one of the greatest problems in contemporary intercollegiate athletics — the problem of effective control of the recruiting of student-athletes. The National Collegiate Athletic Association (NCAA) and the various conferences spend more time on this problem than on any other. Here most of the violations of ethics and rules occur. The second most serious problem which is constantly with us is allied with the first. It is the problem of effective control of various kinds of aid to student-athletes. Both the promise

of aid and the actual granting of it are closely connected with recruiting. Effective control of financial aid and recruiting is a nightmare to all persons connected with intercollegiate athletics.

[8] And here, as Whitehead might have put it, what appears
to be the simple solution is the most bogus. The men who control
athletics in a land-grant institution in the Great Plains snort in de-
rision when an Easterner proposes that all athletic grants-in-aid be
abolished, or representatives of a university in an urban industrial
area suggest that all aid be confined to a work program. Why? Because they know that in some eastern universities and colleges 60
to 80 per cent of all students receive aid in one form or another
— aid which is made possible by endowment funds. Among these
students some surprisingly good athletes will turn up — to the astonishment of no one, particularly the coach. As for a work program
— in a town of 15,000 people, of whom 11,000 are found in the student body, where are enough jobs to be found?

[9] Most of us tend to view the present situation in athletics
from the perspectives of our own collegiate situation, our region or
tradition, or our own procedures and practices. Consequently, we
reason that our athletic problems would be solved if institutions
elsewhere followed our pattern. But the United States is a complex
society, and its universities and colleges display amazing diversity,
not only in their regional environment, but in their academic and
athletic programs. Procedures which may fit the needs and circumstances of an Ivy League school may not meet those of a school in
Texas or Oregon.

[10] In spite of the difficulties involved in working at their
common problems, our universities and colleges have made real
progress in recent years. At the national level, sincere men have
hammered out on the anvils of compromise, rules of control which
have been accepted nationally. No institution, no conference, no
region, no group of any kind, has achieved its ideal of what the purpose and program of intercollegiate athletics should be. But sufficient unity of mind has been achieved to legislate rules within which
all believe they can live. These have served to give the universities
and colleges more effective control over the program of intercollegiate athletics.

[11] The requirements which embody the progressive
achievements that have been made in regulating intercollegiate
athletics may be summarized briefly: (1) the control of the program
must be placed in the hands of the educational institution; (2) all
grants-in-aid must be awarded by the general scholarship or awards
committee of the educational institution; (3) all aid to student-
athletes must be controlled and administered by the institution;
(4) such aids cannot exceed the sum necessary to defray legitimate

educational expenses as these are defined by the institution's catalogue (tuition, board, room, books, and up to $15 a month for incidentals such as laundry, dry-cleaning, and so on); (5) limitations have been imposed on practice and playing seasons; (6) tryouts have been abolished; (7) funds to aid athletes which are supplied by Booster Clubs and similar organizations must go through the regular institutional channels, and the institution is held responsible for violations by such organized groups; and (8) student-athletes must be admitted to college by the same procedures applicable to other students.

[12]Strange as it may seem to many in the face of the news of violations which have occurred, and punishments which have been meted out to educational institutions by conferences and the NCAA, the conditions which existed a few decades ago have been vastly improved. Recently I attended a meeting in Chicago in which two of the participants were men of long experience in intercollegiate athletics. At present they are commissioners of conferences and thus on the firing line. Both agreed that tremendous forward steps had been taken by intercollegiate athletics in recent years.

[13]At the more national level the trend is to tighten up the controls we have and to get more control of unruly sectors. Proposals being considered are (1) limiting participation in intercollegiate athletics to eight semesters or twelve quarters of residence, (2) establishing minimum academic standards which must be met by all applicants for a grant-in-aid, (3) setting up a voluntary pre-registration service in which the universities agree to respect applications for admission of prospective student-athletes which have been accepted by other member institutions, (4) greater use of the criterion of need in arriving at justifiable sums for grants-in-aid to student-athletes, and (5) establishing some procedure in cooperation with state high-school associations to control all-star high-school contests.

[14]Perhaps the most noticeable trend in individual educational institutions is their quite evident desire to affiliate themselves with other institutions in organizing a conference or league, or in joining such a group which is already in operation. Such conference affiliation yields strength to an institution, provides greater opportunities for scheduling contests which are satisfactory, and in turn makes possible more effective control over the program of individual institutions.

[15]The impact of television on sports, generally, has been staggering. Television of major-league baseball has virtually destroyed minor-league baseball. To stem television's adverse effects upon intercollegiate athletics, the NCAA colleges and universities adopted a control program several years ago for football. It has been

generally satisfactory, both to the American public and to the member institutions. Nevertheless, many institutions have found it necessary to cease playing football because the sport became too expensive. [16]Whether American intercollegiate athletics was ever of the English amateur type is a debatable subject. If it ever was, it is not now. Forces in American public education have made the English idea both inappropriate and infeasible in this country. Sports on our campuses should not be limited (or so we believe) to "gentlemen" who indulge in such activities in their leisure time. American institutions of education are agreed that all students should have the opportunity to participate. When time does not permit study, class attendance, and participation along with employment, grants-in-aid have been substituted for financial gain from outside employment. Unless we limit athletic participation to the wealthy, this is probably what we shall have to continue to do. Again, the wise way lies in sound judgment and effective control.

[17]Most of the actions which our educational institutions have taken in the past have been, by force of circumstance, negative and restraining. We have been concerned with effective rules, consistently enforced, for preventing abuses and bad practices. Such regulations have served to stem a rising tide of unethical and vicious practices. Corrective procedures have made possible some advances. However, the time is at hand when more positive programs of action must be inaugurated by our institutions of higher learning.

[18]Of immediate importance is the necessity for a co-operative study of the purpose and program of intercollegiate athletics as a part of the total educational program of our schools. Unfortunately, our colleges and universities have not effectively solved this problem at the institutional level. It may not be solved at the local level until regional and national conferences come to some agreement. The Special Committee on Recruiting and Subsidization of the NCAA recently recommended to the Council of the Association that a thorough study of the purpose and program of intercollegiate athletics be made by a special committee having national representation. The results of this co-operative study would be reported to the members of the Association with recommendations for the adoption of principles and programs growing out of the study. I am convinced that once our colleges and universities see clearly the purpose and program of intercollegiate athletics as it forms a part of our total educational task, the search for solutions of our problems and more effective controls will be greatly assisted.

[19]A further positive program needs to be inaugurated by means of which the values in intercollegiate athletic participation may be made available to greater numbers of young men and women. The number of persons acquiring these values now is far

too limited. Such a program would be costly, but it would be worth the price. The tiger is valuable — if we get positive and effective control of it and lead it in the right direction. [28]

THE SCRAMBLE FOR COLLEGE ATHLETES
by Paul H. Giddens

[1] I have always maintained that college athletics exist primarily for the enjoyment and benefit of students who wish to participate in them, and they should be conducted as an integral part of the educational program. The same is true of all other extracurricular activities — choir, band, student publications, debate, dramatics — which supplement formal classroom learning. They provide outlets for learning by doing, and they contribute to the development of students' special talents and skills. There is little or no justification, educationally speaking, for maintaining intercollegiate athletics, except for the benefit of the players.

[2] The concept that intercollegiate athletics exist primarily for the benefit of the general public and for the purpose of making money has been long in the making. There has been an unprecedented growth of interest in athletic contests of all kinds. First radio and then television have made it possible for millions of people to become ringside spectators at professional baseball, basketball, and football games, and at wrestling and prizefighting matches. The National Broadcasting Company now has a five-year contract to pay $36,000,000 to televise all regular season games of the American Football League. Just recently it purchased the rights to televise the AFL championship and All-Star football games for the next five years for a sum in excess of $7,000,000.

[3] Organized baseball little leagues for the kids from nine to twelve years old have spread all over the country. High schools have expanded their athletic programs, have built large stadiums and established district, regional, and state championship tournaments, are playing night games and post-season games, and are selling rights to broadcast and televise their games. Colleges and universities sell bonds to build large athletic plants and stadiums holding 55,000 to 85,000 people. They also play night games to draw larger crowds and increase gate receipts, participate in postseason tournaments, and compete for the right to play in the Rose Bowl and in other bowl games: Sugar, Cotton, Orange, Gator, Sun, Raisin, and Cigar. These games have become great national spectacles with parades, "million-dollar" marching bands, and half-time shows.

[4] The National Broadcasting Company recently negotiated a two-year contract and agreed to pay $800,000 per game for television rights to the Rose Bowl game. For this mammoth circus in 1965, the gate receipts amounted to about $500,000. After the

expenses of the participating teams were paid, and the travel expenses of bands, Big Ten athletic directors, coaches, and faculty representatives (who were allowed $750 each to travel with their wives), each Big Ten school received over $30,000 as its share of the gate receipts, the highest in history. The Rose Bowl is avowedly big business, with every Big Ten university sharing in the profits. Also indicative of the popularity of college football is the fact that the total attendance for the past four seasons of Big Ten play was 12,534,199.

[5]As a result of this tremendous public interest, intercollegiate athletics have become increasingly commercialized and subjected to pressures wholly alien to an amateur athletic program. In order to win public acclaim, some colleges and universities have resorted to practices which are certainly shoddy, and questionable from an educational point of view. In order to have a winning team, for example, full-time members of the coaching staff are employed the year round to scour the country, scout high school games, interview star players, and offer them all sorts of inducements to enroll at their college or university. They bid for these players as though they were on the auction block. It is not uncommon for a star player to have fifty or sixty or even eighty or more offers.

[6]The chief weapon in this competitive battle for blue-chip athletes is financial aid. Unless financial aid is offered in abundance, coaches say they just can't get enough good players and produce winning teams. The basic question asked by a star student athlete when interviewed by coaches is, "How much?" In the bargaining that takes place, the parents of these boys are as much to blame for what happens as anyone else; they play the role of a broker. According to the National Collegiate Athletics Association, if the amount of financial aid exceeds tuition and fees, room and board, books and supplies, and $15 per month for incidental expenses, it is considered pay for participation. In some colleges, athletes are given preferential treatment in the awarding of financial aid; they get the best scholarships. One college in the Southeast recently reported in the press that of 228 nonresident scholarships awarded, 118 went to athletes.

[7]Georgia Tech announced in January, 1964, that it was quitting the Southeastern Conference and would play as an independent because it could not get the conference to raise its limit of 140 football and basketball scholarships. The announcement said that the rule was too limiting, that Georgia Tech could not field a respectable team under the rule, and that this was not fair to the alumni, to the players, or to the school. Incidentally, by withdrawing from the conference and playing independently, it was estimated that Georgia Tech would increase its revenue by $100,000 on all future televised games and from $25,000 to $50,000 on future televised bowl games.

⁸Colleges and universities may put limits upon the amount of financial aid given to student athletes, but this does not prevent all kinds of under-the-table payments. Jobs are provided where little or no work is required. Special well-known athletic funds, contributed to by businessmen, alumni, and friends, with thousands of dollars in the kitty, provide the wherewithal to get star players. In many cases there is little or no college or university control over these funds or over how they are spent.

⁹The mad scramble for student athletes and their subsidization is not confined to large universities; the small colleges engage in the same practices. They, too, want to win games, championships, and public acclaim and prestige. They cannot possibly compete with the resources and influence of the large universities for star athletes, but that does not prevent them from using similar methods to get the next best talent. Large and small, public and private colleges and universities are engaged in the fierce competitive struggle for student athletes.

¹⁰Over the last ten years the Big Ten schools have tried several plans in search of an acceptable standard as a base for awarding financial aid. In 1961 the need factor was dropped by the Big Ten and a "stringent" grade-average requirement was substituted, making it easier to recruit. In addition to class rank, a freshman must be able to achieve a grade average of 1.7, a D minus, in order to qualify for a scholarship and practice with the freshman team. He must then show a minimum of progress for three seasons of varsity competition — 1.7, 1.8, and 1.9 — to keep the scholarship. He can, therefore, still qualify and get financial aid for four years without attaining even a C average.

¹¹The pressures are so great to get a star athlete that it is often necessary for a college or university to pay his expenses at a preparatory school for a period of study so that he can qualify for admission. For example, this is what the U.S. Military Academy, the U.S. Naval Academy, and the Air Force Academy do. Other colleges and universities "farm out" an inadmissible student to a junior college for a year in order that he may qualify.

¹²Some very respectable academic institutions are even known to have a double standard for admission, one for the athletes and one for all other students. For the desired athletes, they will accept college-entrance examination scores ten to twenty points below those they require for other students.

¹³Once student athletes are admitted to college, they are in many cases given further preferential treatment. They are segregated from other students, lodged in a special dormitory, and given benefits not extended to other students. They are allowed to take a reduced academic schedule during the game season. Special tutors

are provided in case they are not doing well in their studies. For each game they are given complimentary tickets, which can be used by friends or sold to make a little money. Travel uniforms — slacks and sports coats — are provided. If a student athlete fails a course or two and becomes ineligible for the team, there are actually some colleges which are known to have changed the grades in the registrar's office to make the student eligible. Recently the classroom attendance records of a certain college were rigged, resulting in a scandal that led to the resignation of the football coach.

[14] If a potentially good freshman athlete is physically immature or poorly prepared in the fundamentals of the sport, coaches resort to what is called red shirting, whereby a student is deliberately held out of varsity competition for a year so that he may become older, bigger, and stronger, and have a year's additional practice behind him. But this means holding students in school a year longer than necessary merely for the sake of their athletic ability.

[15] Participation in intercollegiate athletics requires long hours in practice sessions. The daily grind is fatiguing, and a student is too tired to study at night. Often there are night sessions. The season is long. Football practice starts in late August or early September, before other students arrive on campus to register. If an invitation to a postseason game or tournament is accepted, this means the season is extended possibly another month with daily practice and play, and the pressure upon student athletes increases. By the time the postseason game has been played, practically a whole semester has passed with a substantial portion of the daily hours devoted to athletics. After a brief interval, spring football practice begins. From an educational point of view, such loss of study time is indefensible.

[16] The pressures to win too often cause coaches to risk playing a student who has not fully recovered from a serious internal injury or a fracture. Winning the game is far more important than the welfare of the student. It would be interesting to know just how many college physicians have been pressured by coaches into letting a player, not fully recovered from an injury, play in a game. It would be equally interesting to know just how many permanent injuries have resulted from playing a student not in the best physical condition.

[17] Recently the National Football Foundation awarded Earl Blaik Fellowships of $500 to each of the eleven outstanding college football players who had an excellent scholastic average. Six were going into medical school, three into engineering, one into law, and one into the ministry. Yes, there are some fine football players who are excellent students. But what about the hundreds of

others who play football? Reports on the "high" scholastic record of athletes are proudly made from year to year by individual colleges and universities, but they are not very convincing. As you examine the report, you wonder how many of these men majored in physical education. How many of these men were in physical education classes taught by their coach or coaches in intercollegiate athletics? How do the marks of those in football and basketball compare with those in swimming, tennis, golf, or wrestling? I recently studied one of these reports made by a Big Ten university. It showed that out of 293 men on the 1964–1965 varsity squads, thirty-seven freshmen, sophomores, and juniors had a grade point average of 3.0 or better (B equals 3.0). But only eight of the thirty-seven came from the baseball, football, and basketball squads. Nineteen came from the golf, tennis, track, wrestling, and hockey squads. And ten of the twenty-nine were on the swimming squad!

[18] In view of the mounting pressures, the growing commercialization of intercollegiate athletics, and college and university practices, it is not surprising that there have been recurring scandals involving cheating, bribery, and dishonesty. In 1945, five Brooklyn College players admitted accepting bribes to throw a basketball game with the University of Akron. Frank Hogan, the district attorney of New York City, later reported evidence that between 1947 and 1950, eighty-six basketball games had been fixed at Madison Square Garden and at arenas in twenty-two other cities in seventeen states by thirty-two players on several teams. In March, 1961, Hogan disclosed another scandal that involved thirty-seven players from twenty-two major colleges who accepted bribes ranging from $700 to $4450 to fix games.

[19] In January, 1965, a major scandal involving intercollegiate athletics at the Air Force Academy rocked the country. It was disclosed that 109 cadets, including about thirty members of the football team, had either cheated on examinations or knew about the cheating and did not report it, and would be separated from the Academy and the Air Force.

[20] A recent study by Columbia University on cheating in college pointed out: "Despite angry denials by coaches and football-minded alumni, the dishonesty among athletes is staggeringly high." The moral fiber of impressionable young men is eroded and broken down when they are bought. If you have peddled yourself to a college or university recruiter, it is only a short step to rationalize that it is perfectly all right to sell yourself to a fixer. According to a recent report of the Commission on Higher Education, National Council of Churches of Christ in the U.S.A., "The colleges teach them how to cheat even before the kids have left high school."

[21] With the rapid growth of professional football and the

keen competition between the two major leagues, a Frankenstein monster has been created within the last five years that threatens to make college football a training ground for professional leagues. Even before the 1964 season, the two professional leagues, battling fiercely for prestige, television income, and gate receipts, began raping college football. Jim Wilson of Georgia signed a contract with the Patriots and played as a pro during his final year in college. Before the season ended, George Sauer, Jr., of the University of Texas signed with the New York Jets, although his college eligibility had not expired. Four key Oklahoma players were dismissed from the squad on the eve of the Gator Bowl game for having signed undated contracts with Houston and the Vikings. One authority estimated that as many as two dozen pro-signed players competed in year-end college bowl games. Others had verbal understandings in advance. When one of the New Year's games on television ended, a pro scout dashed onto the field, corralled one of the stars, led him to the sidelines, set up a makeshift desk, and handed him a pen. Without even reading the contract, the player affixed his signature. The climax of the season was the signing of Joe Namath of Alabama, the number-one college player in the country, by the New York Jets to a three-year contract for $400,000 plus $5000 per year for life.

[22] The National Collegiate Athletic Association and college coaches across the country were indignant about the pros tampering with these players before the expiration of their college eligibility, but there was little that they could do. In commenting upon what had happened, Coach Norm Van Brocklin of the Minnesota Vikings made a spectacular and revealing declaration. He is reported to have said, "I really don't know what to say when people ask me about the ethics of this sort of thing. In our business, we live by results." In the torrent of discussion over the situation, college and university football coaches didn't get much sympathy for several reasons. It came out that possibly two hundred assistant coaches were on pro payrolls as scouts to furnish extensive information on players and to induce players to sign with a particular team. Second, college and university coaches bother star high school athletes all during their senior year, trying to get them to enroll, in the same way that pro scouts lay siege to a senior college player. On ethics in big-time sports, one sports-writer said it is an area "in which neither the pros nor the colleges can stand much scrutiny."

[23] It is heartening to report that four or five years ago the nine presidents of the member colleges of our Minnesota Intercollegiate Athletic Conference began giving greater attention to intercollegiate athletics. Because of rumors and gossip over what this or that college was doing in awarding financial aid to student athletes, each president agreed to submit to all the others an annual report on

the grade average and the amount of financial aid — scholarships, grants, campus jobs, and loans — which his college gave to every man on the eligibility list of every intercollegiate sport. In addition, the presidents agreed to spend one evening together — and we have done this annually — going over these reports and asking pertinent questions. These meetings have been frank, friendly, and helpful. In them we have discussed many problems relating to intercollegiate athletics and made a number of recommendations.

[24]We suffered our greatest humiliation and defeat, however, when in one session the presidents unanimously recommended to the faculty representatives of the Minnesota Intercollegiate Athletic Conference the abolition of all postseason games. The faculty representatives voted down the recommendation of the presidents! Our most recent accomplishment was to agree that the member colleges would not grant any financial aid to a student athlete in excess of the amount indicated in the College Scholarship Service report of family need. We have not solved all the problems, but a beginning has been made.

[25]If intercollegiate athletics continue on their present course and direction and there is no change, they will be gradually abandoned. The small colleges, already hard-pressed for funds sufficient to maintain the quality of their faculty and educational program, cannot afford to continue in the mad race to recruit and subsidize student athletes. Nearly one hundred colleges have abandoned football since 1947. Even larger colleges and universities feel the financial drain; the University of Chicago, the University of Denver, Fordham, Marquette, and more recently, the University of Detroit have abandoned either football or all intercollegiate sports. Even the largest universities are finding the financial burden increasingly heavy. One Big Ten university is reported to be spending $225,000 a year for athletic scholarships. But with their immense resources, the largest universities apparently can afford the luxury for a while.

[26]If intercollegiate athletics are to be saved from extinction, it is high time that college and university presidents, deans, and faculties exert strong and courageous leadership, assert greater control over athletic coaches, eliminate practices not in accord with sound educational principles, and restore intercollegiate athletics to an amateur basis. [29]

CHAPTER EIGHT　*References*

1. From *Webster's Seventh New Collegiate Dictionary*. Copyright © 1967 by G. & C. Merriam Company, Publishers of the Merriam-Webster Dictionaries. By permission.
2. From *Webster's Seventh New Collegiate Dictionary*. Cf. 1.
3. From "Baseball — the Perfect Game" by Roger Angell.
4. Cf. 3.
5. From "On Various Kinds of Thinking" by James Harvey Robinson.
6. From *Patterns of Culture* by Ruth Benedict.
7. From *The American College Dictionary*. By permission of Random House, Inc.
8. From *Webster's Seventh New Collegiate Dictionary*. Cf. 1.
9. From *An Introduction to Literary Criticism* by Marlies K. Danziger and W. Stacey Johnson. Copyright © 1961 by D. C. Heath and Company. By permission.
10. From "Tornadoes" by Morris Tepper. Copyright © 1958 by Scientific American, Inc. All rights reserved.
11. From "A Liberal Education" by Thomas Henry Huxley.
12. "Radicalism and Conservatism" in *New Viewpoints in American History*. Copyright © 1922 by Arthur M. Schlesinger. By permission of Mrs. A. M. Schlesinger.
13. From *Personality and Social Interaction* by Robert H. Dalton. Copyright © 1961 by D. C. Heath and Company. By permission.
14. From *An Introduction to Literary Criticism* by Marlies K. Danziger and W. Stacey Johnson. Cf. 9.
15. From *The Desert Year* by Joseph Wood Krutch. Reprinted by permission of William Morrow and Company, Inc. Copyright © 1952 by Joseph Wood Krutch.
16. From *Word Study* by William Gillis. © 1965 by G. & C. Merriam Company, Publishers of the Merriam-Webster Dictionaries. By permission.
17. From *Volcanoes in History, in Theory, in Eruption*. (University of Texas Press, 1912). By permission.
18. "The Silent Generation," by Thornton Wilder, in *Yale Daily News* (Anniversary Number, 1953). Copyright © 1953 by *Yale Daily News*.

19. "Stevenson — Tragedy and Greatness," by Hans J. Morgenthau. Reprinted by permission of *The New Republic*, © 1965, Harrison-Blaine of New Jersey, Inc.
20. "What's Wrong With the Graduate?" by David Brinkley. Reprinted with permission from Ladies' Home Journal. © 1968 The Curtis Publishing Company.
21. "Why The Devil Don't You Teach Freshmen to Write?" by Edwin R. Clapp, in *The Saturday Review* (February 20, 1965). Reprinted by permission of the author and *The Saturday Review*.
22. "The Case Against Women" by James Thurber. Copyright © 1937 James Thurber. Copyright © 1964 Helen W. Thurber and Rosemary Thurber Sauers. From *Let Your Mind Alone*, published by Harper & Row, New York; originally printed in *The New Yorker*.
23. From *Understanding English* by Paul Roberts. Copyright © 1958 by Paul Roberts. Reprinted by permission of Harper & Row, Publishers.
24. "What To Do When Children Cheat" by Orville Palmer, *Parents' Magazine* (January, 1966). Reprinted by permission of Parents' Magazine Enterprises, Inc.
25. "The Corrosiveness of Prejudice," by McGeorge Bundy in *CTA Journal* (May, 1968). Copyright © 1968 by the California Teachers Association. By permission of the author.
26. "Spoofing and Schtik" by Pauline Kael. First appeared in *The Atlantic Monthly* (December, 1965). The essay now appears in *Kiss Kiss Bang Bang,* by Pauline Kael, Little, Brown and Company.
27. "Where Are We?" by Carl Becker, in *The Cornell Daily Sun*. Reprinted by permission of *The Cornell Daily Sun*.
28. "The Place of Intercollegiate Athletics in Higher Education: Hold That Tiger!" by Frank N. Gardner, in *The Journal of Higher Education*. Copyright © 1960 by The Ohio State University Press and reprinted with its permission.
29. "The Scramble for College Athletes" by Paul H. Giddens. From *The Atlantic Monthly* (December, 1965). By permission of the author.